# Competing for Control

Pyrooz and Decker pull apart the bars on prison gangs to uncover how they compete for control. While there is much speculation about such gangs, there is little solid research. This book draws on interviews with 802 inmates – half of whom were gang members – in two Texas prisons, one of the largest samples of its kind. Using this data, the authors explore how gangs organize and govern, who joins gangs and how they get out, the dark side of gang activities including misconduct and violence, the ways in which gang membership spills onto the street, and the direct and indirect links between the street and prison gangs. *Competing for Control* captures the nature of gangs in a time of transition, as prison gangs become more horizontal and their power is diffused across groups. There is no study like this one.

**David C. Pyrooz** is Associate Professor of Sociology and Faculty Associate of the Institute of Behavioral Science at the University of Colorado Boulder. His research interests are in the area of gangs and criminal networks, developmental and life-course criminology, and incarceration and reentry.

**Scott H. Decker** is Foundation Professor in the School of Criminology at Arizona State University. His main research interests are in gangs, violence, and active offenders. He is the author of *Life in the Gang: Family, Friends and Violence* (1996) and *Policing Immigrants: Local Law Enforcement on the Front Lines* (2016).

D1602809

# Competing for Control

*Gangs and the Social Order of Prisons*

DAVID C. PYROOZ

*Department of Sociology*
*University of Colorado Boulder*

SCOTT H. DECKER

*School of Criminology and Criminal Justice*
*Arizona State University*

WITHDRAWN
UTSA LIBRARIES

CAMBRIDGE
UNIVERSITY PRESS

# CAMBRIDGE
UNIVERSITY PRESS

University Printing House, Cambridge CB2 8BS, United Kingdom

One Liberty Plaza, 20th Floor, New York, NY 10006, USA

477 Williamstown Road, Port Melbourne, VIC 3207, Australia

314–321, 3rd Floor, Plot 3, Splendor Forum, Jasola District Centre,
New Delhi – 110025, India

79 Anson Road, #06–04/06, Singapore 079906

Cambridge University Press is part of the University of Cambridge.

It furthers the University's mission by disseminating knowledge in the pursuit of
education, learning, and research at the highest international levels of excellence.

www.cambridge.org
Information on this title: www.cambridge.org/9781108498357
DOI: 10.1017/9781108653473

© David Pyrooz and Scott Decker 2019

This publication is in copyright. Subject to statutory exception
and to the provisions of relevant collective licensing agreements,
no reproduction of any part may take place without the written
permission of Cambridge University Press.

First published 2019

Printed and bound in Great Britain by Clays Ltd, Elcograf S.p.A.

A catalogue record for this publication is available from the British Library.

ISBN 978-1-108-49835-7 Hardback
ISBN 978-1-108-73574-2 Paperback

Cambridge University Press has no responsibility for the persistence or accuracy of
URLs for external or third-party internet websites referred to in this publication
and does not guarantee that any content on such websites is, or will remain,
accurate or appropriate.

Library
University of Texas
at San Antonio

# Contents

# Figures

# Tables

# Acknowledgments

There are roughly 2,000 prisons in the United States. These institutions are largely an enigma to the general public. They are places people do not visit unless they are confined there, work there, or know someone there. Public knowledge of daily life inside of prisons is typically warped by sensational accounts provided by the media. Unfortunately, few pay attention to what happens inside of prisons unless there are murders, uprisings, or scandals. Although both of the authors of this book had visited and occasionally conducted research inside correctional facilities, prior to the LoneStar Project prisons were in many ways an enigma to us as well. It is one thing to take a class and summarize the state of knowledge on topics related institutional corrections and prisoner reentry; it is something quite different to interview the men who live in these facilities and learn about their life in prison. The LoneStar Project is among the largest and most comprehensive studies of gangs and gang members in prison. Studies like this are never the sole product of the people named as the investigators, nor are books the sole product of the people named as authors. And we are no exception to this.

*Competing for Control* was made possible because of the LoneStar Project, or the Texas Study of Trajectories, Association, and Reentry. Both the Texas Department of Criminal Justice and the National Institute of Justice made a major investment in this study; the former by allowing us to conduct this research in their facilities, the latter by providing the financial support that a project of this nature and scope necessitates. We are thankful to the many people at TDCJ who shared our vision and made it possible to carry it out, including Bryan Collier, Lorie Davis, Bill Stevens, Karen Hall, Alexis Smith, Frances Beitia, Wardens Jones, Carter, Prestwood, O'Hare, and Bailey, and the many captains, majors, lieutenants, sergeants, and officers who worked at the two prisons where we conducted our study. Letting outsiders in a prison poses risks of many kinds, and we appreciate the confidence placed in us and our research team. At NIJ we thank Donna Davis, Jessica Highland, Winnie Reed, Greg Ridgeway, and Phelan Wyrick for supporting the LoneStar Project. Part of the reason gang research in prisons is rare is due to access and support; TDCJ and NIJ allowed us to successfully gain such access.

The LoneStar Project was not "just" 802 baseline interviews with prisoners (and over 1,000 post-release interviews). Both the planning and implementation phases involved more than meets the eye—site visits, survey instrument development and testing, software programming, the hiring and training of interviewers, coordinating interviews, managing field relations, and data analysis. And there are the inevitable unexpected challenges. We were fortunate to have a motivated, diligent, and committed team in place to carry out this project. Vince Webb and Doug Dretke were instrumental in facilitating access and securing permissions, as well as fielding questions about planning and implementation as issues arose. Erin Orrick did a phenomenal job serving as the site coordinator in Texas; it is no small feat to enter a project midway through data collection.

The greatest debt is owed to the four doctoral students—Chantal Fahmy, Kallee McCullough, Meghan Mitchell, and Jun Wu—who worked on the LoneStar Project from start to finish. They were fearless in taking on tasks large and small and experiencing the highs and lows of a project like this. Among the most rewarding parts of the study was witnessing them turn their ideas into doctoral dissertations. We are especially indebted to Meghan Mitchell for her role as the project manager and lifeblood of the study. Many others made important contributions to the study, including Kathryn Doughty, Natasha Khade, and Andrea Tilstra, along with the dozens of graduate and undergraduate students who participated as interviewers. Lastly, we must thank Kendra Clark and Jennifer Tostlebe for all of their efforts in contact management, interviewing, and data analysis, both of whom brought energy to the project when it needed it the most.

We would be remiss if we did not recognize the broad institutional support we received. At Arizona State University, the ASU Foundation and the School of Criminology and Criminal Justice supported this study and the book in both small and large ways. Cassia Spohn, Carrie Hudiburgh, and the IRB office are deserving of special recognition for their support. At the University of Colorado Boulder, the Department of Sociology gave a young assistant professor the latitude to carry out such a major endeavor. The LoneStar Project would not have been nearly as successful if it were not for the support of the Institute of Behavioral Science. There are many people to recognize, but we would especially like to thank those who provided administrative and technological advice and support over the last five years, including Jim Dykes, Del Elliott, Robert Graham, Karl Hill, Dave Huizinga, Jeremy Johnson, Jani Little, Ashton Mellott, Mike Muehlbradt, Marisa Seitz, and Dorothy Watson. We must also thank our colleagues at Sam Houston State University.

A number of our colleagues inside and outside of our departments are deserving of recognition for the feedback they provided on *Competing for Control*. Robert Dreesen and Jackie Grant were a joy to work with at

Cambridge University Press, and we are thankful to the anonymous reviewers who took the time to provide us with excellent feedback. Natasha Khade, Katelyn Loomis, Meghan Mitchell, Jose Sanchez, Jennifer Tostlebe, and Jacob Young read and commented on chapters in the book. Portions of the book were presented during colloquiums held at the Institute of Behavioral Science, Queen's University Belfast, Pennsylvania State University, University of California Irvine, University of Maryland, and University of Pennsylvania, as well as presentations delivered to the Academy of Criminal Justice Sciences and the American Society of Criminology. The feedback we received was especially helpful. Any errors or omissions are the responsibility of the authors.

Our final acknowledgement is the most important one. Thank you to our families. Natty, Cyrus, and Addy for David. JoAnn, Will, Sara, Laura and Liz for Scott. They tolerated the early mornings and late nights, the phone calls, emails, travel, and all of the seemingly endless interruptions that came with the LoneStar Project and *Competing for Control*.

I

# Foundation for the Study

At the turn of the century, James Jacobs, New York University law professor and author of *Stateville* (1977), lamented: "It is hard to understand why the prison gang phenomenon does not attract more attention from the media, scholars, and policy analysts" (2001, vi). Certainly, prisons are dangerous places that impact communities as well as the lives of inmates and those who work there. Over the last several years, prison gangs have made headlines across the country. The 2013 inmate hunger strike in California – involving over 30,000 inmates – was organized by black, Latino, and white gang members housed in solitary confinement for indeterminate sentences (Reiter 2016); the executive director of the Colorado Department of Corrections was executed on the doorstep of his home in 2013 by a recently released 211 Crew prison gang member (Prendergast 2014); and a multi-jurisdictional task force led to the indictments of nearly seventy-five Aryan Brotherhood of Texas gang members, some of whom were implicated in the blowtorch removal of a gang tattoo, the inspiration for a *Sons of Anarchy* episode (Schiller 2016). These are just a few of the events that illustrate the significance of prison gangs for society.

Despite these important events, a recent systematic review and analysis of the study of gangs confirms Jacobs's lament (Pyrooz and Mitchell 2015). For each article, essay, or book written about gangs and gang members under any form of incarceration – juvenile, jail, or prison systems – there were twenty-five works written about gangs and gang members in street settings. Put simply, our knowledge about gangs in institutional settings pales in comparison to what is known in street settings. Such deficits come with unknown costs, particularly with respect to correctional policy and practice. This is the reason Mark Fleisher and Scott Decker (2001b, 2) described prisons as the "final frontier" in gang research. Not a lot has changed in recent years.

It is not as if gangs have magically disappeared from prisons or no longer present serious challenges to the management of prisons. Indeed, gangs remain at the forefront of issues in contemporary corrections as documented by the three events noted above. It is clear that gangs occupy an important place in the social order of prisons despite the fact that gang members constitute a minority of inmates. Gangs are responsible for a disproportionate share of violence and misconduct and maintain a grip on contraband markets in prisons. They also influence housing arrangements and programming, as placing rival gang members in the same cell or classroom could have violent consequences. Gangs have also been implicated in the orchestration of deadly riots and serious disturbances across the nation, not unlike what occurred in California. And, not surprisingly, gang members fare worse than non-gang members when they are released from prison and return to the community, owing to their obligations to the gang.

Issues such as those described above are part of the reason why gangs rank as one of the thorniest problems in contemporary corrections. A survey of executives from twenty-eight state prison systems rated the management of gangs and security threat groups as a major correctional priority (Association of State Correctional Administrators 2013, 9). On a scale from 1 (low agency priority) to 10 (high agency priority), gangs scored an 8. Not one prison administrator assigned a score below 6, and one-fifth assigned scores of 9 or 10. Gangs and security threat groups ranked in the top five as a priority to prison administrators, just behind adhering to the standards of the Prison Rape Elimination Act, staff recruitment and retention, the cost of inmate healthcare, and managing mentally ill offenders. These are clearly important issues. There is convergence between the findings from a small body of research on gangs in prisons and the priorities of the executives of prison systems: gangs in prison pose important risks to the safety and effective management of such institutions. If prison gangs are so important, this begs the question: Why do we know so little about them?

## THE CHALLENGES OF STUDYING GANGS IN PRISON

Researchers study a host of violent settings, including drug dealers and users, war and conflict zones, street gang members, active burglars and robbers, illegal gun dealers, and extremist groups. Why not prison gangs? Robert Fong and Salvador Buentello (1991) held that there were three reasons for the lack of information about gangs and gang members in prison. First, the official documentation of gangs, gang members, and gang-related misconduct was underdeveloped. Many prison systems did not even record information about gangs prior to the 1990s, while others collected this information but in databases that were outdated or poorly maintained. Some argue that even data on the number of gang-related inmates may be among the "most elusive figures in corrections" (Trulson, Marquart, and Kawucha 2006, 26). The state of gang intelligence and management of databases has improved since the observations of Fong and Buentello. However, outside of accessing actual case files of serious misconduct or gang intelligence reports, there is a severe shortage of officially reported information about gangs in prisons. There is no central repository containing national data or even reports about gangs, gang members, or gang violence in prison (Gaston and Huebner 2015), unlike the multiple sources of information about gangs in street settings. Instead, it is often necessary to piece together estimates from disparate sources with unknown reliability and validity to make inferences about the extent and nature of gang-related activity in US prisons.

Second, prison administration is generally reluctant to grant access to outside researchers to study gang activity, which Fong and Buentello (1991) attributed to fears over safety and risk aversion. It is no surprise that most of the research on prison gangs relies not on the words of gang members or observations of the collective behavior of gangs, but on the official data gathered by prison officials and analyzed by researchers. What is undoubtedly the most important work on prison gangs in the last two decades – David Skarbek's (2014) *The Social Order of the Underworld* – was based on data derived from the research literature, official reports, legal documents, memoirs, documentaries, and conversations with correctional staff and ex-inmates. Notably missing from this detailed list are interviews with prison gang members. The same concerns may be raised regarding the important work of political scientist Benjamin Lessing (2010, 2016). Wacquant (2002) noted that researchers deserted the prison scene around the time prisons experienced unprecedented growth. Whether this was due to the shifting winds of interest among researchers, political decisions about isolating prison from public view, or the lack of funding to support such research is unclear. What is clear, however, is that access to prisons is still hard-fought; as Skarbek (2014, 10) observed: "the same walls that keep inmates locked in also keep researchers out. Getting evidence on the inmate community, and specifically prison gangs, therefore presents a substantial challenge." The walls seem even more difficult to penetrate when it comes to research on prison gangs and gang membership because researchers face a dual challenge: gaining permission from prison authorities and securing participation from prison gang members.

The third reason offered by Fong and Buentello is that gangs and gang members housed in prisons are secretive and prohibit the sharing of information with others, including researchers. This secretiveness extends beyond the "convict code" and likely has roots in the need to keep information about the exchange of prison contraband and the organizational structure of the gang discreet. Securing inmate participation and adequate response rates in prison settings is challenging, regardless of the subject of inquiry, as Derek Kreager and his colleagues (2016) have noted. Even if inmates agree to participate in a study, there is also concern that interviewing inmates using structured or even semi-structured surveys may not be an effective method of collecting information. This takes on added significance for gangs, which is why the reliability and validity of street gang members' self-reports have long been the subject of concern and empirical scrutiny (Decker, Pyrooz,

Sweeten, and Moule 2014; Esbensen et al. 2001; Thornberry et al. 2003; Webb, Katz, and Decker 2006). Many believe that gang members will not answer questions truthfully or will purposely mislead researchers about certain subjects. When questions turn to issues related to the gang as a group, rather than the individual gang member relaying information about himself/herself, some argue that gang members – especially prison gang members – must abide by a code of silence (Fong and Buentello 1991). We have witnessed such behavior firsthand. Over the course of gathering data from inmates in a county jail using self-administered surveys, an influential gang member tried to influence the responses of other inmates by reading aloud how he was answering questions pertaining to gang organization. It remains an open question as to whether or not gang members will provide reliable and valid responses during an interview. Despite these considerable barriers to doing research with prison gang members, we believe it is important to push forward on this frontier: there is simply too much at stake to not find out.

Some research on gangs in prison has been conducted. Indeed, a number of studies have been carried out by researchers in prison settings, including ethnographies and extensive surveys (Camp and Camp 1985; Fleisher 1989; Irwin 1970). There is no question that the research can be done. However, like Jacobs (2001), we find it peculiar that so little research has been conducted on gangs, gang members, and gang activities in prison settings. If we were to paint the type of research conducted on gangs in incarcerated settings with broad strokes, the picture would look something like this:

- A handful of **rich qualitative studies** on gangs that are at least somewhat dated due to period effects (e.g., Crouch and Marquart 1989; DiIulio Jr. 1987; Gundur 2018; Hunt et al. 1993; Irwin 1970; Jacobs 1974; Trammell 2012), along with a small but recent group of work conducted outside the United States (Biondi 2016; Maitra, McLean, and Holligan 2017; Phillips 2012);
- A small number of studies that **survey correctional administrators** about gangs in their facilities (Camp and Camp 1985; Pyrooz and Mitchell 2018; Ruddell, Decker, and Egley 2006; Winterdyk and Ruddell 2010; Wood and Adler 2001);
- A small number of **individual studies** that examine the causes or consequences of institutional gang activity that are nested within large, longitudinal surveys (Mears et al. 2013; Pyrooz, Gartner, and Smith 2017);
- Several studies where the **context of gang identity differs** from the context of the behavior of interest, such as surveying about gang membership in prison but behavior before or after prison (Huebner, Varano, and Bynum 2007; Rufino, Fox, and Kercher 2012) or surveying about gang membership before prison and behavior in prison (Huebner 2003);

- A large number of studies that rely only on **official data** to study gang membership or gang activities (e.g., Ralph et al. 1996; Steiner and Wooldredge 2014; Worrall and Morris 2012).

Exceptions to these categories are far and few between. Of course, there are also studies that have carried out ethnographic and survey research in juvenile facilities (e.g., Lopez-Aguado 2016; Maxson et al. 2012; Wood et al. 2014) and county jails (e.g., Fox, Lane, and Akers 2010; Kissner and Pyrooz 2009; Tapia 2013). But, as Maxson (2012; Scott and Maxson 2016) reported in her work in California juvenile correctional facilities, juvenile gangs appear to be different from the adult gangs found in prison. Others have reported that there may be greater similarities between gangs in county jails and prisons, as linkages are perhaps stronger between the two settings as inmates cycle from one institution to another (Tapia, Sparks, and Miller 2014). But that too is a question deserving of greater empirical scrutiny. Together, these prior studies have shed tremendous light on nature, correlates, and perceptions of prison gangs based on official records, media accounts, small samples, and self-administered surveys.

Our argument is that it is necessary to *interview* inmates if we want to learn about the conditions and consequences of incarceration. Self-report surveys of delinquency in non-institutional settings preceded self-report surveys with gang members by a generation. Just as in-person surveys and interviews have been a boon to street gang research, we contend that such methods of data collection are equally important for prison gang research. It is essential to contrast the prison experiences of gang members against those of inmates who have not been involved in gangs on the street or in prison. It is also necessary to gather rich content from prisoners, not just information that is gang-related, but also with respect to theories of criminal and deviant behavior and identity. Understanding the complexities (health, employment, reentry readiness, beliefs in procedural fairness, etc.) of inmate lives is necessary to paint a picture of this population that is more comprehensive, deep, and representative. We further contend that cross-walking this information with numerous other data sources such as prison misconduct data, arrest records, and prior incarceration data will yield a more complete picture about life on the inside of prison and its relationship to life on the outside.

We also argue that the best way to understand the influence of prison and gangs is to interview the same people across multiple time points, particularly as they transition out of prison and return to the community and, in many cases, back to prison. This makes it possible to determine how behaviors and identities change as individuals navigate through old and new structures, belief systems, networks, and relationships when leaving prison behind. It is particularly important to understand how imprisonment affects a gang member's involvement in crime after release. This is true of individuals who enter prison as street gang members, those who affiliate while in prison, and those who disengage from gangs while in prison. In doing so, such a combination of rich and substantive questions, appropriate comparison groups, and longitudinal data goes to great lengths to determine the symbiosis between the street and the prison, including the distinct characteristics of each with respect to gang activity and gang dynamics. Before we can illustrate the benefits of the approach to studying gangs that we are proposing, that is, longitudinal, survey-based interviews, it is first necessary to step back and understand the context in which this circumstance emerged.

## INCARCERATION AND GANGS IN THE UNITED STATES

Incarceration in the United States has seen dramatic peaks and valleys over the last century. Useem and Piehl (2008) identified four distinct periods of prison growth in the United States. While we do not discuss the sources of trends in prison growth because others have done so in great detail (see National Research Council 2014; Pfaff 2017; Pratt 2009; Useem and Piehl 2008), it is useful to consider these periods of growth as they relate to the emergence of gangs in US prisons. After all, gangs were not active in prisons during much of this period, and for some prison systems, gangs are a problem that only emerged in recent years.

Useem and Piehl classified the era from the Great Depression to the beginning of the civil rights movement (1930–1960) as the "trendless trend." Per capita, the number of prisoners in the United States remained steady, around 100 per 100,000 persons. The second period was termed "modest to large decline," where the per capita prison population actually declined by about 20 percent over the course of a decade (1961–1972). The third period of growth between 1973 and 1988, "buildup begins," represents a turning point in punishment and incarceration in the United States. The rate of incarceration jumped from around 100 persons incarcerated per 100,000 people to nearly 250 persons per capita. This led to the period of "accelerated growth," between 1989 and 2005, which is best represented on the National Research Council's cover to the volume, *The Growth of Incarceration in the United States.* By 2005, there were 491 prison inmates for every 100,000 persons in the United States. When policymakers, pundits, and scholars mention mass incarceration, this is the trend to which they are referring.

Figure 1.1 captures much of the latter two periods of prison growth in the United States, while extending Useem and Piehl's (2008) observation another decade using the most recent data from the Bureau of Justice Statistics. Prison growth did not cease in 2005, although it did begin to slow down. Each year through 2009 there were gains in the prison population, and as of 2015 the number of sentenced prisoners still exceeded Useem and Piehl's observations from 2005. However, 2009 represented the zenith in the incarceration trend, where the number of year-end sentenced prisoners topped out at 1,553,574. The country has since moved into a period of decarceration (Mears and

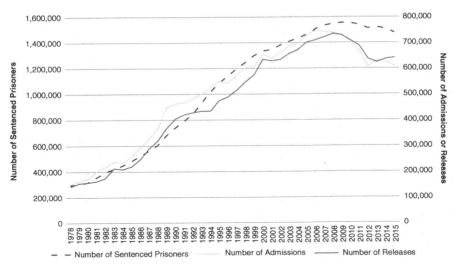

FIGURE 1.1 Year-end sentenced prison population and annual admissions and releases, 1978–2015
Data Source: Bureau of Justice Statistics.

Cochran 2015). Indeed, there were around 80,000 fewer inmates in US prisons in 2015 than in 2009. Such a swing may not seem large, but it is. After all, a shift in the opposite direction – from 1.46 to 1.55 million prisoners – also took about five years to materialize.

Focusing on trends in prison growth tells us a lot about the story of incarceration in the United States. The most obvious observation from this is that our prison population is large, but it has not always been this way. It is safe to conclude that mass incarceration is a rather recent occurrence, emerging in the last two to three decades. While we have seen some evidence of decarceration within some prison systems, there is no doubt that we remain in a period of mass incarceration. But what is most interesting to us typically receives less attention, even though the implications for institutional corrections and communities are of considerable significance, and especially to prisons, gangs, and culture: admissions and releases.

Also included in Figure 1.1 is the annual number of admissions and releases to US prisons. Between 1978 and 2008, there were more admissions to US prisons than there were releases, hence the buildup in the prison population. This buildup, however, occurred across continuous increments rather than with a single shock to the system. Indeed, there were only four years where the prison population experienced double-digit percentage point changes – 1981, 1982, 1989, and 1993 (all increases). But focusing only on aggregate prison growth belies one important fact: both admissions *and* releases rose rapidly over the last four decades. And both admissions and releases are closely related to one another, which indicates that the prison population is constantly churning. The turnover rate in the prison population – the number of releases divided by prisoners – has hovered between 41 and 55 percent. This means that churning is a two-way street: inmates are continually coming in to prison and inmates are leaving prison. In 2015, just over 608,000 people transitioned from "citizen" to "inmate" while 641,000 people transitioned from "inmate" to "citizen." The impact that this magnitude of churning has for individuals and institutions (such as prisons and jails, but also families and the labor force) is not well understood. One thing is clear: such churning is not conducive to producing order either in prisons or the communities that have the highest rates of incarceration (Morenoff and Harding 2014; Western 2018).

Such transitions alter the makeup of prisons, although the implications of this churning are not clear – particularly with respect to gangs. Indeed, such changes in the prison population raise a host of interesting questions about gangs in prison.

- In what ways are gangs involved in misconduct and violence in prison?
- How are gangs in prison organized and structured?
- How do gangs maintain their position in the prison social hierarchy given the constant turnover among members?
- What leads new inmates to want to join the ranks of gangs in prison?
- How do gangs select prospective members of the new class of inmates each year to replenish their numbers?
- What are the consequences of gang affiliation for inmates and prisons?
- How do gangs handle the violations of norms and rules when inmates remain in constant transition?

Before addressing these questions theoretically, as we do in the next chapter, and empirically, as we do in the remaining chapters, we first situate the emergence of gangs in US prisons historically and contemporarily.

There are two overarching issues that we feel are important to address. First, across US prison systems, did gangs emerge before or during the era of mass incarceration? A component of the answer to this is the contribution of the prison gang members to the overall prison population. The second question addresses a related question, but with an emphasis on street gang emergence. Did the emergence of gangs in prison precede or succeed the emergence of gangs on the street? Both are of fundamental importance to prisons and prison gangs, as the answers shed light on the origins of gangs. As we detail in the next chapter, there are conflicting accounts of whether prison gangs are a product of the institution or a product of the street. There is a great deal of theory and research on what gave rise to gangs in street settings, but with a few exceptions the same cannot be said about prison settings. It is therefore important to both understand the emergence of gangs in relation to mass incarceration as well as to determine the sequential order of street and prison gang emergence. In the following analysis, we first present evidence on gang emergence based on a review of the literature, then identify several notable findings in the history of gangs in prison.

Table 1.1 examines the decade when street and prison gangs emerged across the fifty states. To populate this table, we reviewed a host of published documents, including books, articles, and reports, along with surveys that we, as well as others, have conducted (e.g., National Youth Gang Survey; Pyrooz and Mitchell 2018). The reports of gang emergence are based on the first documented activity of gangs in street or prison settings, even though it is known that gang activity waxes and wanes over time (Howell 2015). We did not assess whether the source validated the existence of a given gang according to leading definitions. However, all of the sources we drew on were gang-related studies that underwent some level of peer review. This table complements Klein and Maxson's (2006) documentation of the emergence of street gangs in US cities, while extending our knowledge to include the emergence of gangs in US prison systems. We were unable to locate information on prison for four states – Alaska, Kansas, Louisiana, and Maine – that we treat as missing rather than an absence of gangs.

There are several conclusions we reach based on Table 1.1. First, the 1980s not only marked the buildup to mass incarceration in the United States, but it was also a period that witnessed the widespread emergence of gangs both in street and prison settings. Put simply, gangs went national on the street and in prison. The number of prison systems with gangs nearly doubled, jumping from sixteen prison systems at the conclusion of the 1970s to thirty-one by the end of the 1980s. Just as it was no longer possible to claim that street gangs were a Los Angeles or Chicago problem by the end of the 1980s, it was also no longer possible to claim that prison gangs were a California or Illinois problem.

Second, gangs emerge in street settings before they do in prison systems. Although what we report does not allow us to precisely identify whether street gangs preceded prison gangs by one year or one decade, more states (twenty-one in total) experienced street gang emergence before prison gang emergence. This does not mean that street gangs are a prerequisite for prison gangs, but the high rate of criminal involvement among street gang members (Pyrooz et al. 2016) and the prospect for the importation of culture from the street to prison (Hunt et al. 1993; Irwin and Cressey 1962) does breathe life into this question. If gang members participate in high levels of violent crime and are getting arrested, particularly during the time of the prison boom, they are likely to be imprisoned and to have imported aspects of their membership, alliances, rivalries, and proclivity for violence into institutional settings. Table 1.1 also provides insight into the importation/exportation debate about street and prison gangs. It is clear that street gangs precede prison gangs, suggesting that – at least initially – gang symbols and practices are imported to prison, where they are adapted, changed, and perhaps exported back to the street.

TABLE 1.1  *The emergence of street and prison gangs in the US by decade*

| State | 1950s/ earlier | 1960s | 1970s | 1980s | 1990s | 2000s/ later |
|---|---|---|---|---|---|---|
| Alabama | | | Street | | Prison | |
| Alaska | | | | Street | | |
| Arizona | | Street | Prison | | | |
| Arkansas | | | Prison | Street | | |
| California | Street & Prison | | | | | |
| Colorado | | | Street | Prison | | |
| Connecticut | | | Street & Prison | | | |
| Delaware | | | Street | | Prison | |
| Georgia | | | | Street & Prison | | |
| Florida | | | Street | Prison | | |
| Hawaii | | | | Street & Prison | | |
| Idaho | | | | Prison | Street | |
| Illinois | Street | Prison | | | | |
| Indiana | | Prison | Street | | | |
| Iowa | | Prison | | Street | | |
| Kansas | | | | Street | | |
| Kentucky | | | | Street & Prison | | |
| Louisiana | | | | Street | | |
| Maine | | | | | Street | |
| Maryland | | | | Street & Prison | | |
| Massachusetts | | | Street | | Prison | |
| Michigan | | | Street | Prison | | |
| Minnesota | | | | Street & Prison | | |
| Mississippi | | | | Street | Prison | |
| Missouri | | | | Street & Prison | | |
| Montana | | | | | Street | Prison |
| Nebraska | | | | Street | Prison | |
| Nevada | | | Street & Prison | | | |

(*continued*)

TABLE 1.1 (continued)

| State | 1950s/ earlier | 1960s | 1970s | 1980s | 1990s | 2000s/ later |
|---|---|---|---|---|---|---|
| New Hampshire | | | | | Street & Prison | |
| New Jersey | | | Street | | Prison | |
| New Mexico | | | Street | Prison | | |
| New York | Street | | | Prison | | |
| North Carolina | | | Prison | Street | | |
| North Dakota | | | | | Street & Prison | |
| Ohio | | | | Street & Prison | | |
| Oklahoma | | | | Street & Prison | | |
| Oregon | | | | Street | Prison | |
| Pennsylvania | | Street | Prison | | | |
| Rhode Island | | Prison | | Street | | |
| South Carolina | | | Street | | Prison | |
| South Dakota | | | | Street | Prison | |
| Tennessee | | | | Street | Prison | |
| Texas | | | Street & Prison | | | |
| Utah | | | Prison | Street | | |
| Vermont | | | | | Street | |
| Virginia | | | Prison | Street | | |
| Washington | Prison | | Street | | | |
| West Virginia | | | | Street & Prison | | |
| Wisconsin | | | Prison | Street | | |
| Wyoming | | | | | Street | Prison |

Note: Vermont has no prison gang reports; Alaska, Kansas, Louisiana, and Maine are missing prison gang reports. In California, street gangs emerged before prison gangs, but are combined for display purposes.

Third, there is also considerable evidence of simultaneous street and prison gang emergence as well as prison gang emergence preceding street gang emergence. Fourteen states followed the former pattern (Connecticut, Georgia, Hawaii, Kentucky, Maryland, Minnesota, Missouri, Nevada, New Hampshire, North Dakota, Ohio, Oklahoma, Texas, and West Virginia), while ten states followed the latter pattern (Arkansas, Idaho, Indiana, Iowa, North Carolina, Rhode Island, Utah, Virginia, Washington, and Wisconsin). As we mentioned above, this does not tell us the role prison gangs played in street gang emergence, although it is clear that gang activity that occurs in prison likely does not stay in prison. That is, the reach of gangs extends from the prison to the street, which may also have bearing on street gang emergence and permanence.

Nonetheless, the emergence of gangs in street settings has been documented rather extensively, particularly in large urban centers (Adamson 2000; Howell 2015; Thrasher 1927). There is evidence that prison gangs have existed since the early 1950s, as reported in the works of Camp and Camp (1985), Irwin (1980), and Orlando-Morningstar (1997). It is a matter of some debate, but it is believed that the Gypsy Jokers in Washington state prison was the first prison gang. However, Warden Lewis Lawes (Sing Sing Prison, New York) spoke of the 132 gangs in his prison in 1931 (New York Times 1931). The Gypsy Jokers, an outlaw motorcycle group, remains a notorious group with members in several continents. On the street, outlaw motorcycle groups are different from street gangs, but when confined, they take on the essential features of a prison gang, as we outline in the next section.

Whatever the origins of the first prison gang, other major prison gangs emerged shortly after the Gypsy Jokers. In California prisons, the most well-known Latino gangs, the Mexican Mafia and La Nuestra Familia, formed in 1957 and 1965, respectively. The Mexican Mafia, or *La Eme,* developed out of a group of street gang inmates from East Los Angeles for the purposes of protection, illicit activities, and power. When their predatory actions extended from whites and blacks to other Latinos, particularly Latinos from rural areas of northern California, it gave rise to La Nuestra Familia (Camp and Camp 1985), a fierce rivalry that remains in place today. As the rivalry between northern and southern California gangs emerged among generational lines of Latinos, the remaining racial groups in California prisons soon began forming alliances; black inmates formed the Black Guerilla Family in 1966, aligning with the northern Latinos, while white inmates formed the Aryan Brotherhood in 1967, aligning with the southern Latinos. Both the Aryan Brotherhood and the Black Guerilla Family formed for the purposes of preservation and adopted the philosophy of supremacist movements, the former linked more closely to racial supremacy and the latter more closely to racial militancy. A key feature of these four gangs is their intense focus on race and ethnicity as core qualities of membership and the identification of rivalry, which remains largely true today. Indeed, these four gangs remain among the most dominant in California prisons today.

Many of the gangs that soon emerged in other prison systems took on California prison gangs' namesakes. In some cases this was due to imitation, in others it was due to the migration of gang members from one state to another. In the 1970s gangs such as the Arizona Aryan Brotherhood and the Arizona Old Mexican Mafia emerged, along with the Aryan Brotherhood, Nuestra Familia, and Black Guerilla Family in Utah (Camp and Camp 1985; Orlando-Morningstar 1997). The Texas Syndicate, in fact, did not originate in Texas, but instead developed in the early 1970s in California among a small group of inmates from Texas who banded together for protection (Camp and Camp 1985). These inmates eventually returned to Texas, and ultimately brought the Texas Syndicate into the Texas prison system, which was free of gangs up until that point.

While we have examined prison gang emergence in California linked to one of the US "gang capitals" (Los Angeles), the street gangs of Chicago (the other gang capital) were also linked to the rise to prison gangs in Illinois. The street gangs that emerged in the aftermath of activism in the 1960s were responsible for the bulk of gang activity in Illinois prisons, as documented in detail by Jacobs (1974). Gangs like the Disciples, El Rukns, Latin Kings, and Vice Lords were the most well known, and their presence is felt in several prison systems throughout the United States. More recently, Chicago street gangs have begun to fracture and atomize around neighborhoods and blocks, which will likely have implications for prison dynamics in Illinois.

What our brief review of the history of gang emergence does not reveal is the extent to which gang members are present in US prisons. What proportion of prison inmates are gang members? How has this changed over time? Outside of carceral settings, we have a somewhat reliable understanding of the number of gang members and the proportion of the population who are gang members, owing to extensive efforts to collect data from law enforcement about gang activity in the United States. We view the resulting estimates about non-institutional gang membership as a benchmark to compare to gang membership in the institutional population. One suspects that a higher proportion of inmates are gang members than is the case among citizens in street settings.

The most reliable estimates of gang members were produced by the National Gang Center, which administered the National Youth Gang Survey to a representative sample of law enforcement agencies about gang activity in their jurisdiction. This survey was conducted annually from 1996 to 2012, before being terminated in 2013, unfortunately. Estimates of the number of gang members in the United States ranged from 694,000 to 850,000. The latter estimate came from the most recent survey conducted in 2012. The survey also provided a breakdown of the number of juvenile and adult gang members, with the adult figure providing a more appropriate comparison group to prisons. Adult gang members constituted around 60 percent of all gang members in the United States, translating to about 0.2 percent of the adult population. In other words, about 1 out of every 500 adults in the United States is a gang member. How do these figures compare to the US prison population?

As Shytierra Gaston and Beth Huebner (2015) have pointed out, there is no central repository for information about gangs in prison. Prison systems are not surveyed annually about gang activity in their institutions. The best data on prison inmates come from the Bureau of Justice Statistics as part of its National Inmate Survey and Survey of Inmates in State Correctional Facilities, yet these studies inexplicably lack questions about gang membership in prison. It is therefore necessary to piece together estimates of even the most basic queries – such as, what proportion of US inmates are gang members? – from disparate sources using different definitions and measurement systems.

Figure 1.2 reports the results from six surveys of prison systems that could be considered the most representative portrait of prison gang membership. The first was conducted by Camp and Camp (1985). A total of twenty-three prison systems provided data on the number of gang members in their institutions in 1984, including California and Illinois. Camp and Camp reported that there were 12,634 gang members in these twenty-three prison systems, which translated into about 3 percent of the prison population in these states. Camp and Camp's work was foundational to the study of prison gangs, as it was not only the first to provide estimates of the prevalence of gang membership, but it also offered rich detail about the origins and behaviors of gangs in these prison systems.

The next estimate of gang membership in US prison systems came from Wells and colleagues (2002). Their study was conducted in 2002 as part of the National Major Gang Task Force, and included thirty-nine US prison

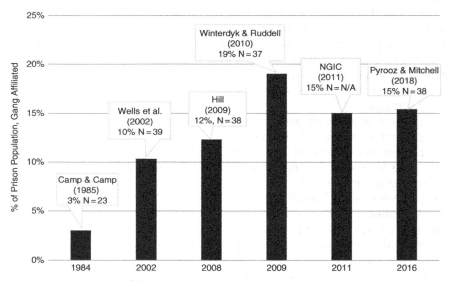

FIGURE 1.2 Estimates of the prevalence of gang membership in US prisons
Notes: Individual prison system data were analyzed to produce national estimates of the prevalence of gang membership in US prisons for Camp and Camp (1985), Hill (2009), Pyrooz and Mitchell (2018), and Wells et al. (2002). The remaining studies only reported state-level average prevalence (Winterdyk and Ruddell 2010) or national count (NGIC [National Gang Intelligence Center] 2011) of gang membership.

systems. The data from these prison systems indicated that there were 112,148 inmates who were Security Threat Group (STG)-involved, or 10 percent of inmates, a sharp jump from what Camp and Camp (1985) observed nearly two decades earlier. Hill (2009) updated these estimates in 2009 based on a survey of thirty-eight prison systems. Recall that 2009 represents the zenith in the era of mass incarceration. Yet, both the frequency and prevalence scores that Hill obtained were not too different from those of Wells and colleagues, even though the survey was conducted seven years later and the prison population had increased by over 12 percent. A little over 132,000 inmates, or 12 percent, were gang members. Together, these studies provide consistent evidence that gang members are disproportionately represented among inmates in US prisons.

The benefit of the Hill (2009) and Wells (2002) studies is that they both reported the number of known gang-involved inmates in each prison system in their study. Two additional surveys of gang members (National Gang Intelligence Center 2011; Winterdyk and Ruddell 2010) that were conducted shortly thereafter did not make such information available, instead only reporting the aggregate number of gang members and/or proportion of gang-involved inmates averaged across prison systems. We also include the figures from the National Gang Intelligence Center, given that it was established by the US Congress and represents an accumulation of knowledge from federal agencies. However, there is too little information about the methodology used in the report to reach sound conclusions about prison gang membership. Winterdyk and Ruddell (2010), alternatively, surveyed thirty-seven prison systems about the number of gang members in their custody. Their results indicate that 19 percent of prison inmates are suspected or confirmed gang members, and is the highest figure reported in such research. It should be noted that their values are not based on using the total number of inmates in the thirty-seven prison systems as the denominator to compute the proportion of gang members. Instead, it was the proportion of gang members averaged across the prison systems. This may have increased the values they report.

Pyrooz and Mitchell (2018) conducted the most recent survey of gang members in prison based on a study focusing on the use of restrictive housing to manage gangs. While their survey included large prison systems like California and Texas, the US Bureau of Prisons and New York were notably excluded – the former because its restrictive housing practices conflicted with survey definitions, the latter because it claimed that answering the questions would disrupt the routines of its personnel. Fortunately, a total of thirty-eight state prison systems provided data on the number of gang members in the respective institutions. Like Winterdyk and Ruddell (2010), these estimates combined suspected and confirmed gang members. Pyrooz and Mitchell found that 15 percent of inmates in US state prison systems were gang members, which translated to around 148,000 of the 963,000 inmates who were covered by their survey. When the authors imputed estimates of gang members for the 13 missing prison systems, they ended up estimating that 213,000 of the 1.5 million prison inmates were gang members, or approximately 14 percent of the custodial population. This represents the most recent estimate of the proportion and frequency of gang members in US prisons. Again, it is important to underscore that there is no centralized or standardized source of prison gang population information.

Prisons in the United States have undergone dramatic changes over the last four decades, most notably the fivefold increase in the number of prisoners between 1978 and 2015. We have shown that this rise in incarceration corresponds with the proliferation of gangs in prison. In general, street gangs emerged before prison gangs in most US prisons. However, the largest growth in prison gang emergence occurred during the earliest stages of the prison boom. Many of the gangs that emerged during that period remain active and powerful today, a testament to the durability of these groups in the presence of constant turnover in the prison population. The best estimates indicate that there are around 200,000 gang members in US prisons, with about one out of every seven inmates affiliated with gangs. Gang members are overrepresented in prisons relative to the general population by a factor of seventy-five. In contrast to non-institutional settings, where in most communities it is rare to come across gang members, institutional settings are places where gang members are commonly found. Hence the comment by James Jacobs (1974, 399): "The 'gang thing' is the most significant reality behind the walls."

What we have presented above establishes when gangs emerged in prison and the pervasiveness of gang members in prisons, but it does not tell us about the essential features of prison gangs. What kind of groups are they? How are they different from or similar to street gangs? And, why is studying gangs in prison important? These questions, we argue, are critically important for research, practice, and policy, and must be answered before embarking on an empirical study of gangs in prisons.

BASICS OF PRISON GANGS

The question of what constitutes a prison gang and a prison gang member has received far less attention from researchers (and practitioners) than what constitutes a street gang and a street gang member. Clearly much of this is due to the inability to conduct research in prison settings. While we deal with this question in greater detail in the next chapter, suffice it to say at this point that the lack of prison gang research and poor definitions of prison gang membership go hand in hand. After all, the search for valid definitions would be among the first tasks on the research agenda for prison gang research.

Klein and Maxson (2006, 4) define a street gang as a "durable, street-oriented youth group whose involvement in illegal activity is part of its group identity." This definition has become the foundation for a good deal of the research on street gangs that has taken place in the United States and Europe for the past decade. It clearly has shortcomings for use in identifying a prison gang. First, a "street-orientation" is not likely to be maintained in prison; the focus would be shifted to institutional activities such as contraband, self-protection, and dominance. In circumstances where prison gangs influence gang activity on the street, however, there could be a street influence. Congregating on "the yard" during recreational time would be the closest parallel, but even then, there are stark differences, especially for gangs whose members are housed in solitary confinement by virtue of their status, as is the case for many individuals in this study. Indeed, the yard is an isolated place for these inmates, for whom human contact occurs only when being shackled (or other forms of physical control) by correctional officers (e.g., Reiter 2016). Second, most individuals in prison are not "youths" but rather adults in their thirties and older. Some of the gang members in our sample are grandparents and others qualify for social security. Thus, a useful definition of prison gang members must focus on adults, rather than even a loose definition of youth. Third, the definition does not include race or ethnicity, among the most important characteristics of prison gang membership. There is a reason it is rare to find gangs that are racially and ethnically diverse in prison. Racial and ethnic identification is a defining feature of most prison gangs and creates the "oppositionality" that fuels group processes such as joining, engaging in fights, and protection. There is also a considerable body of research that finds that self-nomination is a robust way to measure gang membership. However, such a technique has not been used extensively in prison research. As a consequence, we do not know the extent to which self-nomination as a prison gang member shares the same strong measurement properties as it does on the street. There is reason to believe that prison gangs are more secretive and exert more control over their members than do street gangs. Secrecy and control potentially complicate the use of self-nomination, an issue we attend to in the chapters to follow.

Despite some obvious differences, prison gangs and street gangs share many things in common. Most importantly, both engage in high levels of criminal activity. They also share some characteristics in common with other groups that engage in high levels of serious offending, such as drug smugglers, human traffickers, extremist groups, and organized crime groups. The most important of these common characteristics are the commitment to deviant norms and the role of a group process in many activities, especially violence. It is believed that prison gangs can be distinguished from other offending groups, including street gangs. The key difference between street and prison gangs and these other groups is that prison gang membership is of longer duration, has a stronger collective identity, and has more consequences particularly in the exercise of discipline over members. These characteristics reflect the age structure, higher level of organization, and expanded role in illicit activity among prison gangs. At least that is what the current state of knowledge on prison gangs has led us to believe. Such characteristics are also reflected in available definitions of prison gangs. Lyman (1989, 48) defines a prison gang as follows:

"an organization which operates within the prison system as a self-perpetuating criminally oriented entity, consisting of a select group of inmates who have established an organized chain of command and are governed by an established code of conduct."

While this definition is nearly three decades old, it remains widely used despite the lack of empirical validation. The FBI (National Gang Intelligence Center 2011) defines a prison gang with even greater detail:

"Prison gangs are criminal organizations that originated within the penal system and operate within correctional facilities throughout the United States, although released members may be operating on the street. Prison gangs are also self-perpetuating criminal entities that can continue their criminal operations outside the confines of the penal system."

This may be useful as an operational definition, but it ignores the importation of street gangs, gang membership, and gang values into the prison. We believe that importation may play an important role and must be a central element of any study of prison gangs. The final definition that we highlight is provided in the important work of Skarbek (2014, 9), who noted that a prison gang is:

"an inmate organization that operates within a prison system, that has a corporate entity, exists into perpetuity and whose membership is restricted, mutually exclusive, and often requires a lifetime commitment."

Such a definition is highly exclusive, and includes unnecessary defining features of gangs, particularly the requirement of a lifetime commitment. Indeed, our research demonstrates that prison gang membership is not a lifelong commitment, and, in fact, most gang members *leave* gangs in prison.

We did not enter the study with an operational definition of a prison gang. Rather, our thinking on these matters is guided by street gang research; the imposition of some features, such as collective identity, durability, and criminal activity is essential, while others, like organization, are unnecessary and leave out too much. The most prevalent gang in the prison system we study – the Tangos – lack such organizational structure. If we were to exclude the Tangos from our study, we would misrepresent the reality of gangs in Texas prisons. In the end, we launched this project by making a major assumption abrogating us of the responsibility of defining a prison gang: we relied on self-nomination. We saw ourselves in a position similar to Jeff Fagan (1990), who proposed using self-nomination in his research on street gang members to avoid having to define a gang. The young people he studied knew what a gang was, and so do prison inmates.

Table 1.2 provides a preliminary synthesis that compares street gangs and prison gangs based on existing research. A key difference between the groups is that prison gangs are more organized than street gangs. In addition, prison gangs exert higher levels of control and discipline over their members. They also engage in a wider range of entrepreneurial activities than their counterparts on the street. This is manifested in behaviors such as instrumental violence, covert behavior, protection, drug dealing, and stronger allegiance to the gang. In

TABLE 1.2 *A comparison of prison and street gangs*

| Characteristic | Prison gang | Street gang |
|---|---|---|
| Race/ethnicity | Single race or ethnicity | Mostly single race or ethnicity |
| Age | Concentrated in mid-twenties, with members thirties–forties | Average age in upper teens |
| Organizational structure | Hierarchical | Situational/hierarchical |
| Sources of violence | Symbolic and instrumental; Core activity | Symbolic; Core activity |
| Offending style | Entrepreneurial | Cafeteria style |
| Visibility of behavior | Covert | Overt |
| Drug trafficking | Major activity; Organized, collective | Varies; Mostly individualistic |
| Loyalty to gang | Absolute | Weak bonds |
| Key to membership | Unqualified fidelity; Abide by gang rules; Willingness to engage in violence | Real or perceived fidelity; Abide by street rules; Hanging out |
| Key psychological attributes | Oppositional to correctional authorities; Intimidation; Control; Manipulation | Oppositional to authority; Intimidation; Camaraderie |

*Note:* Adopted from Pyrooz, Decker, and Fleisher (2011).

addition, race/ethnicity plays an even more significant role in prison gangs than on the street. It is not an overstatement to observe that race/ethnicity is the defining characteristic of prison gangs. On the street, neighborhood allegiances – which often transcend race or ethnicity – form the core organizing attribute of gang membership. However, for prison gangs, race trumps street or neighborhood allegiances such that street rivals (Bloods and Crips, People and Folks) unite around race or ethnicity in prison (Goodman 2008; Trulson et al. 2006). Street gangs display a fluid membership where leadership is situational, violence is less organized and more symbolic, and economic gain is more individually oriented (Curry, Decker, and Pyrooz 2014; Howell and Griffiths 2015; Klein and Maxson 2006). There is some evidence that gangs in youth facilities look more like street gangs, appearing to be less organized, more dependent on street allegiances, and more prone to symbolic violence.

It is common to refer to "street gangs" and "prison gangs" as if these groups are mutually exclusive. We believe the use of the street/prison adjective is misleading. There are gangs on the street and gangs in prison. The evidence we uncover suggests that this dichotomy is a false one. When we refer to *street* gangs or *prison* gangs, we are referring to the *context of influence* of a gang. For some gangs, such influence exists on the street and in institutions; for other gangs, it exists in only one setting. A single Tango gang member from Texas would have little ability to exert control over others in California prisons. Yet, if enough men from Texas banded together – like the Texas Syndicate did in California – such influence is possible. Just like other social phenomena, gangs also maintain power in numbers.

## ORGANIZATION OF THE BOOK

The purpose of this book is to understand gangs and gang members in prison. The questions that motivate this research include:

(1) How and why do inmates organize themselves into social groups like gangs?
(2) How do these groups govern themselves and maintain external relations inside and outside of prison?
(3) Who gets involved in these groups and how do they join and leave them?
(4) What are the consequences of group involvement for misconduct and victimization in prison?

Each of these questions is central to the social sciences generally, but especially the fields of criminology, economics, political science, psychology, and sociology. As criminologists, we are particularly interested in the norms and rules that social groups like gangs create and violate, as well as the formal and informal responses to such violations. But we are equally interested in the norms and rules that govern gang activity, and how violations of those rules are responded to by the gang.

This book is strongly focused on transitions. By this we refer to the process of moving into or out of a status, group, or role. We typically think of such transitions as becoming a parent or leaving a job, but transitions apply to the context of prison and gangs as well. Transitions can be long-lasting or short-lived; they can be slow or sudden. Some transitions operate as part of the maturational process in the life course, while others are imposed by external forces. Our interest in transitions operates at two levels. The first level is most evident in our focus on prison, that is, the transition from the "free world" to the prison and back to the "free world," as the respondents in our study call it. The other transitions we are interested in involve entry and exit from gangs, particularly in transition to and from prison. Very little is known about how these status transitions interact with physical transitions to and from institutional settings (street, prison), and much of what we think we know about the topic is based on media and journalistic accounts of gangs. Our goal is to bring sound, empirically based knowledge to these issues to learn more about gangs and imprisonment.

Enter the LoneStar Project. We describe the study in greater detail in Chapter 3. But we acknowledge from the outset that this study is the product of a large team of researchers and students. With funding from the National Institute of Justice and support from our respective universities and the Texas Department of Criminal Justice, we embarked on the largest study of prison gang members conducted to date in the United States. We interviewed a cohort of 802 male gang and non-gang members prior to their release from Texas prisons. We also reinterviewed them at two different time periods upon their return to the community, but our focus in this book is on the baseline prison interview. Only men were included in the study, a shortcoming of our work. Though little is known about female gang members in prison, what we do know suggests that gangs play a far greater role in men's prisons than they do in women's prisons and the gender gap in gang membership is far greater among adults than it is among youth. That said, we believe such a study would be important as the needs of women in prison are not well understood (Owen, Wells, and Pollock 2017).

The remainder of the book is organized as follows. Chapter 2 reviews the predominant explanations of gangs and prisons. It contrasts cultural arguments that emphasize inmate codes and importation with structural arguments that emphasize the role of deprivation, social structure, and instrumental activities. It also outlines the role of gangs in prison governance, along with group structure and process arguments. This chapter lays the conceptual foundation for the later empirical chapters (Chapters 4 through 9).

Chapter 3 discusses the methodology of the project in depth, identifying many of the key decisions regarding data collection and measurement. It also provides the broader context for studying these issues in Texas, a state with a large prison population and a violent history of gang activity.

Chapters 4 and 5 address the characteristics of gang members and gangs. The former focuses on what distinguishes gang members from non-gang members, using a rich battery of questions and both official and survey measures of gang membership. It is important to understand whether gang members have demographic, psychological, and social characteristics that are fundamentally different from non-gang inmates. The latter focuses on the characteristics of gangs as groups. We take advantage of the nesting of gang members in gangs and offer a new framework with the express goal of putting "gang" back into gang research. This, along with the introduction of a typology of gangs, allows us to examine variation across gangs and the relationship between gangs in prison and gangs on the street. These are topics that receive much speculation yet are rarely addressed in the research literature.

In Chapter 6 our interest in gangs as groups remains, but we shift our focus to the contribution of gangs to the social order of the prison. We take a close look at the role of gangs in prison governance, as well as the power relations between and within gangs. We also focus on perceptions of gangs – both the positive and negative viewpoints – among gang and non-gang prison inmates, and whether gangs have earned their reputation at the core of the inmate society.

Chapter 7 examines violence and misconduct behind bars. Gang and non-gang members are compared on several dimensions of misconduct, including violence, drug sales, and general forms of misconduct, as well as victimization.

We further determine if there is variation in the criminal activities across gangs based on their organizational characteristics. Examining individual gang members as well as the gang as a collective is an important contribution of this study. It is our contention that the group processes of gangs matter as much in prison as they do on the street.

Chapters 8 and 9 address some of the least understood aspects of prison gang membership, that is, the process of joining, avoiding, and leaving gangs in prison. The gang members in our sample went through a number of transitions in their gang status, both entering into and exiting from gangs. Here we explore the motivations, processes, and consequences of such movement, while also describing the tactics inmates employ to avoid involvement in gangs and the reasons why gang members stay involved in gangs.

We conclude in Chapter 10 with a discussion of what has been learned and what remains to be learned in the realm of prison gangs. We weave together the leading evidence from the LoneStar Project and discuss its relevance for theory, policy, and practice.

# 2

# Understanding Gangs in Prison

We now present a conceptual framework for the study. The first chapter laid the foundation for the book by placing prison and street gangs in the broader context of incarceration. It also established that while gang research has exploded over the past three decades, prisons unfortunately escaped the interest of most social scientists. A number of important conceptual and empirical issues remain to be addressed. We highlight four foundational issues that are central to the interconnected theoretical framework motivating the empirical analysis. Some of these issues are better established than others, but all of them merit the empirical investigation that has largely escaped our understanding of gangs and prison.

First, there is solid evidence to suggest that gangs exist in prisons. Since the first analysis of gangs in prison over three decades ago (Camp and Camp 1985), the existence of gangs in prison has been an accepted fact among researchers and practitioners who work in corrections. Perhaps it is a matter of debate to some who view gangs as revolutionary social movements or a social construction of the prison administration, but such perspectives are rarely found in serious penal scholarship.

Second, it is indisputable that gang members are overrepresented in prison compared to the street. The best studies indicate that the prevalence of gang membership in institutionalized populations, such as prisons, jails, and juvenile facilities, is far greater than the prevalence of gang membership in the general population. The same conclusion is reached whether we rely on police and correctional accounts or individuals' self-accounts of gang membership.

Third, gang members are associated with problem behaviors in prison. A disproportionate amount of serious, violent, and general forms of misconduct has been attributed to gang members in prison. Gangs have been implicated as responsible for prison uprisings, targeted violence, and the control of contraband markets. It is also believed that gangs occupy a central place in the social order of inmate society and prison organization. In this sense, prison gangs exhibit a certain degree of parallelism with street gangs. Both are overrepresented in crime, especially violence, and both exert an influence on the environment in which they live.

Finally, street gangs and prison gangs differ in form and function. Decades of research paint street gangs as horizontally structured, weakly organized, and their criminal activities spontaneous and opportunistic. Prison gangs, alternatively, have been described as the polar opposite; vertically organized, strongly controlling their members, and engaged in instrumental and expressive activities that serve the interests of the gang. We have also contributed to such a representation of prison gangs. Despite these characterizations there has been little empirical research in this area to validate such claims.

While these observations are not settled facts, owing to the limited research on gangs in prison, they do represent themes that must be accounted for in the understanding of gangs in prison. This provides a starting point for building an explanation of the role of gangs in prison and the relationship between street and prison gangs. Even if we were to conclude that these findings represented the reality of life behind bars, it is unclear how these facts arose in the first place. What leads gangs to emerge and persist in prison? What accounts for the problem behaviors of gangs and gang members behind bars? How similar or different are gangs on the street and gangs in prison in their form and function? Each of these questions has both conceptual and practical significance for our understanding of gangs in prison. However, the issue we find most compelling is the relationship between the street and the prison in each of these questions. Indeed, should the activities, culture, and social organization of gangs have their roots in the street, it would necessitate a very different policy prescription and theoretical explanation than if the origins were found in prison.

The purpose of this chapter is to establish a theoretical foundation for the book. This is a large task, given the breadth of our substantive interests. The LoneStar Project was not guided by a single or unified theory but was instead informed by many theoretical perspectives and empirical findings originating inside and outside of prisons. Much like Malcolm Klein's (1971, 28) observations of street gang literature circa 1970, it is our position that theory building has outpaced theory testing in the prison gang literature. Accordingly, we draw on multiple theoretical perspectives and empirical findings to develop a multilevel theoretical foundation for the understanding of gangs in prison. We begin by laying the groundwork for the essential components of the study. This includes a discussion of the interrelationship between street and prison contexts, levels of explanation, modes of cultural transmission, and domains of explanation. We follow this with the presentation of leading theoretical perspectives – both classic and emerging – that guide the analyses in the empirical chapters of the book.

## THEORETICAL GROUNDWORK

Before we introduce theoretical models that summarize what follows in the remainder of this chapter, we must first address more fundamental issues to set the stage for theoretical and empirical analysis.

### Levels of Explanation

We begin with the recognition that any study of gangs – or criminal groups of any type – must be sensitive to the important point made by sociologist Jim Short over thirty years ago. Short (1985) called on gang researchers specifically, and later criminologists generally (Short 1998), to be attentive to the level of explanation in their scholarship. This dictum urges researchers to more accurately specify whether the theory and analyses are operating at individual, group, or institutional levels. This applies to the outcomes of interest as well as explanations for those outcomes. In Short's view, too little attention has been paid to the group context of gangs, particularly situational and interactional processes. Instead researchers tend to focus on individual gang members while inferring the mechanisms underlying behavior to the group. In a sense, the group-level measures are part of the "black box" of gang activity; little understood and seldom studied. This is ironic, of course, because gang activities involve uniting individuals in the effort to achieve common goals and gangs are of interest because they are groups.

We propose cross-level theoretical models to account for the processes and structures addressed in this book. Our theoretical focus is on individuals, groups, and institutions. The unit of analysis in the LoneStar Project is individual prison inmates, although we have a comparative advantage to address Short's critique because we have group-level information, including official data from the prison system and survey data from the respondents, from all gang members and about their gangs. In Chapter 5 this leads us to introduce a new empirical framework to the study of gangs. Given the presence of measures at each level, we pay careful attention to how gang members and gang processes operate across levels of explanation when reaching inferences. This leads to our next point.

Many of the conclusions we reach in this study are with respect to prison life and prison processes. Prison is central to the theoretical models we present shortly. This means that imprisonment is treated as a variable. Of course, everyone in the LoneStar Project was imprisoned at the time of the baseline interview, as we detail in the next chapter. But that does not stop us from concluding that prison operates as a causal explanation of our outcomes of interest, particularly where we document the emergence and change in affiliations, attitudes, beliefs, and behaviors upon admission to or release from prison. For example, life-course principles such as onset, continuity, and disengagement apply to life in prison, particularly with regard to status transitions. Of course, we also have information about the length of imprisonment, number of sentences, and type of institution. If a person joins a gang for the first time upon going to prison, it is our contention that such a status transition was endogenous to the bundle of mechanisms triggered by imprisonment. Ironically, we know very little about how these processes apply to prison gang membership. Our attention to levels of explanation leads to the question: What is in need of explanation?

**Domains of Explanation**

The key domains of explanation in this book include: (1) activities, (2) culture, and (3) social organization. The activities of a group and its members are as important as understanding their culture and social organization. We are interested in several dimensions of activity: individual/group, criminal/conforming, expressive/instrumental, street-based/prison-based, self-supportive/self-destructive, and gang/non-gang. We used dichotomies to illustrate these dimensions in order to highlight how they can vary and interact. For example, there can be activities that are prison-based, criminal, and instrumental, such as the sale of narcotics or other contraband within the institution. Such activities may be gang-directed or individually oriented. Likewise, there may be instances of carrying out violence against rival gangs as part of the ceremonial method of entrance into a gang. Such activities may occur on the street or in prison. These dimensions constitute a thread of continuity in the substantive chapters to follow as we examine the contrasting forms of behavior. As criminologists, our primary interests are in the activities that violate the formal rules of prisons and the informal norms of imprisonment, as well as entering into or exiting from life states that amplify such activities, like gang membership. We also have an interest in the role of prison gangs in creating disorder and order within prison life.

The focus on culture is one of the bedrocks of criminology. The beliefs, customs, practices, and values of individuals and groups have been at the heart of a large body of explanatory work that addresses criminal behaviors, gangs, prisons, and inmates. Key examples of this are found in the *code of the street* (Anderson 1999), the *convict code* (Sykes and Messinger 1960), and the normative orientations of street gang members (Decker and Van Winkle 1996; Short and Strodtbeck 1965) that are central to the descriptions of individual and group misconduct. Meghan Mitchell and her colleagues (2017) found considerable overlap among the values of street offenders, inmates, and street and prison gang members – in other words, there was convergence in culture across context. This both underscores the importance of such values and highlights the similarities across offenders in prison and street groups. A key part of "prisonization," the process of institutionalization and assuming an identity as an inmate, is the acceptance of values consistent with inmate life, such as "don't snitch," "don't cooperate with the guards," "keep to yourself," and "respect other inmates."

Culture is more than values. It includes symbols and collective practices. Symbols can include tattoos, which attain special status in an environment such as prison that induces similarity through clothing, haircuts, and daily regimentation (Rozycki Lozano et al. 2011). Other visible symbols include hand signs, graffiti, group and individual names, and physical interaction. Physical interactions, such as "sitting with the whites" during mealtime or having a public conversation with a gang leader, come with cultural meaning because of what it signals to the prison community (Densley 2013). A function of symbols is to announce to new entrants of a social setting the groups, their roles, rules, and in some cases, the threat they represent. Thus, a newly incarcerated inmate can observe tattoos, signs, and dress to gauge the available groups, the characteristics of their members, and make informed choices about interacting with such individuals. In addition, group practices such as meetings, drills, chanting, and other congregate activities reinforce group membership in the same manner that cultural practices often reinforce instrumental behaviors. These practices also serve the purpose of distinguishing the in-group from the out-group.

The final area of explanation is social organization, which, like activities and culture, takes several forms. More generally, prison social organization refers to the inmate society. This includes status hierarchy, inmate cohesion, social interactions, and valued goods and roles. We are interested in inmate society to the extent that it influences gangs or is influenced by gangs. But we are also interested in other aspects of social organization, particularly with regard to groups. David Skarbek (2014) argued that gangs are central to the social order of prisons, filling a critical void in governance that prison officials are unwilling or incapable of addressing adequately. Such an argument positions gangs at the core of inmate society because they provide critical services and fulfill important functions for a large number of individuals in prisons.

How gangs are able to govern illustrates another important form of social organization. Organizational structure is key to understanding group behavior, as well as group influence on individual behavior. It is useful to think of groups on a continuum from the least organized group that meets only by chance and does not recruit or sustain membership to a highly organized group that interacts regularly and acts as a unit. A common feature of such well-organized groups is the existence of roles, rules, and punishment for the violation of rules. This is not unlike what we expect in corporations or professional sports leagues. Such structures facilitate the effective achievement of group tasks particularly in the face of obstacles to such performance. In prisons, inmates must contend with officers, cameras, and confined structures, as well as the threat of additional punishment like solitary confinement. While gangs certainly attract additional scrutiny and discipline, being part of an organized group also provides a mask and a shield that protects personal identity and deflects responsibility for rule-violating behaviors. Being part of an organized group expands the opportunities for obtaining contraband, seeking protection, or retaliating against threats and attacks. Thus, organized groups take on added importance given the coercive and highly surveilled environments represented by total institutions such as prison. Organization can take place on the street or in prison and can interact with culture in important ways to strengthen groups as well as identify their members.

**An Organizing Theoretical Model**

Having discussed levels of explanation, the context of inference, and key domains of explanation, we turn to the theoretical models presented in Figure 2.1. In this figure, we identify three models that assign varying levels

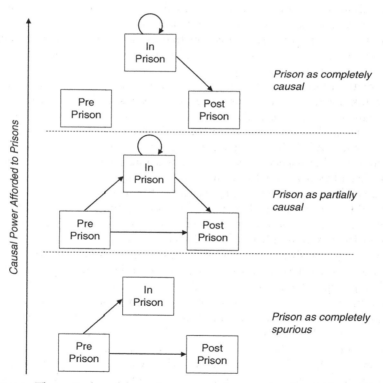

FIGURE 2.1 Theoretical models on the sources of gang-related activities, culture, and organization in prison
Notes: Boxes refer to the context of behavior, culture, and organization. Arrows refer to the causal relationship between and within contexts. No within-context arrows are reported for pre- and post-prison because it is assumed that each influences behavior, culture, and organization in the respective setting.

of causal power to the context of prison to influence gang-related activities, culture, and organization. The bottom and the top of the figure represent opposing viewpoints on the causal influence of prison. Some readers will immediately associate this organizing theoretical model with the classic importation and deprivation perspectives. That is by design. But we avoid such language because the importation and deprivation perspectives are too narrow – they focus only on a subset of prison-exogenous and prison-endogenous explanations of prison and prisoner activities, culture, and organization.

At the bottom of the figure, the *prisons as completely spurious* model suggests that individual and group activities, culture, and social organization in prison are a reflection of the street. In other words, understanding the variables found in the key domains of explanation requires looking not at the prisons but instead at the characteristics and kinds of inmates admitted to prison. From this point of view, should gang members miraculously stop getting arrested and sent to prison, it would mean the end of gangs in prison. The relevance of this viewpoint will become increasingly evident when we seek to understand the sequencing of gang membership in relation to prison and how street and prison gangs may differ.

Alternatively, the *prisons as completely causal* model suggests that explanations for our gang-related variables of interest are found entirely in the prison. From this perspective, while the street may matter for producing the conditions that led the inmate to prison, it is the prison environment that assumes causal power over outcomes both inside of prison and after release from prison. From this perspective, it would not matter if gang members stopped offending since the origins of gang-related activities, culture, and organization are in the prison and not the street.

Finally, the *prisons as partially causal* model recognizes that both exogenous and endogenous mechanisms are working together to influence our key areas of explanation. This is a way to highlight that prison life does not begin with a blank canvas. But it similarly recognizes that the canvas has not been completely painted by the brushes and with the colors of street life. It is unclear if some behaviors, groups, and statuses are more closely linked with one model than another. Although it would be convenient for theory and policy, it is unreasonable to expect that if gang-related violence was attributable to characteristics of the prison environment then selection into gangs in prison must also have its origins in prison.

At this point, it is useful to invoke the public health distinction between "blood-borne" versus "air-borne" origins of infectious agents producing prison activities, culture, and organization. This distinction should be considered in relation to the arrows leading from the street to the prison and from the prison to the street. In other words, how are activities, culture, and organization transmitted from one setting, such as the street, to another, such as prison? Blood-borne pathogens are those that are transmitted by human contact, which requires the physical movement of the infectious agent from one setting to another. A common approach, as we describe below, is to view the admission and release of gang members to and from prison as the agent responsible for transmitting norms and values. Air-borne pathogens, alternatively, are those that are transmitted without physical contact, where the infectious agent moves via non-human contact. Transmission of this sort can occur through non-physical forms of communicating norms and values via media or images promulgated by gang life. Such a distinction was relevant in the street gang literature in the 1990s to understand whether the emergence of gangs outside of traditional gang epicenters (e.g., Chicago and Los Angeles) was due to the physical movement of gangs, "blood-borne pathogens," or the non-physical movement of gang culture, "air-borne pathogens," to new cities (Maxson 1998). This is why communication is a key element for understanding the cultural components of street or prison gangs. It is through patterns and methods of communication that culture is transmitted. Such communication allows one setting to impact the other and may occur through the transfer of persons from one system to the other (street to prison/prison to street). This can be facilitated by prison employees, inmates, phone calls, letters, visitation, or mediated through electronic media such as cellular phones, computers, and other technology.

Before turning to leading theoretical perspectives of gangs, prison, and reentry, the final point to make is with regard to historical context. The organizing theoretical perspective we offer is largely independent of historical context. That is to say, it is common to recognize that prisons were not always crowded, racially diverse, and bureaucratic places, but it is believed that the shifts brought about by mass incarceration had substantial impacts on inmate society (Kreager and Kruttschnitt 2017). To be sure, both our theory and research operate in the era of mass incarceration, an era that witnessed the emergence and institutionalization of prison gangs. Our data are not capable of studying trends or changes at the prison system level, though we discuss the historical context of the emergence of gangs in Texas prisons in the next chapter.

Now that we have addressed the issues needed to establish the theoretical groundwork, we turn our attention to the leading theories of gangs, prison, and reentry. We draw upon these theories to study gang-related activities, culture, and social organization, which combine to motivate the substantive chapters to follow, including: Chapter 5 – the relationship between prison and street gangs; Chapter 6 – gangs, governance, and social order in prison; Chapter 7 – gangs, violence, misconduct, and victimization in prison; Chapter 8 – joining and avoiding in prison; and Chapter 9 – leaving gangs in prison.

## THEORETICAL PERSPECTIVES

We highlight four explanations of gangs in prison that collectively address activities, culture, and organization across levels of explanation. These approaches include cultural explanations, group-based explanations, and structural explanations. In an area of policy, practice, and research that has a solid base of knowledge, it would be less important to offer more than one or two approaches to the issues at hand. However, given the lack of knowledge about prison gangs and gang members, and their growing importance, we believe it is useful to offer a broad review of explanations of gang activities, culture, and organization.

The four theoretical perspectives include: (1) the classic perspectives on deprivation and importation models of inmate society and social organization, (2) emerging governance perspectives posited by economists and political scientists, (3) group structural perspectives on gang continuity and change in street and prison settings, and (4) group process perspectives on how groups influence collective and individual behavior. From these approaches we create specific theoretical propositions nested within our broader organizing theoretical framework to account for both the broad strokes and the fine details of gangs in prison.

## Deprivation and Importation Perspectives

The deprivation and importation perspectives are most closely associated with the organizing theoretical framework presented in Figure 2.1. These two perspectives vary in the significance they attach to the role of prisons in explaining activities, culture, and organization. As such, both perspectives have implications for the remaining empirical chapters.

The deprivation perspective is based on Fishman's (1934) work that emphasized the contrast between the poverty of liberty inside the prison with the freedoms associated with life "outside the walls," or what the men in our study called the "free world." This deprivation affects many aspects of prison life and isolates prisoners from the outside world. Gresham Sykes (1958) described deprivations as the source of the "pains of imprisonment," which in addition to restrictions on liberty, also included absence of rights of ownership, heterosexual relationships, and emotional and physical security. What is perhaps the most significant form of deprivation is stripping inmates of autonomy. Prisons, Erving Goffman (1968) famously noted, are total institutions where there is monolithic structuring of routines. Prisons dictate what inmates eat, what they read, where they walk, and with whom they communicate and live. The prison experience is one that provides regimentation and subjugation of the individual to regulations and externally imposed order.

Clemmer (1940) identified isolation and regimentation as key structural constraints that denied inmates their identity. The process by which this unfolds has been described by Goffman as the "mortification of the self," where inmate social roles shifted and they became mere elements in a system without status as individuals. But this loss of identity, in turn, created a void where new identities could be formed. Prison culture, particularly the convict code, provides alternative sources of identity for inmates. Becoming immersed in prison culture was described by Clemmer as "prisonization." The convict code is an informal set of roles and rules created by the inmates and governs acceptable behavior within prisons. This is posited as an outgrowth of the nature of prison. The five major tenets of the code organized by Sykes and Messinger (1960, 6–9) are as follows:

- Do not interfere with inmate interests – allow inmates to maximize privileges and minimize pains of imprisonment by not snitching or filing grievances on fellow inmates, keeping to oneself, and loyalty to fellow inmates.
- Do not lose your head – avoid conflict with fellow inmates by refraining from quarrels or arguments, playing it cool and doing your own time.
- Do not exploit inmates – avoid force, fraud, or chicanery with fellow inmates, while sharing scarce goods.
- Do not weaken – inmates must maintain self, be tough, avoid whining, and show courage.
- Do not be a sucker – strength lies in inmate solidarity rather than appeals to prison authorities.

These tenets collectively dictate how inmates interact and communicate, their attitudes toward prison staff, the resolution of disputes, and how to earn and afford respect. Of course, not all inmates adhere to the convict code equally. There is a status hierarchy among inmates, where some roles are believed to assume higher status – along with power and control – than others (Kreager et al. 2017). Social roles such as "right guys" (i.e., influential inmate leaders who follow the code), "politicians or shot callers" (i.e., inmates in positions of power), and "merchants or peddlers" (i.e., inmates who control goods and services) are viewed as higher status, while lower-status roles include "new fish" (i.e., newcomers to prison), "punks" (i.e., those who engage in homosexual activities), and "rats" (i.e., those who snitch). These were the roles and rules believed to be central to prison life, all of which are endogenous to the deprivation perspective.

As we established in Chapter 1, gangs typically emerged in US prison systems during the buildup to the prison boom. John Irwin (1980), a "convict criminologist" who served time in the California prison system before becoming a leading correctional scholar, observed that the informal and reputation-based norms of the convict code had weakened by the 1970s. In California and elsewhere, there were large-scale compositional changes taking place in prisons, as they were more crowded and filled with younger, more violent, and racially/ethnically diverse inmates than at any point in history. David Skarbek (2014, 7, 35), when critiquing the deprivation perspective, noted that these were the very features that undermined the convict code of the prisoner community. This is not to say prisonization no longer occurred or that the convict code no longer existed; rather, a decentralized and informal culture of governance was no longer effective because it could not scale up. In an era of mass incarceration, the *types* of deprivations associated with imprisonment – a poverty of liberty, autonomy, goods and services, heterosexual relationships, protection and safety – may not have changed, but their *intensity* did for reasons outlined by Skarbek. Whether it was for the purposes of extra-legal governance or some other form of prison deprivation, gangs emerged as an adaptation to changing prison systems.

While the deprivation perspective sheds light on the emergence of gangs in prison, it also has relevance for the processes associated with gang membership, particularly joining and leaving gangs. Pyrooz, Gartner, and Smith (2017), drawing broadly on prison "endogenous" perspectives that included deprivation, posited this as an *origination* model of the incarceration / gang membership link, arguing that prisoners seek out associations with gangs because the pains of imprisonment can be remedied by the selective incentives that gangs offer. In this sense, gangs provide a collective solution to individual problems. Where prisons deprive inmates of status, safety, governance, and resources, gangs can meet those needs because of their access to goods and services, group organization and structure, and reputation for violence. Prison gangs also provide identity, something missing in total institutions such as prisons. This means that the sources of prison gang membership are far more likely to be found in the prison than the street. This also means that inmates will select into gangs in prison, retain their membership through their prison sentence, and cease their affiliation around the time they are released from prison. After all, if gangs are an adaptation to prison, we would expect that status transitions into and out of gangs would be confined to periods of movement to and from prison.

The final area where the deprivation perspective is relevant to gangs is with regard to the relationship between gangs in street and prison contexts. Differences and similarities between gangs on the street and gangs in prison are expected both in form and function. It is believed that the nature of prisons gives rise to gangs that take on different *forms*, such as organization and structure, and *functions*, such as activities and values and norms, from street gangs, as we reported in Chapter 1. The deprivation model is relevant to this distinction because the nature of prisons may condition how inmates behave and organize. For example, targeted violence against someone who snitched on the gang will require much greater coordination and planning in prison than on the street because movements are restricted, access to units such as protective housing is limited, and activities and communications are monitored. The same strains of deprivation are also believed to condition the organizational structure of groups, which must take greater care to avoid adverse selection of new members, along with turnover of long-standing members, and carve out established roles and responsibilities in a hyper-monitored environment.

The importation perspective takes a very different stance on activities, culture, and organization in prison than does the deprivation perspective. This perspective is most closely associated with the work of John Irwin and

Donald Cressey (1962, 142), who noted that "much of the inmate behavior classified as part of the prison culture is not peculiar to the prison at all." Rather than the "blank slate" that Clemmer (1940) and others argue for, the importation perspective instead maintains that inmates bring characteristics with them into prison that have a bearing on the theoretical, programmatic, and policy interests of social scientists. Indeed, the activities, culture, and organization observed among individual inmates as well as the inmate community have their origins in characteristics found outside rather than inside of prisons. These characteristics include biography, such as geography, race, and adverse child experiences, along with propensities or tendencies, such as cognitive ability, neurological deficits, and self-control. In addition, these characteristics also include involvement in criminal groups, such as gangs, drug traffickers, or organized crime groups, as well as criminal capital from engaging in a variety of crimes, such as theft, armed robbery, and domestic extremism.

Biography and group affiliations would not be relevant if the composition of prisoners remained stable. But the prison population is constantly in flux – there was a 41 percent turnover in inmates in US prisons between 2014 and 2015. This means that two in five prison inmates were newly incarcerated. The influx of the prison population is important and challenges perspectives arguing for endogenous influences of prison: "this indigenous system [prisons], unlike that of primitive tribes, was bombarded with new adults who arrived with full orientations, cultures of their own" (Irwin 1980, 34). Some are unconvinced that deprivations are so great, and prisonization is so all-encompassing, to truly result in the mortification of the self. Irwin, Cressey, and others (e.g., DeLisi et al. 2011; Mears et al. 2013; Wacquant 2001) make sound arguments and offer empirical findings supporting the importation perspective. The size of the incoming population ensures change in the group dynamics of prisons.

In this view, it is the culture, demographics, group affiliation, and personalities transported with inmates from the street to the prison context that produce "prison culture." Recent work by Mitchell and colleagues (2017) examined the overlap between the code of the street and the convict code. This approach builds on the deprivation and importation models, while at the same time comparing the cultural beliefs in different contexts. Mitchell and colleagues present three competing hypotheses to account for prison culture: convergence, independence, and complementarity of prison and street values. The *convergence* hypothesis posits that cultural values overlap so strongly across contexts that they are not independent of each other. The *independence* hypothesis holds the opposite position, that the cultural values are orthogonal; that is, they do not overlap to an appreciable extent. Finally, the *complementarity* hypothesis holds that while unique, each belief system has considerable overlap with the values of others. The review of the evidence on the topic suggested that there were more complementary features across contexts than independent ones – in other words, some features of the convict code (Sykes and Messinger 1960) were indistinguishable from the code of the street.

This is consistent with Wacquant's (2001) claim that the disproportionate incarceration of poor black men makes the ghetto more like the prison and the prison more like the ghetto. In a sense, the explanatory power of the complementarity approach lies in the overlap between independence and convergence, a mixed model so to speak.

The importation perspective takes on even more significance when the activities, culture, and organization of gangs are the targets of explanation. In this view, the origins of prison gangs are found in the street, not the prison. A large proportion of inmates enter prison as individuals who participated in the gang lifestyle *before* coming to prison, bringing with them their individual and cultural histories, including gang affiliations, relationships (both friend and foe), values, behaviors, and predispositions. Inmates then integrate that mix of experience into the larger groups they encounter in prison. In other words, there is a transmission of practices, beliefs, and symbols from the street to the prison. Gang members who go to prison have the ability to structure group norms as well as group behaviors. From this vantage point we would expect there to be few differences in the form and function of gangs in street and prison contexts. After all, prison gangs could be thought of as incarcerated street gangs, a view that finds some support in early studies in California and Illinois (Irwin 1980; Jacobs 1974; Lopez-Aguado 2018). But for any of these observations to be valid from an importation perspective, it is necessary that a sizable volume of gang activity existed on the street before prison gang activity could emerge. If street gangs miraculously vanished it would be detrimental to the emergence and persistence of gangs in prison. Again, since the causal power of prison is negligible, we would expect gang activities, culture, and organization in prison to ebb and flow with the street.

Pyrooz, Gartner, and Smith (2017) referred to the application of importation theory to gangs as a manifestation of the street. Since correctional institutions are merely the recipients of offenders whom the criminal justice system detects, arrests, prosecutes, and sentences, there is nothing unique about the carceral environment. Gang membership amplifies involvement in crime, and the practices of law enforcement target high-rate offenders like gang members. Hence the reason that gang members are overrepresented in juvenile facilities, county jails, and prisons, Pyrooz and colleagues argued, has little to do with the institutional environment. Imprisonment neither initiates nor prolongs trajectories of gang membership. While this view allowed for onset, continuity, and change in gang membership in prisons, these important status transitions would occur at a rate that is indistinguishable from what is observed in non-prison settings. For example, it should be extremely rare for an inmate to join a gang for the first time while in prison – such a status transition should be most likely to occur on the street. Likewise, it would be expected that inmates transition out of their gangs in prison since their gang careers are not enhanced by the prison environment, broadly construed.

This is not to say that *only* deprivation or *only* importation represent the descriptive and explanatory realities of gang activities, culture, and organization in prison. Dan Mears and his colleagues (2013) demonstrated among a sample of incarcerated young people in Iowa and Georgia that street culture interacts with prisoner experiences – such as educational training, religious participation, and family support – to influence misconduct behind bars. The finding that importation and deprivation work together to influence the activities, culture, and organization of inmates is not new. Findings to this effect have been reported for decades (Akers, Hayner, and Gruninger 1977; Irwin and Cressey 1962; Thomas, Petersen, and Zingraff 1978). The question, however, is the extent to which one perspective is more or less powerful in explaining these outcomes of interest than the other. When studying the impact of incarceration on gang membership, Pyrooz, Gartner, and Smith (2017) referred to this blended view as the intensification model. That is, incarceration complicates trajectories of gang membership imported from the street by strengthening gang ties and thwarting efforts to disengage from gangs. Correctional policies and practices, such as limiting programming for gang members and placing gang members in solitary confinement, contribute to these outcomes. State policies, such as mass incarceration and gang crackdowns, have also been implicated in the strengthening of gangs in prisons, arguments that have been promulgated by scholars examining extra-legal governance.

## Extra-legal and Non-state Governance Perspectives

Criminologists and sociologists are not the only social scientists to examine prison gangs. Economists and political scientists also have been active in applying non-cultural explanations to the origins and functions of prison gangs. Long-standing interests in non-state governance – largely in the regulation of the environment, international relations, organized crime and terror groups – have led scholars such as David Skarbek and Benjamin Lessing to bring a lens outside the scope of traditional criminological or sociological theorizing. These works examine the rise of prison gangs and their influence on prison life. Before we explore these perspectives, we first consider established economic perspectives on markets and organized crime.

Fifty years ago, the economist Thomas Schelling (1967) wrote in response to hearings held by the Kefauver Commission regarding organized crime, "rackets," and extortion. Schelling identified five conditions that contributed to the growth and maintenance of such activities, four of which are relevant to prisons and gangs. Key to those conditions was a monopoly over a service or provision of goods. An effective way to gain a monopoly was for those services or goods to be of limited availability and for the monopoly to effectively suppress competition. Under such circumstances, the power of monopoly can be exercised with exclusivity. First, exclusivity is created under circumstances where victims are poor at protecting themselves against others, whether the threats they are protected against are physical or challenges to the distribution of goods and services. Second, the exercise of exclusive power in a market is bolstered by circumstances where victims cannot hide from their assailants. The inability to find asylum or protection makes victims more vulnerable to threats or manipulation. Third, such arrangements thrive when victims can be monitored closely and regularly. Victims who feel as if they can skip a payment or not suffer the consequences for doing so, make poor targets for such rackets. Fourth, extortion works more smoothly in circumstances that have a predictable and routine operation. An expected process and outcome makes it easier for racketeers to extort and for victims to be extorted.

While Schelling wrote specifically in response to what he thought to be a misunderstanding of rackets and organized crime on the part of the Kefauver Commission, it is hard to imagine a set of circumstances that better fit these characteristics than the distribution of illegal goods and contraband in prison. By applying market principles to organized crime, Schelling established a groundwork for a broader understanding of prisons, prison gangs, and the relationship between the prison and the street. What makes the work of Schelling distinctive and relevant to non-state governance perspectives on prisons is that this understanding – from its nascent origins – was not built on culture, let alone the transmission of beliefs and norms from one context to the other. Indeed, concepts like deprivation and importation play no role in the generation of markets or their control from Schelling's perspective. But what is clear from this perspective is that in a prison environment, groups like gangs may be favorably positioned to exercise power.

Both Skarbek and Lessing start with observations similar to our own in Chapter 1: gangs and mass incarceration go hand-in-hand. Both of them, however, offer an alternative interpretation of how mass incarceration gave rise to gangs. Such an argument passes the eye test, but has not been subject to the type of empirical testing one would anticipate before reaching sound conclusions. What is clear from the Skarbek and Lessing work is that the data of criminologists and sociologists are not necessarily the data of economists and political scientists. Fieldwork, interviews with inmates, and individual prison records are of less importance to those whose interest lies in an examination of the exercise of power in institutions. In our view, highlighting the rise of a couple of gangs or gangs in a couple of countries certainly makes for useful anecdotes, but such analyses are not systematic. When seeking to understand *variability* across persons or groups, which has been front and center since the dawn of gang research (Thrasher 1927), a broader and more solid empirical base is necessary.

Skarbek's (2014) primary interests rested with the social order of prison. In applying an extra-legal governance perspective to prison social order, he rejected both the deprivation and importation perspectives for two reasons. First, he held that these perspectives ultimately overlooked the role of and demand for governance in prisons. Governance institutions help define and enforce property rights, capture the benefits of trade, and facilitate collection action. According to Skarbek, formal governance mechanisms are sorely lacking in prison, particularly as cultural sources of social organization – the convict code – broke down with the rise of mass incarceration. Second, he held that the norms of the convict code, regardless of its source, are a means rather than an end. In other words, such norms arise for the purpose of problem solving. Of course, such an argument is enveloped within our larger theoretical perspective of prisons as causal sources of gang activities, culture, and organization.

Gangs, according to Skarbek (2014, 8), play a central role in the social order of prisons. He noted: "prison gangs form to provide extra-legal governance when inmates have a demand for it and official governance mechanisms are ineffective or unavailable." The governance provided by gangs in prison assumes a rational character, providing order through protection, opportunities for generating profit, and social structure. Skarbek notes that many street and prison gangs have similar names and engage in similar activities, but that does not mean they are related. The reach of prison gangs extends into more realms of prison life than does that of street gangs into life on the street. While both facilitate offending and provide instrumental and symbolic benefits, prison gangs are more effective and intrude into more aspects of prison life. This is because of their greater level of organization, restrictions on members, and that they operate in a controlled space. The activity of prison gangs includes enforcing norms and punishments, as well as representing the "interests" of incarcerated individuals. These interests are organized around race/ethnicity, the products of contraband and protection markets, geographical location, and, in some instances, political ideology.

Skarbek's (2014) work is important for many reasons, chief among them is that his theory can situate gangs in time and space – the when, where, and why questions – while also offering an alternative to the deprivation and importation perspectives as explanations of prison life. Skarbek holds that the rise of prison gangs was brought about by increases in racial diversity, violent offenders, and overcrowding in the prison system, which eroded the reputation- and norm-based order in prison social systems. He shifts attention away from cultural explanations of prison life toward structural explanations by emphasizing structural relations and the exchange of commodities. The analysis in support of his theory was based on court documents, aggregate official records, prior criminological and sociological research, declassified law enforcement files, interviews with criminal justice officials, documentaries, media reports, and memoirs. As is the case for most work on prison gangs, interviews with or observations of inmates themselves are notable by their absence, a shortcoming that Skarbek himself recognized.

Across a series of interrelated works, Lessing (2010, 2016, 2017) offers a different perspective from Skarbek (2014), but one that is also rooted outside the cultural emphasis found in criminology and sociology. Lessing contends that there are three overlapping dynamics that account for the rise of prison gangs. The first dynamic is *consolidation*, which refers to the coalescing of power in prisons. Consolidation occurs as a small number of groups swamp less powerful groups and assume control over incentives, such as protection, contraband, and housing and work assignments. Consolidation also coincides with the ability of gangs to mete out punishment or threaten the appearance of safety. The second dynamic is *propagation*, which refers to the extending tentacles of gangs across prison units. Prison transfers and the re-incarceration of gang members enable gangs to gain control and influence in areas where the gang was not previously active. The final dynamic is *projection* of power, which refers to the ability of gangs to influence activities outside of prison. This, writes Lessing in his Brookings Institution paper (2016), is the reason why prison gangs are not just a corrections issue, but a "first-order public-security concern."

From this perspective, the reason prison gangs have emerged as a major security issue has less to do with the gangs themselves than it has to do with state policy. Skarbek (2014) viewed mass incarceration as a problem that stemmed from the composition of inmates. Overpopulation and diversity in criminal history and demographics drove the need for governance. Alternatively, Lessing (2017) argued that policies such as gang crackdowns and prison segregation created the means for gangs to project power. Lessing actually draws on the work of Skarbek (2011) as well as anecdotes to argue that prison gangs leverage power over street gang members (as well as other offenders) due to the increased risk of incarceration in the era of mass incarceration. In one of the few interviews conducted by Lessing, a "former drug boss" noted to him: "What you do on the outside, on the inside you'll have to answer for it" (263). The projection of power allows prison gangs and prison gang members to have an impact on street gangs, street gang members, and criminal enterprises outside of prison. From this view, the walls that hamper the air- and blood-borne transmission of information and people are quite easy to penetrate through the specter of control. In other words, there is a collapse of the barriers between contexts: the prison is the street and the street is the prison.

Like Skarbek, the ideas proposed by Lessing lack the perspective of prison inmates, gang affiliated or otherwise. Lessing does examine official documents, case studies in the United States and Latin America, and a small number of interviews with prison officials. His conclusions are based on these data and formal modeling analysis with strong assumptions about the nature of the data missing from his assessment. Cultural aspects of the projection of power are well known in the street gang literature. There is hardly an acknowledgment of such in the Lessing approach. The major difference is that extra-legal governance perspectives grant gangs far more rationality and organization than revealed by decades of research on street gangs. There are a number of depictions of prison gangs as more instrumental-rational and more organizationally structured than street gangs (including our own). What is lacking from our own observations and those like Skarbek and Lessing, that select on the dependent variable, are systematic studies with large samples of gangs as groups and gang members as individuals. Of course, it is necessary to understand how these groups are structured and how these groups compel individuals to act. These issues receive only brief treatment in governance perspectives, which is why we now turn to a group structure and process perspective where inferences operate on the group level.

## Group Structure Perspectives

Frederic Thrasher's (1927, 45) observation that "No two gangs are just alike" is now a truism in the annals of street gang theory and research. Scholars have pursued strategies to subdivide gangs into classes based on variability in criminal and deviant behaviors (e.g., Cloward and Ohlin 1960; Fagan 1989; Spergel 1964; Taylor 1990), organizational structure (e.g., Decker and Curry 2002; Thrasher 1927), or a mix of group behavior, composition, and organizational structure (e.g., Klein and Maxson 2006; Spindler and Bouchard 2011; Valdez 2003). These distinguishing features of gangs are important not only because they capture variability across gangs, but also because of their implications for differential involvement in criminal activity, fear in the community and schools, and the success of interventions, among other outcomes.

There has been significantly less attention to group-level differences among gangs in prison. It is not uncommon for prison systems to distinguish two tiers of gangs (Pyrooz 2016). The top tier of gangs can be differentiated from the bottom tier by their prison-based origins and activities, organizational structure, and level of threat posed to the institution. California, for example, refers to both tiers of gangs as Security Threat Groups, appending them with "I" or "II." Texas, alternatively, refers to the top tier as Security Threat Groups and the bottom tier as cliques or street gangs. The Federal Bureau of Prisons classifies Disruptive Groups, not unlike STG-Is or STGs in California or Texas, respectively, while recognizing that there is a host of additional gangs and gang members present in their facilities. These are relatively crude distinctions, created for administrative and management purposes.

Table 2.1 reports the work of Salvador Buentello, Robert Fong, and Ronald Vogel (1991), which represents an exception to the failure to describe and understand heterogeneity among prison gangs. Based on a decade of official data and their observations in Texas, as a Texas prison gang specialist (Buentello), special monitor in the *Ruiz* v. *Estelle* lawsuit (Fong), and researcher (Vogel), the authors presented what they termed a theoretical model of prison gang development. Five stages are identified in this perspective, each of which entails an added level of seriousness: Stage 1: "Inmate enters prison"; Stage 2: "Clique"; Stage 3: "Protection Group";

TABLE 2.1 *Elaboration of the prison gang development model*

| Stage | Clique 2 | Protection group 3 | Predator group 4 | Prison gang 5 |
|---|---|---|---|---|
| *Exclusive in-group* | None, relational, homophilous | Yes, but not firm | Yes, avoids adverse selection | Yes, qualification, sharply defined |
| *Long-term commitment* | None, transient | Limited, self-identified | Loyalty to group, but not lifelong commitment | Lifetime membership, tattoos to signify commitment |
| *Group-defined goals and benefits* | Companionship | Protection | Protection, power, profit | Governance, criminal activity |
| *Rules regulating conduct* | None beyond convict code | Minimal, backing up fellow members | Emerging rules, but not formal | Formal rules, constitution |
| *Leadership* | None | Functional, charismatic | Strong, but not formally defined | Strong, formally defined across rank |
| *Group-based criminal activity* | None | Limited, retaliatory | Instrumental crime emerges, intimidation | Crime syndicate, contract violence, established instrumental crime |
| *Locus of influence* | Prison, single units | Prison, several units | Prison, branches across units | Prison system, street |
| *Out-group recognition* | Inmates | Officers | Prison units | Prison system, non-institutional law enforcement |
| *Emergent group process* | Social sorting | Sizable membership, external hostility | Internal organic processes, member-initiated | Power- and violence-based natural selection |

*Note:* Adopted from Buentello et al. (1991) and expanded upon by the current authors.

Stage 4: "Predator Group"; and Stage 5: "Prison Gang." We do not report Stage 1 in Table 2.1 because it captures the social sorting that emerges with individual-level prisonization, where inmates search to find others who share similar demographics and preferences.

Based on our close reading of Buentello and colleagues (1991), we identify nine distinguishing features of the four types of prison groups: exclusive members, long-term commitment, group-defined goals and benefits, rules regulating conduct, leadership, group-based criminal activity, locus of influence, out-group recognition, and emergent group process. Despite their significance, the mechanisms underlying group emergence and evolution were less clear in their writing. After all, what leads a clique to transition to a protection group, a protection group to a predatory group, and a predatory group to a prison gang is critical to understand. It is worth noting that such group processes are generally less well understood than other characteristics of gangs (Decker, Melde, and Pyrooz 2013). If prison officials are concerned with preventing the full-blown emergence of prison gangs, it is necessary to know whether such groups emerge due to processes that are internal or external to the group. Nonetheless, we have tried to represent faithfully what led to the next group stage in each transition. When contrasting the Buentello et al. model against our comparison of prison and street gangs, one could easily associate the characteristics of cliques and protection groups with broad descriptions of street gangs and predator groups and prison gang groups with broad descriptions of prison gangs. Their model allows for group variation within the prison.

When focusing on street gangs, both Julie Ayling (2011) and James Densley (2014) viewed conflict as a central source of gang evolution. Approaching this from an evolutionary perspective, Ayling held that gangs adopt different characteristics based on their environment, which she termed *variation*. In turn, *selection* was dictated not only by the types of variation that gangs adopt, some of which were advantageous to preservation, but also by market forces (i.e., supply and demand for membership, illicit marketplace), competition and conflict (i.e., extra-legal governance, proclivity for fighting), and institutional opposition and support (i.e., law enforcement interdiction, social services and supports). Whether or not the gang persists over time and place is a matter of *replication*, a product of modeling to share cultural identity along with instrumental links to other gangs and crime groups established in prison or otherwise. This is not unlike the stage-based model developed by Densley, who emphasized external threats and financial commitments as a mode of evolution from neighborhood groups to delinquent collectives to criminal enterprises to providers of extra-legal governance. Whether we focus on gangs on the street or gangs in prison, there is little systematic evidence documenting their characteristics at the group level – issues we explore in Chapter 5.

## Group Process Perspectives

Before we delve into the etiological significance of group process, it is useful to take a step back to consider its broader theoretical relevance. Just as there are both legal and extra-legal characteristics that lead people into prison, there are also selection processes that lead individuals into gangs. We can think of selection as something unique to the choice-set (i.e., decision-making process) or the choice-maker (i.e., a characteristic peculiar to the person) that combine to determine non-random movement into certain life states, such as gang membership. Several influential critiques (Gottfredson and Hirschi 1990; Katz and Jackson-Jacobs 2004) have questioned the causal influence of street gangs altogether, ultimately raising the important question: Do gangs attract or create offenders?

Research examining the impact of gang membership on criminal behavior is wedged between the theoretical crosshairs of a thorny debate. One line of thinking, consistent with criminal propensity theories, holds that there is persistent heterogeneity across persons in maladaptive characteristics leading to continuity in poor decision-making and life outcomes. A second line of thinking, consistent with socialization theories, holds that life events and states maintain causal significance on criminogenic attitudes, behaviors, and overall well-being. Terry Thornberry and his colleagues (1993, 2003) seized on the broader theoretical debates characterizing the criminological landscape at the time by introducing a tripartite theoretical model on the gang membership–offending link: (1) the *selection* model is a spuriousness hypothesis, where gangs are merely the recipients of young people with shared deficits who were incapable of or shunned from pursuing prosocial interests; (2) the *facilitation* model is a causal hypothesis, holding that the group context is one that is highly influential on attitudes and behaviors; and (3) the *enhancement* model is a blended hypothesis that recognizes that the "kinds of persons" and "kinds of contexts" combine to influence behavior.

Group process was central to the facilitation and enhancement models proposed by Thornberry et al. (1993, 2003). Group process refers to the influence of the group in encouraging individuals to act in ways they otherwise would not. Much quantitative research treats group process as a black box – an area where our theoretical inferences operate, but are unobserved in empirical research. Qualitative research has more explicitly addressed group process, and exemplary works include Scott Decker and Barrik Van Winkle (1996), Malcolm Klein and Lois Crawford (1967), Jim Short and Fred Strodtbeck (1965), and Diego Vigil (1988), among others. There are many features of group process, which Jean McGloin and Megan Collins (2015) recently organized into intra- and inter-gang micro-level processes. Intra-gang processes include: the *opportunities* found in the environments gangs construct that play out in terms of local life circumstances such as routine activities in unstructured settings; *collective behavior* that involves the diffusion of responsibility and group cohesiveness; the affording of *social status* through appraisals of action and inaction among members; and the *normative influence* of norms and values that promote conformity through group identification. Inter-gang processes concentrate primarily on *external threats* that often result in the escalation and contagion of violence operating through retaliatory channels between gangs. While McGloin and Collins wrote about the ways in which group process amplifies criminal and delinquent behaviors among gang members, the consequences of these processes extend to other important areas, such as worldview, identity, and values, as well as economic, family, and health behavior.

Of course, the group process perspective on gangs has developed almost exclusively in the street gang arena. But we believe that this process extends to the case of prison gangs. The logic of a group process perspective would be applied to individuals who were gang members before entering into prison, who transitioned to a prison gang while in prison, and back to a street gang upon leaving prison. It would also be hypothesized that the activities, experiences, and cultural orientations we examine in the empirical chapters would escalate because of exposure to the prison environment and prison gangs. These are issues we address in more detail in Chapter 7.

## TOWARD A STUDY OF GANGS IN PRISON

An understanding of prison gangs must account for both individuals and groups. The model we propose to examine in this book looks at gang members nested in gangs. Such an understanding must also account for both the prison and the street, as well as how individuals balance the two domains, including the transitions between these domains. Whereas some place the bulk of explanatory power on the characteristics of individual inmates, others assign such power alternatively to the context in which inmates operate. Our response to the different approaches taken by those who emphasize cultural issues such as the inmate code and the street code and those whose focus is on structural arrangements within prison is to marry the two together. Social worlds are not comprised solely of structural relations and processes to the exclusion of values. Similarly, cultural values do not operate in a vacuum, unaffected by structural relations and processes. It is clear, however, that cultural transmission plays an important role in communicating key elements of prison gang life to the street, although it is less clear whether the transmission process follows blood-borne or air-borne pathways.

We address these issues in the remaining chapters, each of which builds from the conceptual framework detailed in this chapter, balancing individual and group factors, street and prison, and culture and structure. First, the study of street gangs has progressed through an understanding of the risk factors for gang membership. Chapter 4, the first empirical chapter, builds an understanding of the characteristics of gang members in prison across several key domains. What differentiates prison gang and non-gang members? The understanding of such risk factors has important implications for gang membership prevention and intervention. To date, however, we know very little about the risk factors for gang membership in prison.

Second, we need a better understanding of the organizational characteristics of prison gangs, including their relationships with other prison gangs and street gangs. Chapter 5 tackles this issue by nesting individuals within groups and describing the differences across prison gangs. This applies to both the criminal and non-criminal aspects of prison gang activities. The relationship between prison and street gangs is also important, not just for how they are different and similar, but also in their explicit linkages. We need to understand how they communicate with each other, what they communicate, and the impact of membership in one form of gang on the other as well as transitions from one to the other. Here we treat prison gangs as variable rather than monolithic. Chapter 6 considers the role of gangs as a form of prison governance. Here, the work of Skarbek, Lessing, and others from the non-state governance perspective is of particular interest as is the evolutionary work of Fong and his colleagues.

A third area we address in Chapter 7 is the impact of prison gang membership on misconduct behind bars. One of the key findings from the street gang literature is the criminogenic effects of gang membership, a finding that should be tested in the prison context. Such a focus must pay particular attention to involvement in violence, as violence is a defining feature of street gang activity that has an impact on non-criminal aspects of street gang life. While there is a strong foundation to suspect that this relationship holds in prison, more detail is certainly needed, both in examining self-reported offending as well as official reports of prison discipline. The importance of controlling the distribution and profits from criminogenic commodities also highlights the need to better understand the role of prison gangs in the illegal prison economy.

Fourth, the street gang literature has only recently begun to understand the entry and exit processes in gangs. Certainly more attention has been addressed to the former. Chapter 8 presents our attempt to bring more empirical attention to this question in terms of joining gangs in prison. In turn, Chapter 9 fills the void in understanding leaving gangs in prison. We know very little about if, when, how, and why individuals leave their prison gangs or disengage from their street gangs upon entering prison. Such analyses are important for any number of reasons, not the least of which is the criminogenic impact of gang membership. Together, these chapters provide a foundation to develop prevention and intervention programming. After all, given that there are a large number of inmates behind bars, generally for fixed periods of duration, there is an interest in preventing inmates from joining gangs as well as intervening in the lives of inmates who are already in gangs.

# 3

# The LoneStar Project

In 2014, we embarked on a large study of gangs and gang members in prison and the community. We termed it the LoneStar Project in our effort to forge an identity for the study. LoneStar is a nod to the nickname of the state of Texas and its unique history as an independent republic, as well as its somewhat distinct history of imprisonment. It is also an acronym that captures the interests of the larger project: the Texas Study of Trajectories, Associations, and Reentry among prison inmates. The LoneStar Project focused on understanding:

(1) the onset, continuity, and change in behavior and identity of incarcerated gang and non-gang members across time;
(2) the small networks of people – family, friends, employers, gang members – who comprise the social lives of prisoners and ex-prisoners; and
(3) the critical transition of inmates from the prison to the street, namely, the reentry experiences of ex-prisoners.

All of these themes are examined in this book, although as outlined in the previous chapters, gangs and gang members occupy a position of prominence in light of our research questions.

The idea for this type of study had been long in the making. The second author of this book interviewed California and Illinois gang members in prison (Decker, Bynum, and Weisel 1998). In 2001, he produced a training manual on gangs on the street and in prison for the American Correctional Association and, together with Mark Fleisher, guest edited a special issue of *Corrections Management Quarterly* on gangs and security threat groups. Fleisher and Decker identified a range of issues related to gangs in prison, while also recognizing the challenges of reintegrating gang members in the community (Fleisher and Decker 2001a, 2001b). One decade later, Jane England, the editor of the *Journal of Aggression, Conflict and Peace Research*, invited Fleisher and Decker to update their work on the topic. Along with the first author of this book, the team reviewed the current state of knowledge on gangs in prison and the reentry experiences of gang members and introduced the comparison of street and prison gangs we reported in Chapter 1. And, through this work, the idea for the LoneStar Project was conceived.

The LoneStar Project was funded primarily by the National Institute of Justice (NIJ). The NIJ has long had interest in issues related to gangs. It hosted a working group meeting in 2011 to identify gaps in knowledge of both basic and applied research on gangs. The relationship between street and prison gangs was identified as a topic of critical importance, though the successful proposal would need iron-clad access to at least one prison. Subsequently, the NIJ posted its request for proposals on issues related to gangs and gang violence in early 2014. Around this time, we had wrapped up multi-site data collection from a Google Ideas-funded study on gangs, technology, and disengagement, and an Office of Juvenile Justice and Delinquency Prevention-funded study on the impact of gang membership over the life course. We were still analyzing data and writing on a variety of topics from both of these projects. In other words, we were busy.

At the time, however, the lead author was a faculty member in the College of Criminal Justice at Sam Houston State University. The university is located in Huntsville, Texas, known colloquially as "Prison City, USA." There are seven prisons in Walker County, five of which are located in the city of Huntsville, including the Huntsville Unit. Better known as "Walls" for its imposing exterior brick walls, this unit was the first prison in the Texas prison system and has been in operation since 1849. It is also one of the most well-known prisons in the country because it is the location of the Texas execution chamber – the busiest of any in the United States. This was the unit where we conducted the vast majority of our interviews. Based on the number of inmates at each of the seven units (around 13,000, according to the online records posted by the *Texas Tribune*), prison inmates constitute nearly 20 percent of Walker County's population. As such, there are few universities better located to study prisons. Indeed, the College of Criminal Justice is just two blocks away from the Huntsville Unit, where roughly 25,000 prisoners are released annually to eagerly awaiting family members and friends. Other inmates board Greyhound buses heading north to Dallas, south to Houston, or west to Austin or San Antonio, while some stick around locally.

There are also few universities with a long-standing relationship with a state prison system. The Texas Department of Criminal Justice (TDCJ) is the only Texas state agency not located in Austin, the state capital. Rather, the agency is headquartered in the outskirts of Huntsville, a short drive from the university. Doug Dretke, the director of the Corrections Management Institute of Texas, housed at the College of Criminal Justice, was previously the director of the Corrections Institutions Division (CID) at the TDCJ. The director of CID is responsible for the management and support operations of the state prisons and jails. In other words, he understands the way the prison system operated. Dretke, along with Vince Webb, then Dean of the College of Criminal Justice, worked to arrange a meeting with the TDCJ about the study in early 2014. Whatever the outcome of the meeting, we knew that this was too great an opportunity to pass up. Studying gang members in prison would be a major and worthwhile endeavor in any prison system; engaging in such a study in Texas is an even greater feat because of the sheer size of the prison system and its tumultuous history of gangs and violence. To our delight, the TDCJ agreed to sign on and shortly thereafter, the NIJ agreed to fund the study.

## TEXAS, PRISONS, AND GANGS

The saying that "everything is bigger in Texas" typically refers to its geographic size (nearly 269,000 square miles) and total population (over 27 million people) – second to only Alaska and California, respectively. The saying also applies to the focus of our study: prisons and gangs.

The state of Texas contains the largest number of sentenced prisoners among the fifty US states. Figure 3.1 reports the number of sentenced prisoners in the custody of the California, Texas, and federal prison systems over the last fifteen years, the three largest US prison systems. During this period, the end-of-year Texas prison population averaged around 159,000 inmates. California's prison population, which until 2006 was the largest of any prison system, fell below Texas's in 2010. It has continued to drop as a result of Assembly Bill 109 (the Public Safety Realignment Act), brought about in response to a federal lawsuit

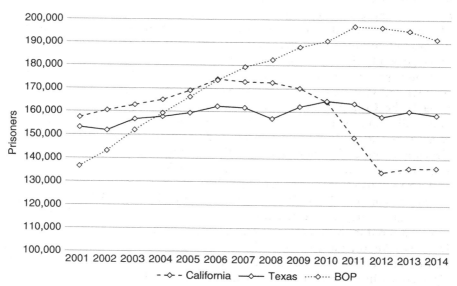

FIGURE 3.1 Number of prisoners in the three largest US prison systems, 2001–2014
Notes: Data are from the Bureau of Justice Statistics. BOP refers to the federal Bureau of Prisons.

on overcrowding in California prisons, which shifted certain lower-level offenders to county jail facilities (Petersilia et al. 2014).

While the state of Texas maintains the largest number of prisoners among the states, it is not the most populous prison system. That title belongs to the federal government, which currently houses 191,000 inmates. During this period, the states of California and Texas saw their prison populations fall and rise by 13.5 percent and 3.6 percent, respectively, while the prison population at the US Bureau of Prisons (BOP) increased by 40.2 percent. Although the prison populations differ in volume between the TDCJ and the BOP, they are remarkably similar in the number of prison facilities: the TDCJ maintains 112 prisons (13 of which are run by private corporations), while the BOP maintains 110 prisons (12 of which are run by private corporations) (Federal Bureau of Prisons 2017; Texas Department of Criminal Justice 2017).

Just like its prison population, the state of Texas also has a substantial amount of gang activity across its cities and prisons. In fact, a lot of gang research in institutional settings has been conducted in the juvenile facilities, county jails, and prisons of Texas. There is good reason for this attention.

We first highlight the level of gang activity in Texas cities by drawing on data from the National Youth Gang Survey (NYGS), which we described in Chapter 1. The benefit of the NYGS is not only that it is representative of law enforcement agencies in the United States, but also that it contains important information about the gang issues in these jurisdictions, including the number of gangs, gang members, and gang-related homicides. We took a snapshot of these issues across a seventeen-year period when the NYGS was administered (1996–2012). Using populations of 100,000 as a cutoff, there were 24 cities in Texas and 211 US cities outside of Texas included in the study. The Texas cities account for 40 percent of the state's population and are the locations with the greatest amount of gang activity.[1]

In a given year, there are about 1,730 gangs, 43,500 gang members, and 109 gang-related homicides in Texas's larger cities. The number of gangs ranks Texas as the highest among the states in the NYGS. The number of gang members and gang-related homicides places Texas behind California and Illinois in sheer volume. But it is well known that cities such as Chicago and Los Angeles drive national statistics on gang activity. Cities in Texas, alternatively, are not considered the cities with chronic and long-standing gang problems under Spergel and Curry's (1993) designation. In fact, most Texas cities reported the onset of gang problems in the late 1980s, right around

---

[1] We thank Arlen Egley Jr. for providing us with the data. All of our estimates are derived from the mean number of gangs, gang members, and gang-related homicides across the seventeen years of data. This better accounts for year-to-year fluctuations in gang activity, as well as the 2001 shift in the sampling strategy employed by the NYGS. And, because most agencies in Texas (~80 percent) and other states maintain gang units based on these data, it improves the reliability and validity of the results (Decker and Pyrooz 2010; see also Katz et al. 2012). Population estimates were based on the 2010 US decennial census.

the time that gang problems erupted in Texas prisons. This stands in contrast to many other large cities in the United States, where there are multiple generations of gang activity (Adamson 2000; Howell 2015).

The Texas prison system has a long history of gang activity, one that is also highly contentious. Crouch and Marquart (1989) documented the early years of gang emergence in their study of litigated reform prompted by the landmark *Ruiz* v. *Estelle* case. In this case, it was ruled that inmate elites ("building tenders") handpicked by the Texas prison system to maintain order was an unconstitutional form of prison governance. It is believed that this ruling led to the unwinding of inmate governance and precipitated a power vacuum that gangs were quick to fill. Indeed, prior to the 1980s gangs and gang violence were rare in the Texas prison system. Only the Texas Syndicate, a gang formed in California's Folsom prison among Latinos from Texas, existed in the 1970s (Fong 1990). The repercussions of *Ruiz* v. *Estelle* were felt almost immediately in the prison system (Beaird 1986; Crouch and Marquart 1989; Pelz, Marquart, and Pelz 1991). A high ratio of inmates to officers, an intelligence network that was essentially dismantled, and increasing racial tensions created a perfect storm that gave rise to the prison gangs of Texas.

Three years after the building tender system was eliminated, the Texas prison system was in crisis. Prison-based gangs such as the Aryan Brotherhood and Texas Mafia emerged alongside the Texas Syndicate. Other gangs, such as the Mexican Mafia, Hermanos de Pistoleros Latinos, and Crips, migrated into Texas prisons from other prisons or from the street (Beaird 1986; Crouch and Marquart 1989; Ralph and Marquart 1991; Texas Department of Public Safety 2015). According to Fong (1990), there was only one gang, the Texas Syndicate, and 56 gang members in March 1983 when the consent decree was put into effect; by September 1985, there were 1,285 gang members in eight different gangs. The Texas prison system witnessed an unprecedented number of acts of violence during the "war years," a 21-month period in 1984–1985. Much of the violence was due to explosive intergroup conflicts primarily between the Texas Syndicate and the Mexican Mafia, but also between the Aryan Brotherhood and Mandingo Warriors. Then, as now, race was a defining feature of prison gang membership and rivalries.

There were fifty-two homicides recorded during the war years – forty-three of them gang-related. With around 35,000 inmates, this translates into an annual homicide rate of about seventy-eight per 100,000 inmates. Perhaps an even more dramatic figure: *about 3 percent of gang members were murdered during this period.* If there were ever a figure or story that could convey to outsiders the origins of gangs and responses to gangs in the Texas prison system, this is it. Indeed, the mortality rates tracked by demographers and epidemiologists rarely reach single percentage points; homicide risk among gang members in the Texas prison system is a clear exception. As a result, in September 1985, the Texas prison system began placing all confirmed and suspected gang members in administrative segregation. As Ralph and Marquart (1991) reported, the prisons went quiet.

Disorder in the Texas prison system has quieted in recent years. The most up-to-date report on mortality in state and federal prison systems (Noonan, Rohloff, and Ginder 2016) indicates that homicides are rare in Texas prisons. According to the inmates we interviewed and when compared to other state prison systems, Texas prisons are now actually relatively safe places. The inmates we interviewed stated that prison today is nothing like it was back in the 1980s and 1990s. There were fifty-four homicides in Texas prisons between 2001 and 2013 – almost equal to the total number of homicides during the "war years" that lasted twenty-one months. In California and the Federal Bureau of Prisons, there were 182 homicides and 116 homicides, respectively. The annual homicide rate of three per 100,000 inmates in Texas is below the national average (~four per 100,000), and well below California (nine per 100,000) and the Bureau of Prisons (five per 100,000). There is no clear-cut explanation for the lower levels of violence in Texas prisons, although the move to place members of prison gangs in administrative segregation (Ralph and Marquart 1991) and very low levels of overcrowding (Carson 2018; Huey and Mcnulty 2005) are plausible explanations. Yet the gangs remain despite the dramatic reduction in violence.

The TDCJ offers no public definition of a gang. A 2007 publication indicates that a Security Threat Group (STG) is "Any group of offenders TDCJ reasonably believes poses a threat to the physical safety of other offenders and staff due to the very nature of said Security Threat Group" (Texas Department of Criminal Justice 2007). How "threat," "physical safety," and "nature" are operationalized by the TDCJ is unclear. Nonetheless, Table 3.1 reports the twelve STGs identified by the Texas prison system, along with the dominant race/ethnic group associated with the gang and whether the members of the gangs are housed automatically in administrative segregation. Many of the twelve gangs identified in this table emerged during the war years, yet they remain active three decades later. This is a testament to the durability of gangs. What is also apparent is that Latino groups dominate the ranks of what the Texas prison system considers STGs. Members of seven of the twelve gangs automatically serve their prison sentences in administrative segregation. The gangs that have earned this controversial dual distinction – labeled as an STG and placed in administrative segregation – are believed to have the greatest propensity to violence and an organizational structure that can wreak havoc on the prison system, a point we return to shortly. However, the dual distinction is not static; in 2015, the Texas Mafia was the latest STG whose confirmed members were no longer placed automatically in administrative segregation. Affiliates of every one of these STGs, along with many cliques and street gangs, participated in the LoneStar Project.

When turning to the definition and operationalization of gang membership, Texas is not unlike prison systems throughout the United States (Carlson 2001). Inmates in the Texas prison system are classified as gang members according to standard protocols derived from intelligence gathered by officials who are knowledgeable about gangs and security threat groups – the Security Threat

TABLE 3.1 *Security Threat Groups in the Texas prison system*

| Gang name | Race/ethnicity | Confirmed members placed in segregated housing |
|---|---|---|
| Aryan Brotherhood of Texas | White | Yes |
| Aryan Circle | White | Yes |
| Barrio Azteca | Latino | Yes |
| Bloods | Black | No |
| Crips | Black | No |
| Hermanos de Pistoleros Latinos | Latino | Yes |
| Mexican Mafia | Latino | Yes |
| Partido Revolucionario Mexicanos | Latino | No |
| Raza Unida | Latino | Yes |
| Texas Chicano Brotherhood | Latino | No |
| Texas Mafia | White | No |
| Texas Syndicate | Latino | Yes |

Group Management Office. Tattoos, self-admission, associating or corresponding with gang members, and possessing gang paraphernalia (e.g., constitutions, rosters, hit lists) are examples of red flags that are entered into an association packet – one or two red flags earns the label of "suspected" while three or more earns the label of "confirmed." Figure 3.2 traces the history of the total number of gang and non-gang inmates in the Texas prison system between 2005 and 2016. These figures are based on published statistics of the prison system.[2] The columns are broken into two subgroups: gang and non-gang inmates. The former includes the confirmed members of the twelve STGs highlighted in Table 3.1, along with the members of cliques and street gangs. The latter is something that bears further consideration.

The story of gangs in prison would be incomplete if we were to focus only on STGs. There are sixty-seven cliques and street gangs present in the Texas prison system. The TDCJ does not classify these groups as STGs because they are less organized, have less formal structure, a lower propensity for violence, and pose a less serious threat to the order of the prison system. Many well-known gangs are not identified as STGs, including: Gangster Disciples, Mandingo Warriors, Mexicles, Surenos, Tri-City Bombers, Vice Lords, White Knights, Wood Pile, and, most importantly, various strains of Tangos – Capirucha, Charcos, Dallas,

---

[2] The divergence in the population counts of inmates reported based on Bureau of Justice Statistics (BJS) data in Figure 3.1 and TDCJ data in Figure 3.2 is due to the latter including the "on hand" population of inmates in prison, state jail, and substance abuse facilities versus the former including all sentenced offenders (e.g., offenders held in county jails awaiting transfer, offenders in intermediate sanction facilities).

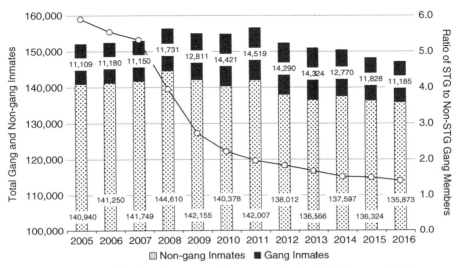

FIGURE 3.2 Count of gang and non-gang inmates and ratio of STG to non-STG inmates in the Texas prison system, 2005–2016
Note: The trend line refers to the ratio of STG to clique/street gang members (secondary axis).

Fort Worth, Houstone, Vallucos, Orejon, and West Texas. Tangos from Austin (Capirucha), Dallas, Houston (Houstone), and Forth Worth are known as the "Four Horsemen," with other cities uniting under the Tango label. Even though there are tensions among sets of Tangos, it is worth pointing out that the Tangos are the largest gang in the Texas prison system, and according to the Texas Department of Public Safety, considered the greatest threat to public safety in the state of Texas (Texas Department of Public Safety 2015). The Tangos are also the gang that is most represented in the LoneStar Project, which is expected given our random sampling of gang and non-gang prison inmates. There are two important points to make about Figure 3.2.

First, the gang population is extremely large – there are over 11,000 confirmed gang members in the Texas prison system. What is perhaps most telling about this figure is that *there are more members of gangs in the Texas prison system than there are prisoners in twenty-one of the fifty state prison systems.* Even if we were to exclude the members of cliques and street gangs, the population of confirmed members of STGs exceeds the entire population of prisoners in fifteen state prison systems (Carson 2015). Indeed, across the dozen years of data reported in Figure 3.2, gang members constitute anywhere from 7.3 percent to 9.4 percent of the prison population, illustrating the sheer volume of the gang population in the Texas prison system. The snapshot from 2016 – the time we were collecting data – indicates that 7.6 percent of the prison population was a member of an STG or clique/street gang. But these figures only include "confirmed" members of STGs and cliques/street gangs, not those inmates who are "suspected" or inmates who have renounced their affiliation with these groups. This means that the estimates of inmate gang involvement in the Texas prison system are conservative.

Second, the STG gang population is declining over time while the clique/street gang population is rising. The secondary axis of Figure 3.2 identifies the ratio of STG gang members to clique/street gang members in the prison system. In 2005, for every member of a clique or street gang in prison there were 6 members of STGs. In 2016, for every member of a clique or street gang in prison there were only 1.4 members of STGs. This is a remarkable drop over such a short period. The explanation for this dramatic fall likely includes the rise of the Tangos, whose origins in the 1990s were a response to the domineering and predatory Latino STGs, or what are termed "families" (Tapia 2013). Indeed, TANGO stands for "Together Against Negative Gang Organizations." The number of clique and street gang members roughly tripled in this short period, while the number of STG members fell by nearly 35 percent. The rise of the Tangos illustrates the dynamic nature of social organization in prison; it changes in response to a variety of internal and external stimuli.

Another possible explanation for this decline is that there are fundamental differences in how the Texas prison system manages STGs and cliques/street gangs. The latter are generally treated much like non-gang inmates – housed in the general population, given wide access to programming, permitted to receive visitors and take phone calls, among other privileges. While those privileges are important, the TDCJ has incentivized severing STG affiliations through programs such as Gang Renouncement and Disassociation (introduced in 2000) and the Administrative Segregation Diversion (introduced in 2014). These programs offer STG members ways to exit segregation or to avoid segregation altogether by renouncing their affiliations with gangs and entering into specialized programming. We discuss these programs in later chapters.

In this context we introduce readers to the LoneStar Project. Although the need is great, there is little research conducted on gangs in prison, and very few studies use survey methods, which have proven especially productive for the generation of knowledge on street gangs (and contributed in significant ways to social science research; see Bernard 2012). Indeed, many of the significant advances in understanding gangs and gang members have come from large-scale studies using survey research design, such as the Causes and Correlates studies in Denver, Pittsburgh, and Rochester, along with the Seattle Social Development Project, Pathways to Desistance, and the first and second evaluations of the Gang Resistance Education and Training program (Krohn and Thornberry 2008). If we are to study gang members in any prison system, Texas is a state that would yield tremendous knowledge about gangs. We now turn to our study methodology, where we introduce readers to the individuals who comprise our sample, including a portrait of who they are, how we selected them, and what we talked to them about when we interviewed them.

## STUDY METHODOLOGY

We learned about the trajectories, associations, and reentry experiences of our respondents by conducting interview-based surveys with them in prison and then re-interviewing them when they returned to the community. Our sample consists of 802 people who were in prison at the baseline interview. The longitudinal study design called for us to re-interview our respondents at multiple points in time upon release from prison. This led us to focus on the changes that could occur immediately upon leaving prison (around one month) and those that might be more drawn out and removed from prison (around one year). The focus of this book is on the baseline interview, which concentrates on gang activity in prison. Figure 3.3 provides a timeline for relevant milestones, which gives readers a sense of the evolution of the project (see also Mitchell et al. 2018).

### Selecting People and Sites

At the early stages of envisioning the LoneStar Project, we were concerned that gang allegiances may interfere with our research design. That is, the norms of gangs may discourage participation in the study, let alone provide us with reliable and valid responses to our questions. A project of this scope and subject matter had never been conducted in prison settings, and there is evidence that STGs like the Mexican Mafia and Aryan Circle in Texas forbid participation in research (Rufino, Fox, and Kercher 2012). While we are on record arguing that the self-report method is indeed a valid approach for gleaning information from active street gang members (Decker, Pyrooz,

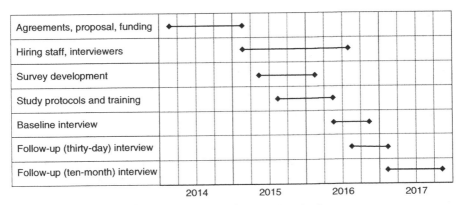

FIGURE 3.3 Timeline of key milestones of the LoneStar Project

Sweeten, and Moule, 2014; Webb, Katz, and Decker 2006), we were uncertain about how well this method would translate to gang members in prison, especially those in administrative segregation. Our conversations with prison officials also factored into this, as they seemed highly skeptical that prison gang members would say anything to us about gang dynamics on the inside. In retrospect, these concerns were exaggerated, which will become clear as we present readers with the evidence we have gathered. Nevertheless, this concern factored into our approach to the research design, where our working assumption was that the potential for interference would wane in the last days of imprisonment.

The second factor impacting our research design was that this was not only a study of gang and non-gang inmates in prison, but also a longitudinal study of trajectories and reentry. There is not a lot of research on reentry experiences. The studies that do exist suggest that reentry looks much different for gang members (Huebner, Varano, and Bynum 2007; Scott 2004). Therefore, we needed to be able to interview inmates during and after imprisonment. This meant that we would exclude inmates who would spend the remainder of their lives in the custody of the Texas prison system – inmates sentenced to death and inmates sentenced to life without parole, both of which are important, but exceptionally small groups, fewer than 1 percent of prisoners.

The final factor that played a major role in our study approach is rather obvious: gangs. If we wanted to learn about the trajectories, associations, and reentry experiences of gang members, as well as the activities, culture, and social organization of gangs, we needed a lot of them in our study. We drew on prior knowledge from a meta-analysis of 179 studies examining the gang membership–criminal offending link (Pyrooz et al. 2016) to determine our target sample size of 800 prison inmates. A sample of this size would allow us to ascertain modest effect sizes when comparing gang and non-gang inmates. We understood from the outset that we would need to oversample gang members in order to secure a large enough sample to conduct subgroup analyses – across black, white, and Latino gang members; across the members of STGs and cliques/street gangs; across those who imported their gang affiliations from the street and those for whom gang affiliations originated in prison. Further, we focused only on male prison inmates, as males constitute the vast majority – 93 percent – of the US prison population (Carson and Anderson 2016) and prior research in female prisons tends to downplay the role of gangs in social organization and facilitating violence (Belknap and Bowers 2016; Lauderdale and Burman 2009).

Our research design called for interviewing inmates within days before their release from prison and re-interviewing them twice upon returning to their communities. To accomplish this, inmates scheduled for release from the Huntsville Unit constituted our sampling frame for the LoneStar Project. This allowed us to intercept inmates at a natural stage of their progression back to the community. Prior to 2010, all inmates exiting the TDCJ – including prison, state jail, and substance abuse facilities – were released out of the Huntsville Unit. Regional releases were introduced to lessen the travel burden for families, but also the TDCJ's logistical and economic challenges of transporting inmates to a single release unit in such a large state. While there are six regional release centers in operation, the Huntsville Unit is responsible for releasing the largest number of prison inmates – about 60 percent of the 43,000 inmates released from state prison each year exit out of the Huntsville Unit. During the eight months we were in the Huntsville Unit conducting interviews, the TDCJ processed nearly 16,000 inmates for release. About 5 percent of these inmates were participants in the LoneStar Project.

A weekly list of scheduled releases was provided to us by the TDCJ executive services office. The list contained information that was relevant to our study purpose – name, date of birth, custody level, projected release date, parole date, gang name, gang/group status, and gang member status. This list was used to initiate the enrollment process into the study, which occurred over four stages. First, disproportionate stratified random sampling was used on a weekly basis to select inmates. Inmates were stratified by official gang and non-gang classifications by the prison system. Sampling fractions differed by gang classification because our goal was to achieve an equal proportion of gang and non-gang members. Inmates with non-zero levels of gang affiliation – former, suspected, and confirmed gang members – were oversampled by a factor of five. Since we seek to generalize our findings to the population of inmates released from the Huntsville Unit during the study period, when appropriate, we apply weights to correct for this oversampling.

The second and third stages of the enrollment process involved determining whether inmates were available and whether they could be approached by correctional staff to be invited to participate in the study.[3] The final stage of enrollment involved inmates who agreed to leave their cell, sat down with project interviewers, and reviewed the consent form. Only forty-eight inmates did not complete an interview at this point – forty-four were refusals and four were partial completions. We sampled with replacements until we reached our approximate target of 800 prison inmates. Each of these limitations to our sampling strategy restricts the inferences we make, but we doubt this would meaningfully change our findings. With some exceptions, official data reveal that our sample largely reflects the population from which it was derived, which we elaborate on below.

---

[3] A total of 398 inmates were selected to participate but were not present at the unit. This usually occurred because inmates did not arrive at Huntsville in time to be invited to participate in the study (e.g., they were transferred and released from the Huntsville Unit on the same day). A total of 460 inmates were present at the unit, but did not leave their cell to meet project staff. This occurred because inmates either refused to leave their cell (e.g., they were tired, or had mental or physical impairments) or as a result of the TDCJ protocols (e.g., they were high-risk or high custody level offenders). Inmates on detainers to other criminal justice agencies were also excluded.

Overall, our final sample consisted of 368 gang and 434 non-gang inmates, as determined by the TDCJ. Our rate of response, which is defined as the number of inmates who enrolled in the study and completed an interview divided by the number of inmates eligible for enrollment, was 61 percent. Our rate of cooperation, which is defined as the number of inmates enrolled in the study and who completed an interview divided by the number of inmates contacted, was 94 percent. These numbers are comparable to well-respected studies involving criminal and high-risk populations (Schubert et al. 2004) and, importantly they demonstrate the feasibility of conducting prison-based interviews with gang members.

## Survey Data Collection

We interviewed inmates in two prisons: the Huntsville Unit and the Estelle Unit. All of our general population custody-level inmate interviews were conducted in the Huntsville Unit, while our high custody-level inmate interviews were conducted in the Estelle Unit. It was necessary to incorporate the Estelle Unit into the study for two reasons. First, gang members were housed disproportionately in administrative segregation. In 2014, the confirmed members of STGs were fewer than 7 percent of the prison population, but constituted slightly over half of the inmates in administrative segregation (Pyrooz 2016). As Reiter (2016) has emphasized in her work in California, even the purported "worst of the worst" get out of prison, even if they are in administrative segregation. This meant that if we wanted a representative sample of gang members exiting prison, we needed to interview inmates in administrative segregation. The second reason we needed to interview at the Estelle Unit was because the Huntsville Unit could not easily accommodate high security-level inmates without impacting the daily routines of the unit, an important consideration that we did not take lightly. We were guests in the prison, and our objective was to have as minimal an impact on its daily operation as possible. This was no simple matter. Interviews began on April 18, 2016 and concluded December 11, 2016. After eight months of near-continuous interviewing, we were in tune with the rhythms of the prison. Our team was in the prisons interviewing 85 percent, or 201, of the days during that period. The exceptions were public holidays (e.g., Fourth of July, Thanksgiving), a brief project administrative hold, and two executions when the prison goes quiet. We were especially sensitive to the latter, as the vast majority of our interviews were conducted in the Huntsville Unit. It bears further mention that all inmates in administrative segregation were released out of the Huntsville Unit (2 percent of all releases), along with all sex offenders (6 percent) and inmates released to electronic monitoring (<1 percent).

Daily interviews were conducted late in the afternoon in the Huntsville Unit, about one to two days before an inmate was released from custody. All of these interviews were conducted in the "bullring," which is about a dozen or so yards and two security doors away from the main entrance of the prison. The bullring consists of two large enclosures made of floor-to-ceiling shined brass bars that are separated by a corridor. An officer stationed in an area above the bullring controlled access to the corridor and the enclosures. Each day correctional staff would holler "east side" and "west side" to allow us access to the bullring where we would conduct the interviews. The bullring terminology arose from the Texas Prison Rodeo, which occurred annually on the prison grounds from 1931 to 1986, a lucrative tourist attraction for the town and prison (Perkinson 2010; Texas State Historical Association 2017).

We would arrive at the Huntsville Unit around 3:45 pm each day, entering our names into the daily log, and having our identification cards reviewed by the officer at the sally port. Before entering the bullring, we would usually see the Warden or Captain, who would check in with us to see how things were going. A ranking officer would lead inmates into the bullring, instruct them to sit down, and remind them to behave. Interviewers were separated from inmates by a concrete, table-like structure that was about twenty feet long, three feet high, and two feet wide. There was enough room to set down laptop cases, consent forms, and rest our elbows, without invading someone's personal space. It was common to see inmates smiling, laughing, and telling stories during these interviews. For many inmates, it was the first opportunity to have a conversation with someone from the free world in years. This atmosphere was far more relaxed than in the Estelle Unit, where we conducted our interviews with inmates in administrative segregation.

Weekly interviews were conducted in the morning or early afternoon at the Estelle Unit. Since these inmates were transferred to the Huntsville Unit several days before release, we tried to secure these interviews almost immediately after having received the list of scheduled releases. There were several times when an interview was cut short or did not occur at all due to an inmate getting pulled out to take the "chain bus" to Huntsville (i.e., transferred to the release unit). It bears mentioning that the Estelle Unit was named after W. J. Estelle Jr., a former prison director and the named defendant in the historic *Ruiz* v. *Estelle* (1980) class-action lawsuit. We interviewed inmates in the administrative segregation building, which is self-contained with separate fencing and unique security protocols, located on the north side of a massive prison compound containing the two separate units, Estelle and Ellis. Accessing the facility required us to be buzzed through the external security fencing and then the main entrance. Our property – shoes, laptop cases, wallets, and belts – would go through CT scanners, while we would walk through metal detectors and then be subject to a pat-down, and sometimes subject to handheld metal detector wand scans. This is what was required even though we could not have physical contact with the inmate, a testament to what was at stake for interviews with such high-custody inmates.

It goes without saying that these interviews were qualitatively different from those conducted in the Huntsville Unit. For starters, these inmates required full shackles and two officers to one inmate for all out-of-cell movement, including to the visiting room where our interviews were conducted. This room is located at the end of the entrance security and contains five stalls for visitation. On the inmate's side, these stalls were concrete, completely enclosed, soundproof, and tagged with graffiti. Unlike the inmates who sat on an immobile stool, interviewers sat on a chair. There was little privacy on the visitor's side, as our backs were to the larger room. Correctional officers would walk in and out, getting snacks or sodas at the vending machine, getting a quick drink of water at the fountain, or visiting the restroom. There was never an incident. Nonetheless, our preference was to err on the side of privacy for the inmates. We were sensitive to the arrivals and departures of correctional officers, pausing our conversations. Most inmates did not mind, though. They would say, "I don't care if they hear me, I am leaving soon." But the complete glass barrier separating us from the inmate made the interview seem more impersonal – picking up on body mannerisms and physical cues was harder when looking at someone in a dimly lit room through a thick plate of glass. Inmates also seemed more distant. It was common to see inmates' eyes darting around the room, especially when the door to the visiting room opened. After all, these inmates were housed in cells not much larger than a parking space and rarely had the chance to see the Texas sunshine, which they could through the security corridor.

Computer-assisted personal interviewing (CAPI) was used for all of the baseline interviews. The TDCJ granted us special permission to bring laptops into the facilities. This was beneficial for two reasons. First, we programmed the survey using software that could account for complex skip patterns. We preloaded our surveys with official data on names, birthdates, release dates, custody level, and gang status. Rather than spending time asking an inmate about his date of birth or age at a certain event, our interviewers were armed with this information on the screen because it was preloaded into individual questions. For example, when asking about the age when they joined a gang, we could relate years to ages and ages to years, to help jog their memory. Also, answering "yes" to "Have you ever been in a street or a prison gang?" would later unlock a battery of questions about gang activity and gang dynamics. And, since we asked inmates about the name of their gang, the answer they provided us would be used rather than a generic listing of "gang" (e.g., Did the [Tango Blast] ever . . .). It is our belief that CAPI increased interview efficiency and accuracy.

The second benefit to CAPI was the electronic format of the data. Both authors have been involved in gang-related survey projects using paper-and-pencil instruments. While there are advantages to such an approach, cost and efficiency are not among them. Indeed, the numeric format of the completed surveys made it so that we could quickly assess a range of important indicators – for example, the ratio of self-reported gang to non-gang inmates, interviewer efficiency, scale properties, and other descriptive statistics. Further, the software allowed us to drill down data to the keystroke level of entry. And, unlike paper and pencil, we encrypted the data immediately upon completing a survey. This not only helped prevent data breaches from a lost or confiscated laptop, but also increased our respondents' confidence in our claims of confidentiality in the interview. Each day, completed interviews were removed from laptops and uploaded to a secure server housed at the University of Colorado Boulder, which was backed up nightly.

## Sources of Data

There were three primary sources of data in the LoneStar Project. First, the *survey data*, which constitute the bulk of the data we report in this book. The survey instrument covered nearly ninety study domains, some of which included questions based on established theoretical constructs, while others included new questions created specifically for this project, particularly in the area of gangs. Examples of study domains include: demographics; ethnic identification; education; military experience; housing; employment; social support; family contact; family crime; peers; physical and mental health; stress; gang embeddedness; legal socialization; self-control; masculinity; collective efficacy; routine activities; prison subculture; prison influence and governance; prison disorder; activism and radicalism; gang membership; gang leaving; gang organization; gang importation and exportation; offending and victimization; service needs; release planning; honesty scale; and contact cards. Our study interests were not confined to gangs – after all, we think gangs are an important, but not the only, part of prison experiences. Nested in the survey data were qualitative data capturing responses to open-ended questions and side conversations that we documented based on information shared by inmates that was prompted by our questions.

The second source of data was derived from *official prison records*, that is, the data collected and managed by the TDCJ. These data are important because they give us the opportunity to contrast what our respondents say about their behaviors and identity against what the prison system says about those same characteristics. These data allow us to compare self-reports of gang membership, misconduct, and victimization, against official reports. Of course, the value of the TDCJ data is not limited to the methodological exercises of assessing convergence and divergence between self- and official-report data. Indeed, official data give us precise information about important events, such as dates of admission to prison, transfers to units, the results of disciplinary hearings, and program participation and completion – these are events that may be difficult for inmates to recall and interpret.

Our final primary source of data is from *statewide law enforcement records*, that is, the Texas Department of Public Safety (DPS). We relied on the DPS data primarily for information about criminal history. These data were critical because they provided us with detailed figures about criminal justice system processing, or the flow from arrest to conviction to case disposition. We could also glean information about the date of first arrest and conviction, as well as the distribution of these events over the life course. Criminal career research in criminology emphasizes the onset, continuity, and change in trajectories of offending over the life course (Piquero, Farrington, and Blumstein 2007). In particular, we could compare the criminal trajectories of gang members to non-gang members. Given the adolescence orientation of much of the research on gangs (Curry 2000; Pyrooz 2014), the DPS data can shed tremendous light on the criminal careers of both our sample and our population.

### Sample and Population Comparisons

Table 3.2 contrasts the characteristics of our sample against the population of inmates who were released from the Huntsville Unit during the eight months we were collecting data. If we are to use our sample to make inferences to the population of releases, the first step is to ensure that our sample resembles the population. We thus concentrate on the sample statistics that are weighted to correct for the oversampling of inmates with gang affiliations. We report a range of relevant comparisons using official data from the Texas Departments of Public Safety and Criminal Justice, respectively.

Overall, we do not identify any red flags that give us pause about generalizing our findings. But we do find some discrepancies that bear mention. Compared to official data, our sample is slightly older (~two years); more likely to have tattoos (~four percentage points), to have been paroled (~three percentage points), a US citizen (~five percentage points), and white (~six percentage points); less likely to be Latino (~five percentage points) and a new receive (recent transfer to the Unit) (~four percentage points). Many of the demographic differences – Latino and citizenship – were due to the inability to interview offenders on detainers, a group that we were not able to screen out initially. Many of these inmates would serve time in TDCJ custody, only to be turned over to Immigration and Customs Enforcement and likely deported. Since Latinos constitute the largest immigrant group in Texas, these individuals were most likely deported to their native country. Many of the inmates who experienced same-day transfer and release, thus escaping the possibility of study enrollment, were generally younger and not parolees. Most importantly, our sample statistics for the gang variables closely approximate the population parameters. Whether these discrepancies would change our results is unknown, but our back-of-the-envelope comparisons of criminal history reveal little reason to be concerned.

Figure 3.4 displays the pre-prison residential location for 652 individuals in our sample. Zip codes are the unit of aggregation, and shaded zip codes contain at least one respondent in our sample. Texas is a large state with around 2,600 zip codes. Yet, our sample consists of individuals from throughout the state. This is important to recognize since the TDCJ now conducts regional releases,

TABLE 3.2 *Sample and population characteristics, official data*

| | Sample (unweighted) n= 802 | | Sample (weighted) n= 802 | | Population N= 15,634 | |
|---|---|---|---|---|---|---|
| | Mean/% | (SD) | Mean/% | (SD) | Mean/% | (SD) |
| Age (in years) [a] | 39.05 | (11.22) | 40.24 | (12.11) | 37.91 | (11.64) |
| Height (in inches) [a] | 69.16 | (3.02) | 69.33 | (3.06) | 69.07 | (3.21) |
| Weight (in lbs) [a] | 184.17 | (36.82) | 184.86 | (36.80) | 181.99 | (37.33) |
| Body mass index [a] | 27.70 | (5.18) | 27.65 | (5.19) | 27.44 | (5.15) |
| Tattoos [a] | 61.72% | | 57.66% | | 54.04% | |
| Race/ethnicity [a] | | | | | | |
|   Latino | 35.91% | | 31.09% | | 36.59% | |
|   White | 33.04% | | 38.22% | | 31.84% | |
|   Black | 30.42% | | 30.26% | | 31.12% | |
|   Asian | 0.25% | | 0.41% | | 0.40% | |
|   American Indian | 0.00% | | 0.00% | | 0.05% | |
| US citizen [a] | 96.50% | | 95.45% | | 90.54% | |
| Custody level [b] | | | | | | |
|   General population | 81.92% | | 79.84% | | 77.58% | |
|   Outside trusty | 4.61% | | 7.67% | | 5.82% | |
|   Segregation | 6.23% | | 2.85% | | 3.17% | |
|   New receive | 2.12% | | 2.80% | | 7.30% | |
|   Safekeeping | 0.12% | | 0.21% | | 0.59% | |
|   Other | 4.99% | | 6.47% | | 5.56% | |
| Gang status [b] | 45.88% | | 9.99% | | 10.02% | |
|   Confirmed/ suspected | 31.17% | | 7.13% | | 7.84% | |
|   Ex/former | 14.71% | | 3.37% | | 2.17% | |
| Non-gang [b] | 54.11% | | 89.51% | | 89.98% | |
| Gang/STG [b] | 28.43% | | 6.50% | | 6.43% | |
| Gang/Clique [b] | 17.46% | | 3.99% | | 3.59% | |
| Criminal history [a] | | | | | | |
|   Prior arrests | 9.29 | (7.33) | 9.77 | (8.51) | 8.50 | (6.39) |
|   Age first arrest | 19.19 | (6.76) | 20.47 | (7.89) | 20.19 | (7.29) |
|   Violent offender | 25.06% | | 26.19% | | 24.63% | |
|   Property offender | 21.45% | | 19.63% | | 15.90% | |
|   Drug offender | 17.70% | | 16.66% | | 19.32% | |
|   Other offender | 35.79% | | 38.77% | | 36.87% | |
| Time served (in years) [a] | 6.13 | (6.10) | 5.09 | (6.10) | 4.19 | (5.50) |
| Parole [b] | 84.91% | | 86.60% | | 83.64% | |

*Notes:* SD = standard deviation. Weighted sample statistics correct for disproportionate sampling of gang/STG gang members. Population refers to all offenders released from TDCJ custody during the period of baseline interviews.
[a]Source of data: Texas Department of Public Safety; [b]Source of data: Texas Department of Criminal Justice.

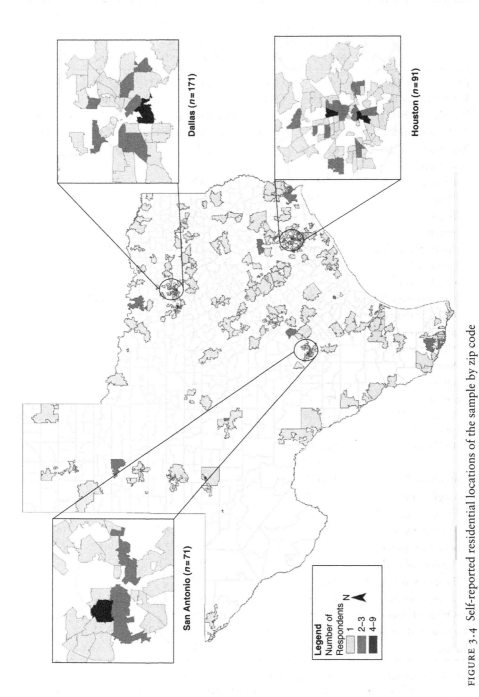

FIGURE 3.4 Self-reported residential locations of the sample by zip code

Note: $N = 652$ due to missing responses to pre-prison spell residential address (homeless, transient, recall of zip code, and prior imprisonment).

yet the Huntsville Unit is likely the most geographically representative of inmate releases among the release units. As expected, large population centers are the drivers of the prison population. Dallas, Houston, and San Antonio, cities with populations that exceed 1 million residents, are reported in boxes due to numerous zip codes. Even then, prison admissions are not evenly distributed across those cities, as evidenced by four to nine respondents being from one to two of the zip codes in the respective cities.

## FIDELITY IN SURVEY RESEARCH WITH GANG AND NON-GANG PRISON INMATES

The final issue – and perhaps the most important – to address in this chapter concerns fidelity in survey research. We do not attribute the paucity of prison gang research entirely to concerns about secrecy among gang members. However, we do agree that this concern has played a role in suppressing responses about gang membership. We liken the state of research on prison gangs to that of street gangs in the late 1980s and early 1990s. At the time, the street gang literature was consumed with defining a gang, enough so that it led some (e.g., Fagan 1990) to propose using self-nomination as the primary method to measure gang membership. This meant letting the individual determine what a gang is and whether he or she is a part of it, rather than the researcher. That, combined with the emergence of numerous longitudinal survey research studies, led to an explosion of knowledge about *street* gang membership (Pyrooz and Mitchell 2015). Can survey research also yield large gains about gang members in prison? The answer to this question is dependent on several factors, including participation rates, survey instruments that can be administered feasibly in prison, inmate perceptions, and concordance rates between official and self-reported data. These are all issues dealt with by research on street gangs.

### Participation Rates

We first asked if gang members – as classified by the prison system – would be willing to even participate in such a study. While we did not portray this as a "gang study," and TDCJ staff were instructed to not mention "gang" when approaching the inmates, our consent form did highlight the role of gangs in our survey. If secrecy was enough to compel gang members to avoid participating in research, we would expect that non-participation rates would be higher among gang members. The evidence suggests otherwise. In fact, we found that gang and non-gang members were just as likely to not enroll in the study after sitting down with us – twenty-three of the non-participants were classified as gang members by the prison system (48 percent of those who declined), while twenty-five of the non-participants were non-gang members (52 percent). This was proportional to our sampling of gang ($n$ = 368, or 46 percent) and non-gang ($n$ = 434, 54 percent) inmates in our sample. Gang members are just as likely to agree to participate in survey research as non-gang inmates, and both groups participated at an exceptionally high rate.

### Survey Duration and Item Response Patterns

Our second step was to determine if the baseline interviews with gang members were fundamentally different from the interviews we conducted with non-gang members. It could be the case that gang members hurry through the survey or refuse to answer questions. We addressed this by comparing the characteristics of survey administration, including the time it took to administer the survey and the item response patterns in the survey. Our software allowed us to drill down to the timing of keystrokes to assess the former, while a range of item non-response patterns allowed us to assess the latter. Overall, we found few differences between gang and non-gang members. In fact, the results were almost identical.

From the first question (obtaining respondent consent) to the last question (interviewer's perception of the respondent's interview) in the survey instrument, the total duration of the survey averaged 113 minutes. While the survey time for gang members (mean = 121 minutes) was longer than non-gang members (mean = 104 minutes), this was expected since we had several sections devoted to gang dynamics. When we partial out those gang sections, we found that the duration of the survey was indistinguishable statistically and substantively between gang members (96 minutes) and non-gang inmates (99 minutes).[4] Whatever is occurring during the survey, it is producing administration times that are equivalent across groups.

At first glance, item response patterns were also different when examining the 1,190 questions in the survey instrument. Gang members answered 751 questions, while non-gang members answered 631. Of course, not all questions applied to everyone. For example, someone who answered "no" to a question about misconduct – e.g., "Have you attacked another inmate with a weapon [during this incarceration]?" – would not be asked about the number of times it occurred in the last six months and the percent of the time it was gang-related. When excluding valid skips, or inapplicable questions, we found that gang and non-gang inmates answered nearly all of the questions posed to them: 97 percent and 98 percent, respectively. This meant that gang and non-gang members were rarely responding with "I don't know" or refusing to answer our questions.

---

[4] Readers might wonder why the survey duration for the non-gang-related items (99 minutes) is not equivalent to the total items (104 minutes) for the non-gang members. There were a number of inmates ($n$ = 73) who were not classified as gang members by the TDCJ, but self-reported to lifetime street and/or prison gang membership in the survey. Since this lifetime measure functioned as the gate item for questions about gang dynamics, inmates who were not classified as gang members would receive these questions.

What is perhaps most important from this exercise is that when we did ask gang members questions about gang dynamics, they answered them. Among the 424 gang-related questions, there was an average of only 0.2 refusals and 3.1 "don't know" responses to our questions. As we suspected, most (80 percent) of the "don't know" responses had to do with group-level questions. Many gang members legitimately did not know the year their gang formed or some criminal activities in which their gang engaged; our interviewers did not suspect that gang members were attempting to conceal information. This gives us confidence that survey research is an effective approach to learn about prison gang members.

## Inmate and Interviewer Perceptions

The third step in assessing survey differences came from our sample itself, as well as the forty-one people we trained to conduct interviews in the prison. We were warned by prison personnel that "word travels quickly," and to not be surprised if gang members have the flow of questions, or even specific questions, memorized because they are required to report external interactions to the gang. We also knew that negative feedback could doom our project, which is why we placed such a premium on training our interviewers and how we described the project to prison officials and inmates. Prior studies, including one in Texas (Rufino et al. 2012), reported the challenges of negative feedback from gang members. But our experiences were just the opposite. Respondents told us across a series of questions that they enjoyed the interview, gave their best effort, listened carefully, and thought the interview was a good use of their time. They also indicated that they were not bored during the interview, and 98 percent of them stated that they answered the questions truthfully. Most importantly, there were no differences across gang and non-gang members for any of these questions.

Did interviewers view things differently? Not really. After completing the interview, each interviewer answered four questions about the interview itself. Overall, there were no differences between gang and non-gang inmates in interviewers' perceptions of honest responses, engagement, and attentiveness during the interview, or likelihood of participation in the follow-up interview. Interviewers did believe that, on average, gang members were more likely to be arrested post-release (as we found out, our interviewers were right). This is not to say that our respondents were saints with perfect recall – there were instances of inmates being evasive and refusing to answer questions. But, we can conclude that such behavior was just as likely to occur among gang members as it was among non-gang members.

## Concordance Rates between Survey and Official Data

Our final test of the reliability and validity of self-reports is perhaps the most important: Are gang members who they claim to be? We assess this by contrasting what the prison system reports about an inmate's gang affiliation against what an inmate says about his gang affiliation. This includes whether or not someone has ever been a gang member in prison and the gang with which they are affiliated. With few exceptions (Curry 2000; Maxson et al. 2012), we do not know much about how self-reports of gang affiliation compare to classifications by the criminal justice system – and we know nothing about this in prisons, where the pressure toward secrecy is perhaps the greatest.

We start by comparing convergence between self-reports and official reports of gang membership. Figure 3.5 includes binomial classification rates of any current or former affiliation with a gang while in prison based on self-reports and official reports.[5] There were 286 "true positives" – the respondent called himself a gang member and so did the prison system. There were 374 "true negatives" – the respondent said he was not a gang member and so did the prison system. This combines to produce a high rate of concordance between the independent sources: about 83 percent. Of course, this also means that 17 percent of our sample either was a false positive (10 percent) or negative (7 percent). In the case of false positives, inmates' claims of not being a gang member ran counter to the gang label assigned by the prison system. The false negatives were inmates for whom their gang membership escaped official detection by the prison system. Our rate of concordance was higher than the 71 percent rate observed by Maxson and colleagues (2012) among juveniles in the California correctional facilities. This is perhaps expected since our data come from prisons, where more resources are devoted to gang intelligence gathering and gang member identity is perhaps more durable and widely known.

If the gang intelligence gathered by the prison system to identify gang members is the criterion used to assess gang affiliation, the convergent validity we are observing satisfies the standards of social science research. We obtained a phi coefficient of 0.66 between the two measures – not a perfect correlation, but one that is very strong. Further, we found that the relationship between self-reports and official reports of gang membership was consistent with the principles of the multi-trait, multi-method matrix introduced by renowned psychologists Campbell and Fiske (1959), which we have outlined in a recent paper (Pyrooz, Decker, and Owens 2018). This suggests to us that we can trust self-reports as a viable source of information about gang membership in prison.

---

[5] We operate under two assumptions here. First, when determining what is "true" versus "false," we base this on self-reports of gang membership because it is our contention that prisoners know more about their affiliations and identity than any other group or organization. Therefore, when determining what is "positive" versus "negative," we base this on official reports of gang membership. After all, it is the prison system assigning these labels, which, in turn, have tremendous implications for a wide range of outcomes in prison. Our second assumption is that gang membership in prison, not old and weaker affiliations on the street, is what matters most for the contingency table. Someone could have been a street gang member, but if that affiliation does not migrate into prison, it does not play any role in these findings.

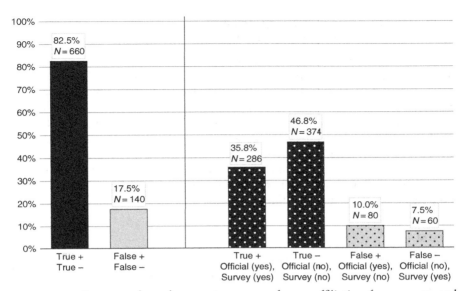

FIGURE 3.5 Correspondence between measures of gang affiliation from survey and administrative data sources
Left columns: overall rate of concordance and discordance.
Right columns: results from 2×2 classification table.
Notes: Valid *N* = 800 due to two refusals. True/false was determined based on survey-based self-report measures; positive/negative based on administrative-based official classification measures.

Getting valid information about gang membership is one thing, but is it also possible to secure accurate information on more sensitive and specific topics, such as gang names? We contrasted the names of gangs provided to us by the prison system for inmates they identified as gang members against the gang names given to us by the inmates who claimed to be gang members. Inmates were not required to name the gang they were a member of, let alone provide us with a valid name. But they did, and at a rate that left us impressed. Out of the 368 inmates identified as gang members by the prison system, we received a concordant gang name from the inmate 86 percent of the time. Here are examples of concordance from the largest gangs represented in the study:

- 85 of the 104 inmates the prison system identified as Tangos also told us they were Tangos;
- 48 of the 51 Crips gang members;
- 45 of the 49 Blood gang members;
- 29 of the 31 Aryan Brotherhood gang members;
- 22 of the 23 Mexican Mafia gang members;
- 18 of the 22 Texas Syndicate gang members;

- 15 of the 15 Aryan Circle gang members;
- 7 of the 8 Barrio Azteca gang members.

Recall that two of the above gangs – Aryan Circle and Mexican Mafia – banned participation in prior research. When turning to the sources of discordance, half of the story could be explained by not self-identifying as a gang member. The other half was legitimate mismatches between self-reported and officially reported gang names – Tango gang members who told us they were members of the Crips and Latino STG members who claimed Tango or a street gang affiliation. Overall, discordance in gang names was the exception rather than the norm. When combined with the above exercises we are confident that it is possible to conduct high-quality survey research with gang members in prison with fidelity.

## SUMMARY

In this chapter, we introduced the LoneStar Project, which has been long in the making, but awaiting the right convergence of parts to pull it off. Texas happened to be the right place and the right time. It is the right place because of the sheer size of the prison system and its tumultuous history of gangs and violence. It was the right time because a strong team was assembled and permissions to launch the project were negotiated. We introduced the sample of prison inmates we interviewed as part of the LoneStar Project, and the population of inmates released during this same period. We also reviewed the sample composition and provided a description of how we selected them, where we interviewed them, and what we talked to them about. We determined with confidence that survey research is possible with gang members in prison. Not only will gang members participate, but their interviews are hardly if at all distinguishable from non-gang members. Most importantly, information on gang member identity and gang characteristics can be gathered with high validity – we can trust the self-reports of gang members as a viable approach to research in prisons. These important lessons serve as a foundation for the remainder of the book. We now shift our focus to a different question: What are the characteristics of gang members and how are they different from inmates who are not in gangs?

# 4

## The Characteristics of Gang Members in Prison

Who are the members of gangs in prison? What attitudes and beliefs do they maintain? What do their social networks look like? And how similar are they to inmates who are not in gangs? In many ways, we see these questions as an extension of Chapter 3 because it provides an additional description of our sample. After all, these are individuals as well as members of a group. We reported in prior chapters that a large majority of prison inmates in the United States are not gang members. In other words, there is a small group of inmates (~15 percent) who affiliate with gangs and a much larger group of inmates who do not. This is also the case in Texas. Both official records and self-reports of prison gang membership confirm this. In this chapter, our objective is to compare gang and non-gang inmates across a range of characteristics. In the community, gang and non-gang members can be distinguished by protective and risk factors, and non-gang members are presumed to have more protective and fewer risk factors than their gang counterparts. We are interested in determining if this also applies in prison. Why is it important to differentiate between gang and non-gang inmates? There are many reasons do to this, but we believe there are two reasons that are the most important.

First, basic description is important when studying social problems we know very little about. As our colleagues Finn-Aage Esbensen and Dena Carson (2012, 466) noted, "it is important, indeed essential, to accurately describe a social problem if we are to understand it, to explain its presence and, more important, to suggest strategies for addressing the problem." They made this statement when outlining their objective to compare gang and non-gang middle school youth in a seven-site US study. We think the need for good description is even greater in prison owing to the difficulties of studying such groups and the limited research on the topic. Indeed, as we detail below, we were only able to find seven studies that have identified the correlates of gang membership in prison. In the absence of such comparisons, politicians, practitioners, and the general public will rely on stereotypes of prison gang members rather than sound, empirical evidence. Science should always trump stereotypes, particularly in the design and implementation of responses to gangs. This leads to our next point.

The second reason to distinguish gang from non-gang inmates is more practical. If differences exist, what are their implications for correctional policies and practices? Jessie Krienert and Mark Fleisher (2001) argued that such aggregate comparisons of the profiles of gang and non-gang inmates are crucial because they offer insights to correctional officials about how to respond to gangs in prison, as well as reveal potential challenges for the safety of inmates with gang affiliations. Perhaps such knowledge would affect housing assignments to protect the safety and security of correctional staff and gang members alike. Background information on education and employment deficits, as well as drug histories, may uncover challenges to institutional programming as well as reentry programming, along with the need for specialized programming for gang-involved inmates. The personal and criminal histories of gang members might suggest the need for alternative programming approaches for this population altogether. Some states offer alternative housing for individuals who have "renounced" their gang membership. We know far too little about "what works" to prevent gang membership or intervene in the lives of gang members; this is true on the street and in prison. Describing the characteristics of gang members in prison is the first step needed to build a foundation for and formulate such responses.

In this chapter, we examine the characteristics that differentiate gang and non-gang inmates. Drawing on protective and risk factor research that assesses susceptibility for gang membership on the street (e.g., Hill et al. 1999; Maxson, Whitlock, and Klein 1998; Thornberry et al. 2003), we concentrate on factors that fit the following domains: (1) demographic and individual, (2) environmental, (3) health, (4) social connections, (5) attitudes and beliefs, and (6) criminal justice system involvement. We start with basic descriptive and bivariate statistics, providing a comprehensive examination of the protective and risk factors for gang membership in prison. We illustrate that no one factor best explains gang membership by assessing cumulative risk across the domains and factors associated with gang membership. In a novel twist, we determine if different measures of gang membership – official reports and self-reports – produce similar results. This is important because it gives us multiple sources to describe the problem, but also to assess whether official and self-reports tell the same story. The comparison of official and self-reports has implications for policy and practice, as well as future research on these matters. Before we present our findings, however, we take stock of what prior studies reveal about the differences and similarities between gang and non-gang members.

## PRIOR RESEARCH ON GANG AND NON-GANG MEMBERS IN PRISON

We identified seven studies that have differentiated between gang and non-gang members in prison with respect to protective and risk factors. These studies are split in their use of survey and official data sources and have been conducted in prison systems in Canada (two studies), an unidentified Midwestern state, Nebraska, Nevada, and Texas (two studies). We highlight the unique contribution of these works in chronological order, as well as the defining characteristics of the studies.

The first comparison of gang and non-gang members in prison was conducted by Shelden (1991). He focused on a random sample of sixty confirmed black and Latino prison gang members in a Nevada prison, then matched them on age and race/ethnicity to non-gang members. He examined information contained in inmates' "prison files" (i.e., official data). When focusing on demographic, economic, and social factors, there were few differences between these groups. In fact, both groups were just as likely to come from intact households, graduate from high school, be born in Nevada, and have similar cognitive ability. But gang members were less likely to have been employed and were more likely to be residing in Nevada when last arrested. In contrast, when arrest histories and substance abuse problems were compared, gang members had more felony arrests, juvenile court referrals, were more likely to be suspected of drug abuse, and to have used weapons. Shelden also found that gang members were involved in more prison misconduct. This work provided clues of what future research on street and prison gangs would reveal – in general, the criminal behaviors of gang members distinguish them from non-gang members more than demographic, social, or economic factors. The differential involvement in crime and violence deserves special mention in this context because of its relevance for future chapters, and is a major conclusion of this book.

The next comparison of gang and non-gang members in prison was conducted in Texas by Ralph and colleagues (1996) using official data from the prison system. Their sample of 14,962 inmates, 12 percent of whom were gang members, was based on discharges from 1980 to 1991. They found that while gang members went to prison at younger ages, they received prison sentences that were about twice as long as non-gang members (sixteen years vs. nine years). Gang members also did more stints in solitary confinement than non-gang members (two and a half years vs. half a year), which would be expected given the Texas policy of automatically segregating gang members, initiated midway (1985) through this study period. Gang members were also more likely to be repeat offenders and violent offenders than non-gang members. When combined with Shelden (1991), these studies point to stark differences between gang and non-gang members in prison, especially with regard to criminal activities.

The work of Krienert and Fleisher (2001) was the first study to rely on survey methodology to compare gang and non-gang members. As we argued in earlier chapters, the benefit of a survey is that it gathers information directly from inmates, untethered to the data gathering and reporting practices and administrative needs of the prison system. Krienert and Fleisher argued that gang membership was a proxy for social deficiencies that could be remedied only with substantial programming. Their study focused on 702 newly admitted inmates to Nebraska prisons, 12 percent of whom were gang members. Unlike Shelden, who matched on demographic characteristics, Krienert and Fleisher found age and race differences between gang and non-gang members. Over 85 percent of gang members were younger than age twenty-five compared to just one-quarter of the non-gang sample, and 47 percent of gang members were black compared to 16 percent of the non-gang sample. Gang members were also less likely to have completed high school, been married, and have children. They also had worse employment histories, including fewer hours worked and less legal income earned. Many of these characteristics – marriage, education, and employment – are important correlates of life-course stability. But the most striking difference, according to Krienert and Fleisher, was the difference in criminal and deviant histories. Gang members had more arrests and first arrests at younger ages, they self-reported more involvement in serious crimes and victimization experiences, and a greater proportion used drugs (94 percent vs. 77 percent). This finding is consistent with what we know about gang membership on the street, suggesting parallels between the offending characteristics of street and prison gang members (a central theme of this book). Krienert and Fleisher contend that the collective social deficiencies of gang members may present serious programming challenges to prison systems as well as with the facilitation of the rehabilitation of these inmates.

Rick Ruddell and his colleagues conducted two studies of gang and non-gang members in Canadian federal prisons. The first used a random sample of inmates admitted between 2006 and 2009 (Ruddell and Gottschall 2011) and the second focused only on females (Scott and Ruddell 2011). These studies are based on extensive intake assessments that were administered to inmates and focused on risks, needs, and reintegration potential. The most notable finding from the Ruddell studies is similar to the social deficiencies argument made by Krienert and Fleisher (2001). Compared to non-gang members, regardless of gender, gang members achieved higher risk scores based on static risk factors (e.g., criminal history), higher needs scores based on dynamic risk factors (e.g., employment, substance abuse), and lower reintegration potential scores based on correlates of recidivism (e.g., risk scores, needs scores, security classification, and motivation). These differences illustrate the challenges associated with programming for gang members in prison, as well as the potential issues gang members experience when they are released from prison.

The final two studies (Varano, Huebner, and Bynum 2011; Rufino, Fox, and Kercher 2012) shared a number of similarities in method, sample, and findings. Both were based on surveys, focused on new prison admits, and sought to distinguish gang from non-gang members. The Varano study was conducted in an unnamed Midwestern state with 179 male gang members and 325 male non-gang members, while the Rufino study was conducted in Texas with 84 male gang members and 133 male non-gang members. The key difference, however, was that the former measured self-reports of gang membership on the street, while the latter measured gang membership using official reports in prison. Despite these measurement and sample composition differences, the findings from this research tell much of the same story as above, particularly with respect to criminal history, demographics (especially age and race), and employment. The Rufino study was notable because it revealed that gang members experienced far more types of victimization on the street than non-gang members. The Varano study was notable because it distinguished between inmates who were members of "organized" and "disorganized" gangs based on respondent self-reports of whether their gang had rules and codes. Members of organized gangs were worse off (engaged in more misconduct), as disorganized gang members did not differ greatly from non-gang members in terms of their pre-incarceration characteristics or misconduct while incarcerated.

We draw several conclusions from this research. First, gang members are more heavily involved in criminal behaviors and institutional misconduct than non-gang members before and during prison. Second, gang members have lower levels of educational attainment and worse employment histories, both of which are closely related and correlates of successful reintegration after release from prison. Third, regardless of whether studies rely on survey or official data to describe the differences between gang and non-gang members, the findings are consistent across data sources. These conclusions are strengthened because we find similar results with different data sources from these studies. Fourth, we know far more about behaviors and background factors than we do attitudes, beliefs, health, and social connections, all of which may reveal important insights about the sources of misconduct, recidivism, and readiness for successful reintegration from prison to society. This void in our knowledge is largely a consequence of the inability of researchers to gain access to prisons to conduct interviews, particularly during a time when gang membership in prison skyrocketed. Lastly, there has been far more research aimed at inmates in the early years of their sentences than the later years, and we know even less about inmates who are close to release.

This foundation leads us to the present analysis of gang and non-gang members in the LoneStar Project. We provide a detailed examination of the protective and risk factors for gang membership. These data address many of the gaps in our current understanding of gang and non-gang differences, particularly as they are drawn from a prison sample shortly before their release to society.

## COMPARING GANG AND NON-GANG MEMBERS IN PRISON

Our goal in this chapter is to compare gang and non-gang members in prison across a wide range of factors from several important domains. Before reporting our findings, it is necessary to first describe the variables used to compare gang and non-gang inmates. Nearly all of these variables are derived from the interviews we conducted with respondents while they were incarcerated. We spend more time describing these variables in this chapter because we also use them later in the book, particularly in Chapters 7, 8, and 9. While only a brief description of the measures is reported in the text, readers who would like more information about the measures may consult an online repository of LoneStar Project resources: www.researchgate.net/project/The-LoneStar-Project.

### Comparative Domains and Measures

#### Demographic and Individual Measures

Several demographic and individual variables known to discriminate between street gang and non-gang members are included in this domain of risk factors. Demographic measures include *age* in years at the time of the interview, along with indicators of the racial or ethnic group the study participant identifies with, including single-race/ethnicity *Latino, black,* and *white,* as well as other or mixed race/ethnicity. Measures of relationship status include dummy indicators for *married, relationship,* and *single.* Study participants self-reported as to whether or not they were a *father* or a *military veteran,* along with *educational attainment,* measured in years (e.g., high school diploma = twelve years). The Wechsler Adult Intelligence Scale-Revised was used to measure *IQ* based on prison administrative data, consistent with past research in prisons (e.g., Worrall and Morris 2012). Our final individual measure is *low self-control,* which is a construct derived from thirteen items in the Brief Self-Control Scale (Tangney, Baumeister, and Boone 2004), such as "You do certain things that are bad for you if they are fun." The items were averaged and coded so that higher scores indicate lower levels of self-control. The scale exhibited acceptable internal consistency (Cronbach's alpha = 0.80, mean inter-item correlation = 0.24).

#### Environmental Measures

In this domain, we asked study participants to report on activities and perceptions in their surrounding environment. In doing so, we differentiate between street and prison contexts. *Street informal social control* and *prison informal social control* are five- and six-item constructs that measure respondents' perceptions of fellow neighbors and inmates' willingness to intervene on behalf of the common good. For each construct, the items were averaged and coded so that higher scores reflected greater informal social control. The scales maintained desirable psychometric properties (street: Cronbach's alpha = 0.83, mean inter-item correlation = 0.50; prison: Cronbach's alpha = 0.80, mean inter-item correlation = 0.40). Dummy indicators of whether the study participants thought their *neighborhood was a good place to live* and whether there were *gangs in the neighborhood* were also included. *Disorder in prison* is a summative index of ten dummy items related to physical and social disorder in prison, such as ignoring informal hygiene and light's-out rules. The final contextual item measures *unstructured routine activities* in prison, which is the number of hours in a typical day the inmate spends hanging out with fellow inmates outside of the observation of authorities.

## Health Measures

The measures in this domain tackle an area of research we know little about in criminology generally, particularly among gang members and prison inmates. *Stress* is a construct derived from five Likert-scaled items in the perceived stress scale (Cohen, Kamarck, and Mermelstein 1983). The items were coded so that higher scores reflect greater stress, and the reliability of the items approaches acceptable levels (Cronbach's alpha = 0.63, mean inter-item correlation = 0.25). *Self-rated health*, a scale from the RAND Health Survey, asked study participants to report whether their health was poor, fair, good, or excellent, and is an established measure of health used by epidemiologists. *BMI*, or body mass index, is based on official records of height and weight. *Exposure to violence* is a summative index of four dummy items related to witnessing violence, such as fights, or having someone close to them commit suicide. *Self-esteem* is a five-item construct derived from the Rosenberg (1965) self-esteem scale. The Likert-scaled items were coded so that higher scores reflect greater self-esteem and the construct, which was based on the average of the items, maintained strong psychometric properties (Cronbach's alpha = 0.80, mean inter-item correlation = 0.44). Finally, we asked our study participants about their *projected age of death*, which we capped at 150 years.

## Social Connections

We include five measures in the domain of social connections, which broadly taps the qualitative features of, and resources found within, the social networks in which our sample is situated. *Gang embeddedness* taps individual immersion within enduring deviant networks (Pyrooz, Sweeten, and Piquero 2013), and was generated using a mixed graded response model with seven items about ties to the gang – position, importance, violence, signs and symbols, contact, friends, and influence – that was standardized (mean = 0, standard deviation = 1). *Social distance* consists of five Likert-scaled items that measure isolation from others (Wooldredge 1998), which were averaged and exhibited acceptable internal consistency (Cronbach's alpha = 0.71, mean inter-item correlation = 0.33). *Family social support* and *friend social support* each consist of three Likert-scaled items that tap non-instrumental forms of support, such as family or friends they can rely on. Both constructs had Cronbach's alpha and mean inter-item correlations that exceeded 0.75. Seven items were averaged to generate a construct of *criminal peers*, which contains information about whether study participants' current friends have, for example, been arrested, incarcerated, or sold drugs.

### Attitudes and Beliefs

Attitudes and beliefs are measured by seven constructs. All of the constructs were generated by taking the average of the items; each of them maintains sound psychometric properties that meet standards of acceptable measurement (Cronbach's alphas > 0.70; mean inter-item correlations > 0.30). *Code of the street* consists of six items that measure adherence to hyper-masculine norms of interpersonal behavior, including aggression, dispute resolution, and earning and maintaining respect (Stewart, Schreck, and Simons 2006). Two constructs are included that measure Tom Tyler's notion of legal orientations (Kirk and Papachristos 2011; Reisig and Mesko 2009; Tyler and Jackson 2014), including (1) an eleven-item construct of *legitimacy* that measures inmates' belief in the legitimacy of correctional officers' authority, and (2) a seven-item construct of *procedural justice* that measures inmates' perceptions of fairness in how they were treated by correctional officers. *Ethnic identification* consists of two constructs, *cultural* and *social*, based on eight items that measure pride and understanding of the study participant's ethnic background and willingness to participate in social relationships and situations with other racial and ethnic groups (Phinney 1992).

### Criminal Justice System Involvement

Based on official records from the Texas Department of Criminal Justice and the Texas Department of Public Safety, we include several measures of criminal history and incarceration among members of our sample in Texas. We rely on Texas data since that is where the members of our sample were sentenced (and released). *Age at first arrest* is the age in years at the time of the first recorded arrest. *Number of arrests* is a count of the total number of arrests. *Prison stints* refers to the number of times an individual was in state jails or prisons. *Years incarcerated* is the number of years spent incarcerated for the current prison stint. *Violent offender* refers to the most serious conviction for the incarcerating offense, as determined by the prison system.

### Analytic Plan

We organize these results into three sections. First, we examine the descriptive characteristics of gang and non-gang members by comparative domains, using both official and self-reports of gang membership. This section reveals whether the characteristics that describe gang members differ from the characteristics that describe non-gang members. Second, we examine odds ratios and differences in the predicted probabilities of gang membership derived from a series of bivariate logistic regression analyses. Unlike the descriptive statistics section described above, here we concentrate on how unit changes in the measures found in the comparative domains correspond to differences in the likelihood of gang membership.

This is a subtle distinction in language, but a sharp distinction in analysis. Indeed, our first section of the analysis presents the characteristics of gang and non-gang members where the denominators are the respective groups (i.e., gang membership is the independent variable), while our second section reveals how these characteristics correspond with changes in the likelihood of gang membership where the denominators are derived from scores on the protective and risk factors (i.e., gang membership is the dependent variable).

Finally, and based on the bivariate results, we examine the cumulative risk posed by gang membership. In the community, researchers have found that no single protective or risk factor best explains gang membership, and instead is best represented as an accumulation of these factors (Esbensen et al. 2010; Thornberry et al. 2003). We created risk factor dummy scores using mean cut-points for each of the variables that were related statistically to gang membership. We then divided our sample into ten groups based on the total number of risk factors. In turn, we examined the proportion of people within each group who were gang members, differentiating cumulative risk by official and survey measures of gang membership.

All of these analyses are weighted to correct for the oversampling of gang members, which makes the results generalizable to the population of male offenders exiting the most populous release unit in the Texas prison system during the study period. In order to make our sample representative, the weighting lowers the proportion of inmates officially designated as gang members and increases the proportion of officially designated non-gang members. The weighting ensures that the fraction of gang and non-gang members is equivalent to the larger population of inmates from which our sample was generated.

## DESCRIPTIVE CHARACTERISTICS OF GANG AND NON-GANG MEMBERS

Table 4.1 answers two basic questions: (1) What are the characteristics of gang and non-gang members in prison? and (2) Does the picture of gang and non-gang members painted by one data source reproduce itself in the other data source? We elaborate in further detail on the first question in the next section, but even a cursory glance at Table 4.1 reveals that the answer to the second question is "yes." We regard the measurement issues (self-report vs. official records) to be as important as the substantive outcomes. Some of the discrepancies are highlighted, but we reserve further discussion for our concluding section. It is important to note that the denominator for these comparisons is within the columns. That is, we are reporting descriptive characteristics among four groups: *officially designated* gang ($n = 368$) and non-gang ($n = 434$) members, along with *self-reported* gang ($n = 346$) and non-gang ($n = 454$) members.

TABLE 4.1 *Descriptive characteristics of gang and non-gang members, by official and self-reports of gang membership*

| Measures | Official gang membership | | | | Survey gang membership | | | |
|---|---|---|---|---|---|---|---|---|
| | Non-gang (N = 434) | | Gang (N = 368) | | Non-gang (N = 454) | | Gang (N = 346) | |
| | Mean/ % | (SD) | Mean/ % | (SD) | Mean/ % | (SD) | Mean/ % | (SD) |
| **Demographic** | | | | | | | | |
| Age in years | 40.57 | (9.59) | 37.27 | (19.75) * | 41.64 | (10.40) | 34.55 | (13.67) * |
| Latino | 28.8% | | 45.7% | * | 27.8% | | 41.3% | * |
| Black | 27.4% | | 25.5% | | 28.7% | | 21.3% | |
| White | 34.8% | | 17.7% | * | 35.7% | | 22.4% | * |
| Married | 13.9% | | 15.5% | | 13.9% | | 14.8% | |
| In a relationship | 16.2% | | 17.2% | | 15.6% | | 19.0% | |
| Single | 70.0% | | 67.3% | | 70.6% | | 66.2% | |
| Father | 68.0% | | 72.6% | | 67.6% | | 72.1% | |
| Military veteran | 10.6% | | 3.0% | * | 10.9% | | 5.5% | |
| Education | 11.66 | (1.49) | 10.90 | (3.52) * | 11.74 | (1.65) | 10.95 | (2.27) * |
| IQ | 93.28 | (9.96) | 91.05 | (25.03) * | 93.33 | (10.88) | 91.96 | (17.71) |
| Low self-control | 1.37 | (0.59) | 1.46 | (1.61) | 1.33 | (0.63) | 1.56 | (1.11) * |
| **Environmental** | | | | | | | | |
| Informal social control | 2.85 | (0.74) | 2.66 | (2.10) * | 2.90 | (0.79) | 2.55 | (1.45) * |
| Prison social control | 1.77 | (0.71) | 1.80 | (1.90) | 1.79 | (0.78) | 1.71 | (1.26) |
| Good place to live | 73.3% | | 64.7% | * | 74.8% | | 63.2% | * |
| Gangs in neighborhood | 49.0% | | 65.3% | * | 44.8% | | 73.4% | * |
| Disorder in the prison | 7.50 | (1.72) | 8.35 | (3.98) * | 7.32 | (1.87) | 8.66 | (2.57) * |
| Unstructured routines | 2.26 | (3.11) | 2.36 | (6.99) | 2.24 | (3.40) | 2.36 | (5.17) |
| **Health** | | | | | | | | |
| Stress | 0.83 | (0.44) | 0.91 | (1.23) * | 0.80 | (0.49) | 0.96 | (0.84) * |
| Self-rated health | 2.03 | (0.65) | 2.22 | (1.65) * | 2.01 | (0.70) | 2.23 | (1.16) * |
| BMI | 27.67 | (4.11) | 27.80 | (10.68) | 27.69 | (4.40) | 27.66 | (8.01) |
| Exposure to violence | 1.69 | (0.81) | 2.12 | (2.17) * | 1.60 | (0.87) | 2.26 | (1.39) * |
| Self-esteem | 2.12 | (0.41) | 2.14 | (1.15) | 2.13 | (0.44) | 2.09 | (0.80) |
| Projected age of death | 86.44 | (14.99) | 86.80 | (44.27) | 86.21 | (15.85) | 87.52 | (32.03) |
| **Social connections** | | | | | | | | |
| Embeddedness in gangs | -0.26 | (0.66) | 0.31 | (2.25) * | -0.44 | (0.54) | 0.73 | (1.59) * |
| Social distance | 1.05 | (0.39) | 1.01 | (1.05) | 1.03 | (0.42) | 1.09 | (0.72) |
| Family social support | 2.38 | (0.60) | 2.46 | (1.44) | 2.36 | (0.65) | 2.50 | (1.02) * |
| Friend social support | 1.87 | (0.72) | 1.75 | (2.06) | 1.86 | (0.79) | 1.87 | (1.34) |
| Criminal peers | 0.69 | (0.56) | 0.90 | (1.66) * | 0.65 | (0.59) | 0.97 | (1.17) * |

*(continued)*

TABLE 4.1 (*continued*)

| | Official gang membership | | | | Survey gang membership | | | |
| | Non-gang (N = 434) | | Gang (N = 368) | | Non-gang (N = 454) | | Gang (N = 346) | |
| Measures | Mean/ % | (SD) | Mean/ % | (SD) | Mean/ % | (SD) | Mean/ % | (SD) |
|---|---|---|---|---|---|---|---|---|
| **Attitudes and beliefs** | | | | | | | | |
| Code of the street | 1.96 | (0.65) | 2.24 | (1.85) * | 1.88 | (0.70) | 2.42 | (1.14) * |
| Convict code | 2.52 | (0.45) | 2.72 | (1.24) * | 2.47 | (0.48) | 2.80 | (0.78) * |
| Legitimacy | 1.57 | (0.40) | 1.36 | (1.12) * | 1.59 | (0.43) | 1.37 | (0.74) * |
| Procedural justice | 1.13 | (0.45) | 0.98 | (1.18) * | 1.14 | (0.50) | 0.99 | (0.77) * |
| Ethnic ID – cultural | 3.09 | (0.45) | 3.15 | (1.21) * | 3.07 | (0.49) | 3.20 | (0.86) |
| Ethnic ID – social | 3.14 | (0.51) | 3.15 | (1.45) | 3.18 | (0.53) | 3.01 | (1.13) * |
| Spirituality/religiosity | 3.05 | (0.71) | 2.99 | (1.84) | 3.07 | (0.78) | 2.93 | (1.27) |
| **Criminal justice system** | | | | | | | | |
| Age at first arrest | 20.81 | (6.29) | 17.29 | (8.22) * | 21.05 | (6.87) | 18.09 | (8.73) * |
| Number of arrests | 8.44 | (4.59) | 9.97 | (12.85) * | 8.47 | (5.04) | 9.08 | (8.53) |
| Prison stints | 1.80 | (0.95) | 2.21 | (2.57) * | 1.87 | (1.08) | 1.73 | (1.43) |
| Years incarcerated | 4.28 | (4.12) | 5.65 | (12.41) * | 4.33 | (4.63) | 4.78 | (7.31) |
| Violent offender | 39.4% | | 39.7% | | 38.4% | | 43.7% | |

*Notes:* All values are weighted to correct for sampling.

\* $p < 0.05$ (gang and non-gang members differ statistically).

There are sharp demographic differences between gang and non-gang inmates in prison. Gang members are younger than non-gang members by several years, particularly when examining self-report data. The race and ethnicity of gang members also differ from non-gang members. By a large margin, gang members are more likely to be Latino and less likely to be white than non-gang members. Most of the remaining gang members reported that they are mixed race, and a select few were Asian or Native American. But in Texas prisons, the modal gang member is Latino, while the entire custodial population is pretty evenly split across black, white, and Latino inmates. The family characteristics of gang and non-gang members are statistically indistinguishable from one another. Both groups of inmates are just as likely to be married and in a relationship; they are also just as likely to be fathers. Indeed, around 70 percent of the people in our sample were parents, illustrating one of the collateral consequences of incarceration. There were socioeconomic differences between gang and non-gang members as well. Notably, the mean educational level for both groups was less than a high school degree, reflecting one of the key challenges to reintegrating prisoners into the economy upon reentry, but about three-fourths of a year lower for gang members. Gang members were less likely to have served in the military than non-gang members. There was mixed evidence between the data sources in levels of IQ and self-control. The official measure suggested that gang members maintained lower IQ scores while the survey measure did not. With regard to the latter, consistent with self-control theory, the survey measure suggested that gang members maintained lower levels of self-control than non-gang members, while the official measure did not.

The neighborhoods where gang members lived before arriving at prison differed from non-gang members, regardless of data source. Non-gang members reported that their neighborhoods had higher levels of informal social control and were a better place to live, while also having less gang activity, than the gang members. In contrast, when we turn to the prison environment, reports of informal social control and unstructured routine activities do not differ between gang and non-gang members. This is perhaps expected, as the ability of prisons as total institutions to structure inmate environments is far greater than any street setting and affects gang and non-gang members more or less equally. Of course, it should also be noted that gang members observed more disorder in prison. Whether this difference is a consequence of gang members contributing to and participating in this disorder or having a strong tendency to identify signs of disorder is not entirely clear. Nonetheless, observing disorder is one of the few prison environmental features that distinguishes these groups statistically. As a total institution, it appears that prison is effective in creating a consistent environment across groups, at least for the measures we examined.

In general, gang members rate themselves as being healthier than non-gang members. On its face, one of the puzzling findings from correctional research is that prisoners may be healthier while incarcerated than when not (Baćak and Wildeman 2015). This makes sense when one considers that the state is mandated to provide some level of health care while these individuals are in its custody, whereas on the street no such mandate exists. While gang members assign themselves higher scores on overall health, they also report greater stress and exposure to violence than non-gang members. Stress and violence are intimately linked to one another in the research literature (Sharkey et al. 2012). The relationship between gang membership and involvement in violence likely has health consequences in prison that we do not understand fully. Despite this, gang members project to live to an average of eighty-six years of age, which is not different statistically from that reported by non-gang members. Such age projections hardly reflect the fatalism often assumed to apply to inmate self-perceptions and gang members. Reports of self-esteem are also equivalent across the gang and non-gang groups. The relationship between prison gang membership and health is curious, raising questions about the mechanisms that lead to such reports and requiring further study (Fahmy 2018).

Gang researchers point to gang-related group processes when they seek to explain why gang members have higher rates of crime, misconduct, and victimization than non-gang members (Decker, Melde, and Pyrooz 2013; Klein and Maxson 2006). While we do not measure group process directly, we do have information about the social networks of inmates that promote collective action. There are large differences in gang embeddedness between gang and non-gang inmates, not a surprising finding at first glance. However, embeddedness in gangs is not limited only to gang members, a finding many would not expect to see. Our data revealed that there were many non-gang members who were embedded in gangs, as evidenced by a standard deviation of 0.66. In fact, some non-gang members were more deeply embedded in gangs than gang members – connected for family or social reasons, but not formally affiliated – although this was clearly an exception rather than the norm. The social support networks were very similar for gang and non-gang members; both groups believed that they had family and friends they could count on. But the friendship networks of gang members consisted of people who have engaged in more types of criminal activity than non-gang members. This is something that we expected to find, as gang members tell us that many, if not most, of their friends are other gang members. The social connections of gang members, we suspect, are the principal explanation for increased risk of recidivism, as gang members may lack the connections to individuals engaged in positive activities who may be in a position to assist them when returning to the community. Although we do not investigate that proposition in this book, it is something we will be examining.

When turning to the attitudes and beliefs of members of our sample, several striking differences emerged that are consistent with a long line of research on gang members in street settings, a parallelism between street and prison gangs. There is solid criminological evidence that many of the attitudes and beliefs we examine predict criminal activity. These are also the attitudes and beliefs that are impacted adversely when someone gets involved in gangs. We observe consistent findings across data sources that gang members, when compared to non-gang members, maintain a greater adherence to the code of the street and the convict code, view the authority of correctional officers with less legitimacy, and view the actions of correctional officers as procedurally unfair. Much of this will not come as a surprise to those familiar with criminological and gang research. Indeed, the codes that govern the extra-legal resolution of interpersonal disputes are heightened in gang circles and decades of specialized police and correctional practices that target the behaviors and statuses of gang members have led to distrustful views of the criminal justice system (Matsuda et al. 2013; Papachristos, Meares, and Fagan 2012). Such rejection of authority is based on years of negative experiences with institutions – police, schools, the job market – that are told and re-told within the gang. However, we were surprised to find that gang members did not adopt more racially and ethnically homogenous cultural and social views. Differences between the groups did exist, but only for the survey measure of gang membership. This stands in contrast to popular beliefs about prison gangs whose identity and membership are built upon strict enforcement of racial/ ethnic identity. One would suspect that out of all inmates, those who affiliated with race-based groups would shun relationships and activities with races/ ethnicities other than their own and culturally be most in tune with their in-group. We simply do not find that, although actions certainly speak louder than words, and we are measuring subjective perceptions rather than objective behaviors.

Our final comparisons are made in the domain of criminal justice system involvement. The results reveal greater involvement in the criminal justice system for gang members. Gang members were arrested at younger ages, arrested and imprisoned with greater frequency, and spent more years incarcerated than non-gang members. Indeed, the links between gang members and the criminal justice system are stronger than they are for non-gang members. This is the case even though non-gang members were several years older than gang members, which would give them more time and opportunities for interaction with the system. Our data suggest otherwise. There is something unique about gang membership that leads to deeper involvement in the criminal justice system. Recall that this also was the strongest and most consistent finding across the previous studies of gang membership on the street as well as those few which exist for prison.

Overall, official and survey measures of gang membership reveal a rather similar story. If we simply focus on statistical significance and examine the differences between gang and non-gang members we get the same story for thirty-four out of the forty-one (83 percent) comparisons that we make. Most of the differences in the relationships were found in terms of risk propensities and criminal justice system involvement. Official gang members were simply more deeply immersed in the system – more arrests, more prison stints, and more years incarcerated. There were also fluctuations between the data sources in the magnitude of the differences. Nonetheless, we remain impressed that different gang membership measurement procedures can produce such similar results. We now move away from descriptive comparisons between gang and non-gang members to focus on the protective and risk factors that predict gang membership.

## PREDICTORS OF GANG MEMBERSHIP IN PRISON

If what we describe above viewed gang membership as an independent variable, what we describe next views gang membership as a dependent variable. Even though at first glance the results in Table 4.1 do not appear to differ greatly from the results reported in Table 4.2, there is a critical distinction between them: the denominators that yield the findings are different. Gang and non-gang members, respectively, constitute the denominator in Table 4.1, which addresses questions such as: What percent of gang members (or non-gang members) are Latino or lived in gang-active neighborhoods before prison? Alternatively, the denominator in Table 4.2 is the entire sample of inmates in our study, and addresses questions such as: How do rates of gang membership differ between Latino and non-Latino inmates or those who lived or did not live in gang-active neighborhoods before prison? In the former case, we examine differences in the profiles of gang and non-gang members, while in the latter we examine how rates of gang membership change when our sample scores lower or higher on the variables we study.

Our goal in this approach is to determine what increases or decreases "risk" for gang membership in prison among all inmates. When we rely on official data, the base rate of gang membership is 10 percent, since our sample was derived from the population of inmates stratified by gang and non-gang official designations (i.e., gang members were 10 percent of the sampling frame). When we rely on survey data, the base rate of gang membership is higher – 20 percent. This is due to inmates who were not classified as gang members by the prison system and, in turn, our weighting corrects for them.

We provide readers with two ways to interpret the measures associated with gang membership. First, we report odds ratios, which tell us the odds of gang membership for a given response category (e.g., Latino gang members divided by Latino non-gang members) compared to the odds of gang membership for another given response category (e.g., non-Latino gang members divided by non-Latino non-gang members). Odds ratios that are equivalent to 1, or have 95 percent confidence intervals above and below 1, indicate that there is no association between the variable of interest and gang membership. Alternatively, variables with odds ratios that exceed or fall below 1 (along with the upper and lower 95 percent confidence intervals), indicate a positive or negative relationship between the variable of interest and gang membership.

Second, we report the marginal effect for the variable of interest, which is expressed in percentage point differences. This is the difference in proportions of members in each of the groups who are in a gang. That is, the proportion of those in a gang who score 1 compared to the proportion of those in gang who score 0. Again, using Latinos as the example, the marginal effect would be the percentage point difference in the proportion of Latinos who are gang members and the proportion of non-Latinos who are gang members. Whereas an odds ratio could, in theory, equal a minimum of zero or an infinite maximum, the marginal effect could vary from a minimum of zero to a maximum difference of 100 percentage points.

There is one final point to note: we standardized all measures that are not dummy variables (measures with more than two response categories) because it allows us to provide an even playing field to compare the effect sizes. All index and interval measures thus have a mean of 0 and standard deviation of 1. The marginal effect for dummy variables and non-dummy variables indicates the difference in the predicted probability of gang membership associated with shifting from a score of 0 to 1. With this in mind, we report the results from a series of bivariate logistic regression models predicting gang membership using both official and survey measures.

## Bivariate Results

Age is negatively associated with prison gang membership. Older inmates are less likely to report membership in gangs than younger inmates. For example, inmates who are aged fifty-two years (a one standard deviation increase) are anywhere from 25 percent (official measure) to 47 percent (survey measure) less likely to report gang membership than inmates who are aged forty years (the mean age of the sample). Latino inmates were about twice as likely to be in gangs as non-Latinos, while white inmates were less than half as likely as non-white inmates to be in gangs. Higher levels of educational attainment were also negatively related to gang membership; an increase of about two years of education lowered the risk of gang membership by 33 percent. There were three discrepancies between the official and survey measures of gang membership: (1) official measures indicated a negative relationship (74 percent lower likelihood) between military status and gang membership, while survey measures indicate no relationship; (2) IQ was negatively related to official measures of gang membership (17 percent lower likelihood), but unrelated to self-report measures of gang membership; and (3) low self-control was positively related (35 percent higher likelihood) to survey measures of gang membership, but no such relationship was observed for official measures. It is important to note for each discrepancy that the relationship was not in the opposite direction, rather, simply no relationship existed for one of the categories.

Alternatively, environmental factors were consistent across the official and survey measures of gang membership. Perceptions of higher levels of pre-prison neighborhood informal social control lower the risk of prison gang membership by 17 percent (official) and 29 percent (survey). Likewise, respondents who thought that their neighborhood was a good place to live were less likely to be involved in gangs in prison, while respondents who reported gang activity in their neighborhood were more likely to be involved in gangs in prison. Thus, the social context of communities of origin has an impact on affiliations and behavior in prison. Perceptions of prison disorder were also positively associated with prison gang membership. Disorder, wherever it exists, has negative consequences for individuals, a finding consistent with prior research on the street and in prison. This appears consistent with a parallelism argument between the two settings.

Several characteristics in the health domain also increased the risk for prison gang membership, and each of these relationships was consistent across official

TABLE 4.2 *Bivariate logistic regression models predicting official and self-reports of gang membership*

| Measures | Official gang membership | | | Survey gang membership | | |
|---|---|---|---|---|---|---|
| | Odds ratio | Marginal effect | | Odds ratio | Marginal effect | |
| **Demographic/individual** | | | | | | |
| Age in years[a] | 0.750 | –0.027 | * | 0.523 | –0.100 | * |
| Latino[b] | 2.076 | 0.068 | * | 1.826 | 0.097 | * |
| Black[b] | 0.908 | –0.009 | | 0.669 | –0.065 | |
| White[b] | 0.402 | –0.085 | * | 0.519 | –0.105 | * |
| Married[b] | 1.143 | 0.013 | | 1.076 | 0.012 | |
| In a relationship[b] | 1.075 | 0.067 | | 1.274 | 0.040 | |
| Single[b] | 0.883 | –0.012 | | 0.817 | –0.033 | |
| Father[b] | 1.245 | 0.021 | | 1.240 | 0.035 | |
| Military veteran[b] | 0.260 | –0.126 | * | 0.480 | –0.119 | |
| Educational attainment[b] | 0.667 | –0.037 | * | 0.650 | –0.068 | * |
| IQ[a] | 0.834 | –0.017 | * | 0.897 | –0.018 | |
| Low self-control[a] | 1.133 | 0.012 | | 1.345 | 0.048 | * |
| **Environmental** | | | | | | |
| Street informal social control[a] | 0.833 | –0.017 | * | 0.705 | –0.056 | * |
| Prison informal social control[a] | 1.034 | 0.003 | | 0.911 | –0.015 | |
| Good place to live[b] | 0.668 | –0.038 | * | 0.579 | –0.088 | * |
| Gangs in the neighborhood[b] | 1.962 | 0.063 | * | 3.403 | 0.189 | * |
| Disorder in the prison[a] | 1.586 | 0.043 | * | 2.304 | 0.127 | * |
| Unstructured routines[a] | 1.025 | 0.002 | | 1.031 | 0.005 | |
| **Health** | | | | | | |
| Stress[a] | 1.145 | 0.013 | | 1.290 | 0.041 | * |
| Self-rated health[a] | 1.277 | 0.023 | * | 1.324 | 0.045 | * |
| BMI[a] | 1.025 | 0.002 | | 0.994 | 0.001 | |
| Exposure to violence[a] | 1.545 | 0.040 | * | 2.031 | 0.108 | * |
| Self-esteem[a] | 1.041 | 0.004 | | 0.928 | –0.012 | |
| Projected age of death[a] | 1.018 | 0.002 | | 1.068 | 0.011 | |
| **Social connections** | | | | | | |
| Embeddedness in gangs[a] | 1.737 | 0.050 | * | 3.942 | 0.158 | * |
| Social distance[a] | 0.930 | –0.007 | | 1.123 | 0.019 | |
| Family social support[a] | 1.126 | 0.011 | | 1.222 | 0.033 | |
| Friend social support[a] | 0.882 | –0.012 | | 1.015 | 0.002 | |
| Criminal peers[a] | 1.301 | 0.025 | * | 1.508 | 0.065 | * |

(*continued*)

TABLE 4.2 (*continued*)

| | Official gang membership | | Survey gang membership | | |
|---|---|---|---|---|---|
| Measures | Odds ratio | Marginal effect | | Odds ratio | Marginal effect | |
| **Attitudes and beliefs** | | | | | | |
| Code of the street[a] | 1.401 | 0.031 | * | 1.978 | 0.103 | * |
| Convict code[a] | 1.426 | 0.033 | * | 1.869 | 0.096 | * |
| Legitimacy[a] | 0.664 | −0.038 | * | 0.643 | −0.070 | * |
| Procedural justice[a] | 0.622 | −0.044 | * | 0.622 | −0.077 | * |
| Ethnic ID – cultural[a] | 1.125 | 0.011 | | 1.269 | 0.039 | * |
| Ethnic ID – social[a] | 1.022 | 0.002 | | 0.788 | −0.038 | * |
| Spirituality/religiosity[a] | 0.938 | −0.006 | | 0.860 | −0.024 | |
| **Criminal justice system** | | | | | | |
| Age at first arrest[a] | 0.396 | −0.085 | * | 0.553 | −0.094 | * |
| Number of arrests[a] | 1.264 | 0.022 | * | 1.105 | 0.016 | |
| Prison stints[a] | 1.320 | 0.026 | * | 0.886 | −0.020 | |
| Years incarcerated[a] | 1.237 | 0.020 | * | 1.083 | 0.013 | |
| Violent offender[b] | 1.011 | 0.001 | | 1.244 | 0.036 | |

*Notes:* All values are weighted to correct for sampling.
* $p < 0.05$ (variable predicts gang membership statistically). [a]standardized variable; [b]binary variable.

and survey measures. Inmates with higher levels of stress and greater exposure to violence were more likely to be gang members in prison than those with lower stress levels or less exposure to violence. Yet, this did not appear to detract from gang members' self-rating of their health. Inmates with higher self-rated health were 28–32 percent more likely to be in gangs in prison than inmates with lower self-rated health. Why this might be the case is not entirely clear, although this could be related to an invincibility often associated with gang members' self-perceptions (Decker and Van Winkle 1996).

Two measures in the social connections domain were also related to a greater likelihood of gang membership: embeddedness and criminal peers. While both measures were consistently related to prison gang membership (regardless of whether they were measured by official or survey indicators of gang membership) it is notable just how much larger the association was using self-reports of prison gang membership. Indeed, a standard deviation increase in embeddedness corresponded with 3.9 times the likelihood of self-reports of prison gang membership, compared to "only" 74 percent of official reports of prison gang membership. Clearly, embeddedness was a much better predictor of survey than official gang membership, as evidenced by the marginal effects.

A number of attitudes and beliefs were related to prison gang membership. Higher levels of adherence to street code and convict code values were related positively to both measures of gang membership, while a stronger belief in the legitimacy of correctional officers or perceptions of correctional officers as procedurally fair was related negatively. There are notable differences when comparing the marginal effects between the official and survey measures of gang membership. The marginal effects in the latter were at least twice as large as the former. While highly related, there remain differences between official and self-reported measures of gang membership.

The final domain measures criminal justice system involvement. Here, the only consistent discriminating factor was age at first arrest. A one standard deviation increase (around eight years) in the age of first arrest lowered the likelihood of prison gang membership by anywhere from 45 percent (survey measure) to 60 percent (official measure). This is consistent with our finding for age. The number of prison stints and the number of years incarcerated were both positively related to prison gang membership using the official measure, but unrelated when using the survey measure.

## Cumulative Risk

Figure 4.1 reports the univariate distribution of risk factors across the men in our sample. The lower and upper tails of the distribution contain a small proportion of people, which is what we would expect given how we constructed the risk scores. Nonetheless, it is notable to observe that no one was recorded as having zero risk factors and, by the same token, no one was recorded as having all of the risk factors.[1] We then used a software program to create ten groups based on the distribution of risk factors based on sensible boundaries. Whereas true deciles would separate people with the same number of risk factors, this program aimed to group people with similar numbers of risk factors instead of similar numbers of people.

Figure 4.2 compares how rates of gang membership are related to the number of risk factors. There are two observations that immediately jump out from this figure. First, there is a rather linear and positive relationship between the number of risk factors in a group and the proportion of the group with a history of prison gang membership. This applies regardless of the data source used to measure gang membership. Second, the relationship between the rank order of the group and the proportion of the group in a gang is different based on which measure of gang membership was used. In general, these group classifications resulted in about twice the proportion of gang membership using survey measures of gang membership rather than official measures. Among the

---

[1] This would be nearly impossible, particularly with the dummy variables, since the former would be applicable only to white military veterans and the latter would be applicable only to Latino non-military veterans, much less having been recorded for all of the remaining risks.

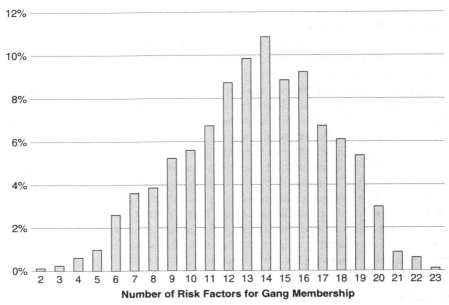

FIGURE 4.1 Proportional distribution of cumulative risk factors for gang membership

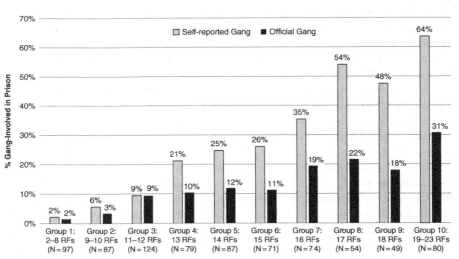

FIGURE 4.2 Cumulative risk of gang membership in prison by survey and official measures of gang membership

Notes: Unequal N size quantiles (groups) were determined in Stata 14.0 based on category counts of risk factors (RFs). Percentages are rounded.

eighty respondents with nineteen or more risk factors, nearly two-thirds self-reported gang membership, yet only about one-third were officially classified as gang members. Of course, the weighting of our sample contributes to these discrepancies (the unweighted values are nearly identical, but lack the ability to generalize to the population of prisoner releases). The correlation between the rank order of groups and the proportion in a gang is 0.46 for survey measures and 0.37 for official measures. While those values do not appear as discrepant, the conclusion we reach in Figure 4.2 is that the protective and risk factors we examined in this study do a better job predicting survey measures of gang membership than official measures. This is perhaps expected given that our survey represents an up-to-date snapshot of the men in the LoneStar Project, whereas an official measure of gang membership could be based on dated gang histories (hence the larger differences in criminal justice system involvement among officially classified gang members).

## CONCLUSION

Our goal in this chapter was to describe the gang and non-gang members in prison. We aimed to determine if factors from a wide range of domains could distinguish gang from non-gang members. Our answer is a ringing "yes." This is important for two reasons. First, the scientific underpinnings of our understanding of the impact of gang membership – in and out of prison – are enhanced by such knowledge. This includes having confidence in the measurement properties of the self-reported gang membership. Second, such a knowledge base adds to our ability to respond more effectively to the needs of prison gang members both in the institution as well as upon their release. Our work here builds on the "multiple social deficiencies" perspective identified by Krienert and Fleisher (2001) to describe gang members. Our analysis of cumulative risk shows that gang members have more troublesome risk factors and fewer protective factors than non-gang members. Gang members have deficiencies in areas important for successful reentry – attitudes, criminal history, education, employment, and social connections – that are likely to impede a successful transition back to society, both in terms of program readiness inside of prison and reentry readiness outside of prison.

Our results revealed that the protective and risk factors we analyzed discriminated between these groups rather effectively. In fact, our analysis indicated that we predicted gang membership in prison – using both measures – about as well as prior research has predicted street gang membership. This is evidence of parallelism between street and prison gang members on these measures. However, we can conclude that prison gang members differ in significant ways from imprisoned non-gang members, extending the literature on this topic based on a rich survey with a large sample of gang members. Factors from all of the six domains contributed to predicting gang membership, but four of these domains stood out: demographics (i.e., ethnicity, Latino), environment (e.g., pre-prison neighborhood), social connections (i.e., gang embeddedness), and criminal justice system involvement (i.e., age at first arrest, prison stints).

We also sought to determine whether the same story emerged if we relied on measures of gang membership generated from different measurement procedures. The results are less clear in that regard. Indeed, the similarity observed in the bivariate results largely eroded when we shifted to cumulative risk. The fact that official measures of gang membership were explained best by records from the criminal justice system suggests that prison authorities might be relying on available information – albeit distal or outdated – to ascertain prison gang membership. Survey data capture information that is largely hidden or unobserved by prison authorities. This is likely why we do a better job explaining survey measures of gang membership than official measures of gang membership.

Against this backdrop, it is important to point out that no single factor or domain was chiefly responsible for predicting gang membership. Multiple factors across multiple domains were at work in differentiating gang and non-gang members. This is consistent with a long line of research on street gangs, which identifies cumulative risk as the principal source of gang membership (Esbensen et al. 2010; Thornberry et al. 2003). This again reflects the multiple social deficiencies possessed by prison gang members, highlighting the challenges of dealing with them and their challenges in relating with social institutions.

We conclude by noting that if we were pressed to choose a source of data to best measure gang membership, we would advocate for survey-based approaches. Our logic in this is that inmates know more about themselves – especially their identities and historical associations – than prison authorities. Official measures of gang membership are generally slower to adapt to the evolving gang landscape, especially in the absence of conflict or violence that often uncovers such affiliations. Surveys can capture these subtle changes. Yet, we recognize that surveys are not always practical, for reasons we have highlighted in previous chapters. It should be understood that even when there is considerable overlap in official designations and self-reports of gang membership, it does not guarantee that the correlates of gang membership will be identical using either measure. Given the current state of knowledge regarding prison gang members, researchers who gain the opportunity to use official measures but are denied the chance to do surveys can still provide useful information from official sources. We believe that triangulating multiple data sources continues to be the best way forward, and where possible, combining official and survey data sources should produce the most useful, valid, and reliable outcomes.

Having described the characteristics of gang and non-gang members, emphasizing the features that differentiate these groups of inmates, we shift the focus to gangs as groups. We believe that group processes are what generate many of the aforementioned protective and risk factors. As a consequence, it is necessary to understand the group characteristics and processes of gangs in prison. What do these groups look like? How are they organized and structured? What types of activities are they involved in? And, perhaps most importantly, what role do they play in the social organization of prisons? We now turn our attention to these questions.

# 5

# The Characteristics of Gangs in Prison

In 1927, Frederic Thrasher observed that "No two gangs are just alike" (1927, 45). Of course, the point of Thrasher's emphasis was heuristic; it directed attention to the diversity within gangs identified in his fieldwork in Chicago. This chapter is motivated by Thrasher's early observations and uses data from the LoneStar Project to examine this claim quantitatively with application to prisons. If gangs are not all alike, in what ways are they different? If they are indeed different, what explains the differences and similarities across gangs? And, most importantly, what role does prison play in explaining variation in the group-level characteristics of prison gangs? While these questions guide our interests in this chapter, our overarching goal is to describe the characteristics of gangs in prison.

In the previous chapter, we examined individual-level differences between gang and non-gang members in prison. The focus on individual-level characteristics is an important part of understanding prison gangs and gang members. But it is their group nature that makes prison gangs so important – and difficult – to understand. Thus, a discussion of the links between prison gangs and street gangs is the first focus of this chapter. This important issue has implications for understanding the activities, culture, and organization of both prison and street gangs. If street and prison gangs are one and the same, or cut from the same cloth, it would mean that we could translate knowledge from one setting to the other. Despite its significance, there has been little systematic research on this topic. Yet, the general public seems to have a consistent view of prison gangs, driven by media and law enforcement reports (and academic reports, to be sure). This is what our colleague Jacob Young calls eminence-based knowledge.

The description of prison gangs is not unlike how organized crime groups have been described (Paoli 2014; von Lampe 2016). Indeed, some of the most influential works on prison gangs describe them as vertically structured social organizations, carrying out highly coordinated and instrumental violence, monopolizing protection and contraband markets, and extending their influence from the prison to the street (Camp and Camp 1985; Fong 1990; Irwin 1980; Jacobs 1974; Lessing 2016; Skarbek 2014). This stands in sharp contrast to the ways in which street gangs are described: horizontally structured, spontaneous and symbolic violence, and a proscribed influence on the illegal market (Curry, Decker, and Pyrooz 2014; Howell and Griffiths 2015; Klein and Maxson 2006). If a student devoted a year reading the gang literature – one semester to street gangs, the second to prison gangs – they would walk away with the conclusion that the two groups are physically separate and qualitatively different from each other in important ways. What are lacking from the aforementioned accounts are systematic data gathered from gang members who are situated within gangs that operate on the street and in prison. This is the first aim of this chapter.

Our second aim is to examine the characteristics of gangs as groups. We focus on five major characteristics of gangs, including their structural, instrumental, expressive, profit-generation, and communication features. A key goal of this book is to put the "gang" back into gang research, which is why gangs, and not gang members, constitute our unit of aggregation. Accordingly, our methodological approach diverges from earlier chapters as we introduce a new framework to the study of group-level characteristics of gangs, that is, multilevel modeling. Given that this framework is critical to the remainder of the book, we spend more time introducing it to readers. Moving toward the empirical study of gangs as groups is an important advancement for theory, research, and responses to gangs. Such an approach puts the group front and center in the analysis rather than individual gang members. The benefit of studying gangs as groups is that it will open new doors for testing theories and assessing group-level responses to gangs for programs and policies.

## SEPARATE AND UNEQUAL OR TOGETHER AND SIMILAR?

One of the primary interests of this book is the relationship between gangs in prison and gangs on the street. In this context, we are concerned with the extent to which prison gangs and gang members are independent from or are linked to street gangs and gang members. This focuses attention on three key processes: (1) the *movement* of people and structure between prison and the street, (2) the *transmission* of culture from one setting to the other, and (3) the *explicit links* between activities on the street to the prison and from prison to the street. The processes by which relationships between street gangs and prison gangs are established and maintained are not well understood. However, the concepts of importation and exportation (outlined in Chapter 2) offer a conceptual framework to begin the development of such an understanding. The *importation model* argues that many aspects of the street are imported into prison by individuals who bring prior relationships, affiliations, culture, and experiences to an institutional setting. From this perspective, gangs in prison have direct ties to street gangs because offenders are admitted to prison with their gang affiliations, rivalries, and structures. But "importation" is not simply the movement of street gangs to the prison. Clearly there must be an adaptation process as the prison environment exerts an impact on the membership, structure, processes, and activities of street gangs. Some of this may be due to the gangs themselves, although some of this may also be a consequence of prison policies and practices (e.g., dispersion, concentration, or isolation housing).

Prisons may also *export* their influence to the street through the cycling of individuals in and out of prison (Hummer and Ahlin 2018). When inmates leave prison and return home, they bring to the street assets and deficits they have accumulated in prison. These may include relationships as well as organizational assets such as discipline, structure, and a sharpened focus on instrumental ends over symbolic ones. Cunha (2014) posits that over time there has been a convergence between prison and community, particularly among gangs, largely as a consequence of mass incarceration. This argument parallels Wacquant's (2001, 2009) observation of the fungibility between street and prison, where the boundaries between prison and society have become more permeable with mass incarceration, allowing individuals, norms, and structures to be transmitted between and reproduced within each setting. If newly sentenced prisoners bring their street affiliations with them to prison, prison gangs should reflect elements of the street. Similarly, if the beliefs and structures acquired in prison are exported to the street, street gangs should reflect elements of prison life. This is consistent with the importation/exportation model.

Figure 5.1 provides a graphical representation of the potential relationships between street and prison gangs that range from completely overlapping to completely independent. We developed this comparative model in our work with Gary LaFree and Patrick James comparing gangs and domestic political extremists (Pyrooz, LaFree, Decker, and James 2018). The model is flexible enough to apply to a range of criminal groups, and we extend it here to compare prison and street gangs. We treat prison as a variable in this model. Physical separation, informal social organization, and formal social control processes of imprisonment are afforded more or less weight in the explanation of similarities and explicit linkages between gangs on the street and gangs in prison.

Model A, what is termed *interchangeability*, is consistent with what we have described above. It views prison and street gangs to be one and the same. This model depicts the greatest overlap between street and prison gangs, which is why it is placed in the lower left quadrant of Figure 5.1: the differences are minimal and the role of prison for inducing similarities is also minimal. In this case, there are strong importation and exportation processes at work, as members cycle between the street and the prison bringing relationships, norms, rivalries, and structure from one domain to the other. This reflects the large-scale churning of individuals from the street to the prison and back again in the era of mass incarceration. Support for this approach comes from Hunt et al. (1993, 407) who observed, "it may be more useful and accurate to see the culture and organization of prison and street life as inextricably intertwined,

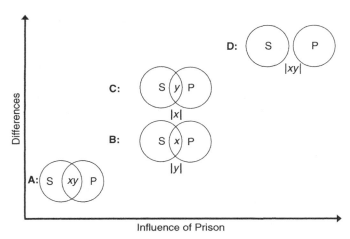

FIGURE 5.1 Models of the relationship between prison and street gangs
Notes: Abbreviations: S = street gang, P = prison gang, SP = prison and street gang, $x$ = comparative predictor variable (cause), $y$ = comparative outcome variable (consequence), | | = dissimilar.

with lines of influence flowing in both directions." Such an argument is consistent with Buentello, Fong, and Vogel's (1991) "prison gang" class of their typology as well as Moore et al.'s (1978) observations in Los Angeles. The walls that keep the general public out of prison do not contain the influence of gangs within the prison.

Based on our organizing theoretical model presented in Chapter 2, prison is treated as a variable and is expected to explain the differences between street and prison gangs. Because prisons operate as total institutions, they structure the daily routines, social relationships, ties to the free world, and access to programming. As a consequence, we expect prisons to moderate the form and function of the gangs that operate within the institution. Therefore, moving up the y-axis in Figure 5.1 reflects greater differences between street and prison gangs, while moving across (left to right) the x-axis reveals a stronger influence of prison. Each of the remaining models holds that there should be differences between street and prison gangs and the prison should contribute to distinguishing between the groups.

Models B and C distinguish between prison and street gangs based on their causes (origins) and their characteristics (form and function). Model B is termed *fundamental cause* while Model C is termed *common core*. Both models view prison and street gangs as having distinct features, but for different reasons. The fundamental cause model views the mechanisms underlying the origins of prison and street gangs and the gang behaviors as similar, while the common core model views them as distinct. The fundamental cause model also views the characteristics of prison and street gangs to be different, while the common core model views them as overlapping. Of course, we present these models as ideal types, but the reality is certainly a blend of the two. We discuss these two models together because each views prison and street gangs as being distinct from one another and the deprivations of prison contributing to the distinction. There may be movement of gang members between the street and the prison, the transmission of culture between the settings, and environmental stimuli generating activity in both contexts, but the explicit formal linkages are largely missing.

This does not mean that there is no exchange between the street and prison, but such exchanges are limited in nature. For example, there may be communication between street gangs and prison gangs but the communication is largely social, or if instrumental it occurs infrequently and is not intended to create formal linkages between the two. It makes sense that many of the bonds of gang membership created on the street would continue to have an influence on the behavior of gang members in prison, but that the physical separation would weaken such bonds and their influence on behavior over time. This model is largely built on the exchange of information between parties of roughly equal status and power. Such communication is facilitated through a number of means including the movement of individuals from the prison to the street, from the street to the prison, through information passed on by visitors and prison employees, phone calls and letters, and occasionally through electronic means such as cell phones or internet. The primary overlap is in the exchange of information rather than control exerted by one group (prison vs. street) over another.

Model D, our final model, takes the extreme opposite position of the interchangeability model. It is termed *independence* because it affords complete power to the ability of prisons to moderate the activities, culture, and organization of gangs. This view contends that prison life – groups, values, and experiences – is largely independent of the street. Such independence is primarily a consequence of the physical separation of individuals in prison from those on the street, but also the unique influences of the institutions, staff, and inmates. Physical separation also has consequences for structure, communication, movement, and the possible influence of one sphere on another (i.e., prison to street, street to prison). The independence model supports the separate study of and responses to street and prison gangs, not unlike what is reflected in the current state of knowledge of prison gangs. Yet, street gang research suggests that there is heterogeneity in the characteristics of gangs.

## THE COMPARATIVE FEATURES OF GANGS

Five characteristics are essential for understanding heterogeneity across gangs: structural, instrumental, expressive, profit-generation, and communication features. Each of these types of characteristics relates either to the activities of the gang, culture of the gang, including its norms and values, or organization and structure of the gang.

Structure refers to the individual and organizational characteristics of gangs. The Maxson–Klein structural typology has been used to differentiate across gangs based on the number of members, subgroups, age range of members, length of existence, territoriality, and criminal versatility (Maxson and Klein 1995; Klein and Maxson 2006). Some gangs are structured more horizontally and others more vertically. Horizontally structured gangs are decentralized and include fewer positions of authority and shorter chains of command, while vertically structured gangs are centralized with hierarchies and take on greater differentiation and specialization across members. Rajeev Gundur (2018), who conducted interviews with former prisoners who returned to the community in Arizona, Illinois, and Texas, reported that prison gangs have been viewed traditionally as maintaining vertical structures. However, he held that prison gangs are becoming increasingly horizontally structured. Structure can also include compositional factors, especially based on demographics such as age and gender. For example, gangs with a larger proportion of females engage in crime at different rates than gangs with a smaller proportion of females (Peterson, Carson, and Fowler 2018).

We think of instrumental features as characteristics that allow gangs to pursue goals and common interests to produce gain or advantage. Groups should produce efficiencies that could not be accomplished through individual effort. In other words, group efforts should result in joint products. These are characteristics seen within corporations, non-governmental organizations, and governments that allow them to achieve group goals. These are also characteristics that we would expect to find in gangs: leadership, claiming ownership over turf or territory, holding meetings to discuss matters important to the gang, the existence of responsibilities and rules (e.g., constitutions), and punishment for violating rules. This should lead groups to operate efficiently and effectively. In the absence of these characteristics, these groups would either cease to exist or function with little control or purpose.

The expressive features of gangs are less about their manifest functions than about the symbolic features of the gang. It is well known that most gang violence stems not from conflicts associated with instrumental pursuits, but instead from acts that have symbolic meaning to gangs (Decker 1996). By this we mean perceptions of disrespect and weakness, such as letting rivals X-out your graffiti or insult your gang without retaliation. Based on his research on the social structure of gang violence in Chicago, Papachristos (2009) demonstrated that violent interactions between gangs had less to do with the "risk factors" found among individuals or neighborhoods than they did the relational features of gangs (i.e., retaliation). Intergang disputes were driven by social networks that placed a premium on rival goods, such as reputation, status, and dominance. Therefore, by focusing on the expressive characteristics of gangs we learn what they define as their "red line" that, when crossed, will warrant a response.

Profit-generation refers to the ability of gangs to raise and leverage funds. One of the vexing issues in gang research is disentangling the pursuit of individual self-interest from those pursuant to the interest of the collective, especially for illegal income (Decker and Van Winkle 1996; Hagedorn 1994). We concentrate on the various ways in which gangs may be able to compensate for their members' inability to achieve stable jobs and high incomes in an economy that requires the types of capital – cultural, human, and social – that are less likely to be found in the environments where gangs operate, including prisons. And we are also interested in whether the returns from illicit enterprise end up invested in the gang rather than lining the pockets of individual members (Decker, Bynum, and Weisel 1998; Venkatesh and Levitt 2000).

The final characteristic of gangs that interests us is the ways in which members of a group communicate with one another. Communication comes in many forms. The advent of computer-mediated communication has expanded the ways in which individuals and groups communicate (DiMaggio et al. 2001; Rogers 2010). It is notable that computer-mediated communication is largely values-neutral and can be used to further many gang goals. There are varying forms of communication and intensity (the frequency of communication). Both are important in understanding gangs. But questions of this type are particularly interesting in the context of prisons, for two reasons. First, the pressures placed on groups by surveillance from correctional authorities have an impact on the form of communication, producing creative ways to communicate (e.g., Reiter 2016). And, second, the diffusion of members across places, not only cities and neighborhoods, but also over 100 prison units in a state like Texas, necessitates multiple modes of communication.

## METHODS FOR UNDERSTANDING GANG-LEVEL CHARACTERISTICS

The empirical goals of this chapter are threefold. The first is to gauge the ability to study gangs as groups and not just the individuals who comprise these groups. We do this by examining the group-level features of gangs based on reports from the gang members themselves and aim to put the "gang" back into gang research. To accomplish this, we join a larger analytic tradition in the social sciences that examines the nested nature of social behaviors and relationships – that is, multilevel analysis. It goes without saying that any population of gang members is situated within gangs. However, gang research is really gang *member* research both on the street and in prisons. Individual behavior does not occur in a social vacuum and collective behavior is not activated without the efforts of individuals, a critical point made by Jim Short (1985, 1998). It is necessary to measure and analyze group-level characteristics if we are to understand them. The importance of group context leads to our next point.

Second, there is a need to examine Thrasher's (1927) earliest statement – "No two gangs are just alike" – because it remains largely untested despite a century of research on gangs. To what extent is there heterogeneity across gangs in their group-level characteristics? This question is important to advance theory, research, and responses to gangs. After all, if all gangs are alike and lack variability in their group-level characteristics, then it must also be the case that we can ignore these very characteristics in the empirical study of gang members and the translation of interventions from one gang to another must only be concerned with characteristics of the neighborhoods where these gangs are situated. The lack of empirical answers to this question points to the failure of gang research specifically, and group research more generally, to employ research designs that have a comparative component, a point driven home by Malcolm Klein (2005) in the call for more comparative research on gangs.

The final goal is an attempt to explain differences in the group-level characteristics of gangs. In the LoneStar Project we set out to assess whether street and prison gangs are different from one another. It is one thing to conduct synthetic comparative reviews of the extant literature on street and prison gangs, as we have (Pyrooz, Decker, and Fleisher 2011); it is something very different to empirically test for these differences. Is it accurate to describe street and prison gangs as a dichotomy? That is, do they differ enough (structure, activities, beliefs, relationships with other groups, involvement in crime) to be considered separate groups? While there has been a good deal of speculation about this topic, there is little actual data to address the issue. In addition, we draw heavily on the typology of prison gangs presented nearly three decades ago by Buentello et al. (1991), and elaborated upon in Chapter 2. This typology illustrates that the context of influence for prison gangs may not be contained to prisons; that is, does the prison gang extend its influence to the street? Lastly, if there is heterogeneity across gangs in their group-level characteristics, which gangs end up scoring higher on the essential features we described above – structural, instrumental, expressive, profit-generation, and communication?

Although we hoped that a comparative analysis across gangs was possible, we were not certain that our sampling strategy would produce enough members of specific gangs to permit such an assessment. We knew that the random sampling of prisoners combined with an oversample of gang members would increase the probability of being able to nest gang members in gangs. Still, we could not be certain that self-reports of gang affiliation would grant us the statistical power needed to conduct multilevel analysis. After all, it is necessary to have a large number of groups and multiple individuals nested within each group in order to compare them to each other. Fortunately, as readers will see in the following discussion, we were able to secure the participation from gang members who were nested within a large number of gangs to address the three major goals of this chapter. Before we turn to what we learned about the five group-level characteristics of gangs, it is necessary for us to first describe the measures we relied upon to compare gangs to one another.

## Measures of Group-Level Characteristics

We outlined above the conceptual foundation for focusing on five essential characteristics of groups – historical/compositional, instrumental, expressive, profit-generation, and communication – as they illustrate key dimensions of prison gangs. Several items are used to tap varying dimensions of each of these constructs. Some of these items are based on established indices of gang organizational structure, drawn from our own research conducted over the last two decades (Decker, Katz, and Webb 2008; Moule, Pyrooz, and Decker 2014). But most of these items were created for the specific purpose of expanding our knowledge of the group-level characteristics of gangs. The following thirty-three items were presented to respondents who, in turn, were asked to answer these questions with regard to the gang(s) in which they were involved.

*Historical/compositional* measures focus on the global and demographic characteristics of gangs. We focus on one historical and six compositional measures of gangs and include the following: (1) the year the gang formed, or length in years of existence; (2) the number of members in the gang in Texas; (3) the percent of the gang that is female; (4) the typical age of members in the gang; and (5–7) whether the predominant racial or ethnic group in the gang is Latino, white, black, or another racial/ethnic category.

*Instrumental* measures concentrate on the characteristics of gangs that allow them to pursue common goals and interests. We include eight items asking respondents about the instrumental characteristics of their gang: (1) leaders who make decisions about the gang; (2) claims a turf or territory; (3) defends the areas it claims from other gangs at all costs; (4) has meetings where gang business is discussed; (5) follows a chain of command for making decisions; (6) has rules that gang members are supposed to follow; (7) will punish members who violate the rules of the gang; and (8) everybody in the gang has responsibilities. These nine items exhibited high reliability (Cronbach's alpha = 0.84, mean inter-item correlation = 0.40).

*Expressive* measures tap the symbolic features of the gang. Five items are used to measure the expressive characteristics of gangs: (1) disciplines its own members if they make the gang look weak or bad; (2) reputation is everything; (3) does not hesitate to use violence versus another gang regardless of the cost; (4) punishes someone who claims to be a member but really isn't; and (5) will target police or correctional officers if they cross the line. The psychometric properties of these five items were largely acceptable based on conventional standards (Cronbach's alpha = 0.69, mean inter-item correlation = 0.30).

*Profit-generation* measures are indicators of the ability of gangs to generate and invest funds. Seven items capture types of profit-generation and group reinvestment: (1) makes money selling drugs, contraband, or other substances;

(2) makes money selling sex through prostitution; (3) makes money taxing the sales of drug dealers; (4) makes money taxing the sales of legitimate businesses; (5) makes money providing protection to people or groups; (6) makes money transporting people or goods between cities, states, or countries; and (7) invests profits back into the gangs. These items maintained strong internal reliability (Cronbach's alpha = 0.82, mean inter-item correlation = 0.39).

*Communication* measures focus on the types of ways groups communicate with one another. We focus on four forms of communication within gangs: (1) online using social media such as Facebook, Twitter, or YouTube; (2) using cell phones; (3) using typed or handwritten letters; and (4) in person. Unlike the previous construct, the communication items did not covary as strongly and fell short of conventional standards of reliability. Items 1 and 2 were moderately related (correlation = 0.47), but the remainder of the correlations fell below 0.25. We nonetheless retain the four items but urge readers to interpret our measure of communication more consistent with an index than a construct.

The response categories for the twenty-four non-structural items were identical. Individuals were asked to report "how true" this statement was of their gang. Five responses were possible: 0 percent true, 25 percent true, 50 percent true, 75 percent true, and 100 percent true. We employed this approach because our pre-testing with prisoners revealed that this was the most versatile response set, allowing us to ask multiple variants of group-level characteristics. We treated these as Likert responses rather than probabilities, which is more appropriate for these types of items with categorical responses. While we report on the nine items in the structural domain individually for descriptive purposes, we combine the items found in the instrumental, expressive, profit-generation, and communication domain by calculating the mean score for the valid items in each domain.

*Context of influence* refers to the setting – street or prison – in which gangs operate. At an earlier point in the interview, we asked our respondents to name the gangs they were affiliated with, from the most to the least recent. Of the 441 individuals who self-reported involvement in a gang over their lifetime, 429 provided us with gang names for the gang they were most recently a member of. All 47 individuals who reported involvement in a second gang provided us with a name. In sum, we obtained 476 gang names. When a gang name was identified by a respondent they were then asked a series of descriptive questions about the gang, including: "Does this gang operate on the street, in prison, or both?" As we describe below, aggregate group-level responses to this item are used along with Texas Department of Criminal Justice (TDCJ) and Department of Public Safety (DPS) records, published research, and personal knowledge to classify gangs into four groups: *street-oriented, prison-oriented, Security Threat Group (STG) – no segregation,* and *STG – segregation.* The latter two response categories are based on the twelve gangs that the TDCJ classifies as STGs, distinguished by whether or not the members of these gangs are automatically placed into administrative segregation housing (refer to Table 3.1).

While there are valid data on gang names for 429 individuals and 476 person-gangs, our analytic sample is much larger. For all items of group-level characteristics, we asked our respondents to report about the gang they were involved in on the street and in prison, respectively. This might seem odd at first glance. After all, the gang members in our study were affiliated predominantly with a single gang rather than with distinct street and prison gangs. But our a priori assumption – based on our read of the literature and our prior experiences – was that there would be a sharp distinction between street and prison gang reports. For example, reported characteristics of the Aryan Brotherhood may differ depending on the setting in which they were asked. Thus, it would be more appropriate to allow the gang members themselves to report on the instrumental, expressive, profit-generation, and communication characteristics separately by context rather than imposing equivalence. In the best-case scenario, this approach would appreciate differences in the context of influence and increase statistical power since we would have more observations. In the worst-case scenario, this approach would induce differences between street and prison gangs by asking for distinct reports of group-level characteristics. And since gang members are incarcerated, they are likely more familiar with the happenings of the gang inside rather than outside of prison. Either way, we could test for these differences empirically based on whether a respondent was reporting about the same gang or a different gang in the respective setting. The street and prison gang was the same for 169 persons (i.e., 338 person-gangs), different for 43 persons (i.e., 86 person-gangs), and a single street or prison gang was reported for the remaining 214 persons, resulting in an analytic sample of 638 person-gang contexts.

## Analytic Plan

The empirical goals of this chapter are more descriptive than explanatory. We are interested in frequencies and proportions when examining the context of influence among the 476 person-gangs in the LoneStar Project. Indeed, we report a straightforward breakdown of the frequency of self-reports of specific gangs being street only, prison only, or street/prison. We also report the proportions across these three categories, which we used to classify specific gangs into four groups. This simple exercise addresses whether or not a street gang–prison gang dichotomy best represents our understanding of these gangs in the largest study of gang members in prison to date. We employ the same descriptive approach when turning to the historical and compositional characteristics of gangs, where we aggregate information across the individuals nested within specific gangs. To the best of our knowledge, the information we report about the context of influence, historical, and compositional characteristics of gangs represents the largest sample of *gangs as groups* studied to date.

The next part of the analysis is more complicated analytically, but the goals remain largely descriptive. Here, we turn to multilevel statistical modeling, an analytical approach that has become commonplace in criminological, educational, psychological, and sociological research (for an excellent discussion of its applicability to criminology, see Johnson 2010). This approach explicitly recognizes multiple levels of analysis. In our case, individual gang members (level 1) are nested within gangs (level 2). We turn to the many benefits of multilevel modeling shortly, but one of its aims is to overcome fallacies that have plagued social scientific research – the ecological fallacy, where individual inferences are incorrectly made from higher-order or aggregate data, and the atomistic fallacy, where aggregate-level inferences are made from individual data.

The atomistic fallacy abounds in gang research. It is common to make group inferences when relying on individual data. With our colleagues, Jill Turanovic and Jun Wu (Pyrooz et al. 2016), we documented 179 studies where researchers quantified the association between gang membership and criminal offending. It is not problematic to reach group-level inferences based on *individual* attributes. It is possible to argue that the empirical evidence suggests that membership in a gang appears to have a causal effect on criminal offending. Longitudinal studies reveal that criminal activity rises and falls as young people enter and exit gangs, respectively. However, it is problematic to reach group-level inferences using individual data based on *group* attributes. This is especially problematic without knowing the groups that individuals affiliate with – after all, observations are not independent from one another, a key violation in leading regression-based modeling strategies. These points were made by Papachristos (2011) in advocating for a "networked" criminology while also harkening back to debates about tautology in gang definitions (Curry 2015; Short 1996).

One of the debates in gang research (and research on groups involved in crime in general) is how the characteristics of the gang influence the behavior of members, particularly crime and delinquency. This debate has generally concentrated on two group-level characteristics: (1) gang organization (Bouchard and Spindler 2010; Decker et al. 2008; Moule et al. 2014; Pyrooz et al. 2012), and (2) gang cohesiveness (Hughes 2013; Klein and Crawford 1967; Short and Strodtbeck 1965). There are sound reasons to expect that the organization and cohesiveness of gangs, respectively, could be related positively or negatively to individual offending. The problem, however, is that relating individual self-reports of gang organization or cohesiveness to individual behavior creates what Johnson (2010, 626) termed "false power" – an artificially inflated number of observations. These studies, in turn, have inflated statistical power because they are unaware of the relatedness among gang members in the sample, increasing the likelihood of identifying a statistically significant effect – false positives, or Type I error. Take for instance a study of 200 gang members nested within 25 gangs. Studies that ignore the nestedness of gang members appear to have a sample of 200 people. This is (mostly) unproblematic for studying individual attributes, but not for group attributes. There are 25 gangs in the study, not 200. As a consequence, the study is overpowered and may lead to incorrect inferences.

Having a randomly sampled single representative from a population of gangs would be less problematic to the extent he or she has a sound understanding of gang-level characteristics. But we know little about the reliability and validity of individual reporting and rarely capture the relatedness of the individual gang members in a sample. On the former point, it is well known that gang members have a tendency to exaggerate the violence propensity of their group, a protective mechanism that Marcus Felson (2006) called "big gang theory." On the latter point, the studies containing the largest sample of gang members, which are useful for more representative findings of individual attributes, lack information about group attributes. In commenting on the Gang Resistance Education and Training study, consisting of nearly 1,000 youth gang members (Esbensen et al. 2001), Klein and Maxson (2006, 172) noted that "its formulation did not include a deliberate gang structure investigation." This is characteristic of single-city (Denver, Pittsburgh, Rochester, Seattle) and representative (Add Health, NLSY97) longitudinal studies that have come to define gang research over the last quarter-century (Pyrooz and Mitchell 2015). If we are to learn about gangs as groups, we ought to ask group-level questions when surveying gang members.

The work of Lori Hughes (2013) constitutes a rare exception to this atomized approach to the study of gangs. She revisited the debate about conflicting findings on the relationships between gang cohesiveness and delinquency by reviving the data collected by Short and Strodtbeck (1965) on 248 boys involved in eleven gangs in Chicago. Social network methods were used to examine the connectedness of the boys in the eleven gangs, relating that measure to delinquency to find evidence in support of the classic Short and Strodtbeck finding – more cohesiveness equated to lower delinquency. Of course, Hughes's work stands apart from much of the individual-level approaches, but illustrates that analyses of group attributes must consider alternative research designs to reach group-level conclusions.

The advantages of multilevel modeling become apparent when turning to the analysis of the group-level characteristics of gangs. For our purposes, the multilevel model is an extension of ordinary least squares (OLS) regression modeling. The major difference being that variation is decomposed across submodels, one at the individual level and one at the group level.[1] The chief

---

[1] The model takes the following form:

Level 1: $Y_{ij} = \beta_{0j} + \varepsilon_{ij}$

Level 2: $\beta_{0j} = \gamma_{00} + \mu_{0j}$

where the Level 1 equation models individual reports of group-level characteristics, $Y$, for person $i$ in group $j$. The key distinction between standard OLS regression and multilevel modeling is advantage of this approach is that non-independence or group dependencies are considered. This not only addresses key violations in regression assumptions, but also provides more accurate standard errors; true rather than false power for null hypothesis significance testing. Another advantage is that multilevel modeling can account for both individual and group characteristics – compositional, contextual, and global effects – simultaneously in random intercept models, though the equation in the footnote ignores explanatory variables for the moment. In addition, it is possible to examine variation in these individual- and group-level variables across groups in random coefficient models. For example, it would be possible to determine whether the effect of gang cohesiveness or organization influenced gang member offending uniformly across gangs. If not, it would be worthwhile to understand why the effects were stronger or weaker across gangs.

Our goals in this chapter are rather modest analytically. Indeed, we aim to decompose variance between and within gangs to produce valid estimates of group-level characteristics. Therefore, we estimate a fully unconditional multilevel model consisting of 593 person-gang contexts nested within thirty-eight gangs. This differs slightly from the analytic sample (646 person-gang-contexts) mentioned above, owing to the fact that we dropped gangs composed of a single individual represented in the LoneStar Project. After all, the goal of reinserting "gang" into gang research requires us to ascertain more than one observation per gang. Our multilevel model allows us to gather optimally weighted group-level information about gangs through empirical Bayes predictions (Rabe-Hesketh and Skrondal 2008; Raudenbush and Bryk 2002). The advantage of this approach, as opposed to simply taking group means, is that it adjusts scores based on the reliability of group-level reporting, which is highly dependent on the number of observations in a group. The estimates of group-level characteristics "shrink" toward the overall mean across gangs (i.e., the prior distribution) for groups with less reliable reporting, while remaining similar to the specific group mean (i.e., likelihood distribution) for groups with more reliable reporting. Overall, this provides us with a more accurate picture of the group-level characteristics of gangs, one that simultaneously takes into account information between and within gangs.

---

that the Level 1 intercept, $\beta_{0j}$, takes on different values for different groups. In a fully unconditional model, that is, a model without any predictors, the intercept closely approximates the group-level mean for a given outcome. What is more, rather than representing individual deviations from the sample mean, as in standard OLS regression, the Level 1 error term, $\varepsilon_{ij}$, represents deviations in individual scores from group-level means. In turn, the Level 1 intercept, $\beta_{0j}$, is modeled as an outcome at Level 2, making this a "multilevel" analysis, or what is sometimes referred to as "intercepts as outcomes." Whereas the $N$ at Level 1 is the number of individuals, the $N$ at Level 2 is the number of gangs included in the study. The error term, $\mu_{0j}$, at Level 2 represents group-level differences. These are deviations in single group scores from the mean across groups. In the end, the multilevel model is not much different from the standard OLS model, with the main exception being the addition of a group-level error term.

## THE GROUP-LEVEL CHARACTERISTICS OF GANGS

### Gangs on the Street, Gangs in the Prison, or Both?

Are street and prison gangs distinct or overlapping entities? If a dichotomy of gangs existed, distinguished by the institutional context in which they operate, we would expect to find that gang members in the LoneStar Project would strongly endorse responses that their gang was "street only" or "prison only." Alternatively, if there was collapse between the street and prison, much like there is between online and offline activities (e.g., Lane 2018), we would expect to find that gang members would respond that their gang operated in both settings. As Buentello and his colleagues (1991) noted, a prison gang is not just a gang in prison; its reach extends from prison to the street.

The results presented in Table 5.1 are telling. Overall, 71 respondents indicated that their gang was "street only," 79 indicated that their gang was "prison only," and 326 indicated that their gang operated on the street and in prison. The fact that two-thirds of the respondents rejected a street–prison gang dichotomy and endorsed the presence of their gang both on the street and in prison is suggestive. Indeed, it appears that describing gangs as "street-based" and "prison-based" is inconsistent with the views of the gang members themselves. If anything, the seemingly impenetrable walls of prisons do not prevent gangs from exerting influence in one setting or another. While there are street gangs and there are prison gangs, it would be injudicious to describe these groups as a dichotomy. "Street" gangs are in prison, while "prison" gangs are on the street. Even though we sampled based on incarcerated persons, it is notable that nearly an even proportion of respondents indicated that their gang operated on the "street only" (15 percent) or "prison only" (17 percent).

This simple exercise raises an important question: What are the characteristics of gangs with influence in both street and prison settings? Table 5.1 provides a glimpse. The gangs with influence that overlapped across contexts were more likely to be classified as STGs than the gangs whose influence was confined only to the street or prison. Indeed, 94 percent of the 260 respondents who self-reported membership in an STG indicated that their gang operated in both street and prison settings. In contrast, only 39 percent of the remaining 216 respondents – who were involved in fifty-six gangs not considered STGs – identified their groups similarly. This is a large distinction, one that might suggest that the organizational structure and place-based orientations of gangs may explain why some groups operate in both settings while others operate only in a single setting. After all, the TDCJ only classifies gangs as STGs if they are active in the prison, present a threat to the institutional order of the prison system, are organized and structured, and have a propensity for violence. It may be the case that the non-STG gangs lack these characteristics. If so, our multilevel models should be able to capture differences in organization and structure.

TABLE 5.1 *Gang types based on self-reported gang affiliation*

| | Street only | Prison only | Street/ prison | Total | Any street | Any prison |
|---|---|---|---|---|---|---|
| | f | f | f | f | % | % |
| **STG: administratively segregated** | | | | | | |
| Aryan Brotherhood | 0 | 0 | 34 | 34 | 100% | 100% |
| Aryan Circle | 0 | 0 | 17 | 17 | 100% | 100% |
| Barrio Azteca | 0 | 0 | 9 | 9 | 100% | 100% |
| Hermanos Pistoleros Latinos | 0 | 0 | 5 | 5 | 100% | 100% |
| Mexican Mafia | 0 | 0 | 25 | 25 | 100% | 100% |
| Raza Unida | 0 | 0 | 7 | 7 | 100% | 100% |
| Texas Syndicate | 0 | 2 | 16 | 18 | 89% | 100% |
| *Gang type total* | 0 | 2 | 113 | 115 | 98% | 100% |
| **STG: not administratively segregated** | | | | | | |
| Bloods (all) | 7 | 0 | 52 | 59 | 100% | 88% |
| Crips (all) | 6 | 0 | 64 | 70 | 100% | 91% |
| Partido Revolucionario Mexicanos | 0 | 1 | 3 | 4 | 75% | 100% |
| Texas Chicano Brotherhood | 0 | 0 | 8 | 8 | 100% | 100% |
| Texas Mafia | 0 | 1 | 3 | 4 | 75% | 100% |
| *Gang type total* | 13 | 2 | 130 | 145 | 99% | 91% |
| **Prison-oriented** | | | | | | |
| Mandingo Warriors | 0 | 2 | 0 | 2 | 0% | 100% |
| Mexicles | 0 | 2 | 2 | 4 | 50% | 100% |
| Peckerwood | 0 | 6 | 4 | 10 | 40% | 100% |
| Tangos | 1 | 63 | 47 | 111 | 43% | 99% |
| Single-representative gangs | 0 | 2 | 0 | 2 | 0% | 100% |
| *Gang type total* | 1 | 75 | 53 | 129 | 42% | 99% |
| **Street-oriented** | | | | | | |
| 18th street – other | 2 | 0 | 1 | 3 | 100% | 33% |
| 18th street – Vagos | 2 | 0 | 0 | 2 | 100% | 0% |
| Aryan Nation | 0 | 0 | 2 | 2 | 100% | 100% |
| Bad Boys | 2 | 0 | 0 | 2 | 100% | 0% |
| Black Disciples | 0 | 0 | 3 | 3 | 100% | 100% |
| Black Widows | 2 | 0 | 0 | 2 | 100% | 0% |
| Gangster Disciples | 2 | 0 | 9 | 11 | 100% | 83% |
| Latin Kings | 2 | 0 | 2 | 4 | 100% | 50% |
| Northsiders | 4 | 0 | 0 | 4 | 100% | 0% |
| Surenos – other | 6 | 0 | 4 | 10 | 100% | 40% |
| Surenos – eastside | 3 | 0 | 0 | 3 | 100% | 0% |
| Vice Lords | 0 | 0 | 3 | 3 | 100% | 100% |
| Single-representative gangs | 32 | 0 | 6 | 38 | 100% | 16% |
| *Gang type total* | 57 | 0 | 30 | 87 | 100% | 34% |

*Notes:* N = 439, N*G = 476.
STG = Security Threat Group; *f* = frequency.

The TDCJ further distinguishes between gangs with members who necessitate placement in administrative segregation from those who do not. The former group was even more likely to endorse street/prison overlap (98 percent) than the latter group (90 percent), which further suggests that there are distinctions among STGs. Not a single member of the seven gangs placed in administrative segregation indicated that their gang was "street only." Only two members of the Texas Syndicate indicated that their gang was "prison only" whereas the remaining sixteen members in our study indicated street/ prison overlap. When turning to the non-segregated STGs, only the Texas Chicano Brotherhood resembled the segregated STGs – all eight of their members told us that they operated on the street and in prison. Out of the 129 Blood and Crip gang members, 13 indicated that their gang was "street only." This is notable not only because the Bloods and Crips are the only black STGs in the Texas prison system, but also because these 13 responses were the only ones that indicated "street only" gangs among all 260 STG gang members. Of course, the Bloods and the Crips have an established history on the streets of Texas cities, which is why these responses are not at all surprising.

We will revisit the street/prison overlap in Chapters 8 and 9, when we examine patterns of joining and leaving gangs in prisons. It is likely the context of influence conditioned the type of gang our respondents joined – membership in street-only gangs was imported into prison, while membership in prison-only gangs originated in prison. We now turn to whether we can discern group-level differences in the characteristics of the gangs represented in the LoneStar Project. We start by turning to the historical and composition characteristics of gangs.

## Historical and Compositional Gang Characteristics

There are two key pieces of information related to the historical and compositional characteristics of gangs found in Table 5.2. First, we report the descriptive statistics for the thirty-eight gangs with more than one member represented in the LoneStar Project. The unit of aggregation is the group, which entails reporting information about group norms (i.e., means) and dissensus (i.e., standard deviation). Second, we compare scores across groups of gangs according to our four-part typology of gangs. Here, we report group-level descriptive statistics across gangs that fall within each part of the typology. Whereas the sample size for the rows reporting on the single gangs is the number of members, the sample size for the rows reporting on the four-part typology is the number of gangs.

Gang emergence, or the year the gang formed, is an important variable. It tells us when a group transitions from being considered – internally or externally – a playgroup to a gang. It is notable that the first digit across all thirty-eight gangs is "1"; every single gang we have documented in the LoneStar Project had their origins in the twentieth century. In fact, we find that at the time of data collection, all of the gangs had been in existence for over twenty-five years. This should not come across as a surprise to observers of Texas prison gang activity, as the 1980s were a tumultuous period for formal and informal governance of the prison system. The oldest gangs were street-oriented. But much of this had to do with gangs with Chicago origins – Latin Kings, 1940; Ambrose Folk Nation, 1955; Vice Lords, 1957 – driving down the averages. The youngest gangs were prison-oriented, and an outgrowth of the latter half of the 1980s. We highlight the Tangos because they were the most recent gang to form, a testament to their delayed origins relative to the "war years" between 1983 and 1985. Most of the non-street-oriented gangs emerged in the years before or after this period. The fact that these gangs remain in existence speaks to the durability of these groups, as well as the inadequacy of approaches aimed at ending the influence of gangs in prison.

When turning to the size of gangs, we should note from the outset that we do not put a lot of stock in these numbers. Unlike corporations or universities, knowledge of the number of employees or size of the student body is not well understood in extra-legal groups like gangs. Since there is "power in numbers," gangs may aim to project more power than they truly have by inflating membership estimates, thus these are gross estimates. After all, the sum of the group size for the thirty-eight gangs is approximately 380,000 individuals. The most recent estimates (from 2012) from the National Gang Center suggest that there are approximately 850,000 gang members in the United States. The national estimates, of course, are from law enforcement, and it is understood that a large proportion of gang members go undetected by police. Still, estimates of this sort shake our confidence about reaching valid conclusions about the size of gangs. That said, these might represent the most accurate estimates of group size in the literature on gangs, since we are reporting the average based on reports from multiple members nested within the same gang. Indeed, the wisdom of crowds has been shown to have its advantages for things such as fairgoers' estimates of the weight of an ox to predicting the stock market and voting trends (Surowiecki 2005), and could be telling for the size of gangs.

Walter Miller (1975, 23) proposed a general estimate that 10 percent or less of the gang members were female in the cities he studied using law enforcement reports. Of course, survey research with juveniles suggests that proportion is much higher – at least 30 percent (Esbensen and Carson 2012; Pyrooz and Sweeten 2015). The gang members in the LoneStar Project told us, on average, that females composed 13 percent of the members of their gangs, ranging from none to 40 percent. The STG-segregated gangs indicated that females were a small minority of their gangs – just 6 percent, and no more than 16 percent in the Aryan Circle. In contrast, the remaining three classes of the typology told us that, on average, females composed more than 10 percent of their gang – 18 percent of the members of STG-non-segregated, 11 percent of the members of prison-oriented, and 15 percent of the members of street-oriented gangs. On the one hand, if the group size estimates could be trusted, it would suggest that there are a large number of female gang members associated with these gangs. On the other hand, this suggests that in the eyes of male gang members, females maintain only a minority presence on the rosters of gangs.

When reviewing the column associated with age, it is notable that the average "common age" was in the teens for only three of the thirty-eight gangs – Texas Chicano Brotherhood, Bad Boys, and Northsiders. The members of most gangs were older, typically in their mid-twenties. Several gangs, such as the Aryan Brotherhood, Barrio Azteca, Texas Mafia, Mandingo Warriors, Aryan Nation, and Black Widows, told us that their typical member was age thirty or older. These findings should come with the caveat that our measure of age was not ideal, as we provided only seven response categories collapsed by pre-teen, teen, twenties, thirties, forties, and fifties periods, which we then associated with the midpoint age of eleven, sixteen, twenty-five, thirty-five, and forty-five years (no one responded below eleven or above fifty). Nonetheless, this provides useful information to get a sense of the typical age of members in these thirty-eight gangs. Perhaps the most telling finding is that there is an entire population of gang members that goes unobserved in most of the research on gangs that concentrates only on juveniles, a point first made by our colleague David Curry (2000) and reiterated by the first author (2014). As we will show in Chapter 8, many people join gangs for the first time in their life not as teenagers, but as adults in prison.

Our last compositional observation is with regard to race/ethnicity. We computed the racial/ethnic composition of the thirty-eight gangs based on their respective members represented in the study. This score was highly correlated with what the individual members told us about the "main race/ ethnicity" in their gang: Latino gangs ($r = 0.84$), white gangs ($r = 0.95$), and black gangs ($r = 0.85$). Indeed, there was not a single instance where the racial/ ethnic group that comprised the largest share of a gang was not identified as the "main race/ethnicity" of the gang. Each gang's score that does not summate across the three races or ethnicity to 1 (or 100 percent) refers to "other" and multiracial group categories. For example, 87 percent of the 125 observations for the Tangos were "Latino – single race/ethnicity" and 4 percent were "white – single race/ethnicity," whereas the remaining 9 percent were of other or mixed-race heritage.

Outside of the Bloods and Crips, there was no mixing of non-dominant single-race Latino, white, or black groups for the twelve STGs. Indeed, only a single racial/ethnic group was recognized in the other ten STGs. For example, of the forty-eight observations of the Aryan Brotherhood, 92 percent reported being white single race. The remaining four observations were either mixed American Indian and white or single-race American Indian. Over half of the twenty-seven gangs reported in Table 5.2 were composed of 90 percent or more of a single race/ethnicity. And with one exception (Gangster Disciples), a single racial/ethnic group constituted the majority of the gang. The gangs in Texas prisons are largely Latino and highly racialized. Indeed, over half of the thirty-

TABLE 5.2 *Historical and compositional characteristics gangs*

| | N | G | Year formed Mean (SD) | Group size ÷ 1000 Mean (SD) | Percent female Mean (SD) | Main age Mean (SD) | Race/ethnic composition Latino Mean | White Mean | Black Mean |
|---|---|---|---|---|---|---|---|---|---|
| *STG-segregated* | | 7 | **1979 (8.9)** | **12.574 (10.9)** | **0.06 (0.05)** | **28.5 (3.9)** | **0.57** | **0.27** | **0.00** |
| Aryan Brotherhood | 48 | | 1974 (14.7) | 12.572 (23.0) | 0.05 (0.09) | 30.4 (6.8) | 0.00 | 0.92 | 0.00 |
| Aryan Circle | 25 | | 1985 (1.5) | 3.689 (3.7) | 0.16 (0.18) | 29.6 (5.9) | 0.00 | 0.96 | 0.00 |
| Barrio Azteca | 12 | | 1984 (8.2) | 5.700 (4.30) | 0.05 (0.10) | 34.2 (9.0) | 0.92 | 0.00 | 0.00 |
| Hermanos Pistoleros Latinos | 6 | | 1981 (3.3) | 5.725 (7.9) | 0.03 (0.04) | 21.4 (4.9) | 0.33 | 0.00 | 0.00 |
| La Raza Unida | 8 | | 1983 (2.7) | 17.071 (36.7) | 0.06 (0.11) | 26.3 (3.5) | 1.00 | 0.00 | 0.00 |
| Mexican Mafia | 38 | | 1982 (4.8) | 8.342 (10.9) | 0.03 (0.07) | 29.6 (6.9) | 0.84 | 0.00 | 0.00 |
| Texas Syndicate | 25 | | 1960 (32.0) | 34.921 (45.5) | 0.03 (0.07) | 27.9 (5.5) | 0.92 | 0.00 | 0.00 |
| *STG-not segregated* | | 9 | **1975 (5.4)** | **30.346 (19.5)** | **0.18 (0.09)** | **23.1 (4.3)** | **0.27** | **0.22** | **0.36** |
| Bloods – all | 92 | | 1973 (10.7) | 52.055 (44.9) | 0.19 (0.17) | 21.7 (4.9) | 0.05 | 0.06 | 0.68 |
| Crips – all | 113 | | 1973 (9.0) | 36.872 (38.9) | 0.21 (0.18) | 22.4 (7.1) | 0.04 | 0.01 | 0.78 |
| Texas Chicano Brotherhood | 14 | | 1989 (3.4) | 6.454 (5.8) | 0.07 (0.18) | 16.3 (7.2) | 1.00 | 0.00 | 0.00 |
| Texas Mafia | 5 | | 1974 (5.9) | 3.250 (4.5) | 0.01 (0.01) | 31.7 (5.8) | 0.00 | 0.80 | 0.00 |
| *Prison-oriented* | | 8 | **1987 (2.9)** | **17.762 (10.9)** | **0.11 (0.12)** | **26.9 (5.3)** | **0.47** | **0.26** | **0.25** |
| Mandingo Warriors | 2 | | 1985 (–) | 4.000 (–) | 0.40 (0.56) | 40.0 (7.1) | 0.00 | 0.00 | 1.00 |
| Mexicles | 4 | | 1989 (19.1) | 10.000 (–) | 0.13 (0.19) | 25.0 (0) | 1.00 | 0.00 | 0.00 |
| Peckerwood | 10 | | 1989 (5.7) | 7.250 (8.7) | 0.01 (0.02) | 25.0 (0) | 0.00 | 1.00 | 0.00 |
| Tangos – all | 125 | | 1990 (8.3) | 27.923 (35.7) | 0.07 (0.12) | 25.2 (4.7) | 0.87 | 0.04 | 0.00 |

*(continued)*

TABLE 5.2 *(continued)*

| | N | G | Year formed Mean (SD) | Group size ÷ 1000 Mean (SD) | Percent female Mean (SD) | Main age Mean (SD) | Race/ethnic composition | | |
| --- | --- | --- | --- | --- | --- | --- | --- | --- | --- |
| | | | | | | | Latino Mean | White Mean | Black Mean |
| *Street-oriented* | | **14** | **1973 (14.7)** | **12.444 (18.2)** | **0.15 (0.10)** | **22.7 (4.8)** | **0.54** | **0.12** | **0.17** |
| 18th Street – all | 4 | | 1978 (21.7) | 0.226 (0.2) | 0.15 (0.14) | 20.5 (5.2) | 0.75 | 0.00 | 0.00 |
| Ambrose Folk Nation | 2 | | 1955 (21.2) | 3.500 (2.1) | 0.03 (0.04) | 20.5 (6.4) | 0.50 | 0.00 | 0.00 |
| Aryan Nation | 2 | | 1975 (26.2) | 0.300 (–) | 0 (–) | 30.0 (7.1) | 0.00 | 1.00 | 0.00 |
| Bad Boys | 2 | | 1986 (3.5) | 0.760 (1.1) | 0.13 (0.18) | 16 (–) | 0.50 | 0.00 | 0.00 |
| Black Disciples | 6 | | 1964 (5.4) | 28.300 (41.2) | 0.25 (0.17) | 21.2 (6.1) | 0.00 | 0.00 | 0.67 |
| Black Widows | 2 | | 1988 (–) | 0.150 (0.07) | 0.02 (0.01) | 30.0 (7.1) | 1.00 | 0.00 | 0.00 |
| Gangster Disciples | 17 | | 1964 (4.4) | 43.863 (46.1) | 0.25 (0.24) | 27.7 (5.8) | 0.06 | 0.18 | 0.41 |
| Latin Kings | 4 | | 1940 (–) | 8.000 (10.4) | 0.38 (0.14) | 25.3 (9.5) | 0.75 | 0.25 | 0.00 |
| Northsiders | 4 | | 1978 (11.5) | 0.182 (11.5) | 0.18 (0.19) | 14.8 (2.5) | 1.00 | 0.00 | 0.00 |
| Party of Mexican Revolution | 4 | | 1988 (5.6) | 38.333 (53.5) | 0.08 (0.15) | 25.0 (0) | 1.00 | 0.00 | 0.00 |
| Surenos – all | 15 | | 1985 (11.3) | 1.996 (3.8) | 0.12 (0.14) | 21.3 (10.4) | 0.93 | 0.07 | 0.00 |
| Vice Lords | 5 | | 1957 (32.0) | 46.667 (46.2) | 0.19 (0.19) | 25.2 (6.7) | 0.00 | 0.00 | 1.00 |
| *All gangs* | | **38** | **1978 (11.4)** | **17.828 (17.1)** | **0.13 (0.10)** | **24.7 (5.1)** | **0.50** | **0.20** | **0.17** |

*Notes:* G = the count of gangs. Bolded values are for G gangs in the part of the typology.

eight gangs in our sample were Latino, reflecting the gang member demographics. This illustrates key points we made in Chapters 3 and 4. When we study gangs on the street, neighborhood is the driver of social sorting. But when we turn to gangs in prison, it appears that race and ethnicity serve an equivalent purpose. The evidence we provide affirms the points that others have made, albeit with survey data based on demographic composition (Goodman 2008; Trulson and Marquart 2010). Put simply, gang members stick to gangs of their own race or ethnicity.

### Group-Level Characteristics of Gangs in Multilevel Context

Is it possible to research the group-level characteristics of gangs by relying on the self-reported perceptions of gang members? We answer this question with an affirmative. Although, one must be prepared for substantial variation in the reports of group-level characteristics *within* gangs. Overall, we found significant variance across gangs for all four of the outcomes: instrumental – 13 percent, expressive – 19 percent, profit-generation – 20 percent, and communication – 5 percent. On the flip side, anywhere from 80 percent to 95 percent of the variation for these respective characteristics was found *within* gangs. This is a clear sign of fluctuation in reports about group-level characteristics across the members of a given gang. Of course, such variation does not prevent us from employing this method to study gangs. After all, the classic work from Sampson, Raudenbush, and Earls (1997) found that 79 percent of the variance in perceptions of collective efficacy was within the neighborhoods they studied in Chicago. Put simply, intersubjective agreement will vary across social collectives, whether the in-group is defined by the neighborhoods where people live, the schools that students attend, or the groups with whom people affiliate.

We can attribute some of the intersubjective agreement in within-gang responses to perceptions of group-level characteristics. Some of these findings are intuitive, while others are not. Age was one explanation. For instrumental, expressive, and communication outcomes, older gang members scored their gangs higher than younger gang members. This could be due to retrospective reinterpretation of group-level characteristics, or perhaps memory recall. It also may be the case that the stronger features of gangs have relented since the "war years" in Texas, which the older gang members recall from personal experience, while the young gang members recall from hearsay. Notably, gang members with higher IQ scores (as measured by the prison system using the Wechsler Adult Intelligence Scale) viewed their gang as having lower instrumental, profit-generation, and communicative features. It is possible that they may have a more accurate understanding of group-level characteristics. We also find that the gang members whom our interviewers perceived as more honest scored higher on the instrumental, expressive, and communicative features of gangs. Not unlike IQ, it is conceivable that these gang members shared more accurate information about their gang. There were some racial differences in reporting, where black and white gang members viewed their gangs as having higher instrumental features than Latino gang members – this, undoubtedly, was related to the large proportion of Tangos in the sample. White gang members also viewed their gang as having a higher profit-generation commitment than Latino gang members. Current gang members reported that their gangs maintained lower profit-generation and communicative features than former gang members, which may have an explanation similar to age. But there were no differences in reports between current and former gang members among the instrumental and expressive group-level characteristics.

There were several other notable null findings, including whether or not a gang member was reporting about a street or prison gang. Indeed, there were no differences between street and prison gangs among gang member perceptions of the instrumental, expressive, profit-generation, and communicative features. This finding is noteworthy for reasons that extend beyond correcting for intersubjectivity in responses. Indeed, it tells us that a large sample of incarcerated gang members who have been active in gangs on the street and gangs in prison report no differences between gangs in either setting. If the above section dispensed with the notion of a dichotomy of street and prison gangs, this is further evidence that the characteristics of gangs in either setting are, on balance, no different from one another on a number of important group-level characteristics. Before such a hard conclusion could be reached, obviously, it would be necessary to draw information on a population of street gang members, much like our random sample of prison gang members. But these findings constitute the first available evidence to address this subject matter.

Some gangs maintained more consistent reporting among their members than others. For example, the STG-segregation gangs maintained more consistent reporting for instrumental group features than the street- and prison-oriented groups. STG-no segregation had more consistent reporting than prison-oriented gangs, but were no different from street-oriented gangs.

Overall, there is variation across gangs in their group-level characteristics. The likelihood-ratio tests in our multilevel variance decomposition models were statistically significant. This means that gangs are not homogenous on any of their group-level characteristics we measured. On the one hand, this is a good sign, as it suggests that there is variation across gangs that can and should be understood. On the other hand, the results indicate that this variation must be acknowledged and considered when reaching inferences about the individuals nested within gangs. We are interested in the former, and start by examining variability in the instrumental, expressive, profit-generation, and communicative features across thirty-eight gangs.

Figure 5.2 reports the empirical Bayes predictions derived from the fully unconditional multilevel models. This figure captures these predictions for all

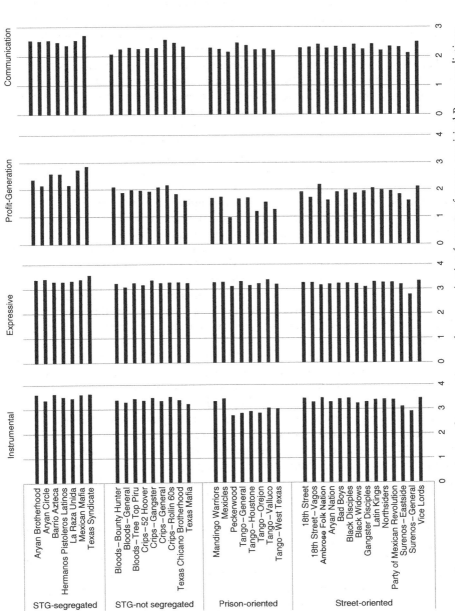

FIGURE 5.2 Instrumental, expressive, profit-generation, and communication features of gangs, empirical Bayes predictions

gangs across all outcomes. The vertical axis contains a list of names for the thirty-eight gangs that are represented in the study, organized by the four gang classifications mentioned above – STG-segregation, STG-no segregation, prison-oriented, and street-oriented. The horizontal axis ranges from 0 to 4, the lower and upper bounds for the average scores on the four outcomes, each of which is represented in the respective columns.

The mean score on the instrumental characteristics of gangs was 3.30, which suggests gangs are perceived by their members as maintaining rather high values on their organizational characteristics. There was significant variation across gangs, as noted above. The prison-oriented gangs consistently scored lower than the street-oriented (Cohen's $d$ = –0.57), STG-segregation ($d$ = –1.06), and STG-no segregation ($d$ = –0.67) gangs. It was the norm among the prison-oriented gangs (and especially the Tangos) to score below 3, whereas both types of STG gangs were consistently above 3. Yet, there was a noticeable difference between the STG-segregation and STG-non-segregation gangs – the former scored about one-half standard deviation higher than the latter ($d$ = 0.42). There was more variation among the street-oriented gangs than the STGs. The predicted values for some street-oriented gangs, like the Black Disciples and the Vice Lords, were comparable to STG gangs. Whereas the street-oriented gangs scored, on average, lower than the STG-segregated gangs ($d$ = –0.49), they were statistically indistinguishable from the STG-non-segregated gangs ($d$ = –0.17, $p$ = 0.30) and higher than the prison-oriented gangs ($d$ = 0.45). These results not only convey that there is variation in the instrumental characteristics of gangs, but that this variation is captured by our gang classification.

Turning to the expressive features of gangs, it is notable that while the mean score was comparable to that for instrumental characteristics, the dispersion across groups was tighter. That is, gangs had less consensus regarding their instrumental characteristics than they did their expressive characteristics. With one exception (Surenos – general), all of the gangs scored above a 3 on this outcome, with gangs like the Aryan Circle and Texas Syndicate scoring above 3.40. Nonetheless, there were statistically meaningful differences across the four classes of gangs. Indeed, the STG-segregation gangs exhibited higher scores than the STG-non-segregated ($d$ = 0.50), prison-oriented ($d$ = 0.33), and street-oriented ($d$ = 0.65) gangs. Beyond that, however, there were no statistically significant differences between the remainder of the gangs. It appears that the expressive feature of gangs is the strongest among STG-segregated gangs, then remains rather equal for STG-non-segregated, prison-oriented, and street-oriented gangs. Of course, it should be mentioned that symbolism among gangs cuts to the core of their collective identity. But it seems to rank even stronger in the priority of STG gangs who are subject to placement in solitary confinement; perhaps such an emphasis on expressive characteristics is necessary as a result of the TDCJ's managerial practices.

The profit-generation outcome is distinguishable from the other outcomes because the overall scores are noticeably lower across all of the gangs – there is not a single instance of a gang more highly endorsing profit-generation outcomes than another outcome. There is also another point of distinction. Whereas the expressive outcome exhibited the least amount of between-gang variation, the profit-generation outcome maintained the most variation between gangs. That variation is evident in Figure 5.2, not only between the classes of gangs, but also within the classes. Prison-oriented gangs were yet again distinguishable from the other three classes due to their low scores in this domain. On average, the prison-oriented gangs scored slightly above a 1, the equivalent of "25 percent true of my gang." The differences between prison-oriented gangs and STG-segregated ($d$ = 1.27), STG-non-segregated ($d$ = −0.58), and street-oriented ($d$ = 0.45) were moderate to large. Nonetheless, the STG-segregated gangs still stand out from the remaining gangs based on their profit-generation scores. Not only did we observe large differences relative to prison-oriented gangs, but there were also moderate to large differences in relation to STG-non-segregated ($d$ = 0.67) and street-oriented ($d$ = 0.80) gangs. And, again, the STG-non-segregated and street-oriented gangs were indistinguishable from one another statistically. We continue to find evidence of important variation across gangs, this time in terms of their profit-generation activities.

Our final group-level comparison is made with respect to communication. A story similar to the expressive outcome emerges. While there is slightly more variation across gangs in their communication characteristics than we observed in the expressive outcome, there remain consistent differences only between the STG-segregation and the comparative classes: STG-non-segregation ($d$ = 0.46), prison-oriented ($d$ = 0.40), and street-oriented ($d$ = 0.58). There was some variation within each of the three classifications that were not STG-segregation. For example, compare the Bounty Hunter Bloods to the Rollin 60s Crips, the Peckerwoods to the Tangos, and the Surenos to the Vice Lords. Yet, the gangs that fell within three broader classes were not different from one another statistically. It may be the case that the unique circumstances of an STG being placed in administrative segregation would require their members to pursue multiple and creative means to communicate with one another.

CONCLUSION

Overall, this chapter leads to several important conclusions. First, we can dispense with the notion of a street gang/prison gang dichotomy. The gang members did not endorse a dichotomy when reporting on the context of influence of their gang. Nor did we find that group-level characteristics could be meaningfully distinguished based on whether a gang member was reporting on a street gang or a prison gang. Indeed, we explicitly tested for this finding, but it did not exist in our data based on our entire sample, just focusing on the individuals who were in the same street and prison gang, or individuals who were in different street and prison gangs. We thus find the conclusion reached by Hunt et al. (1993, 407) to be compelling: "it may be more useful and accurate to see the culture and organization of prison and street life as inextricably intertwined, with lines of influence flowing in both directions." Such a conclusion also means that the independence model of street and prison gangs finds itself outside of the purview of a reasonable explanation, at least based on our data.

Second, we find that it is possible to study the group-level characteristics of gangs based on the self-reports of gang members about their gangs, even if there is substantial variation within gangs. Multilevel modeling can account for this wide variation and produce sound predicted values that are optimally weighted based on individual and group information. This is a large advantage that could result in putting "gang" back into gang research.

Third, we find substantial heterogeneity across gangs in their group-level characteristics. This variation must be modeled if we are to reach valid inferences about the individual attitudes and behaviors of gang members. After all, there are group dependencies that make the members of a gang more similar to one another than they are to the members of other gangs. It is not a stretch to envision how geography, family, prison units, and other forms of social sorting could produce these group dependencies. Social scientists ignore these dependences at our own peril. Indeed, not understanding the nestedness of members within gangs could result in the inaccurate conclusion that a program was effective when it really was not or the conclusion that a program works uniformly across gangs when it really does not.

Fourth, gangs that were placed in administrative segregation by the TDCJ were fundamentally different across all of the group-level characteristics than gangs that were not subject to this managerial practice. There are three important points that stem from such an observation. The first point is that the Texas prison system is identifying groups for placement in these circumstances based on practices that are validated independently by survey research. The second point is that this research provides a strong test of concurrent validity for measures of group-level characteristics. After all, if the Texas prison system has invested its resources in identifying the gangs it deems the most organized and structured, this suggests that the measures we have used are also being independently validated. This supports prior research that relies primarily on the instrumental measures. The final point to make is that the scheme we use to classify gangs accounts for nearly all of the variation between gangs. This means that controlling for their group-level characteristic would allow researchers to avoid the need to rely on multilevel modeling. Although multilevel modeling has numerous advantageous features, it is a high bar to meet in survey research because of the number of gangs and observations per gang required. We see this as a productive direction for gang research.

Fifth, there are fewer differences between STGs that are not placed in segregation and prison-oriented and street-oriented gangs. If anything, we find that street-oriented gangs are largely indistinguishable from STG-non-segregated gangs, alluding to our first point. Finally, prison-oriented gangs – represented largely by Tangos – are distinguished from the other gangs based on their low levels of instrumental and profit-generation characteristics. These gangs do not resemble prison gangs in the traditional sense, underscoring their distinctive features and their unique history in the Texas prison system.

These results are unique not just because of the opportunities afforded us by the nature of the data. They provide solid evidence that street and prison gangs overlap not only in activities and structure, but also in membership. These findings are not only important for understanding gangs, but may also have implications for other groups involved in crime, whose members routinely circulate from the street to prison and back again. The organizational characteristics of gangs are durable and portable. The key methodological insight from this chapter makes it possible to build a reliable description of the group from individual-level data. These conclusions provide a transition to our next chapter, which takes up the issues of governance, order, and power among street gangs.

# 6

## The Role of Gangs in the Social Order of Prisons

Imagine a prison without formal oversight or regulation. No governance or rules. No correctional officers or authorities. No cameras or monitoring. Such a prison might resemble a Hobbesian state of nature where there is a constant war of atomized individuals engaged in hedonistic pursuits of control and power. Such a state would be intolerable, or, as Hobbes described it: solitary, poor, nasty, brutish, and short. Only in the most extreme and infrequent circumstances – the riots in Attica, New Mexico, and South Carolina (Thompson 2017; Useem 1985) – are US prisons described in these terms. The specter of living in such a Hobbesian state leads people to either cede certain privileges or cooperate with each other in ways that reduce the worst of such disorder. This is another way of saying that order is ubiquitous in institutions, including prisons. In the abstract, orderly prisons are those where operations and routines are largely predictable and stable (Useem and Piehl 2008). Or, as John DiIulio (1987, 11) noted in starker terms, "no assaults, rapes, or riots." Contrary to popular belief, prisons are orderly and relatively safe institutions, especially compared to the neighborhoods from which most inmates come. Evidence from the Bureau of Justice Statistics (Noonan, Rohloff, and Ginder 2016) indicates that the risk of homicide victimization is actually lower inside of prisons than outside of them.

What contributes to social order in prisons? The obvious answer is the prison staff. The custodial officers, treatment personnel, and administrative supervisors set and enforce the rules, afford and regulate privileges, and are legally responsible for structure and routines within institutions. Prison administrators and staff seek to produce compliance through formal mechanisms. This is what Sparks, Bottoms, and Hays (1996) called the problem of order that is intrinsic to prisons, places where people are held against their will. In such conditions, inmates are "cowed into submission" by prison staff who impose their authority physically and psychologically. However, this is an incomplete explanation of social order in prisons. As David Skarbek (2014, 18) noted, "it is not that simple." In fact, the findings from decades of research in prison indicate that the rules set by the prison administration and enforced by custodial staff constitute only part of the equation for social order. After all, formal social control only goes so far whether in the free world or behind prison walls. Despite the fact that prisons are total institutions, the inmates contribute substantially to the broader social order of prisons. The history of correctional institutions (Boin and Rattray 2004; Rothman 2002) is replete with examples of the crucial role that inmates play in regulating prison conduct. These are extra-legal sources of social order and control, owing to their lack of officially recognized authority. Extra-legal control takes on an informal character in the form of prison norms and values, but also has a formal character, when inmate groups influence the social order through the imposition of rules and punishment.

In this chapter, we examine the extra-legal sources of social order in prisons. Perspectives that emphasize the role of deprivation during incarceration point to the role of the inmate code in producing order. Others (Crouch and Marquart 1989; Jacobs 1974; Lessing 2016; Skarbek 2014) point specifically to the role of gangs in producing order in prison. A key element in producing and maintaining order in prison is the provision and control of illegal commodities and services. Some claim that the significance of gangs extends beyond the inmate status hierarchy and is at the core of social order in prisons. If gangs create order in prisons – for both inmates and the institutions – we would expect that gang and non-gang members alike would recognize this fact. From this vantage point, we would expect that gangs should play a key role in a variety of activities, including the regulation of contraband markets, rule setting and norm enforcement, and the provision of governance. But there are differences among gangs as well, as we have shown in the previous chapter. Some are recognized as Security Threat Groups (STGs) and classified as such by prison authorities. In many cases, STGs are recognized as such extreme threats to social order that their members are placed in administrative segregation, while other STGs find their members intermingled in the general population. Other gangs in prison maintain ties and allegiances to their street gangs, while others are a product of imprisonment.

Rather than speculate about the role of gangs in the social order of prisons or rely on the perceptions of prison authorities or their administrative records, we draw on interviews with the inmates themselves. Explanations that rely on administrative records or secondhand accounts may not reflect the reality of social order experienced by inmates. In measurement terms, we rely on direct rather than secondhand measures of these concepts. If the sources of control and order in institutions align more in the domain of gangs than in the domains of inmate society or prison staff, it is all the more reason to focus on informal and quasi-formal inmate groups and organizations like gangs to understand prison (dis)order.

WHO RUNS THE JOINT? AND HOW?

Societies function due to their ability to regulate conduct and integrate individuals into a broad consensus about how to behave (Durkheim 1951). We believe that institutions such as prisons are much the same. The question of who "runs" prisons is important because it reveals much about the maintenance of order as well as the control of contraband in prison. The question also includes the regulation of inmate behavior. There is no doubt that the prison staff exercises great influence on the social order in prison. That is by design. The prison staff has the legal authority to create and regulate total institutions (Goffman 1968). Prisons impose severe restrictions on inmate autonomy, conventional status attainment, communication with loved ones, and sexual relationships. Prisons also dictate what inmates eat and read, where they walk, and with whom they live. From the outside looking in the answer is clear: the prison staff run the joint. But formal social control only goes so far. As with most institutions, informal social control plays a central role in regulating conduct in prison. We know this to be true in institutions such as schools, businesses, and hospitals, where group process and structure, along with norms and values, are crucial to the social order. If formal social control (officers, laws, and prison rules) cannot explain the entirety of social order in prisons, it is important to learn about the origins, forms, and components of informal or extra-legal sources.

As we discussed in Chapter 2, there are alternative interpretations of the extra-legal sources of social order in prison. Prison sociology attributes this social order to inmate society. In short, a convict code or inmate culture exists in prison and ultimately plays a part in regulating inmate behavior and social order. The major tenets of the code – don't cooperate with the guards, don't lose your head, don't exploit other inmates, don't be weak, and don't be a sucker – constitute the norms and values of inmate society (Mitchell et al. 2017; Sykes and Messinger 1960). The origins of inmate society have been debated intensely, particularly whether they are internal or external to the prison. Some view the regulating forces of inmate society as a functional adaptation to the deprivations associated with the "pains of imprisonment," while others view these forces as a reflection of the inmate values and organization imported into prison from the street. Whatever the reality, what is important is that the importation perspective recognizes that gangs are a key player in inmate society. Based on his participant observation work in Illinois's Stateville prison, Jacobs (1974) reported that street gangs reproduce themselves in function if not form inside of prison, bringing with them their street activities, hierarchies, ideologies, and intergroup relations. He noted that "No area of prison life has remained unaffected by the mass influx of gang members" (405). In other words, if inmate society is a source of social order, it is one that is dependent on gangs.

David Skarbek (2014) also placed gangs at the core of inmate society, but his governance-based argument is a departure from the deprivation–importation debate. In his view, prison gangs were neither a reproduction of the street nor an adaptation to prison. Instead, prison gangs were a response to mass incarceration, increased racial and ethnic stratification in prison, and the increased violence faced by many institutions in the 1970s and beyond. Inmate society could no longer be governed by a decentralized system based on norms and reputation, such as the convict code. This stemmed from a breakdown of trust. Prisons became increasingly racially and ethnically diverse and composed of more violent inmates. Despite this, the need for some level of self-governance remained; such governance had to define and enforce rules, capture the benefits of contraband trade, and help inmates act collectively. Prison administration and custodial staff were incapable of providing such order, according to Skarbek, owing to their shirking of responsibilities and limited resources for dispute management. He held that since norm-based governance does not "scale up," someone needed to fill the power vacuum. Gangs assumed that role often through violent means. Skarbek describes a community responsibility system in which the "community" is the group-based gang affiliation. Gangs share a responsibility for the actions of their members and cultivate a reputation that members capitalize on for a variety of purposes, including the regulation of contraband markets. Ultimately, gangs serve an important role in the regulation of prison conduct and norms. Skarbek goes so far as to contend that the social order generated by gangs contributes to the safety of prisons. There does indeed appear to be a prima facie inverse relationship between the rise of gangs (Chapter 1) and the fall of violence (Useem and Piehl 2008) in prison, although we are unaware of research that has formally tested that claim.

How do gangs contribute to the social order in prisons? After all, gang members constitute a minority of prisoners across institutions throughout the United States and are overrepresented in prison misconduct. Gangs must maintain *power* for their influence to extend beyond their own group. Because power is the way gangs translate their priorities into action, we are interested in knowing how power is exercised, especially its forms and sources. In his trenchant analysis of the exercise of power in international relations, Nye (2004, 2) begins with an operational definition of power: "one's ability to affect the behavior of others to get what one wants." In this context, he distinguishes between hard and soft power. Soft power depends on the use of what Nye calls attraction. This is the exercise of influence through appeal or persuasion to get people to follow your intentions. If soft power is the carrot, hard power is the stick. Whereas co-opting others represents the use of soft power to achieve goals, hard power employs coercion. While Nye applied these concepts to international relations, notably terrorism, they certainly have value in explanations of control in prison. After all, inmates have both forms of power at their disposal. They can use violence, threats, and intimidation (hard power) as well as seduction, ideology, norms, and rules (soft power).

We contend that if gangs exert control in prison, hard power is a distinguishing feature of their involvement in the creation and enforcement of social order. It is through the projection *and* use of hard power that gangs in prison come to control behavior and commodities in prison. Indeed, in many instances displays of symbolic power (marching, controlling a yard, hunger strikes) can have instrumental ends. Skarbek (2014) alludes mostly to the deployment of hard power in prison, while Lessing (2016) focuses mostly on the projection of hard power to the street from prison. Our view of the way gangs exercise power in prison aligns more with Nye's (2009) view of "smart power," which blends soft and hard power and is situationally based.

Cambridge University criminologist Ben Crewe (2012) identified four "elementary forms of social power" in correctional institutions. The first of these is *coercion*; the threat or use of force or deprivation. This is hard power in its raw form. It is also, according to Crewe, typically a last rather than first resort and unsustainable in prison because it is a "provocative, inefficient and illegitimate means of enforcing order" (81). Gangs deploy violence both for instrumental (e.g., sale of contraband) and symbolic (e.g., misuse of symbols or disrespect, "extreme" assaults) purposes (Butler, Slade, and Dias 2018; Skarbek 2014). While such violent displays of power are used sparingly they contribute to the reputation or brand of the gang. After all, too much violence is bad for business. But what is reported about violence in prison resembles the mythic violence and narrative stories reported in the street gang literature (Felson 2006; Klein 1971; Lauger 2012). This is part of the reason why gang members who "debrief" or snitch on the gang may be placed in protective custody – it is the *potential* for violence that can achieve compliance. Gang members would rather remain in solitary confinement – what the United Nations has labeled torture – than to turn on the gang and return to the general population. And, as we demonstrate in Chapter 8, inmates turn to gangs in prison because they see it as a refuge from a dangerous and volatile atmosphere. Even if these inmates end up on the receiving end of violence, it is likely that victimization will be more controlled and predictable than if they were unaffiliated, similar to what has been observed among street gang members (e.g., Melde, Taylor, and Esbensen 2009). Ironically, street gang members cite "protection" as a major reason for joining their gang, despite considerable objective and episodic evidence to the contrary. A similar failure to accurately calculate the risks of gang joining in prison also appears to be the case.

The second mechanism of power is *manipulation or inducement*, a less forceful means to achieve compliance than coercion, but certainly a hard rather than soft form of power. Control over the provision of rewards and punishments can result in the manipulation of inmates, and hence social order. Gangs are able to consolidate control over privileges and contraband and thus manipulate their distribution. Jacobs's (1974) classic work on Stateville described how gang leaders dictated which prison industry jobs members would receive and how gangs could undermine the authority of prison staff and the success of programs. Johnson and Densley (2018) recently reported how gang leaders in a Brazilian prison dictated everything from the mundane, such as who would sleep where, to the magnificent, such as orchestrating riots. Of course, there is the matter of contraband in prisons, including drugs and cell phones, which can generate major revenues. In prison, contraband is power. From California (Skarbek 2014) to Texas (Gundur 2018), Brazil (Johnson and Densley 2018) to Kyrgyzstan (Butler et al. 2018), it is gangs rather than individual entrepreneurs who govern these markets. The control of contraband markets affords gangs considerable power to shape the social order in prison. Everything from simple suggestions to direct demands made by gang members to non-gang inmates could get others to "fall in line" with directives; ignoring them could result in the loss of privileges or the loss of life, and everything in between.

A third mechanism of power is what Crewe termed *habit, ritual,* or *fatalistic resignation* that produces routine behavior. The monolithic structuring of routines and the deprivations of the prison environment are a source of much of this type of control. But this mode of power may take a more sinister turn when inmate groups impose structure on inmate routines. This is exemplified by the racialized gang politics in prison. While prisonization is described as the process of becoming acculturated to norms and routines in prison, such acculturation now includes the intersection of "race" and "gang." This structuring of daily life includes where inmates sit during meals, where they congregate on the yard, and with whom they share a cell. In prison, seemingly trivial matters and possessions are magnified in significance – glances or stares, seats in the cafeteria, clippers for haircuts, TV stations in the dayroom, and the sharing or taxing of goods purchased from the canteen or commissary. Gangs take strides to keep the peace between racial groups and avoid unplanned and public violence. Jacobs (1974) described the "international rules" that applied to intergang relations, including self-discipline. Inmates who are "out of line" with other gangs or racial groups typically get "checked" by their own, a process that can range from apologies to physical punishment. Skarbek (2014) contends that these efforts to avoid warfare occur because lockdowns throttle contraband markets. Of course, certain "harms" are too great to resolve peacefully, such as getting spat on, disrespected, or violating long-standing rules of control. Regardless, inmates must be socialized to the racial/gang politics in prison; these politics may directly or indirectly produce routines in inmate behavior. The whole prison can suffer the consequences if these routines are ignored.

Compliance that is gained through habit or resignation differs from compliance achieved through legitimate mechanisms, the fourth and final form of power. The forms of *normative justification* or *commitment* involve (1) personal moral agreement with directives, (2) a shared commitment to the beliefs or values of others, and (3) the assigned legitimacy to the ordained power of others. Much of the final form of social (soft) power can be conceived in terms of the social exchange that occurs among inmates, where compliance is produced as an outgrowth of the relationships that generate mutual obligations and expectations among offenders (Schaefer et al. 2017; Weerman 2003). The power exercised by gangs often assumes this status, as gangs evolve into a source of quasi-legitimate power in prisons. While we have already mentioned conflict resolution among gangs, this also appears to exist in prison, where gangs "hold court" and weigh the evidence regarding claims of "snitching" or impose punishments of executions upon adjudication (Johnson and Densley 2018). This suggests a level of deference and legitimacy afforded to gangs by other inmates. This is not unlike the efforts of gang members housed indeterminately in Pelican Bay secure housing units to encourage over 30,000 inmates in California to partake in a hunger strike (Reiter 2014). Submitting oneself to the conditions of starvation indicates a broader attachment to the power of gangs by the general prison population.

## METHODS TO UNDERSTAND GANGS AND PRISON SOCIAL ORDER

We report the views of inmates – gang and non-gang members alike – regarding the contribution of gangs to prison social order. Ironically, while there are various reports that provide the views of prison employees (wardens, officers, etc.) on this topic, there have been few attempts to understand the perspective of inmates themselves on the issue of prison control. Our analysis begins with the premise that the views of both gang and non-gang inmates are important. If there is convergence between the two groups regarding the role of gangs in prison social order, then the influence of gangs in the generation of such order should be widespread and extend to non-gang inmates. However, if there are differences in the assessments of the role of gangs in prison social order, we would likely ascribe such differences to the braggadocio and inflation of importance so common among gang members. Of course, this may not be entirely true. Instead, it is possible that the gang members occupy a vantage point that allows them to possess a more complete understanding of the contribution of gangs to prison social order. If that is the case, we should observe marked differences across gangs. This is a major reason why we provide a comparison between the four types of gangs identified in Chapter 5 (STG-segregated, STG-non-segregated, prison-oriented, and street-oriented) in their assessments of the role of gangs in the various measures of social order.

## Measuring the Contribution of Gangs to Prison Social Order

We examine three domains of social order: rules, order, and control of contraband. As the earlier discussion in this chapter demonstrates, these are core components of inmate social order and involve the exercise of both hard and soft power. To measure *rules*, we begin with three comparative questions regarding the relative power of prisoners, prison staff, and gangs. This allows us to assess the views of all inmates of the importance of each of the key groups involved in prison social control: gangs, inmates, and prison staff. We asked respondents to state their level of agreement with the following three items: (1) it is more important to follow the rules gangs set than prisoners set; (2) it is more important to follow the rules gangs set than the prison staff; and (3) it is more important to follow the rules prisoners set than the prison staff. Inmates who responded with "strongly disagree" were coded 0 and a "strongly agree" response was coded 4. A corollary to the importance of each group's rules is the fearfulness of punishment from each group. Thus, we also ask how fearful a respondent would be of punishment by each of the three groups: prisoners, gangs, and prison staff. These include the following three statements and elicit responses on a three-point Likert scale, where "not at all fearful" was coded 0 and "extremely fearful" was coded 2. We asked respondents to state their level of fearfulness of punishment for violated rules set by: (1) prisoners, (2) gangs, and (3) prison staff. Together, how respondents answer these questions should give us a reliable glimpse into the social order of prisons.

A second set of questions are measures of the role of gangs in the maintenance of *order* in prison. The measures of order capture the role of gangs in specific and general areas of prison social order, collectively tapping aspects of governance, trust, protection, and dispute resolution. Respondents were provided statements to which they indicated a level of agreement on a five-point scale ranging from "strongly disagree" (coded 0) to "strongly agree" (coded 4). These items are worded as follows: (1) prisons would be much more violent without gangs; (2) gangs help maintain order in prisons; (3) gangs are better at fixing problems than the prison staff; (4) if there are problems between gangs, the whole prison suffers the consequences; (5) prison staff need to talk to gangs before making any major changes; (6) gangs make you feel safer in prison; (7) inmates who don't affiliate with gangs will have a hard time in prison; and (8) if you have a problem, you would trust gangs to resolve it and not the prison staff. If gang and non-gang inmates believe that gangs play a major role in prison social order, we would expect higher scores across these measures.

The third set of questions concerns the selling of contraband and profits from such activity. The goal here is to ascertain the extent to which command over contraband is within the control of gangs. These four questions also use a five-point Likert scale, which range from "strongly disagree" (coded 0) to "strongly agree" (coded 4). We are interested in the extent to which the sale of various forms of contraband sales requires the approval of gangs, including: (1) drugs, (2) cell phones, and (3) other goods or forms of contraband. One additional question related to illicit markets was included and was worded as follows: "gangs get a cut of all profits from goods that are sold in prison." If gangs exert control over the illicit marketplace, we would expect that they would dictate who is able to sell forms of contraband but also tax the sale of contraband. After all, providing "governance" in prisons includes allowing inmate groups to capture the benefits of contraband trade.

## Analytic Plan

We begin with a univariate assessment of the responses to these items for the full sample. This will provide us with an overall understanding of the contribution of gangs to prison social order. Low values in this assessment would stand in stark contrast to research that shows high levels of gang control based on the views of correctional personnel, the media, or case studies or studies with small samples. In contrast, high values that indicate considerable agreement with statements about the contribution of gangs to prison social order would validate these views.

We then partition the results by gang status, comparing gang to non-gang members. As noted earlier, we regard complementarity in responses across these two groups as stronger evidence that prison gangs play a significant role in creating social order within the prison. Our final comparison is across the four gang types developed in Chapter 5 and identified above. We are interested in differences across gang and non-gang members and across the gang typology, as well as overall levels of agreement. The chapter concludes with an examination of the qualitative responses to issues regarding the role of prison gangs in the creation of social order in the prison. In the review of the qualitative responses we follow the structure of analysis here, looking first at rules, then at order, and finally at the control of contraband.

### VIEWS ON GANGS AND THE SOCIAL ORDER IN PRISON

The literature leads us to expect strong control of order, rules, and contraband by prison gangs. Lessing (2016) and Skarbek (2014) are the most outspoken proponents of this position. In an earlier essay (Pyrooz, Decker, and Fleisher 2011) we argued that compared to their counterparts on the street, prison gangs were better organized and more effective in exerting control over the behavior of their members, an atmosphere of control that extended to non-gang inmates and staff as well. However, there was little empirical evidence at the time to reinforce such conclusions and our conclusions were drawn on tenuous evidence.

### Univariate Analysis of All Prisoners

Table 6.1 presents the responses of the full sample to the three domains of questions. The first three items compare the relative importance of following rules set by the three key groups in prison: prisoners generally, gangs specifically, and the prison staff. The scale ranges from "0" (strongly disagree)

TABLE 6.1 *Descriptive statistics for prison social order variables, full sample*

| Rules | N | Mean | (SD) | Strongly disagree | Disagree | Neutral | Agree | Strongly agree |
|---|---|---|---|---|---|---|---|---|
| *It is more important to follow the rules:* | | | | | | | | |
| … gangs set than prisoners set | 800 | 1.67 | (1.26) | 16.4% | 37.6% | 17.6% | 19.4% | 9.0% |
| … gangs set than the prison staff | 802 | 1.64 | (1.20) | 16.0% | 40.0% | 16.2% | 19.5% | 8.4% |
| … prisoners set than the prison staff | 802 | 1.94 | (1.15) | 10.1% | 31.7% | 20.2% | 30.4% | 7.6% |
| | N | Mean | (SD) | | | Not at all | Somewhat | Extremely |
| *How fearful of punishment for violating:* | | | | | | | | |
| … the rules that prisoners set | 802 | 0.62 | (0.65) | | | 47.3% | 43.4% | 9.4% |
| … the rules that gangs set | 797 | 0.80 | (0.74) | | | 39.2% | 41.4% | 19.5% |
| … the rules that prison staff set | 802 | 0.60 | (0.69) | | | 51.5% | 37.0% | 11.5% |
| **Order** | N | Mean | (SD) | Strongly disagree | Disagree | Neutral | Agree | Strongly agree |
| Prisons would be more violent w/o gangs | 801 | 1.49 | (1.15) | 17.1% | 47.8% | 9.7% | 19.7% | 5.6% |
| Gangs help maintain order in prisons | 799 | 2.09 | (1.21) | 10.3% | 28.3% | 13.5% | 37.8% | 10.1% |
| Gangs fix problems better than COs | 800 | 1.98 | (1.23) | 11.9% | 30.4% | 15.4% | 32.4% | 10.0% |
| Prison suffers when gangs have problems | 800 | 2.96 | (0.95) | 1.9% | 9.4% | 7.4% | 53.5% | 27.9% |
| COs must talk to gangs to make changes | 799 | 1.96 | (1.19) | 10.6% | 32.8% | 14.9% | 33.7% | 8.0% |
| Gangs make you feel safer in prison | 799 | 1.15 | (0.89) | 21.2% | 54.4% | 14.5% | 8.5% | 1.4% |
| Non-gang inmates have hard time | 799 | 1.62 | (1.14) | 14.6% | 41.9% | 15.9% | 21.8% | 5.8% |
| I trust gangs to fix my problems, not COs | 799 | 1.59 | (1.10) | 13.6% | 43.8% | 17.3% | 20.5% | 4.8% |
| **Control** | N | Mean | (SD) | Strongly disagree | Disagree | Neutral | Agree | Strongly agree |
| *Approval of gangs is required for selling:* | | | | | | | | |
| … drugs | 766 | 1.86 | (1.14) | 8.9% | 39.3% | 15.1% | 29.9% | 6.8% |
| … cell phones | 751 | 1.75 | (1.12) | 9.2% | 44.3% | 14.4% | 26.1% | 6.0% |
| … other contraband | 766 | 1.64 | (1.12) | 10.8% | 46.7% | 14.4% | 23.5% | 4.6% |
| Gangs get a cut of contraband profits | 766 | 1.60 | (1.09) | 12.0% | 46.6% | 15.7% | 21.1% | 4.6% |

*Note:* COs = correctional officers.

to "4" (strongly agree), and a "2" indicates a neutral position of neither agreeing nor disagreeing. The mean levels of agreement for gangs compared to prisoners (1.67) and gangs compared to prison staff (1.64) show little preference for following gang rules. This suggests that the general inmate population sees little difference in the importance of rules set by gangs or staff and that – on balance – the broader inmate population mostly disagrees with both statements. In fact, the majority of respondents disagreed with both statements, and only a small minority (<10 percent) strongly agreed with either. The respondents perceived the importance of following rules set by prisoners as roughly equivalent to those set by prison staff (1.94). What is clear from these results is that inmates do not identify a single group as wielding the most influence in terms of rule setting in prison. When we ask which group is most feared if their rules are violated, a similar story emerges. The response scale ranges from "0" (not at all), to "1" (somewhat) and "2" (extremely). The mean responses regarding a fear of violating the rules that prisoners set (0.62) and prison staff set (0.60) are quite similar. This indicates low levels of fear in violating the rules set by each of those groups. The score for level of fear in violating gang rules was higher (0.80) but still between "not at all" and "somewhat," although nearly one in five respondents indicated "extreme" fear for violating gang rules. Still, these results indicate generally low levels of fear of punishment for violating the rules of either of the three groups and relatively low levels of importance assigned to the rules of gangs, inmates, or staff. These findings are not consistent with the belief that gangs exercise high levels of rule-based control over prison life. If that were the case, inmates would have more fear of violating such rules. Of course, these findings are susceptible to the possibility that inmates were feigning fearlessness in the attempt to project a more masculine image.

The second panel of eight responses provides measures of order in prison. Again, we use a five-point scale that ranges from "0" (strongly disagree) to "4" (strongly agree). Only two of the eight measures ("gangs help maintain order in prisons" and "the whole prison suffers when gangs have problems") reached a value of "2," which indicates greater agreement than disagreement in the contribution of gangs to the social order in prison. Since only two of the eight measures reached "neutral" and one of those "agree," it suggests low levels of support for the hypothesis that the social order in prison is established or maintained by gangs. The majority of respondents indicated that prisons would be safer without gangs, that gangs make them feel less safe in prison, they prefer prison staff to resolve problems rather than gangs, and that non-gang inmates do not have a harder time in prison than gang inmates. These findings stand in contrast to the prevailing understanding of gangs and the social order in prison.

We conclude the findings for the entire sample by looking at perceptions of the degree to which the approval of prison gangs is needed for selling three types of contraband (drugs, cell phones, and other) and whether gangs receive a "cut" from profits in prison. Control of contraband may be the most widely held belief about the role of gangs in prison, a belief fueled by media and academics alike (Mizzi 2015; Roth and Skarbek 2014; Thompson 2018). Recall that on our scale a score of 2.0 is a "neutral" response on a question. Each of our contraband measures include a score below 2.0; drugs (1.86), cell phones (1.75), and other contraband (1.64) were all regarded by inmates as not requiring approval from prison gangs to be sold in prison. There was more disagreement than agreement for each of these items. In addition, the premise that gangs get a "cut" of the profits from contraband sales received the lowest level of agreement of the four measures (1.6).

Taken together, these findings from the sample *writ large* suggest that the role of gangs in creating or maintaining social order is limited compared to the way it is depicted in the media and in accounts based on secondary documents and data (e.g., staff and administrative interviews, prison riots). Whether we examined rules, order, or contraband we arrived at a similar set of findings: prison gangs are not feared by inmates more than other prisoners or staff, they provide only some contribution to the prison social order, and are not seen as having a monopolistic hold on the sale of contraband in prison. What is more, this is the view of *all* inmates, nearly half of whom are gang members. We decompose the relationship between gangs and social order further in the sections that follow. At this point, one thing is clear: if prison gang members make important contributions to the social order of the prison, those contributions do not appear to be highly recognized by non-gang inmates. If prison gangs exert power over day-to-day activities in prison, knowledge of such power may be confined to gang members alone.

## Comparing Gang and Non-gang Members

It is possible that variation in inmate responses is masked by only looking at scores for the entire sample. Combining the scores of gang and non-gang members (as we did in Table 6.1) allows us to determine whether gang members are seen as fulfilling a special role in prison social order by inmates at large. But do gang and non-gang members see that role differently? To address this, we break out gang and non-gang members in Table 6.2 based on responses to self-reported involvement in gangs while incarcerated. The logic of our comparisons in Table 6.1 is replicated here, where we look at the three categories: rules, order, and contraband. To save space, responses are condensed into any form of agreement and disagreement (our conclusions do not change based on the use of a three- or five-point scale).

We begin by comparing the measures of the importance of following the rules set by gangs, inmates, and staff. The mean for the importance of gang rules compared to other prisoners is twice as high (1.08 to 0.48) for gang members than non-gang members. A similar finding emerges when the importance of gang rules is compared to the rules of the staff. While the difference between

TABLE 6.2 *Descriptive statistics for prison social order variables, by prison gang and non-gang members*

| Rules | Non-gang members (N = 454) | | | | | Gang members (N = 346) | | | | | Cohen's d |
|---|---|---|---|---|---|---|---|---|---|---|---|
| | Mean | (SD) | Disagree | Neutral | Agree | Mean | (SD) | Disagree | Neutral | Agree | |
| *It is more important to follow the rules:* | | | | | | | | | | | |
| ...gangs set than prisoners set | 0.48 | (0.75) | 67.9% | 16.4% | 15.7% | 1.08 | (0.90) | 36.1% | 19.4% | 44.5% | 1.04* |
| ...gangs set than the prison staff | 0.48 | (0.78) | 69.6% | 12.8% | 17.7% | 1.02 | (0.89) | 38.4% | 20.8% | 40.8% | 0.92* |
| ...prisoners set than the prison staff | 0.82 | (0.87) | 48.7% | 20.9% | 30.4% | 1.15 | (0.89) | 33.0% | 19.4% | 47.7% | 0.53* |
| | Mean | (SD) | Not at all | Somewhat | Extremely | Mean | (SD) | Not at all | Somewhat | Extremely | |
| *How fearful of punishment for violating:* | | | | | | | | | | | |
| ...the rules that prisoners set | 0.59 | (0.62) | 47.4% | 45.8% | 6.8% | 0.66 | (0.69) | 46.8% | 40.5% | 12.7% | 0.14 |
| ...the rules that gangs set | 0.71 | (0.73) | 45.3% | 38.4% | 16.2% | 0.92 | (0.74) | 31.0% | 45.5% | 23.5% | 0.42* |
| ...the rules that prison staff set | 0.68 | (0.70) | 45.2% | 41.4% | 13.4% | 0.49 | (0.66) | 59.5% | 31.5% | 9.0% | -0.39* |
| Order | Mean | (SD) | Disagree | Neutral | Agree | Mean | (SD) | Disagree | Neutral | Agree | |
| Prisons would be more violent w/o gangs | 0.47 | (0.79) | 71.5% | 9.9% | 18.5% | 0.78 | (0.93) | 56.4% | 9.5% | 34.1% | 0.51* |
| Gangs help maintain order in prisons | 0.83 | (0.91) | 50.8% | 15.1% | 34.2% | 1.43 | (0.84) | 22.8% | 11.6% | 65.6% | 0.96* |
| Gangs fix problems better than COs | 0.73 | (0.87) | 55.3% | 16.6% | 28.1% | 1.35 | (0.86) | 25.4% | 13.9% | 60.7% | 1.02* |
| Prison suffers when gangs have problems | 1.71 | (0.66) | 11.3% | 6.9% | 81.9% | 1.70 | (0.66) | 11.0% | 8.1% | 80.9% | -0.01 |

(continued)

| | Mean | (SD) | Disagree | Neutral | Agree | Mean | (SD) | Disagree | Neutral | Agree | |
|---|---|---|---|---|---|---|---|---|---|---|---|
| COs must talk to gangs to make changes | 0.88 | (0.91) | 47.9% | 15.7% | 36.4% | 1.10 | (0.92) | 37.9% | 13.9% | 48.3% | 0.34* |
| Gangs make you feel safer in prison | 0.24 | (0.56) | 81.9% | 11.9% | 6.2% | 0.48 | (0.74) | 67.3% | 18.0% | 14.8% | 0.50* |
| Non-gang inmates have hard time | 0.65 | (0.86) | 60.8% | 13.3% | 25.9% | 0.78 | (0.87) | 51.2% | 19.4% | 29.5% | 0.22* |
| I trust gangs to fix my problems, not COs | 0.46 | (0.74) | 69.3% | 15.7% | 15.0% | 0.97 | (0.90) | 42.2% | 19.1% | 38.7% | 0.87* |
| **Control** | Mean | (SD) | Disagree | Neutral | Agree | Mean | (SD) | Disagree | Neutral | Agree | |
| *Approval of gangs is required for selling:* | | | | | | | | | | | |
| ... drugs | 0.77 | (0.87) | 51.7% | 19.5% | 28.8% | 1.02 | (0.95) | 44.1% | 9.6% | 46.4% | 0.39* |
| ... cell phones | 0.67 | (0.84) | 57.3% | 18.5% | 24.2% | 0.93 | (0.95) | 48.8% | 9.4% | 41.8% | 0.41* |
| ... other contraband | 0.60 | (0.81) | 61.2% | 18.1% | 20.7% | 0.84 | (0.94) | 53.0% | 9.9% | 37.1% | 0.40* |
| Gangs get a cut of contraband profits | 0.58 | (0.81) | 62.5% | 16.7% | 20.8% | 0.78 | (0.90) | 53.8% | 14.5% | 31.7% | 0.32* |

*Notes:* Response categories for all of the measures range between 0 and 2. Any disagreement (strongly or not) was coded 0; neutral was coded 1. Any agreement (strongly or not) was coded 2. Independent sample $t$-test statistics were used to determine statistically significance differences between gang and non-gang members. COs = correctional officers. *$p < 0.05$ (two-tailed). Cohen's $d$ refers to standardized differences in the means between gang and non-gang members.

non-gang and gang inmates is not as large, gang members indicate that following the rules set by prisoners is more important than those set by staff. Each of these means is different at conventional levels of significance. Though the differences between gang and non-gang respondents are not as great, it remains the case that gang members are more fearful of violating the rules that gangs set, and less so of those set by prison staff. Each of these differences is statistically significant, adding confidence to the finding. Interestingly, non-gang members were more fearful of violating rules set by prison staff than were gang members. This may reflect the widely supported belief that a key feature of gang members is their oppositional stance toward authority as well as the importance of their own rules. However, it is notable that gang and non-gang members alike are mostly not fearful of violating the rules of prisoners and prison staff, although most gang members are expectedly fearful of violating gang rules while non-gang members are not. It appears as if non-gang members view themselves as not being vulnerable to the rules and punishments of the "gang game."

We next examine the eight measures of order. For seven of the eight measures, gang members agree at a higher level than do non-gang members and in each case the difference observed is statistically significant. Only for the measure "prison suffers when gangs have problems" are the mean responses from non-gang and gang groups similar. Perhaps not surprisingly, the biggest divergence in responses for gang and non-gang members was for the measure of whether gangs help maintain order in prison. Recall that this is a primary contention of the non-state governance perspective on prison gangs – that gangs play a key role in keeping order – citing evidence of declines in prison riots coinciding with the rise of prison gangs. The premise of this argument was in part that disorder in prisons was "bad for business" and that the control and sale of contraband was a primary way gangs maintained control over other inmates. What is perhaps the most notable finding is that even the majority of *gang members* hold that gangs do not make prisons less violent, that gangs do not make prisoners feel safer, and that non-gang members will not experience hardship in prison.

Contraband is the final category we use to assess whether prison gangs control the social order of the prison. Again, we find consistent differences in the extent to which non-gang and gang members in prison believe that prison gangs control contraband, all of which are statistically significant. There is a higher level of agreement with these statements regarding the role of gangs in each of the four comparisons (drugs, cell phones, other contraband, and gangs getting a cut of the profit from contraband). Gang members report that gangs control these market behaviors more than do non-gang members. That said, it is worth examining the values of the gang responses. In every case of contraband except for drug sales, the average score for gang members is below 1.0. This means that while a higher percentage of gang members report that gangs control contraband, the answers do not approach the "neutral" category and fall somewhere between disagree and neutral. This falls short of being an overwhelming endorsement of the power of prison gangs in what is regarded as the most important and lucrative activity in prison life: the control and sale of contraband. The participation of non-gang members in contraband markets is not evidence of the monolithic power of prison gangs.

Comparing the results from Tables 6.1 and 6.2 demonstrates (not surprisingly) that the inmate responses in Table 6.1 fall in between the non-gang and gang responses recorded in Table 6.2. Thus the belief expressed above that averaging the two groups was masking important group differences is confirmed. While the differences between gang and non-gang groups in Table 6.2 are small and consistently depict a greater role for gangs in rules, order, and contraband of small proportions, they are statistically significant for fifteen of the eighteen comparisons. We conclude that the perceptions of gang members differ from those of non-gang members across a wide variety of domains and measures, which is what we expected either due to exaggerated views of the importance of gangs or due to privileged views of the role that gangs play.

In sum, gangs are not recognized as highly powerful in the creation and enforcement of rules, the maintenance of order, and the sale of contraband by non-gang members. Even gang members describe the role of prison gangs in the social order of the prison as somewhat weak. The area of contraband deserves special mention owing to its significance in prison and the considerable media and scholarly attention that it receives. While gang members perceive a larger role for gangs in contraband sales than do non-gang members, it hardly rises to the iron-fisted and monopolistic control often ascribed to gangs. Street gang research has made important contributions to the understanding of the organizational structure of gangs on the street (e.g., Decker, Katz, and Webb 2008). Based largely on law enforcement and media images, street gangs were described in terms that emphasized their formal-rational character. The reality of many such gangs was that they had situational leadership, with informal and diffused structures. This research (Decker and Van Winkle 1994; Hagedorn 1994) also noted that while a large number of gang members participated in the street-level drug trade, gangs did little to organize such sales nor did the gang members who sold drugs on the street view the gang as controlling the sales or deserving of the profit from such sales. Our observations run parallel to those findings. One study is too little evidence from which to generalize, but the evidence here is consistent that even gang members see a less prominent role for gangs in the social order of the prison than is depicted in much of the extant journalistic and social science accounts.

## Comparisons across a Typology of Gangs

Recognizing the variation in prison gangs, in Chapter 5 we developed and examined a four-category typology of prison gangs. That typology included STG gangs housed in administrative segregation, STG gangs not in segregation, prison-oriented gangs, and street-oriented gangs. We now extend the logic of transitioning from the general inmate population (Table 6.1) and gang and non-gang comparisons (Table 6.2) to these four categories of gangs. Here we use the same scale values ("0" Disagree, "1" Neutral, "2" Agree) as in the previous discussion of Table 6.2, but only report agreement in Table 6.3. This allows a fuller set of comparisons across the specific measures themselves within gang type as well as across gang types. We also report the standardized differences between the gang types in Table 6.4 to give readers a sense of the magnitude of the differences.

What jumps out first in Table 6.3 is that the STG-segregation gangs score consistently lower than the other three gang types on the measures of rules. Given their confinement in solitary and isolation from other inmates, that is perhaps not surprising. After all, rules are the result of social interaction, something missing in solitary confinement. The standardized differences (Cohen's *d*) were as small as $-0.15$ (rules of gangs vs. prisoners compared to STG-no segregation) and as large as $-0.64$ (rules of prisoners vs. prison staff compared to street-oriented gang members). In contrast, the remaining three gang types shared a similar vision about following rules, although the prison-oriented gangs appeared to stand out in their endorsement of following the rules that gangs set relative to the rules of prisoners ($d > 0.30$). When turning to punishments for rule violations, the story was less consistent across the gang typology. The STG-segregated gang members were most fearful of violating gang rules, while the STG-non-segregated gang members were the least fearful. The prison-oriented gang members were most fearful of violating prisoner rules, while the street-oriented gang members were the least fearful. What is perhaps the most notable finding is that the STG-segregated gang members were the most fearful of violating the rules of prison staff – their mean score was on par with non-gang inmates. The standardized differences were large (*d* ranging from 0.32 to 0.48) compared to the other three gang types. Of course, this was expected given that these are gang members who are subject to solitary confinement, where their activities are closely tracked and rule violations could prevent inmates from leaving these conditions.

For the eight measures of order, it appears that the groups with the lowest level of organizational structure view gangs as providing the greatest amount of order in prison. Of course, there are some exceptions, but the members of prison-oriented gangs were the most likely group to endorse items such as: prisons would be more violent without gangs; gangs help maintain order in prisons; gangs fix problems better than prison staff; and trust in gangs rather than prison staff to fix problems. The remaining order of endorsing the contribution of gangs to prison order went as follows: street-oriented gangs, STG-non-segregated, and STG-segregated. This is not to say these patterns are uniform. In fact, the STG-segregated gang members were most likely to recognize that the "prison suffers when gangs have problems." Yet, it is rather remarkable that the majority of members of gangs in all four gang

TABLE 6.3 *Descriptive statistics for prison social order variables, by gang typology*

| | Gang type | | | | | | | | | | | |
|---|---|---|---|---|---|---|---|---|---|---|---|---|
| | STG-segregation (N = 115) | | | STG-no segregation (N = 145) | | | Prison-oriented (N = 129) | | | Street-oriented (N = 87) | | |
| **Rules** | Mean | (SD) | Agree | Mean | (SD) | Agree | Mean | (SD) | Agree | Mean | (SD) | Agree |
| *It is more important to follow the rules:* | | | | | | | | | | | | |
| …gangs set than prisoners set | 0.87 | (0.91) | 35.1% | 0.96 | (0.89) | 37.8% | 1.20 | (0.87) | 49.6% | 1.02 | (0.89) | 39.6% |
| …gangs set than the prison staff | 0.80 | (0.88) | 30.7% | 1.00 | (0.91) | 40.7% | 1.06 | (0.88) | 41.7% | 1.02 | (0.93) | 43.4% |
| …prisoners set than the prison staff | 0.91 | (0.93) | 38.6% | 1.11 | (0.89) | 45.2% | 1.24 | (0.87) | 52.8% | 1.30 | (0.80) | 50.9% |
| | Mean | (SD) | Fearful | Mean | (SD) | Fearful | Mean | (SD) | Fearful | Mean | (SD) | Fearful |
| *How fearful of punishment for violating:* | | | | | | | | | | | | |
| …the rules that prisoners set | 0.63 | (0.67) | 52.6% | 0.61 | (0.71) | 47.4% | 0.71 | (0.70) | 56.7% | 0.53 | (0.58) | 49.1% |
| …the rules that gangs set | 0.94 | (0.76) | 68.4% | 0.78 | (0.75) | 58.5% | 0.90 | (0.74) | 66.9% | 0.87 | (0.76) | 64.2% |
| …the rules that prison staff set | 0.68 | (0.78) | 49.1% | 0.47 | (0.61) | 41.5% | 0.44 | (0.64) | 36.2% | 0.53 | (0.61) | 47.2% |
| **Order** | Mean | (SD) | Agree | Mean | (SD) | Agree | Mean | (SD) | Agree | Mean | (SD) | Agree |
| Prisons would be more violent w/o gangs | 0.62 | (0.90) | 28.1% | 0.57 | (0.86) | 24.4% | 0.93 | (0.93) | 39.4% | 0.72 | (0.91) | 30.2% |
| Gangs help maintain order in prisons | 1.14 | (0.95) | 52.6% | 1.36 | (0.87) | 62.2% | 1.49 | (0.75) | 64.6% | 1.47 | (0.77) | 64.2% |
| Gangs fix problems better than COs | 1.11 | (0.93) | 49.1% | 1.30 | (0.88) | 57.8% | 1.43 | (0.81) | 63.0% | 1.26 | (0.86) | 52.8% |
| Prison suffers when gangs have problems | 1.82 | (0.55) | 90.4% | 1.59 | (0.76) | 75.6% | 1.72 | (0.63) | 81.1% | 1.55 | (0.80) | 73.6% |
| COs must talk to gangs to make changes | 1.07 | (0.95) | 48.3% | 1.17 | (0.91) | 51.1% | 1.10 | (0.92) | 48.0% | 0.92 | (0.94) | 39.6% |
| Gangs make you feel safer in prison | 0.39 | (0.71) | 13.2% | 0.31 | (0.57) | 5.2% | 0.58 | (0.79) | 18.9% | 0.60 | (0.82) | 21.2% |

(continued)

TABLE 6.3 (*continued*)

| Rules | Gang type | | | | | | | | | | | |
|---|---|---|---|---|---|---|---|---|---|---|---|---|
| | STG-segregation (N = 115) | | | STG-no segregation (N = 145) | | | Prison-oriented (N = 129) | | | Street-oriented (N = 87) | | |
| | Mean | (SD) | Agree | Mean | (SD) | Agree | Mean | (SD) | Agree | Mean | (SD) | Agree |
| Non-gang inmates have hard time | 0.74 | (0.86) | 27.2% | 0.79 | (0.89) | 31.1% | 0.80 | (0.85) | 28.4% | 0.98 | (0.93) | 41.5% |
| I trust gangs to fix my problems, not COs | 0.80 | (0.92) | 34.2% | 0.89 | (0.89) | 34.1% | 1.03 | (0.88) | 40.2% | 0.85 | (0.93) | 35.9% |
| Control | Mean | (SD) | Agree | Mean | (SD) | Agree | Mean | (SD) | Agree | Mean | (SD) | Agree |
| *Approval of gangs is required for selling:* | | | | | | | | | | | | |
| ... drugs | 1.16 | (0.94) | 53.1% | 0.75 | (0.91) | 32.1% | 1.02 | (0.95) | 45.7% | 0.73 | (0.87) | 27.5% |
| ... cell phones | 1.03 | (0.96) | 47.3% | 0.68 | (0.88) | 27.8% | 0.95 | (0.94) | 41.9% | 0.56 | (0.84) | 22.0% |
| ... other contraband | 0.91 | (0.96) | 41.6% | 0.60 | (0.85) | 23.9% | 0.92 | (0.93) | 39.4% | 0.48 | (0.79) | 18.0% |
| Gangs get a cut of contraband profits | 0.98 | (0.94) | 42.5% | 0.61 | (0.83) | 22.2% | 0.72 | (0.87) | 27.8% | 0.42 | (0.80) | 18.9% |

*Notes:* Response categories for all of the measures range between 0 and 2. The only response category reported in percent is agreement. Any agreement (strongly or not) was coded 2; neutral was coded 1; any disagreement (strongly or not) was coded 0. COs = correctional officers. Cohen's *d* refers to standardized differences in the means between gang and non-gang members.

TABLE 6.4 *Standardized differences in prison social order variables by gang typology, Cohen's d*

| | Gang type | | | | | | | | | | | |
|---|---|---|---|---|---|---|---|---|---|---|---|---|
| | STG-segregation (N = 115) | | | STG-no segregation (N = 145) | | | Prison-oriented (N = 129) | | | Street-oriented (N = 87) | | |
| **Focal group** | 1 | | | 0 | | | 2 | | | 3 | | |
| **Comparison group** | 0 | 2 | 3 | 1 | 2 | 3 | 0 | 1 | 3 | 0 | 1 | 2 |
| **Rules** | *d* | *d* | *d* | *d* | *d* | *d* | *d* | *d* | *d* | *d* | *d* | *d* |
| *It is more important to follow the rules:* | | | | | | | | | | | | |
| …gangs set than prisoners set | −0.15 | −0.54 | −0.24 | +0.15 | −0.39 | − | +0.39 | +0.54 | +0.30 | + | +0.24 | −0.30 |
| …gangs set than the prison staff | −0.32 | −0.42 | −0.34 | +0.32 | − | − | + | +0.42 | + | + | +0.34 | − |
| …prisoners set than the prison staff | −0.31 | −0.52 | −0.64 | +0.31 | −0.21 | −0.32 | +0.21 | +0.52 | − | +0.32 | +0.64 | + |
| *How fearful of punishment for violating:* | | | | | | | | | | | | |
| …the rules that prisoners set | + | −0.16 | +0.23 | − | −0.20 | +0.17 | +0.20 | +0.16 | +0.40 | −0.17 | −0.23 | −0.40 |
| …the rules that gangs set | +0.30 | + | +0.13 | −0.30 | −0.23 | −0.17 | +0.23 | − | + | +0.17 | −0.13 | − |
| …the rules that prison staff set | +0.42 | +0.48 | +0.32 | −0.42 | + | −0.13 | − | −0.48 | −0.20 | +0.13 | −0.32 | +0.20 |
| **Order** | | | | | | | | | | | | |
| Prisons would be more violent w/o gangs | + | −0.48 | −0.15 | − | −0.57 | −0.23 | +0.57 | +0.48 | +0.33 | +0.23 | +0.15 | −0.33 |
| Gangs help maintain order in prisons | −0.34 | −0.57 | −0.54 | +0.34 | −0.22 | −0.19 | +0.22 | +0.57 | + | +0.19 | +0.54 | − |
| Gangs fix problems better than COs | −0.28 | −0.50 | −0.24 | +0.28 | −0.22 | + | +0.22 | +0.50 | +0.27 | − | +0.24 | −0.27 |
| Prison suffers when gangs have problems | +0.50 | +0.26 | +0.57 | −0.50 | −0.26 | + | +0.26 | −0.26 | +0.33 | − | −0.57 | −0.33 |
| COs must talk to gangs to make changes | −0.15 | − | +0.22 | +0.15 | +0.10 | +0.38 | −0.10 | + | +0.27 | −0.38 | −0.22 | −0.27 |
| Gangs make you feel safer in prison | +0.18 | −0.35 | −0.37 | −0.18 | −0.56 | −0.57 | +0.56 | +0.35 | − | +0.57 | +0.37 | + |
| Non-gang inmates have hard time | − | −0.11 | −0.39 | + | − | −0.30 | + | +0.11 | −0.28 | +0.30 | +0.39 | +0.28 |
| I trust gangs to fix my problems, not COs | −0.14 | −0.37 | − | +0.14 | −0.23 | + | +0.23 | +0.37 | +0.29 | − | + | −0.29 |

*(continued)*

TABLE 6.4 (continued)

| | Gang type | | | | | | | | | | | |
| --- | --- | --- | --- | --- | --- | --- | --- | --- | --- | --- | --- | --- |
| | STG-segregation (N = 115) | | | STG-no segregation (N = 145) | | | Prison-oriented (N = 129) | | | Street-oriented (N = 87) | | |
| **Focal group** | 0 | | | 1 | | | 2 | | | 3 | | |
| **Comparison group** | 1 | 2 | 3 | 0 | 2 | 3 | 0 | 1 | 3 | 0 | 1 | 2 |
| **Rules** | d | d | d | d | d | d | d | d | d | d | d | d |
| **Control** | | | | | | | | | | | | |
| *Approval of gangs is required for selling:* | | | | | | | | | | | | |
| …drugs | +0.62 | +0.20 | +0.68 | −0.62 | −0.41 | +0.04 | −0.20 | +0.41 | +0.46 | −0.68 | −0.04 | −0.46 |
| …cell phones | +0.52 | +0.11 | +0.73 | −0.52 | −0.41 | +0.20 | −0.11 | +0.41 | +0.62 | −0.73 | −0.20 | −0.62 |
| …other contraband | +0.49 | – | +0.69 | −0.49 | −0.51 | +0.20 | + | +0.51 | +0.72 | −0.69 | −0.20 | −0.72 |
| Gangs get a cut of contraband profits | +0.59 | +0.41 | +0.92 | −0.59 | −0.18 | +0.35 | −0.41 | +0.18 | +0.52 | −0.92 | −0.35 | −0.52 |

*Notes:* All cells contain a standardized difference between the focal group and comparison group. Cells containing positive values are shaded. Cells containing negative values are white. Cells with Cohen's *d*s below |0.10| indicate only the direction (positive = "+"; negative = "–") of differences. Cells with effect sizes exceeding |0.10| contain numeric values. The font is bolded in cells with Cohen's *d*s exceeding |0.20|. COs = correctional officers.

types agree that prisons would be safer without gangs, that gangs do not make respondents feel safer, and that they do not entrust gangs to resolve their personal problems.

The traditional view that gangs provide order in prison does appear to be supported by the gang groups in the domain of the control of contraband. The responses of STG-segregation gangs stood out on the contraband measures. Indeed, they had the highest levels of agreement on eleven of the twelve comparisons to the other three gang types, and were statistically equivalent to prison-oriented gang members in the control of "other contraband." Clearly these individuals saw prison gangs as exerting higher levels of control, including getting a cut of the profits made from selling contraband, than did the other gangs. Perhaps the challenges of distributing contraband in segregated units put a premium on the involvement of prison gangs in distribution.

## QUALITATIVE RESULTS FROM OPEN-ENDED QUESTIONS

While data from the LoneStar Project are primarily quantitative, we did include several open-ended questions and recorded the responses to those questions verbatim as well as recording comments when offered by respondents, cataloging around 14,000 entries. We review the major response categories of prison social order to provide more depth to the quantitative analysis. Responses to the open-ended questions are organized into four categories: (1) rules and the social order of the prison, (2) the control of contraband, (3) how prison gangs have changed over time, and (4) the relationship between street and prison gangs. The responses to questions regarding rules and prison governance showed considerable variation, with respondents identifying a wide range of behaviors that contribute to the social order of the prison. Many of those behaviors included trivial things like keeping your cell and personal hygiene in good order. Another consistent theme was how much prisons had changed in the course of the last several decades. A number of respondents pointed to the waning power of the gang "families" in prison; that is, the STGs like the Mexican Mafia and Texas Syndicate, arguing that more horizontally organized groups such as the Tangos exerted considerable influence over prison behavior. This is consistent with the argument made by Gundur (2018) in his discussion about changes in prison social organizations that emphasizes the "flattening" of such groups in response to changing markets in prison.

## Rules and the Social Order of the Prison

The majority of what we learned about social order in prison describes somewhat benign or "soft" norms that focused on the routines of everyday life in prison and contribute to creating order in prison. But there was a "harder" side to many of the rules and much of the control in prison. Many of the rules had a formal character and specifically identified gangs as their locus of origin as well as enforcement. Territoriality is generally viewed as one of the key features of street gangs. Consistent with this, we heard about gang boundaries and territory in prison as well. Inmates quickly learned the locations to avoid in the yard and cell blocks, particularly if they were members of a different prison gang. One of the key features that defines territoriality is race. When asked about the rules for gang members to follow in prison, one respondent told us, "Jump in on your side of a race riot is the main one [rule]." This was a theme we heard echoed throughout the qualitative data; whatever your gang affiliation was, standing up for your race was important.

Many of our respondents told us that there was considerable overlap between inmate rules and gang rules, but that when you were in a gang, the rules of the gang trumped all other rules. While many respondents (gang and non-gang involved) told us "only gang members have to worry about following gang rules" a number of gang members indicated: "you can find a way to do both [inmate code and gang rules] but it is most important to follow the gang." The status of prison rules and directives from the prison staff is interesting to note. We commonly heard from inmates that the prison rules and prison staff took a secondary status compared to gang rules, particularly among gang members, because the staff were few in numbers and were not around "24/7."

However, somewhat pragmatically, a number of inmates told us that the staff (particularly correctional officers) were more important the closer one got to a parole date, owing to the ability of COs to "write them up" and possibly jeopardize their release. Other norms that structured prison conduct involved whether to intervene when a CO was engaged in physical threats from inmates. Three specific circumstances were noted where such behavior was permissible: the CO was a female, the CO had been decent toward inmates, and the CO was involved in transporting contraband into the prison for gang members. Many of the units (prisons) had cameras and the presence of the cameras fulfilled a surveillance function that made protection (from staff or other inmates) less important. A small number of inmates specifically mentioned that the Prison Rape Elimination Act (PREA) had led to more safety in prison. Ironically, increased use of administrative segregation for gang members was frequently cited as a contributing factor to prison safety, noting that removing many gang members made prison more "mellow."

What we heard about most were the mundane norms of everyday life, particularly, "Don't snitch and mind your own business." Not snitching or cooperating with the correctional officers was a very common refrain as was "keeping to yourself." These are not the rules of governance, but contribute to the routine social order of the prison, helping to create the patterns of daily life inside the walls. Another such norm was to "keep to your own race" a guideline that extended to things such as drinking, eating, or sitting with members of another race. Some inmates told us that the logic behind this was that most of the serious fights and even riots were interracial, and this was a way to reduce tensions and prevent such incidents from occurring. The third set of norms that regulate every day conduct included the exhortation to "respect yourself and others." For example, we were told by one inmate that people who were sleeping should be respected and left alone because, "you aren't in prison when you are asleep." Norms of respect were accomplished through demonstrating personal cleanliness as well as keeping your clothes washed and your cell neat. This extended to other forms of conduct, including masturbation and homosexuality, both of which were viewed as signs of a lack of self-respect among many inmates. Antipathy toward homosexuality among prisoners was also noted by Hensley (2000) who reported that such beliefs are quite common among inmates.

But not all of the "rules of conduct" were so benign and focused on the patterns of everyday life in prison. Many of the rules had a more formal character and specifically identified gangs as their locus of origin as well as enforcement. Such rules included prohibitions against cooperation with authorities or deliberately acting in ways that could provoke violence, such as gambling with nothing to pay off a debt incurred by losses.

## Control of Contraband

Our respondents provided a different set of descriptions of the rules and norms surrounding the trafficking and sale of contraband in prison than our quantitative data reflected. Rather than focusing on minor instances of contraband with vague accounts, they provided clear and specific descriptions of the role of gangs in controlling contraband in prison. Put simply, the respondents who provided qualitative data told us that gangs in prison control the sales and profits from contraband sold in prison. This included "hard" goods such alcohol, narcotics, and cell phones, as well as things such as protection. These transactions represented one aspect of prison life where gang and non-gang members interacted with each other. Some of our subjects went so far as to observe that when illegal goods were being moved, prison violence was kept at a low ebb so as not to disturb the important commercial transactions involved in moving larger quantities as well as individual sales of contraband. While drugs and cell phones were the primary items of contraband, protection was also important. Our respondents provided a consistent response to questions about what would happen if someone else tried to move in on gang-controlled contraband: swift, certain, and severe punishment would follow. Indeed, one inmate went so far as to say, "If you're not in the gang, you're not going to sell nothing." A number of respondents underscored that prison gangs already had control of contraband and that control was a considerable source of their power and attractiveness in prison. That said, few specific descriptions were given of punishments for violators who infringed on gang privilege in the selling of contraband.

Our qualitative results diverge from the quantitative results in the area of contraband. We find evidence of a broader market that extends beyond gangs in the quantitative results, while a model of control that more closely resembles the monopoly held by gang members over contraband in prison is found in the qualitative data. Prison gang control of contraband appeared to be strongest for commodities such as drugs and cell phones, with prices for the latter set at $1,000 or more. Clearly the organizational network in prison and between prison and the street (where gangs have access to drugs) facilitates contraband trafficking. The discrepancy between qualitative and quantitative data may be a matter of sampling. Cell blocks often function differently, and while gangs may control contraband in one, they may not in another. Gang members who responded to our open-ended questions also may have had experience in other units (prisons) in the Texas system. Regardless, our results raise questions about the iron fist of gang control in prison contraband sales. The discrepancy may also lie in the mythologizing done by gang members regarding the control over contraband exercised by prison gangs. This would not be the first time that gang members inflated the role of their gang.

The details of moving contraband inevitably involved cooperation from correctional officers. Such interactions did not occur on an ad hoc basis, rather they reflected a patterned practice that prison gangs seemed to control. One inmate familiar with contraband told us:

Only if you are affiliated with them [prison gangs] – they have guidelines. If they want to get something dropped out they get a "basketball" (literally) which is full of cellphones, drugs, etc. Once the people [gang members] get it they are supposed to split it between the person and their family [gang]. That is why you get so much at one time.

The movement of such a volume of contraband requires connections in and out of the prison.

## The Changing Role of Prison Gangs

We were interested also in learning how prison gangs and their role in the maintenance of social order in the prison had changed. Responses to these questions uniformly supported the idea that race and ethnicity continue to play a central role in the social organization of inmates and their relationships in prison. That said, many respondents indicated that gangs have lost power over the course of the past decade or so.

"The gangs don't have near the respect they had way back [referring to the war years and its aftermath] ... because gang membership doesn't mean as much to each member as it used to."

Of course, this is a common refrain when talking to veterans or OGs ("Original Gangsters"), as we have observed in both the LoneStar Project and other studies over the years. Hunt and colleagues (1993) first documented this refrain in California prisons over twenty-five years ago, noting the emergence of "warring camps" of inmates who lack respect for old heads in prison. In Texas, the turn of the century was cited by a number of inmates as the time during which prison gangs changed and began to lose control over prison life. This coincided with the continued growth of the use of administrative segregation as well as the growth of the Tangos, a prison gang with a flatter organizational structure, which we detailed in Chapter 3. Many inmates also told us that the need for gang membership, particularly in the area of protection from violence and sexual assault, was considerably less than twenty years ago. PREA was mentioned by several individuals in this regard, owing to the inability to avoid detection of misconduct due to the obligations of COs to report rule violations. Perhaps the balkanization of gang organizations reflects changes on the streets, or a natural evolutionary process in group formation. Clearly, as Gundur (2018) notes, many contemporary gangs find a horizontal structure to be more effective in meeting their needs than the vertical structures of twenty years ago. The Tangos represent the largest such group in Texas prisons (as is reflected in our sample; see Chapter 5). Comprised primarily of Latino men from large cities in Texas, this group reflects a different orientation than traditional, vertically organized prison gangs. While still involved in the sale and control of contraband, many inmates told us that the Tangos were less violent than the traditional ethnic gangs they have begun to replace in prisons. This is an empirical question that we investigate in the next chapter. But the dynamic nature of social groups, particularly as they interact with a changing environment (in prison and on the street) and the steady cycling of individual members through gangs make it only logical that prison gangs would undergo change. This underscores the need for more research attention focused on such groups.

Another common refrain among gang and non-gang members was that the prison gangs in the aggregate had lost their power and respect among inmates. Whatever its cause (e.g., administrative segregation, changes on the street, prison management), we frequently heard that the control over the social order of the prison that was once extensive had eroded. A lack of discipline and loyalty was perceived to be stronger among younger inmates. One member simply told us that, "The gang set has fallen apart and there is no loyalty anymore." Another observed that:

Prison is washed up. It is not what it used to be. It used to be more disciplined and gangs meant something. Now the gangs don't mean anything and nothing means anything anymore.

Words like "mellow" and "watered down" were used to describe the prison atmosphere (perhaps a bit of hyperbole in the use of the word "mellow"). One veteran prison gang member captured the sentiments of many individuals who weighed in on this issue:

Everything has gotten watered down, calmed down. It is not as violent as it used to be. It's a new generation, a younger generation, that doesn't necessarily have the same morals as what the older generation does.

Many gang members pointed to the weakening of gang control as a factor in intra-gang violence. As one prison gang member told us, there is: "Less violence now. More inner strife within the family itself. You don't really see opposite gangs go at each other." Another individual observed that more violence occurred against members of the same gang than "rivals" and others told us that violence occurred within gangs. While this parallels some findings from the street (Decker and Curry 2002) we lack the hard data on the combatants in gang violence to fully answer this question.

## The Locus of Control: Street Gangs or Prison Gangs?

Earlier commentary (including some of our own) identified prison gangs as well-organized entities from whom power and control flowed to street gangs. Not all aspects of street gang behavior (by a long shot) were controlled by prison gangs, but it seemed clear that the dominant "partner" in the relationship was the prison gang and the subordinate partner was the street gang. Our results are not consistent with this view, and we do not find consensus among our respondents about the direction or nature of control in this relationship.

Respondents were split among views that street gangs influenced prison gangs, prison gangs influenced street gangs, and a middle ground that reflected some form of reciprocity. The relationship appeared to change, depending on the nature of an issue. The three key issues were the impact of violence on the street on violence in prison, the communication of "news" and priorities (especially involving contraband) regarding street gangs, and the role of the street gang (if any) in supporting families of imprisoned gang members. There was consensus that street gang violence could be reflected in patterns and targets of prison violence. Specifically, individuals in prison could be held accountable by the gang for acts of violence they committed against gang members or their families while on the street – consistent with Lessing's "projection of power." This could involve group characteristics, such as a "race riot" or "gang rivalry" on the street that would migrate to prison. But it could also be an individual matter, as one respondent told us: "If they was having trouble with someone in the street or somebody snitched on them, then that person comes to prison, then they send word to prison we take care of it here." The reliance of prison gangs on street gangs is seen most clearly in instrumental activities that require access to commodities, particularly contraband such as narcotics, liquor, or cell phones. Often the complicity of correctional officers or family members who visit someone in prison is secured through contacts outside the prison by street gang members with access to contraband who can interact more easily about such matters than prison gang members. Street gang members also have access to the cash necessary to conduct such transactions, paying for the contraband itself as well as the cooperation of COs or family members.

Expressive activities – particularly those that involve the use of violence to settle scores or exact discipline from gang members – do not have their origins exclusively in the prison or on the street. Instead, these behaviors may have their locus in either source. This reflects a symbiosis between prison and street gangs whereby each has a level of dependence on the other. One respondent described this as a relationship that could be inside/out or outside/in. The constant recycling of individuals from the street to prison and within prison back to the street reinforces the relationship between the two and gives it some degree of reciprocity:

Sometimes when dudes still got ties on the street, they still have ties in here that leads to the streets and back to prison.

If there's a war going on in the world, in the penitentiary, the same rival gang, there's a war, whatever goes on the outside goes on inside, it works outside in.

The third model of the prison–street gang relationships is that the prison gang dictates what goes on in the streets. This conforms to the model depicted by Buentello, Fong, and Vogel (1991), Fong (1990), Jacobs (1977), and Pyrooz et al. (2011) where the prison gangs take the superordinate role in the relationship. This conforms with the view of "super gangs" whose control over prison gangs was clearly more extensive than it is today and whose control over the streets, if not absolute, was quite consequential. One respondent characterized the relationship as follows:

The inside pretty much controls the outside. So they didn't really do much on the outside if the inside didn't let them.

Yet another individual told us that

The street gang responds to the prison gang; the prison gang tries to make decisions because the top leaders are in prison.

This model of control reveals something both about the structure and control in prison and street gangs. The communication of information between the street and the prison has never been a large challenge save for the use of administrative segregation. Prison gang members tend to be older and more experienced offenders than their street gang counterparts, so it makes sense that they would continue to at least attempt to exert control over the street. That said, this role appears to be somewhat circumscribed.

It is important to contrast our qualitative findings with the quantitative results. The quantitative results in the areas of rules and order did not meet our expectations. That is, based on decades of research we expected to find high levels of agreement that the rules set by gangs and the attendant punishments for violations of those rules influenced both gang and non-gang members alike. Instead, we found that even among gang members, gang rules were not ascendant in prison, nor were there many concerns about punishments for violating gang rules. To reiterate, this was the case for both gang and non-gang members. Even when we examined the responses from members of specific gangs, only the prison-oriented gangs expressed much concern about following rules set by prison gang members. In the case of order in prison, neither gang nor non-gang members saw a dominant role for gang members in this process. This conclusion held for both the qualitative and quantitative data. It was only in the case of the control of contraband in prison that the qualitative and quantitative data diverged. While the quantitative data indicated higher levels of control of contraband by gangs than were found for the role of gangs in rules or order, they did not rise to a level supporting the conclusion that gang members were clearly in control of illegal trade in drugs, cell phones, or other forms of contraband. While the role of gangs in acquiring and selling contraband was acknowledged by gang and non-gang respondents alike, the extent of control by gangs appears weaker than has been described in other accounts. This seems consistent with the descriptions of gangs as having lost power in prisons and their more horizontal structure. While the qualitative findings did provide support for the position that prison gangs still control contraband, this may be a matter of sampling, or perhaps contraband is tightly controlled by prison gangs and knowledge of the inner workings of that process are not widely known beyond a small circle of gang members.

CONCLUSION

How do we account for these findings about control and the social order of prisons? They clearly diverge from our expectations based on the literature and what little prior research has been done in this area. The contrast between what we expected and what we found requires elaboration, as does the divergence between the qualitative and quantitative findings.

We first offer a conclusion based on the findings in this chapter: gangs in prison show considerable variation. They vary in organization, purposes, composition, and activity. We established that in Chapter 5 and observed the variation across gang types in this chapter. The four-gang typology created in Chapter 5 demonstrates that there is considerable variation among gangs, variation that has consequences for the exercise of rules and control in prison. These gangs hardly fit the image of hard power, control, and domination depicted by Jacobs, Lessing, and Skarbek. Another key finding from our sample was that while there were some similarities between gang and non-gang members in their assessments of the role of gangs in the social order of prison life, for the most part, gang members saw a larger role for the gang in such activity than did non-gang inmates. This suggests that gang control is neither so widespread nor effective that it is perceived as highly important by non-gang members. Indeed, non-gang members responded that rules set by the staff were of more importance than those set by gangs. In addition, non-gang members did not report that gangs control contraband nearly to the extent that gang members did. This suggests that the ascendancy of gangs in prison is seen as much more powerful among gang members and may not extend fully to non-gang members. This would seem to limit gang control in prison primarily to other gang members, a response we heard from our respondents on many occasions. The role and control of gangs in prisons appears to be changing toward less control and less loyalty in the face of tighter administrative control and expanded use of administrative segregation.

There are differences between the quantitative and the qualitative results we presented regarding the locus of gang control. The quantitative results depicted gang control as diffused, and largely operational among prison gang members. The influence of the prison gangs on non-gang members was weaker and more indirect than that found in studies of earlier decades. The largest divergence between the quantitative and qualitative results was in the area of contraband. In the quantitative results, even prison gang members acknowledged that the grip of the group was not what it once was. This is a different version of the control of contraband found in our qualitative results where gang control of contraband in prison was described in strong terms. Our qualitative results found that even non-gang members acknowledged the primacy played by prison gang members in the movement of contraband. Of course, our qualitative sample is considerably smaller and may represent the inmates most involved in gangs and contraband. It may also be the case that such depictions of gang control of the movement of contraband may reflect the bravado and "inflation" often found in gang responses about the influence and power of their gang.

The divergence between the responses of gang and non-gang members suggests that the control exercised by gangs is not far-reaching and extends primarily to gang members. Clearly one reason for this may be the nature of our sample. We include both gang and non-gang members in our sample. Much of the prior work that has established the power of gangs in prison has relied on administrative records, interviews with prison staff (especially management), and limited interviews with gang members that focused exclusively on information about gangs. In a sense this is sampling on the independent variable, that is to say sampling only the category of interest. Without another group to contrast gang members against, it is hard to know whether their responses regarding control are high, medium, or low compared to those of other inmates. The exclusive focus on gang members overinflates their role in the control of prison social order. This conclusion is supported by the lack of findings for a gang role in social control in the responses of non-gang members. Since non-gang members do not recognize the authority of gangs or their role in the rules, control, and contraband distribution mechanisms we argue that gang control does not penetrate significantly beyond gang members and groups. Gang members recognize the ubiquity of gang power but the impact of such power does not appear to extend beyond the gang. It is our argument that interviewing both gang and non-gang members in similar settings is an important step in understanding the role of gangs in prison across a wide variety of domains.

Of course, it is possible that the nature of the design or execution of the study plan accounted for the findings here. The measures used in the questionnaire for rules, order, and contraband have not been used in another study before and therefore have not been validated. Perhaps another reason that the results diverged from expectations built on the literature is that the sensitive nature of the topics produced underreporting of the level of control by both gang and non-gang members. After all, our interviewers could be observed during the interview process (usually through the glass of a closed door) and were clearly present through the agreement of the prison administration.

A plausible alternative to these concerns is the observation that little of the knowledge about prison gangs is current nor does much of it come from inmates themselves. After all, there have been few direct studies of prison gang members, so the knowledge base is hardly well established. For example, the work of Jacobs (1977) is over forty years old and the Buentello et al. (1991) study is over twenty-five years old. The work of Skarbek (2014), although more recent, was based in California, which shares a tumultuous history of gangs like Texas, while Lessing's (2016) research is based outside of the United States. Mass incarceration was much more a reality in the 2000s than the 1980s or 1990s. In addition, the growth and nature of gangs on the street has changed dramatically since those earlier prison-based studies. Prisons are dynamic institutions with a steady churning in and out of new inmates, and gang affiliations on the street are also dynamic. These factors combine to produce changes in the nature of gang behavior and control in institutional settings. Indeed, the widespread public availability of cell phones is a relatively recent phenomenon but one that has affected the social order in prison. The Tangos were the most recent gang to appear in Texas prisons, as we showed in the previous chapter. They are an example of a horizontal gang that includes cliques from major cities across Texas. Such groups represent a change from traditional Latino gangs such as the Mexican Mafia or Texas Syndicate and are generally less formal. In addition, as we have noted earlier, administrative records are not collected for research purposes (independent, validated, hypothesis testing) and administrative records exaggerate gang control because they are so heavily focused on prison misconduct and discipline.

In conclusion, our findings support a role for prison gangs in contributing to the rules and social order of the prison. However, that role appears to be limited mostly to other gang members and may not be given credence or widely recognized by non-gang members. It appears gang and non-gang inmates operate in different social worlds. It is clear that gang members participate in the distribution of contraband, but do not appear to control such distribution with an iron fist. Our qualitative findings contrast with changes in the structure of prison life across the past decade or so where the power of prison gangs has been weakened and prison gangs have assumed a horizontal structure. Two points derived from research on street gangs seem to apply here: that gangs are dynamic, and that they are also diverse. Having established the role of prison gangs in the establishment and maintenance of social order within the prison, we move to Chapter 7 and an examination of violence and misconduct in prison, outcomes that are perhaps most closely linked to gangs.

# 7

## Misconduct and Victimization in Prison

Despite being highly controlled environments, crime and victimization occur in prisons. According to a report from the Bureau of Justice Statistics, eighty-three inmates were the victims of homicide in federal and state prisons in 2014 (Noonan, Rohloff, and Ginder 2016). The homicide rate among inmates reached historic lows in the first decade of the twenty-first century (Mumola 2005), but has crept up in recent years and now exceeds the homicide risk in the general population. Just like on the streets, homicide remains a rare event in prison – for example, the Texas prison system averaged four homicides per year between 2001 and 2014. But this does not mean victimization is rare. Indeed, inmates are subject to a wide variety of types of victimization, including theft, extortion, and robbery. A representative survey of inmates held in state prisons revealed that 29 percent had been written up by authorities for engaging in violence and 15 percent had been the victim of an intentional injury (Toman 2017). This suggests that violent misconduct and victimization are rather common inside prisons. Their occurrence has consequences for how life is lived by inmates. The potential for victimization is an undercurrent in prison that motivates inmate group affiliation and activity, as we demonstrate in the next chapter. Prison staff, visitors, and inmates are all potential targets of offending, as well as potential offenders. The behaviors of interest may include violations of law (e.g., aggravated assault, drug sales) or violations of institutional rules (e.g., refusing treatment, excessive noise).

It is our contention in this chapter that gangs and gang membership play a key role in prison misconduct and victimization, just as they do on the street. We believe that explanations of misconduct, victimization, and the overlap between the two cannot be described accurately without including a measure of gang membership. Yet, as we have noted consistently throughout the book, there is a paucity of research on gangs, gang members, and prison. We believe that this is due to the difficulties of conducting research in prison settings, whether that difficulty is linked to the challenges of gaining access to official data, the challenges of data collection in prisons, or a general aversion to "getting dirty" (Hepburn 2013). Consequently, our knowledge base for policy and theory is more limited than it should be (Fox, Lane, and Turner 2018).

This general observation about the state of research in prison is especially true in understanding misconduct and victimization. These topics are of critical importance for understanding life in prison, though perhaps not ones prison administrators find easy to discuss. After all, individuals are sent to prison as punishment and are expected to serve their sentences in a lawful manner. Misconduct and victimization in prison are often taken as a sign that the prison has failed in controlling the behavior of inmates and creating a safe environment. Many lawsuits are based on the victimization of individuals while in prison, further complicating the issue of access to data, correctional officers, or interviews with inmates. Indeed, many individuals who have conducted research in prison have at some point found their access restricted or questionnaires limited. We believe that multiple sources of data on this topic are needed for a full explanation of these issues, including official records, self-reports of inmates, and staff surveys.

This chapter examines the relationship between gang membership, misconduct, and victimization in prison. These outcomes (misconduct and victimization) are considered jointly because in many ways they are two sides of the same coin. Thus, we examine them individually as well as together, consistent with a long tradition in criminology (Berg 2012). Since we lack an established theoretical or empirical base to study the relationship between gang membership, misconduct, and victimization in prison, we turn to the literature on street gangs as our launching point. Group process is central to understanding the actions and behaviors of street gangs, and we contend that this is also the case in prison. Accordingly, we contrast levels of misconduct and victimization by gang status, since we would expect active gang members to be more susceptible to the mores, obligations, and routines of life in the gang than are former gang members and especially non-gang inmates. In a notable twist, new to the study of gangs, we determine if *gang activity* is principally responsible for the amplification of misconduct and victimization among gang members. In other words, we ask whether gang-related misconduct and victimization drive up the overall levels of these outcomes. To boost confidence in our results, we examine whether survey and official data tell the same story, adding a measure of reliability to the findings. Lastly, we assess whether there is heterogeneity in the link between gang membership, misconduct, and victimization across gangs. In this context we ask whether some gangs are more involved in misconduct and susceptible to victimization than others. This chapter provides the most comprehensive investigation of the relationship between gang membership, misconduct, and victimization to date, an area of great theoretical and policy significance.

IS PRISON A MIRROR IMAGE OF THE STREET?

Throughout this book, we have examined the utility of what we know about street gangs for our understanding of prison gangs. We refer to this as the "parallelism" between gang behaviors, processes, and structures on the street and in prison. This juxtaposition clearly invokes the deprivation/importation dichotomy outlined in Chapter 2. Similarities in the behaviors, processes, and structures of gangs in street and prison settings would be consistent with the importation perspective, while differences would be consistent with the deprivation perspective. We believe that this consideration is particularly important for the general question about misconduct and victimization in prison. Several of the most consistent findings about street gangs are invoked by such a comparison, including the following:

- Gang membership plays a key role in elevating the prevalence and frequency of *criminal offending*. This conclusion enjoys widespread support regardless of the sample characteristics, site of the study, method of data collection, or type of crime studied (Pyrooz et al. 2016).
- Gang membership is a major risk factor for *victimization*. This is a conclusion that also enjoys widespread support in gang research, but, unlike offending, this relationship appears to be more sensitive to controls for factors endogenous to and exogenous from gang membership (Fox 2013; Gibson et al. 2012).
- The *victim–offender overlap*, one of the most established findings in criminology (Jennings, Piquero, and Reingle 2012), appears to be stronger among gang members than non-gang members (Pyrooz, Moule, and Decker 2014), which is perhaps expected owing to the aforementioned observations.
- Gang membership is a life state that people *enter and exit*, and researchers find that levels of criminal offending and victimization rise when someone joins a gang, then decline when someone leaves a gang, although not necessarily returning to pre-gang levels (Melde and Esbensen 2014; Sweeten, Pyrooz, and Piquero 2013; Weerman, Lovegrove, and Thornberry 2015; Wu and Pyrooz 2015).
- There is *heterogeneity* in criminal activity and victimization across gangs. Studies reveal that some gangs are more likely than other gangs to be perpetrators and receivers of violence (Maxson and Klein 1995; Papachristos 2009; Papachristos, Hureau, and Braga 2013).

How do we account for these empirical observations? The tripartite model developed by Terry Thornberry and his colleagues (1993) posited selection, facilitation, and enhancement as three possible explanations for these findings, as we noted in Chapter 2. Clearly, facilitation and enhancement have received the most empirical support as possible explanations for the spikes in offending and victimization during gang membership. Thornberry and colleagues anchored the facilitation and enhancement models to *group process*, which is a means to account for the dramatically higher levels of gang participation in offending and victimization. Group processes include a bevy of collective actions and normative orientations that influence individual and group behaviors, such as the perpetration of offending and susceptibility to victimization. These influences are located at the group level, not simply by individuals who comprise these groups or the communities in which they reside. Group process is the thread of continuity across gangs, according to Klein and Maxson (2006), not composition or ecology.

## MISCONDUCT, VICTIMIZATION, AND THEIR OVERLAP: A GROUP PROCESS PERSPECTIVE

Can a group process argument be applied to gangs in the context of prison? It is our contention that group processes among gangs in prison should produce results that are comparable to what is observed on the street. We draw on the work of Jean McGloin and Megan Collins (2015), who organized the state of theory and research on gang-related group processes that give rise to higher offending and victimization. First, the *opportunities* found in the environments that gangs construct in prison will influence risk for misconduct and victimization. Gang membership entails routine engagement with both dangerous actors and dangerous places (Huebner et al. 2016; Taylor et al. 2008). Gang membership creates risk for offending and victimization through physical proximity to other gang members, such as hanging out on the yard or in the dayroom, as well as physical proximity to coveted locations or space, such as benches or exercise equipment. Although criminal opportunities are restricted in solitary confinement, we must recognize the ubiquity of opportunities for rule violations in prison, as misconduct also includes acts that are not violations of the legal code.

Second, the *collective behavior* of gangs involves the diffusion of responsibility and group cohesiveness. Whereas the person is assigned the status of perpetrator or victim in non-gang behaviors, the *group* is assigned such a status in gang-related behaviors. This is what social psychologists describe as entitativity, where group affiliation masks individual identity. Entitativity is also the reason why Eduardo Vasquez and colleagues (2015) noted, when applying this concept to gangs, that "any of them will do" when a group considers targets for retaliation. In other words, incidents of gang violence include an expansive pool of perpetrators and victims. Group cohesiveness captures the connectedness of a gang, how they traverse space and time as a group, and act collectively in times of conflict (Klein and Crawford 1967). The collective behavior of gangs should have as much validity in prison as it does on the street, particularly as tattoos and collective action signal affiliation and congregate activities diffuse responsibility across members.

Third, *social status* is afforded through the appraisals of action and inaction among gang members. Gang members who engage in certain actions are rewarded with positive appraisals (Short and Strodtbeck 1965). For example, if a white inmate associated with the Peckerwoods is getting jumped on the yard by members of the Tangos, other Peckerwoods are expected to join the fray. Members who defend the Peckerwood – regardless of the physical toll it takes – will be positively rewarded, while those who do not will be shunned, or perhaps worse, end up a target for their inaction or lack of heart. This dynamic plays out in various ways beyond (in)action in times of conflict, including investing in illicit gang activities (i.e., putting in work), co-opting witnesses and prison staff for group gain, and assuming individual responsibility for group action (i.e., taking heat).

The final component of group process within the gang is *normative influence*, which refers to the norms and values that promote intra-gang conformity through group identification. This obviously overlaps with social status, but here we are focused more explicitly on the expectations and obligations that come with gang membership, not simply whether or not one receives positive or negative appraisal. Normative influence is perhaps best exemplified by focusing on intergang conflict. For example, Andrew Papachristos (2009) described an act of violence between gangs as a "gift" because it is something that must be reciprocated. If a member of the Texas Syndicate attacks a member of the Tangos, there is an obligation for the Tangos to respond with violence. Of course, this is a broader set of obligations that is shared among members of the Tangos. If the Texas Syndicate get away with the violence – that is, they escape retaliation – the Tangos end up looking weak not only to other gangs in prison, but also on the street, as well to other inmates and even prison staff. Normative influence thus captures the cultural orientations of gangs, such as their adherence to norms of retaliation and valuation of respect, which ultimately increase risks of both offending and victimization, especially with the intensification of the cycle of gang violence (Decker 1996).

Whether these mechanisms apply to prison gangs remains an open question, one that we attempt to tackle in this chapter. But we believe that the basic processes of enhancement and facilitation of offending among gang members apply to the prison context as well as the street and serve to diffuse the risks of victimization and motives for offending throughout the group. In fact, a closed environment such as prison may result in a more efficient and quicker spread of information to communicate threats and retaliatory targets than on the street.

Figure 7.1 gives us some confidence that gang-related group processes are existent in prison. We asked all of our self-reported gang members to reveal to us their gang's "biggest rival," which we used to construct a rivalry network of prison gangs in Texas.[1] The rivalry network indicates that most edges or ties between gangs are within rather than between racial and ethnic groups, consistent with

---

[1] For presentation purposes, we removed the street-oriented gangs unless a tie (i.e., rival) existed to a gang with a locus of influence in prison.

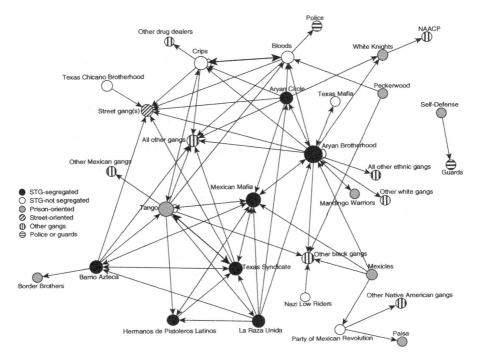

FIGURE 7.1 Rivalry network of gangs in prison

Notes: Circles are nodes, which represent a single gang. Larger nodes are gangs with more respondents represented in our sample. For presentation purposes, only gangs with a locus of gang influence in prison are reported, although rivals without such a locus are collapsed into broader groups (street-oriented gangs, other gangs, and police/guards). Arrowed lines are edges, which represent a reported rivalry between nodes. The width of the edge is larger if more individual gang members claim a rivalry. Incoming arrows are indegree, representing a rivalry reported from a gang member to a node; outgoing arrows are outdegree, representing a rivalry reported by a gang member to a node.

street gang research (Gravel et al. 2018). For example, nearly all of the ties pointing toward the Tangos are directed from other Latino gangs (save for the single tie with the Crips). Some of these rivalries are stronger than others, as evidenced by the size of the line between gangs such as the Tangos–Texas Syndicate, Bloods–Crips, and Aryan Brotherhood–Aryan Circle. Several gangs are embedded in multiplex rivalries, such as the Aryan Brotherhood that appears to be at odds with multiple gangs of multiple races and ethnicities. Black gangs – Bloods and Crips – do not name entire races or ethnicities as rivals, whereas this was more common among Latino (e.g., Tangos) and white (e.g., Aryan Brotherhood) gangs. The fact that these rivalries are in place is suggestive of the underlying ability for group processes to be activated, and as a consequence, result in higher rates of misconduct and victimization among gang members.

## PRISON RESEARCH ON GANG MEMBERSHIP, MISCONDUCT, AND VICTIMIZATION

What does the empirical research say about the relationship between gang membership, misconduct, and victimization in prison? Marie Griffin and John Hepburn (2006) examined the official records of 2,318 male inmates in a southwestern state prison system in 1996. They focused on disciplinary reports during the first three years of confinement, and compared these reports based on whether inmates were in gangs (17 percent) or not (83 percent). Nearly half of street (41 percent) and prison (48 percent) gang affiliates engaged in violent misconduct (weapons, threats, fights, or assaults), compared to one-quarter of non-gang inmates. Gang affiliation was among the strongest predictors of violent misconduct even when accounting for other relevant demographic and criminal justice system risk factors. This theme is reiterated in much of the research relying on official data (e.g., Ralph et al. 1996; Shelden 1991; Worrall and Morris 2012).

As we have noted throughout this book, surveys of inmates are rare in research on gangs. The work of Beth Huebner (2003) constitutes one of the few exceptions. She examined data from the 1991 Survey of Inmates of State Correctional Facilities, which is notable for two reasons. First, there have been seven surveys – 1974, 1979, 1986, 1991, 1997, 2004, and 2016 – conducted over three decades, yet only the 1991 survey contained measures of individual gang involvement. Second, both gang involvement and misconduct were measured in the survey, as opposed to relying on administrative data for one or the other. Huebner found that gang involvement was positively related to inmate-on-staff and inmate-on-inmate assaults, net of individual factors as well as prison-level factors.

Research from the Federal Bureau of Prisons (Gaes et al. 2002) is generally cited as evidence of the disproportionate level of misconduct attributed to gang affiliates. Much like the work of Griffin and Hepburn (2006) and others, this research also relies solely on official data. The notable distinction is the group-level analysis found in the work of Gaes and colleagues. Of the 82,504 inmates included in their study, nearly 7,500 of them were gang affiliated, which gave them ample statistical power to determine if some gangs are involved in more violence and misconduct than other gangs. Compared to unaffiliated inmates, the members of twenty of the twenty-seven gangs were involved in more violence. The evidence from that study suggests that gangs like the Bloods, Vice Lords, Drug Cartels, Jamaican Posse, and New York City street gangs maintained higher counts of violence.

In terms of victimization, the evidence is far less clear, partly because more studies focus on misconduct than victimization. As we learned in our own work in the LoneStar Project, it is easier to gain access to official reports of misconduct than victimization. John Wooldredge and Ben Steiner have conducted the leading work on this topic (2012, 2014; see Steiner, Butler, and

Ellison 2014) based on their sample of nearly 6,000 inmates in forty-six prisons in Kentucky and Ohio. They found that gang membership, based on official data, was unrelated to assault victimization and negatively related to theft victimization. The allure of protection is a strong motivator for gang involvement, and the evidence produced by Wooldredge and Steiner suggests that in contrast to research findings on the victimization of street gang members, gangs in prison might actually fulfill such a promise.

In summary, although the need is great, we lack a sound theoretical and empirical foundation for understanding the relationship between gang membership, misconduct, and victimization in prison. There is no doubt that the work of Jacobs (1974), among others, established a central role for gangs in prison misconduct and violence, and offers qualitative evidence consistent with the importation of violence from the prison to the street. But that must be contrasted against the arguments of Skarbek (2014), among others, who contends that gangs bring order to institutions. And with order we would expect less violence. The literature is too varied and inconsistent to reach strong conclusions, and as we highlight below, there is a need to bring multiple sources of data, examine several types of misconduct and victimization, disentangle current and former gang status, and better analyze group-level differences among gangs.

## STUDYING GANGS, MISCONDUCT, AND VICTIMIZATION

Our first goal in this chapter is to provide a comprehensive investigation of the relationship between gang membership, misconduct, and victimization in prison. To do this, we draw on multiple measures of misconduct and victimization, including self-reports and official records, as well as distinguishing between current, former, and non-gang members. As we have established, it is rare to have data from both inmates and administrative records. It is also rare to distinguish between current and former gang members. Only recently has this occurred in research on street gangs; we are unaware of any instance of researchers studying former gang members separately from current gang members in institutional corrections. Perhaps it is a reflection of the long-standing belief – one that has been dispelled among street gangs – that once an inmate joins a gang they can never leave.

Another goal of this chapter is to assess whether gang activity is responsible for higher levels of misconduct and victimization among gang members. This might sound like an obvious proposition, but there are few data sources that systematically document the gang-relatedness of misconduct and victimization. After all, not all misconduct perpetrated and victimization experienced by gang members has to do with gangs. Finally, and consistent with Chapter 5, we assess heterogeneity in misconduct and victimization across gangs as groups. Are some gangs involved in more misconduct than others? Do some gangs experience more victimization than others? Our aim is to address these questions in the prison environment.

## Measures of Misconduct and Victimization

Data on officially recorded disciplinary incidents of misconduct were provided to us by the Texas prison system. Unfortunately, at the time of this writing we were not able to secure official data on victimization. We received information on 6,081 disciplinary incidents involving our respondents during their most recent incarceration spell. Nested within these incidents were 7,216 offenses recorded by the prison system. We included 65 offenses in our analysis, which we group into the following four categories: *disorder* (thirty-two types, e.g., "failure to obey orders"), *violence* (fifteen types, e.g., "fight/assault offender with a weapon with non-serious injury"), *instrumental* or property (eleven types, e.g., "soliciting money or gifts"), and *substance*-related (seven types, e.g., "unauthorized drug use or possession"). We summed the total number of offenses within each category to generate counts, and then examined the following outcomes:

* *incarceration spell*: (1) all forms, (2) disorder, (3) violence, (4) instrumental or property, and (5) substance-related;
* *last six months*: (6) all forms, (7) disorder, (8) violence, (9) instrumental or property, and (10) substance-related.

Will self-report data from inmates tell the same story as administrative data? If the relationship between gang membership and misconduct is consistent across the two data sources, it gives us confidence that this finding is an empirical reality and not an artifact of prison practices (e.g., enhanced surveillance of gang members). To determine this, we asked our respondents about their involvement in seventeen forms of misconduct and their experience with thirteen forms of victimization, drawing from leading questionnaires that were adapted for a prison environment. The use of self-reports to measure misconduct and victimization enjoys a long history in criminology (Cantor and Lynch 2000; Thornberry and Krohn 2000), and has been shown to produce reliable and valid measures of misconduct and victimization on the street (e.g., Krohn et al. 2010) and in prison (e.g., Steiner and Wooldredge 2014). Although, our own work on the subject matter suggests that misconduct is underrecorded in administrative data (Pyrooz, Decker, and Owens 2018), not unlike what researchers find on the street, which is known as the "dark figure" of crime and victimization (Biderman and Reiss Jr. 1967; Hart and Rennison 2003).

The items used to measure prison misconduct included: (1) burglary (i.e., personal living space); (2) theft of property (e.g., from other inmates or the prison system); (3) fraud via illegitimate means (e.g., counterfeit money); (4) fraud via the sale of illegitimate goods; (5) damaging property; (6) weapon carrying; (7) robbery; (8) assaulting prison staff with a weapon; (9) assaulting prison staff without a weapon; (10) group-based assault of an inmate with a weapon; (11) group-based assault of an inmate without a weapon; (12)

individual assault of an inmate with a weapon; (13) individual assault of an inmate without a weapon; (14) threatening to hurt someone; (15) sexual assault; (16) the sale of illegal goods; and (17) disobeying prison staff orders. Together, these items capture a wide range of misconduct behavior that spans violence, instrumental, property, and disorder. For the purposes of examining specific forms of misconduct, we group items 1–7 to create an instrumental/property scale and items 7–15 to create a violence scale.

The items used to measure prison victimization included: (1) fraud via the sale of illegitimate goods; (2) identity-related fraud; (3) property damage; (4) burglary; (5) theft of property; (6) robbery; (7) threats of harm with a weapon; (8) threats of harm without a weapon; (9) group-based assault with a weapon; (10) group-based assault without a weapon; (11) individual assault with a weapon; (12) individual assault without a weapon; and (13) sexual assault. Similar to misconduct, these items capture a wide range of victimizations, and were grouped together to generate scales of instrumental/property victimization (items 1–6) and violence (items 6–13).

Our survey instrument queried respondents about whether a misconduct or victimization event occurred during their current incarceration spell, similar to nationally representative surveys of inmates (e.g., Survey of Inmates in State and Federal Correctional Facilities). A "yes" response generated a follow-up question asking the number of times it occurred in the last six months of imprisonment. This allowed us to establish the time order for incidents of misconduct and victimization and the measures of events, states, and attitudinal correlates gathered at the post-release interview. Of course, we cannot make causal inferences with these data, but ensuring the temporal overlap of gang membership and misconduct and victimization increases the internal validity of our findings, especially when including a broad set of covariates to control for spuriousness, described below.

Respondents who provided us with non-zero responses to our measures of misconduct and victimization were asked to report the percent of the time the event was *gang-related*. For some respondents, who had trouble estimating the breakdown of gang- and non-gang-related incidents, we provided them with response categories of 0 ("never"), 25 ("sometimes"), 50 ("half"), 75 ("most times"), and 100 ("every time"). The purpose of these questions was to determine whether the bulk of misconduct and victimization was gang-related or not. There are three comparisons that are relevant to this topic: (1) overall levels of misconduct and victimization, which is what most researchers study; and then the decomposition of the overall score into (2) non-gang-related misconduct and victimization and (3) gang-related misconduct and victimization. If we were to find that *non-gang-related* misconduct and victimization were equivalent between gang and non-gang inmates, yet *overall* misconduct and victimization differed, it would suggest that *gang-related* activity is what drives the relationship between gang membership, misconduct, and victimization. Yet, if gang-related misconduct and victimization were equal among gang and non-gang inmates, while overall levels were higher among gang members, it would suggest that gang activity is not what is driving up the problem behavior of gang members. In other words, this approach is one attempt at isolating the contribution of gang activity (not simply gang membership) to misconduct and victimization.

Criminologists have debated how to best scale measures of crime and victimization. A frequency scale, which is the sum of incidents over a designated period, is a common approach, but it is dominated by less serious events. A dichotomous scale, which measures whether any crime or victimization has occurred, also very common, obscures patterns of variation and is equally susceptible to less serious events. Sweeten (2012, 533) demonstrated that variety scales are preferred to alternative methods of measurement because they are "easy to construct, possess high reliability and validity, and are not compromised by high frequency non-serious crime types." Therefore, we construct a series of variety scales for our self-report measures, where we take the sum of dichotomous items of misconduct and victimization, which can be interpreted as the number of forms of misconduct and victimization. We organize our survey measures as follows:

- *incarceration spell – misconduct*: (1) all forms, (2) violent, (3) instrumental/ property;
- *incarceration spell – victimization*: (4) all forms, (5) violent, (6) instrumental/property;
- *last six months – misconduct*: (7) all forms, all motives; (8) all forms, gang-related; (9) all forms, non-gang-related; (10) violent, all motives; (11) violent, gang-related; (12) violent, non-gang-related;
- *last six months – victimization*: (13) all forms, all motives; (14) all forms, gang-related; (15) all forms, non-gang-related; (16) violent, all motives; (17) violent, gang-related; (18) violent, non-gang-related.

## Measuring Gang Membership

Whereas misconduct and victimization constitute our key outcome variables, gang status is our primary explanatory variable. Gang status consists of three mutually exclusive groups of inmates: (1) current gang members, or inmates who told us that they were actively involved in a gang; (2) former gang members, or inmates who told us that they were no longer an active gang member in prison; and (3) non-gang members, or inmates who told us they had never been in a gang in prison. The last group constitutes the reference group for all of our analyses, although we report tests for similar levels of misconduct and victimization between current and former gang members. Including former gang members allows us to determine whether leaving the gang produces reductions in both of these behaviors, although we should be clear from the outset that our measures do not allow us to fully address time order. While the baseline data from the LoneStar Project are cross-sectional, these measures do represent a notable advance over prior research to ensure that gang membership overlaps with the behaviors and experiences we are examining.

## Controls for Spuriousness

Gang membership is not a life state that people enter at random. Many of the factors that give rise to gang membership are also related to crime and victimization. Not accounting for these joint influences would make the correlation between gang membership, misconduct, and victimization appear larger than it truly is. At the same time, gang membership is not a life state that one-dimensionally influences crime and victimization. Gang membership is conceived as a turning point or snare in the life course because it triggers shifts in routine activities, the worsening of attitudes and beliefs, and assuming new roles and social networks (Melde and Esbensen 2011). These factors also heighten risks for crime and victimization. As we learned in our meta-analysis of 179 studies examining the gang membership–offending link (Pyrooz et al. 2016), focusing only on the bivariate association likely overestimates this relationship, while examining comprehensive multivariate associations likely underestimates this relationship. Of course, we would rather find ourselves in the latter predicament than the former, given that there is nothing inherently criminal about being a gang member. It is necessary to control for spuriousness to avoid misspecifying the relationship between gang membership, misconduct, and victimization.

To this end, all of our analyses include a rich set of covariates as controls, which we organize into demographic, criminal justice history, and theoretical domains. Demographic controls include measures of age (linear and quadratic), race and ethnicity (black, Latino, and mixed/other, with whites as the reference group), educational attainment, marriage, and IQ. Criminal justice system controls include the number of prior arrests, years incarcerated for the current spell, and custody level (restrictive housing and other custody levels, with general population as the reference group). Theoretical controls include low self-control, code of the street, convict code, procedural justice, legitimacy, self-esteem, prosocial peers, and religiosity. All of the covariates have been described in more detail in prior chapters, which is why we do not provide additional information about them here. Together, these covariates constitute many of the leading explanations of crime and victimization (Cullen, Agnew, and Wilcox 2017), and appear to maintain validity in the prison environment (Steiner et al. 2014).

## Analytic Plan

Our analytic plan unfolds in five stages. We begin by examining the relationship between gang status and officially recorded misconduct across the incarceration spell and the last six months of imprisonment, respectively. We report our findings for all forms of misconduct, as well as disorder, violence, instrumental/property, and substance-related. Together, this gives us a broad sense of the gang/misconduct relationship and whether it is sensitive to different forms of misconduct. It also establishes a baseline comparison to the survey data. After all, nearly all of the research on the relationship between gang status and misconduct in prison is based on official rather than survey data.

The second stage of our analysis examines the relationship between gang status and self-reported misconduct and victimization across the incarceration spell and the last six months. All forms and violent forms of misconduct and victimization are the two outcomes we examine. Here, we focus on whether the statistical associations for these outcomes in the survey data are comparable to administrative data. We would expect to find a similar pattern of associations across both data sources. We focus on statistical (i.e., where the association is different from zero) rather than substantive (i.e., magnitude of the association) significance given that the measurement practices and scaling procedures between the two data sources diverge.

The third stage of our analysis relies only on the survey data to tackle a long-standing and heretofore untested assumption in research on gang membership, misconduct, and victimization: Is gang activity responsible for elevated rates of misconduct and victimization among gang members? The alternative hypothesis is that gang members offend with impunity and are more susceptible to victimization for reasons that have nothing to do with gangs. We test for this by comparing rates of misconduct and victimization – all forms and violence only – for gang-related and non-gang-related offense categories. We anticipate that gang and non-gang members are equivalent on *non-gang-related* levels of misconduct and victimization, but diverge from one another in their *overall* levels of misconduct and victimization due to gang-related activities.

We also assess the victim–offender overlap in prison. We determine if the overlap between perpetrators and victims of violence is stronger among gang members than it is among non-gang members, which is what we have observed in street settings. There is good reason to believe – owing to gang-related group processes – that this observation should extend from the street to prison, even when accounting for leading alternative explanations.

Our final step removes non-gang members from the analysis to examine how misconduct and victimization vary across gangs measured at the group level. We do this by introducing gang-level fixed effects for the thirty-one groups with more than one member in our sample. Since respondents are reporting about their own behavior and experiences rather than group-level characteristics, we do not generate empirical Bayes predictions like we did in Chapter 5. Instead, we generate aggregate estimates of misconduct and victimization (all forms and violent) across groups and across the four-part gang typology, adjusting for the same covariates we described above.

## MISCONDUCT AND VICTIMIZATION AMONG GANG AND NON-GANG MEMBERS

### Officially Recorded Misconduct

Over 85 percent of our respondents were written up for a disciplinary incident, indicating just how common this practice was in prison. In the six months prior to release from prison, just under half of the sample (48 percent) was reported for a rule violation. The bulk of rule violations were related to disorder – refusing to work, possessing tattoo paraphernalia, establishing inappropriate relationships with staff. That does not mean that other forms of misconduct were infrequent. Indeed, over the course of incarceration spells, about one-third of our respondents were recorded for having engaged in violence, one-quarter in instrumental misconduct, and nearly half in substance-related misconduct. A similar pattern across misconduct categories emerges when turning to six-month observation periods.

How are levels of misconduct distributed by gang status? Figure 7.2 shows that inmates involved in gangs engage in more misconduct than non-gang inmates do. The adjusted number of offenses for current and former gang

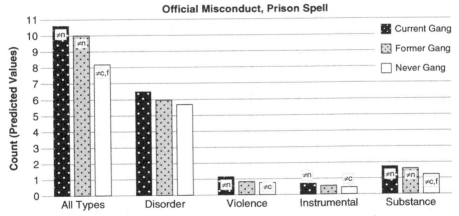

FIGURE 7.2 Predicted values of official disciplinary incident counts by gang status, prison spell

Notes: Column labels indicate statistically significant differences ("≠," $p < 0.05$) in the predicted value between gang status groups (c = current gang member, f = former gang member, n = never gang member) based on negative binomial regression models adjusting for the following covariates: age, age quadratic, black, Latino, race/ethnicity mixed/other, educational attainment, IQ, low self-control, code of the street, convict code, correctional officer legitimacy, correctional officer procedural justice, self-esteem, peer support, religiosity, prior arrests, years of incarceration, restrictive housing, and other non-general population custody level.

members is 10.6 and 10.0, respectively. In contrast, non-gang members were recorded for engaging in 8.2 adjusted offenses. These are standardized differences of about 0.20 and 0.15 (Cohen's *d*), which would rank gang membership in the high tier of prison misconduct correlates. The difference between current and former gang members is negligible statistically and substantively. In other words, the key distinction in misconduct is between inmates with any history of gang affiliation and inmates without it.

When turning to the four misconduct categories, disorder is notable by the absence of differences across gang status. Each of the three groups was represented at high levels of disorder-related write-ups, an incident that involves considerable discretion on the part of correctional officers. If gang members were subject to heightened surveillance and scrutiny, we would have anticipated greater differences in write-ups for minor disciplinary infractions like disorder, but that is not what we are observing.

Current gang members were involved in more violent, instrumental, and substance offenses than non-gang members while incarcerated. The scale of the y-axis makes it appear as if these differences are not large, but that is not the case. The standardized differences between these groups were 0.18, 0.17, and 0.24, respectively. However, we would have anticipated larger effect sizes for violence than the other categories, owing to the group processes of gangs. Nonetheless, these findings are on par with a lengthy body of research on gangs and, generally, the literature on prison misconduct. Former gang members were also involved in more substance offenses than non-gang members, which helped contribute to the overall difference in offense counts between former gang and non-gang members.

If we focus only on the last six months of incarceration, as reported in Figure 7.3, all the differences we have described above wash away. Indeed, not a single multivariate difference existed between current, former, and non-gang members for the five outcomes – all types, disorder, violence, instrumental, or substance possession or use. The similarity in levels of misconduct across gang statuses was pretty remarkable – all of the standardized differences fell below |0.10|. Of course, there were some bivariate differences in the proportion of current and former gang members recorded for violating rules against violence and disorder (as well as all misconduct types), but those differences appeared to be explained by factors other than gang membership. This is not to say that the factors that render the gang membership–misconduct link spurious were not endogenous to gang membership. Still, it appears as if shifting to six-month recall periods removed the variation we observed between gang and non-gang members when we examined entire incarceration spells. This could be due to the shorter recall period or the fact that inmates are all preparing for release. Should we expect similar findings when turning to our survey data?

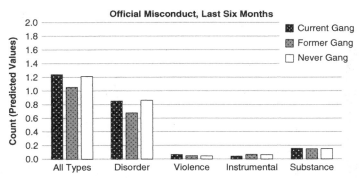

FIGURE 7.3 Predicted values of official disciplinary incident counts by gang status, last six months

Notes: None of the differences between the columns were statistically significant ("≠," $p < 0.05$) in the predicted value between gang status groups (c = current gang member, f = former gang member, n = never gang member) based on negative binomial regression models adjusting for the following covariates: age, age quadratic, black, Latino, race/ethnicity mixed/other, educational attainment, IQ, low self-control, code of the street, convict code, correctional officer legitimacy, correctional officer procedural justice, self-esteem, peer support, religiosity, prior arrests, years of incarceration, restrictive housing, and other non-general population custody level.

## Self-Reported Misconduct and Victimization

Figure 7.4 shows that both current and former gang members reported higher levels of misconduct and victimization over the course of their incarceration. These differences were large in magnitude, especially for all forms and violent forms of misconduct ($d > 0.57$) and victimization ($d > 0.38$). There were also differences across gang status in instrumental forms of misconduct and victimization, but they were less pronounced. Since survey data largely mirror the findings of official data, it provides us with greater confidence to conclude that the patterns of misconduct and victimization during incarceration spells diverge sharply between gang and non-gang inmates.

Unlike what we observed in the official data, the results presented in Figure 7.5 indicate that shifting to six-month recall periods does not drastically change the relationship between gang status and all forms of misconduct, with one major exception. For former gang members, levels of misconduct and victimization are comparable to non-gang rather than current gang members. The great divide in misconduct is no longer whether or not someone has a history as a gang member, but instead whether or not someone was an *active* gang member. This is exactly what we would expect since former gang members are less likely to be subject to the group processes of the gang. It is also notable that there were no statistically significant differences in victimization across gang status. Whereas the relationship between gang membership and

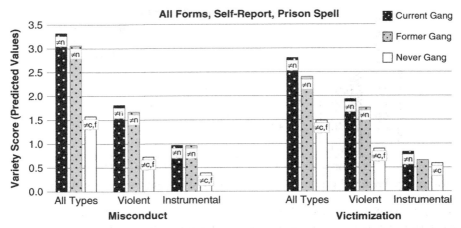

FIGURE 7.4 Predicted values of all types, violent, and instrumental misconduct and victimization by gang status, prison spell
Notes: Column labels indicate statistically significant differences ("≠," $p < 0.05$) in the predicted value between gang status groups (c = current gang member, f = former gang member, n = never gang member) based on negative binomial regression models adjusting for the following covariates: age, age quadratic, black, Latino, race/ethnicity mixed/other, educational attainment, IQ, low self-control, code of the street, convict code, correctional officer legitimacy, correctional officer procedural justice, self-esteem, peer support, religiosity, prior arrests, years of incarceration, restrictive housing, and other non-general population custody level.

offending ranks among the strongest in criminological research, the gang membership–victimization link appears to be more susceptible to controls for confounding and mediating factors.

We expected *gang-related* misconduct and victimization to be the driving factor distinguishing current, former, and non-gang members. The evidence suggests that we were only partially correct. Whereas gang-related misconduct was substantially higher among current than former ($d = 0.88$) and non-gang ($d = 0.98$) members, there were still differences in the level of *non-gang-related* misconduct. It could be the case that gang membership emboldens inmates to offend with greater impunity regardless of whether the motivations are gang-related or otherwise. Former gang members, too, engaged in gang-related misconduct at rates that were statistically greater than non-gang members, although the differences were substantively minimal ($d = 0.11$). Former and non-gang members were statistically equivalent to one another in their levels of non-gang-related misconduct, which is what we would expect to find.

In terms of all forms of victimization, the right columns of Figure 7.5 show that the differences across gang status were more muted. As expected, current gang members experienced more gang-related victimization than non-gang members. However, these differences were not so great as to drive overall

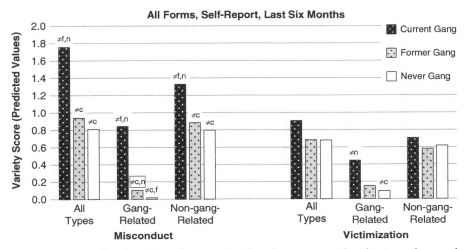

FIGURE 7.5 Predicted values of gang-related and non-gang-related misconduct and victimization by gang status, last six months

Notes: Column labels indicate statistically significant differences ("≠," $p < 0.05$) in the predicted value between gang status groups (c = current gang member, f = former gang member, n = never gang member) based on negative binomial regression models adjusting for the following covariates: age, age quadratic, black, Latino, race/ethnicity mixed/other, educational attainment, IQ, low self-control, code of the street, convict code, correctional officer legitimacy, correctional officer procedural justice, self-esteem, peer support, religiosity, prior arrests, years of incarceration, restrictive housing, and other non-general population custody level.

differences in victimization between these groups. Both former and non-gang members report experiencing gang-related victimization, although at a level much lower than non-gang-related victimization, which is what we would expect to observe.

Figure 7.6 shifts our focus to violent misconduct and victimization. Given that both theory and research have linked gang membership to violence, we would anticipate stronger differences across gang status that are comparable if not larger than all forms of misconduct. The results in Figure 7.6 are practically a mirror image of Figure 7.5. Current gang members engaged in more gang-related and non-gang-related forms of violence, while both former and non-gang members engaged in very little gang-related misconduct, and both experienced slightly more gang-related victimization. The biggest distinction when examining violence is that *gang-related* violence appears to be elevating overall differences in violent victimization between current and non-gang members. Indeed, there are statistically and substantively significant ($d = 0.25$) differences in overall violent victimization between current and non-gang members. Whereas gangs are viewed as providing a protective function to their members, that is perhaps only the case when the violence is unrelated to gangs.

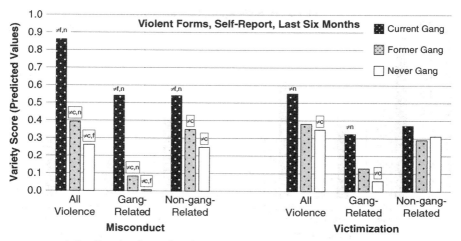

FIGURE 7.6 Predicted values of violent gang-related and non-gang-related misconduct and victimization by gang status, last six months
Notes: Column labels indicate statistically significant differences ("≠," $p < 0.05$) in the predicted value between gang status groups (c = current gang member, f = former gang member, n = never gang member) based on negative binomial regression models adjusting for the following covariates: age, age quadratic, black, Latino, race/ethnicity mixed/other, educational attainment, IQ, low self-control, code of the street, convict code, correctional officer legitimacy, correctional officer procedural justice, self-esteem, peer support, religiosity, prior arrests, years of incarceration, restrictive housing, and other non-general population custody level.

As we mentioned at the start of the chapter, the victim–offender overlap is one of the most established findings in the criminological literature. There is good reason to believe that this overlap should extend from the street to prison and be stronger among gang members than non-gang members, largely owing to the group processes we described earlier in the chapter. Figure 7.7 confirms this expectation. It contains the proportion of each gang status who fall into four different groups of victims and offenders: (1) victims *and* offenders, (2) only offenders, (3) only victims, and (4) neither victims nor offenders. These results adjust for correlates of the victim–offender overlap. Regardless of whether we focus on misconduct and victimization over the incarceration spell or the last six months, it is clear that active gang members are more likely to be victims *and* offenders than are former or non-gang members. There are three sets of comparisons to highlight: current to non-gang, current to former gang, and former to non-gang.

First, current gang members are more likely to fall in the victim–offender overlap category than are non-gang members for every outcome, and by a large margin. Over the entire incarceration period, there was a twenty percentage point difference for all misconduct and victimization and a twenty-eight

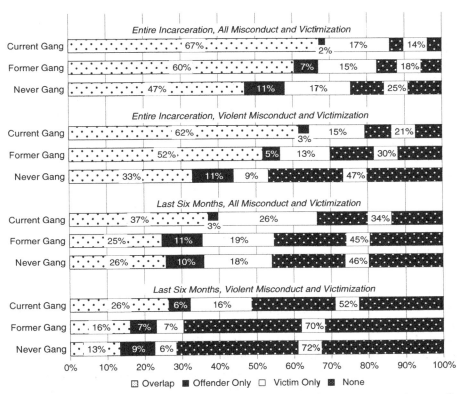

FIGURE 7.7 Predicted values of the victim–offender overlap by gang status, prison spell, and last six months

Notes: Predicted values for the victim–offender overlap are reported in the rows based on multinomial regression models adjusting for the following covariates: age, age quadratic, black, Latino, race/ethnicity mixed/other, educational attainment, IQ, low self-control, code of the street, convict code, correctional officer legitimacy, correctional officer procedural justice, self-esteem, peer support, religiosity, prior arrests, years of incarceration, restrictive housing, and other non-general population custody level.

percentage point difference for violence. Over the last six months, these differences shrink to eleven (all types) and thirteen (violence) percentage points but were still statistically distinct from zero.

Second, there were no statistically significant differences between current and former gang members over the entire incarceration period (although violence appears substantively greater). This changed when shifting to the last six months, as we would have anticipated. Current gang members were more likely to be victims and offenders than former gang members for all forms of misconduct and victimization (twelve percentage points) as well as violent forms of misconduct and victimization (ten percentage points).

Finally, and in the opposite direction of the current/former gang member results, former gang members were statistically similar to non-gang members in the victim–offender overlap over the last six months, but distinct when examining the entire incarceration period for all forms of misconduct and victimization (thirteen percentage points) and violent forms (nineteen percentage points). These results underscore that the victim–offender overlap not only exists in prison, but that it is stronger among gang members and it is sensitive to the contours of gang membership.

We have established that levels of misconduct and victimization are greater among gang members than non-gang members. Now we turn our attention to group-level variation across gangs. It is too strong an assumption to believe that the differences between gang and non-gang members hold for each of the gangs represented in the LoneStar Project. After all, as we demonstrated empirically in Chapter 5, not all gangs are alike in their group-level characteristics. There is good reason to expect that such variation also extends to misconduct and victimization in prison.

### Gang-Level Differences in Misconduct and Victimization

Are patterns of misconduct and victimization equal among gangs in prison? Across the thirty-one gangs with two or more members included in this analysis, we find that some engage in higher levels of misconduct than others, while some groups experience victimization at higher levels than others. To get a statistical sense of how much variation exists across gangs, we focus on a measure of dispersion: standard deviations. In doing so, we find substantial variation when focusing on official data (disorder SD = 9.9; violence = 1.9; instrumental = 1.3; substance = 3.5) and when focusing on survey data (all misconduct SD = 2.9; violent misconduct = 1.9; all victimization = 3.5; violent victimization = 2.6). This is pretty clear evidence that the patterns of misconduct and victimization are not equal across gangs, regardless of the source of data.

To get a visual sense of variation in misconduct and victimization across gangs, Figures 7.8 and 7.9 report the adjusted values (i.e., controlling for demographic, criminal justice, theoretical, and gang correlates) for each gang. This set of findings further confirms our suspicion that the collective behavior and experiences of gang members are not equivalent across gangs. Figure 7.8 shows that some gangs are recorded for having engaged in a larger number of official misconduct offenses than others. The most obvious difference is comparing the segregated Security Threat Groups (STGs) to the remaining three classes of gangs. Across the board, the total number of disciplinary reports for prison disorder and violence are statistically lower among the members of segregated STGs (mean = 3.8 offenses) than the three other groups (STG-non-segregated mean = 8.1; prison-oriented mean = 9.1; street-oriented mean = 9.8). With the exception of the Aryan Brotherhood, the segregated STGs were recorded for fewer than five disorder offenses; in

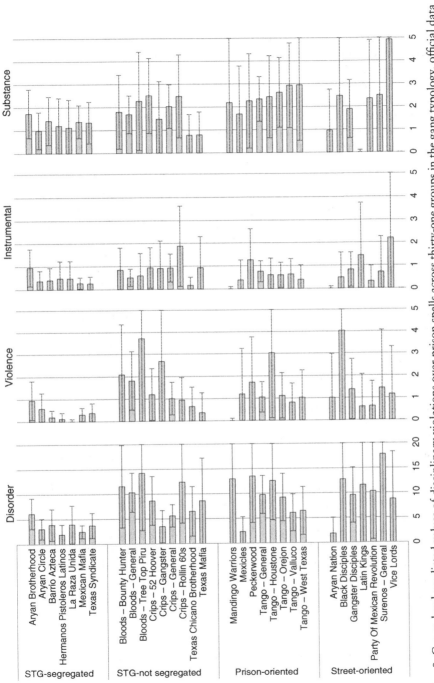

FIGURE 7.8 Group-level predicted values of disciplinary violations over prison spells across thirty-one groups in the gang typology, official data
Notes: Subsample of self-reported members of gangs with two or more respondents. Predicted values are reported based on negative binomial regression models adjusting for the following covariates: age, age quadratic, black, Latino, race/ethnicity mixed/other, educational attainment, IQ, low self-control, code of the street, convict code, correctional officer legitimacy, correctional officer procedural justice, self-esteem, peer support, religiosity, prior arrests, years of incarceration, restrictive housing, and other non-general population custody level.

contrast, very few of the remaining twenty-four gangs were recorded for fewer than five disorder offenses. A similar dynamic is observed when focusing on violent misconduct. The members of segregated STGs were recorded for violating half the number of violent misconduct offenses than the remaining gangs. We want to be clear that these results do not implicate solitary confinement as a mechanism of prevention for misconduct; the solitary confinement designation is the policy applied to the gang, not the gang member (i.e., only confirmed members are placed in solitary confinement).

When turning to instrumental and substance-related disciplinary infractions, the members of segregated STGs are no longer as clearly distinguishable from the other groups by their lower levels of misconduct. Instrumental violations were more of a mixed bag across the gangs and gang types, whereas substance-related violations were notably higher among prison-oriented gang members than members of both STG gangs. This finding could be reflective of the organizational structure of these gangs, which lack the more rigid imposition of discipline on their members. And, while the members of street-oriented gangs were recorded for disciplinary infractions at a rate similar to prison-oriented gang members, they were also statistically equivalent to the members of both STG types.

As reported in Figure 7.9, the story changes only slightly when examining misconduct and victimization using survey data. In terms of misconduct, it is the prison-oriented gang members who engage in the most types of misconduct, including violence. The remaining groups are statistically equivalent to one another. Of course, there are exceptions in each category. For example, La Raza Unida maintained the lowest levels of misconduct among the STG-segregated gangs, whereas the Hermanos de Pistoleros Latinos and Texas Syndicate were the highest. Misconduct for the latter gangs was more comparable to the prison-oriented gangs.

Consistent with the victim–offender overlap, prison-oriented gang members were also more likely to experience victimization than the members of STGs (and equivalent to the street-oriented gang members). On balance, more gangs engaged in higher levels of misconduct than experienced victimization. In fact, only seven gangs (Barrio Azteca, Crips – 52 Hoover, Texas Chicano Brotherhood, Tango – West Texas, Black Disciples, Party of the Mexican Revolution, and Vice Lords) reported more victimization than misconduct. However, when we shift to violent victimization, that number increases to sixteen gangs, and is more evenly distributed across the gangs in the typology.

CONCLUSION

The imprisonment of offenders does not stop the further perpetration of crime or susceptibility to victimization. Despite the typical respondent in the LoneStar Project having served around five years in prison before we interviewed him, the

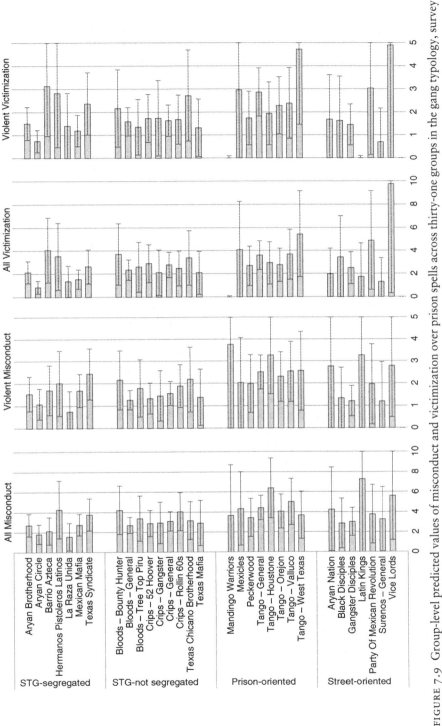

FIGURE 7.9 Group-level predicted values of misconduct and victimization over prison spells across thirty-one groups in the gang typology, survey data

Notes: Subsample of self-reported members of gangs with two or more respondents. Predicted values are reported based on negative binomial regression models adjusting for the following covariates: age, age quadratic, black, Latino, race/ethnicity mixed/other, educational attainment, IQ, low self-control, code of the street, convict code, correctional officer legitimacy, correctional officer procedural justice, self-esteem, peer support, religiosity, prior arrests, years of incarceration, restrictive housing, and other non-general population custody level.

*majority* of these men told us that they engaged in violent misconduct (54 percent) and had been victimized (51 percent) while incarcerated. Population representative surveys in the United States do not yield such high rates of violence perpetration or victimization over such a brief period in the life course. This suggests to us that something occurs in prison that places significant pressure on inmates to violate rules and increases susceptibility to personal violence. In our minds, that "something" is group process, the collective responsibility to respond to threats and the liability of increased targeting for victimization that comes with being a gang member.

Our focus was on a group of offenders who are rarely studied: imprisoned gang members. Based on our findings, we hold that any study of incarcerated individuals that excludes a measure of gang membership runs the risk of putting forth an incomplete explanation of misconduct and victimization. As we have demonstrated above, our results support such a conclusion. Here is a simple way to demonstrate this: if we were to exclude current and former gang members from the survey analysis, and only focus on non-gang members, the majority of the sample no longer reports having engaged in violence or being victimized while incarcerated. Indeed, just over one-third of non-gang members engaged in violence and were violently victimized during their incarceration spell. In contrast, adding the gang members back in pushes those proportions into the majority. This suggests to us that our parallelism hypothesis is largely true: the relationship between gang membership, misconduct, and victimization in prison largely mirrors what decades of criminological research reveal on the street.

In putting forth our group process perspective, we held that neither an individual or ecological perspective best accounts for the relationship between gang membership, misconduct, and victimization. Instead, it was our contention that there are group processes that lie at the core of our findings. Three pieces of evidence support this conclusion.

First, an amplification of involvement in misconduct and susceptibility to victimization occurs during active periods of gang membership. Non-gang and former gang members are not subject to the gang processes like current gang members. This is why we find that the patterns of misconduct and victimization for former gang members resemble those of current gang members when examining them over the incarceration spell but resemble non-gang members when shifting to six-month recall periods. Former gang members, and especially non-gang members, are not influenced by the same gang-related opportunity structures, collective actions, social status, and normative influences as current gang members. While the rules of gangs overlap with the rules of prisoners, each group responds to a different authority, a point made by Mitchell et al. (2017), which is further supported in Chapter 6. Just like offending and victimization covary with the contours of gang membership on the street, we find evidence that these contours are also quite important for explaining these outcomes in prison.

Second, it is the gang-related forms of misconduct and victimization that are driving up overall levels of these outcomes. Stated another way, even for current gang members, in the absence of gang-related activity, levels of misconduct and victimization among gang and non-gang members would be much more similar to one another. The functions of group processes are related to gang-related outcomes, not non-gang-related outcomes. Prison disturbances involving multiple gang members, particularly riots, are reflective of the collective behavior of the gang (Huff and Meyer 1997). The return of profits from the sale of contraband to the gang are the product of the opportunities and normative influences of the gang. If these motivations for collective action were eliminated, and group processes ceased to exist or shifted to prosocial orientations, the misconduct and victimization of gang members would not be much different from that of non-gang members.

The final empirical evidence that is relevant to the group process argument is that of the victim–offender overlap. The major theories of the overlap place an emphasis on individual predispositions to offend, vulnerability to victimization, subcultural orientations that shun legal in favor of vigilante justice, and the lifestyles and routine activities of offenders and victims (Berg 2012). Yet none of these explanations, nor any other factor we took into consideration, could fully explain why the victim–offender overlap is stronger among gang members. Our contention is that this difference is attributable to group processes. After all, gang violence is highly retaliatory, which means the triggerman of today is the dead man of tomorrow. Entitativity in gangs also means that when a member of Gang A is stabbed by a member of Gang B, the pool of targets in Gang B expands to the entire group; it also means that the pool of offenders in Gang A expands beyond the victim, owing to the obligation to retaliate. The diffusion of responsibility increases offending but also diffuses liability, and thus vulnerability to victimization among gang members. The rivalry network of gangs in Texas prisons suggests that at any given time there is a large pool of inmates at odds with one another awaiting the activation of group processes facilitative of misconduct and victimization.

We found that it is too strong an assumption to expect that these group processes are equally consequential across gangs. In fact, there was wide variation across gangs in misconduct and victimization at the group level. Some gangs were more likely to be perpetrators of violence, while others were more likely to be victims. Of course, the story is not as clear as it was in Chapter 5. Instead, we tend to find that the members of segregated STGs engaged in the least amount of official misconduct, while the prison-oriented gangs engaged in the most misconduct using a survey measure. There were exceptions to this, both within and between the different categories of the gang typology. But this is precisely what we would expect to find, given that gang-related activities ebb and flow, often in tandem with conflict with a rival gang.

In conclusion, there is a considerable amount of misconduct and victimization that occurs behind bars, but gang members are disproportionately involved in and experience both. Our argument that the group processes of gangs is a sound theory for explaining this dynamic finds support in the temporal overlap between active periods of gang membership and the outcomes (offending and victimization). Gang-related activity accounts for the bulk of the overall differences in these outcomes, as well as the statistically and substantively significant relationship between gang membership and the outcomes net of leading alternative explanations. Prison gang membership is a leading explanation for misconduct and victimization, and ignoring this fact misrepresents our understanding of their occurrence in prison.

# 8

# Joining and Avoiding Gangs in Prison

Life is a series of transitions across institutions, relationships, and roles. People age, develop new identities, assume new roles, and change associates, friends, and even family. Joining a gang is one of the critical transitions that may occur in the life course. Although group processes and structures are both central to this book, up to this point we have paid more empirical attention to the latter. We have compared the members of gangs to inmates who were not affiliated with gangs. In addition, we examined the form and function of the different structures of gangs behind bars, including their role in the governance of prisons as well as misconduct and victimization. In this chapter, we focus on a crucial aspect of group process: joining a gang. If transitions into new identities, roles, and statuses are consequential for the life course, we ought to learn about how such transitions unfold, especially if they occur in places like prisons that are tasked with the job of rehabilitation. Understanding these transitions addresses another important goal of this book. Joining is a key feature of understanding groups, perhaps as important as understanding their origins. After all, if a group is to be sustained it must have a means of generating new membership. This is true of nuns in a convent, physicians in a medical practice, set designers in Hollywood, and, yes, prison gangs. Gangs cannot compete for the informal control of institutions if they are unable to replenish their ranks.

Gang membership in prison may have its locus of origin on the street or in the institution, leading to four possible patterns of involvement. First, there is the *street importation* pattern. Clearly, many individuals sent to prison have a gang affiliation before entering the prison system that they bring with them (Jacobs 1974). This pattern is consistent with the classic importation perspective on the origins of prison social organization, where biography, predispositions, and cultural capital do not suddenly bend or break to the expectations and rhythms of the prison (i.e., Irwin and Cressey 1962). Such individuals may find that their hometown affiliations and rivalries are subsumed in the larger gang structure of the institution (Lopez-Aguado 2018; Skarbek 2014). Those who import their gang membership from the street can affect communication between the prison and the street, particularly as such communication may involve the movement of contraband or cash, as well as information about the use of violence against rivals or about exercising discipline against members, as we saw in prior chapters.

Second, there is the *prison origination* pattern. Whereas the socialization to gangs for the street importation group occurs outside of prison, such processes occur inside of prison for this group. These are individuals who were not affiliated with a gang on the street but decided to become gang members once in prison. This pattern is consistent with the classic deprivation perspective (Clemmer 1940), where transitions into gangs are thought to be a response to the deprivations faced in prison. Such deprivations may include threats to personal safety, lack of personal relationships, loss of personal identity, and access to alcohol, drugs, or other contraband. Joining in prison may represent a coping mechanism for dealing with the challenges of life in prison (Reid and Listwan 2018). Although the onset of gang membership is thought to have its origins in adolescence, a national study revealed that a large proportion of gang members do not join a gang until adulthood (Pyrooz 2014). Could this be a consequence of imprisonment?

There are two additional patterns of gang involvement, both of which we think of as prison *gang avoiders*. The street-only gang avoidance pattern refers to a group of gang members who initiate, but also contain, their involvement in gangs to the street. These individuals either dropped out of gangs well before becoming incarcerated or decided upon becoming incarcerated that they no longer wish to have a gang affiliation, perhaps in the belief that serving their time can be done most expeditiously by avoiding the influences on criminal involvement brought about by gangs. The final pattern represents complete gang avoidance: these are individuals who were not street gang members and choose not to affiliate in prison, thus avoiding gang membership in both contexts. We believe that the third and fourth groups present interesting insights for policy and programmatic efforts, an issue we pursue later in the book.

This chapter examines both joining and avoiding gangs in prison. We focus on a series of questions that stem from the aforementioned patterns of involvement in a representative sample of inmates: (1) How common are these patterns? (2) Why and how do people join gangs? (3) Why and how do people avoid gangs? (4) What differentiates – demographics, environment, health, social connections, attitudes and beliefs, and criminal justice system involvement – people for whom the origins of gang membership are found on the street or in prison? We believe that the dynamics of joining a gang in prison differ from joining a gang on the street. Likewise, we believe that gang avoidance strategies in prison, where gang members occupy a large and overt proportion of inmates, also diverge from the street, where movement is freer and gangs are less prominent (e.g., Carson and Esbensen 2017). Although we are interested in the group process of entry, we would be remiss to ignore how group structure conditions such outcomes. This is why we examine the dynamics of gang joining across the four-part typology of gangs: Security Threat Group (STG)-segregated, STG-non-segregated, prison-oriented, and street-oriented gangs. With over 200,000 gang members in US prisons, our goal is to learn about the origins of membership, as well as the strategies employed by the majority of inmates to avoid involvement in gangs.

## UNDERSTANDING GANG JOINING AND AVOIDING

The dynamics of gang joining have been a major focus of research and policy (Decker and Van Winkle 1996; Esbensen et al. 2010; Howell and Griffiths 2015; Simon, Ritter, and Mahendra 2013). Learning how and why people join gangs reveals a lot about the group processes of gangs, a topic of considerable interest to researchers. This research, in turn, is used to inform programmatic efforts to prevent gang membership. James Densley (2015, 2018) provides two comprehensive reviews of the issue, emphasizing the motivations and methods of joining.

In terms of motivations, Densley's review of gang joining points to the common distinction between "pushes" and "pulls" into the gang. Pushes represent coercive negative forces such as pressure, violence, or deprivation for gang joining. Indeed, fear of violence is a commonly voiced motive for gang joining. Pulls, on the other hand, represent more positive attractions to the gang, such as the chance to make money, form friendship bonds, or lead "the gang life." It is not clear how, if at all, these motives change among prison inmates, particularly those who enter confinement with a history of gang affiliation. However, the processes represented by pushes and pulls take place in the larger context of gangs in the community. In locations where gangs are scarce, the pressures and opportunities to join gangs are considerably lower than in locations rife with gangs that actively recruit members. As state prisons draw from a wide range of diverse locations (especially in a state like Texas), the opportunities to join a gang before being sent to prison will be highly variable. If gangs do not exist in the activity spaces of people, joining a gang is simply "off the table," owing to the opportunity structure. Or, to paraphrase Densley (2015): no gang, no gang member. Very few people are the founding members of a gang.

Similarly, the methods of joining a street gang have received considerable attention in the literature. Densley (2018) distinguishes between "formal" and "informal" processes. The former includes more ceremonial aspects to join than do the latter, often including initiation rites in which the prospective gang member must prove their toughness or loyalty to the gang. Being "beaten in" to a gang is perhaps the most-discussed method of joining when gang members are interviewed about how they joined, which Descormiers and Corrado (2016) termed "the ego violent event." A beating is endured to demonstrate a toughness that may be needed as a gang member. But, it is not uncommon for gang members to report that they were required to commit a crime or "go on a mission" to demonstrate their loyalty to the gang (see Bolden 2013). This may mean engaging in a resource-generating crime such as drug sales or robbery, but more often includes committing an act of violence against a rival gang member. Many gang members talk about being "blessed in," a non-violent method of joining. This may be the privilege afforded an individual with an older sibling or parent in the gang, who grew up in the neighborhood where the gang got its start, or who has some affiliational tie to leadership in the gang. The symbolic need of gangs to communicate their toughness and willingness to engage in violence leads to the stories about being beaten in or going on a mission as part of the method of joining a gang. But, on the street, such violence is exaggerated as part of the swagger that gang membership requires.

Gang avoidance is another process that we believe is important to understand, although it has received less scrutiny from researchers. Indeed, most studies are concerned with why and how people join gangs, not the motives and methods for avoiding them. But gang avoidance takes on added significance because studies reveal that most youth do not join gangs. This is true even in the most high-crime, disadvantaged, and gang-active neighborhoods, as evidenced in research in Rochester, New York (Thornberry et al. 2003) and Seattle, Washington (Hill et al. 1999). In these environments, the pressures to join a gang are considerable, yet most youth are able to resist. How do they do this? Dena Carson and Finn-Aage Esbensen (2017) reported how youth negotiate gang-active spaces in the school context. Although all the youth in their study were involved in gangs, it was common – especially for former and suspected gang members – to actively avoid gangs. They would distance themselves physically and socially from gang members, avoiding involvement in the fights, disruptions, and incivilities brought about by gangs. In many ways, Carson and Esbensen described a delimited school context of two worlds, one occupied by gang youth and a second occupied by non-gang youth. This bears a striking resemblance to our findings on prisons, gangs, and governance from Chapter 6 where prison gang control was exercised primarily over other gang members. At the same time, understanding *why* youth do not want to involve themselves in gangs (despite the opportunity) is an area in which we know very little. Learning about the characteristics, motivations, and methods for avoidance are important for both theoretical and policy reasons.

## PRIOR RESEARCH ON JOINING AND AVOIDING GANGS IN PRISON

But what does the above research tell us about joining a gang in prison, particularly adult prisons? Most of the research has focused exclusively on gang joining on the street, not prisons, much less institutions such as county jails and juvenile facilities. Our argument is that this is driven primarily by the reasons we discussed in Chapter 1 (e.g., Fong and Buentello 1991), although there is more to it than simply blaming "lack of data." Indeed, we liken the "blinders" applied to gang joining in prison to what Frank Cullen (2011) observed in his Edwin Sutherland address to the American Society of Criminology, where the field is "adolescence limited" in its focus on criminal behavior. Gang research is also adolescence limited. Longitudinal studies stop asking questions about gang membership in adulthood. Adult samples of gang members are rare or confined to ethnographic observation. More importantly, there is the view that the origins of gang membership are found in adolescence, not adulthood (e.g., Pyrooz 2014), and that incarceration is a consequence, not a cause, of gang membership.

Although there are several studies that allude to the gang-joining patterns we outlined above in institutional settings (e.g., Maxson et al. 2012; Pyrooz, Gartner, and Smith 2017; Stone 1999), only Narag and Lee (2018) focused exclusively on adult institutions. These works underscored that violence is a prominent feature of gang life behind bars, which in turn has implications for the motives and methods of joining a gang in institutional settings, not unlike what is emphasized in research on gang joining on the street. Narag and Lee, based on their research in the Philippines, held that all jail inmates experienced the strains of imprisonment. The difference for individuals who joined *pangkats*, or Filipino jail gangs, was that they maintained less social support from conventional sources. Gangs, then, provided these individuals the instrumental and social supports they were lacking in jail. These included feelings of safety, belonging and identity, and resources such as material goods. In contrast, the non-gang inmates, or *querna*, reported neither the pushes nor the pulls that made *pangkat* appealing.

Narag and Lee (2018) also outlined how *querna* inmates viewed the *pangkat* in Philippine jails, shedding light on avoidance strategies. These inmates reported that the *pangkats* were too risky, too childish, and reflected a tribe mentality. Instead, *querna* inmates wanted independence in their identity and to avoid the obligations that come with gang involvement. They also felt that *querna* inmates provided the instrumental and social supports comparable to gangs without the negative influences of gangs. Although within the juvenile system, Reid and Listwan's (2018) research on violence avoidance in California also aligns nicely with our interest in gang avoidance. They found both passive and active forms of avoidance, the former involving delimitation (e.g., head down, keeping to self) comparable to the work of Carson and Esbensen (2017), while the latter involved either acting aggressively by maintaining a tough posture or carefully managing risk through interactions with gang members. Gang members were overrepresented in the aggressive group, involving themselves in fights as a preemptive strategy to avoid violence at later points in time by building a reputation.

It is one thing to extrapolate from life in a street gang to prison gang life and quite another to have the data to address important questions such as the motives and methods for gang joining and avoidance. There is good reason to believe that joining a gang in prison differs from joining on the street. First, and most importantly, the gangs are different, as we have demonstrated in Chapter 5. The STG-segregated gangs in Texas prisons are more organized and structured than other gangs. Of course, there are other options for gang joining, such as the prison-oriented or STG-non-segregated gangs. Second, and regardless of the gang joined, the prison environment is different. Prisons constrain behaviors in ways that are unlike the street. Owing to this, gang joining in prison may entail more elaborate entrance practices that prospects may feel obligated to follow or run this risk of serious consequences. Anonymity is scarce in prison, as is the ability to transfer to different facilities. Lastly, the people in prisons are different, including the gang members, who maintain extensive criminal and gang careers. Prison is part of the allure of gangs (Venkatesh and Levitt 2000), and those who are incarcerated are viewed differently owing to their time in prison. This is the reason that gang members claim that the "real gangbanging is in prison" (Decker and Pyrooz 2015). If the streets are primary education, prison is higher education. Hence, the process for joining a gang may be different. And, if prison is indeed different, then we would also expect that the gang avoidance strategies – both the motives and methods – also diverge from what is reported on the street.

## METHODS TO LEARN ABOUT JOINING AND AVOIDING GANGS

To learn about how and why people join and avoid gangs in prison and on the street, we asked our 802 gang and non-gang respondents a series of closed- and open-ended questions about this topic. We began by asking about gang joining. All of our respondents were asked: "Have you ever been in a street or a prison gang?" We then aimed to reconstruct key transitions in the life course that form the basis for learning about the relationship between imprisonment and gang joining. First, respondents were asked whether they were in a gang while they were incarcerated or while they were on the street. Second, we asked if the respondent was incarcerated at the time they joined the gang. The answers to these questions allowed us to determine whether the origins of their gang membership are found on the street or in prison, and whether gang membership is imported into prison or exported out of prison. We also asked respondents to report the age at which they joined a gang (or the month-year or season for those who had difficulty recalling). Since 11 percent of our gang subsample had joined more than one gang over their lifetime, this information was useful for mapping age of onset to the patterns of prison admissions and releases. Overall, these measures allowed us to generate three main pathways: (1) street-only gang members, (2) street-to-prison importation gang members, and (3) prison origination gang members.

### Measuring the Motives and Methods for Joining Gangs

Next, we learned about the motivations for gang joining by asking anyone who had self-identified as having a history of gang membership: "What was the main reason why you joined this gang?" It would have been more straightforward to recycle response categories from an established body of findings on why people join street gangs. Yet, we know very little about why people join gangs in prison. This is why we decided to make this an open-ended response, which proved to be a good decision. Based on consensus coding of qualitative responses, we identified new themes as well as variants on existing themes about joining gangs on the street and in prison. We organize these themes into a push/pull framework, where pushes refer to factors external to the gang and pulls refer to factors internal to the gang. The themes include the following:

- Adjustment/guidance (push): personal help and coping with challenging circumstances, seeking direction and guidance;
- Normative influence (push): normative views on becoming a gang member based on imprisonment, family, friends, and neighborhood influences;
- Belonging (pull): companionship and friendship found in gangs, loyalty and trust, or sense of family;
- Economic (pull): gang membership as a career, access to drugs for sales or use, or monetary and contraband returns to the gang membership;
- Ideological (pull): alignment of personal beliefs and norms with the gang, including race, shared rivals, religiosity, and purpose;
- Protection (pull): the gang as an avenue to ensure personal safety, familial safety, or racial safety;
- Status (pull): genuine attraction to gang lifestyle or valued the status and respect associated with life in the gang.

Turning to methods of joining, our interest in the selection process shifts to *how* someone joined a gang. Similar to the question of motivations, we relied upon an open-ended question to learn about methods for gang joining: "What did you have to do to join this gang?" Consensus coding of the qualitative data revealed several important themes, which we organize into active/passive forms of entry. Active forms involve the engagement in activities or tasks that aim to evaluate the "drive" and "heart" and "loyalty" of a gang prospect. Passive forms of entry do not entail ceremony or extreme acts; people simply become members. The following were the forms of entry:

- Attacked rivals/exes (active): targeted rival or ex-gang members with violence;
- Jumped in (active): withstood a physical beating from members of the gang the prospect sought to join;
- Engaged in other violent crime (active): hurt unspecified people to advance the interests of the gang;
- Engaged in other non-violent crime (active): engaged in non-violent criminal activity to advance the interests of the gang;
- Prospected (active): underwent a period of observation to demonstrate character and heart, educated about gang rules and regulations, made financial

commitments to the gang, or was responsible for maintaining "books" or gang paraphernalia;

- Gang ties (passive): connections to gang leaders, familial gang members, or neighborhood gang association;
- Nothing (passive): entry did not require active methods or social connections to bypass active methods.


## Measuring the Correlates of Gang-Joining Patterns

Are the people who join gangs on the street different from the people who join gangs in prison? And, are the people who import their gang membership from the street to the prison similar to those who leave their affiliations on the street or who initiate affiliation in prison? These are the questions we address among the 441 lifetime gang members in our sample. There are good reasons to believe that these three groups of gang members differ along a number of dimensions, including the following domains and items, which we first introduced in Chapter 4:

- Demographic characteristics include age in years, race and ethnicity (black, Latino, and white), relationship status (married, non-marriage relationship), father, military veteran, educational attainment in years, IQ, and low self-control.
- Environment characteristics include informal social control (pre-prison residence), prison informal social control, pre-prison neighborhood as a good place to live, whether there were gangs in pre-prison neighborhood, disorder in prison, and unstructured routines in prison.
- Health characteristics include stress, self-rated health, BMI, exposure to violence in prison, self-esteem, and projected age of death.
- Social connections includes embeddedness in gangs, social distance with correctional officers, family and friend social support, and criminal peers.
- Attitudes and beliefs captures a variety of worldviews and antisocial outlooks, including the code of the street, the convict code, legitimacy of correctional officers, procedural justice during imprisonment, cultural and social ethnic identification, and spirituality/religiosity.
- Criminal justice system involvement, measures based on Texas prison or public safety data, includes age at first arrest, number of arrests, number of prison spells, number of years imprisoned, and whether the respondent was most recently convicted and sentenced for a violent offense.
- Gang-related includes the age at first joining a gang, whether the respondent is a current or former gang member, the number of years since leaving a gang (former gang members only), the number of years in a gang, and the type of gang – from our four-part typology – of which the respondent was most recently a member.

## Measuring the Motives and Methods for Avoiding Gangs

Whereas the focus in the questions above is on joining a gang, we flip this around and ask equally important questions: Why did they *not* join? And, perhaps more importantly, how did they *not* get involved in (i.e., avoid) gangs in either setting? If we are to promote gang prevention in prison (and on the street), we can learn as much from those who avoid gangs as we can from those who join them. We believe that this is a novel yet important approach to the study of gangs with relevance for other groups involved in crime.

All of the respondents who did not self-identify as having a history of gang membership on the street were asked questions about *street* gang avoidance, while respondents who responded the same about prison were asked questions about *prison* gang avoidance. First, we were interested in knowing: "Did you ever consider joining a street/prison gang?" A "no" response would then elicit an open-ended question: "Why not?" These responses were coded to identify key emergent themes, which include the following:

- See no benefits: gang membership is a waste of time, there is no use in it, nothing comes out of it, or no real reason to join;
- Independent: leader not a follower, do not want to be told what to do, or life in the gang is too consuming or requires too much;
- Disinterested: not into gangs, gangs are not my thing, or not interested in joining;
- Gangs are trouble: put off by the violence and hurting people, gangs only do bad rather than good, leads to more prison time or denial of parole, or want to avoid unlawful behavior;
- Values/politics: do not share beliefs in racial supremacy, despise the values of gangs, or view gangs as ideologically impure;
- Gangs are childish/cowardly: gangs are for stupid, weak, or immature people;
- No opportunity: there were not gangs in my location (prison unit, neighborhood, or city) or never approached about getting involved in a gang;
- Too busy: did not have the time to join, busy with job, school, religious, or athletic activities;
- Already in a gang: maintained allegiance to my street gang when incarcerated.

Second, we were interested in knowing: "How did you avoid getting involved with a gang on the street/prison?" Similar to motives, the question of methods was also open-ended, allowing us to gather rich information about avoidance strategies, which include the following:

- Declined invitation: approached about joining, but declined on the grounds of independence, future goals, or disinterest;
- Kept my head down: stayed away from gangs, did not associate with gang members, or minded my own business;

- No gangs to join: there were no gangs in my neighborhood or prison unit;
- Too busy (non-religious): too involved in education, programs, jobs, school, or athletics to join;
- Too busy (religious): too involved in religious activities to join a gang;
- Family/friend guidance: family members and/or friends steered me away from gangs;
- Nothing (not recruited): was not approached about joining or maintained characteristics (e.g., gay, sex offender) that precluded affiliation;
- Nothing (reputation): carried self in a manner that precluded gang membership or maintained a reputation that avoided disrespect from other inmates or gangs;
- Fighting: fought with the gangs to avoid their recruitment or harassment.

Finally, we were interested in understanding the personal contact that non-gang respondents had with gangs either in prison or on the street. There is some debate about whether "recruitment" is truly a reality among street gangs. Whereas risk factor and motivations research views gang entry as a one-way street, that is, the deficits and agency of only the prospective gang member are at work, more theoretical and qualitative research views gang entry as a two-way street, where both the prospective gang member *and* the interests and strategies of the gang are at work. We therefore asked: "Did a street/prison gang ever try to recruit you?" If recruitment is a valid concept for understanding gang joining, we would expect to observe it in an environment where groups maintain the need to replenish their ranks through competing for prospective members. Whereas recruiting could be thought of as a "harder" form of contact, we were also interested in a "softer" form of contact, one that is relevant to avoidance specifically but also to the contribution of gangs to the social order of prisons generally: "At prison admission, did gang members ask you if you were affiliated with a gang?" The extent to which non-gang inmates endorse such practices reveals that gangs are integrally involved in vetting the credentials of inmates in prison.

## Analytic Plan

Our plan of analysis in this chapter has four parts. First, we report on the patterning of gang onset in relation to imprisonment. Based on self-reports of the location and age of entry into gangs, we examine the extent to which gang membership originates on the street or in prison, as well as whether it migrates from the former setting to the latter. Weighted and unweighted values are reported to provide a sense of the typical pathways into gangs in relation to admission into prison, based on our representative sample. We also highlight examples of gang onset and prison admission, both for one-gang or multiple-gang members. This provides us with a good starting point for understanding how and why people join and avoid gangs on the street or in prison.

Second, we shift our focus to the methods and motives for joining gangs. Based on our consensus coding of the qualitative data, we report the prevalence of identifying the aforementioned responses provided regarding the methods and motives for joining a gang. We distinguish these outcomes across multiple strata: (1) location of where someone left a gang, whether it was on the street or in prison, and (2) the four-part gang typology, which includes STG-segregation, STG-no-segregation, prison-oriented, and street-oriented gangs. Representative quotes based on our thematic analysis are provided for the core themes that emerged in our data, including themes that distinguished gang joining across key stratifications.

The third portion of our analysis focuses on distinguishing the three core patterns of gang onset in relation to imprisonment: (1) street-only gang members, (2) street-to-prison importation gang members, and (3) prison origination gang members. We quantitatively compare these three groups across demographic, environmental, health, social connections, attitudes and beliefs, criminal justice system, and gang-related domains.

Finally, our attention turns to the people who were able to avoid gangs on the street or in prison. Similar to the methods and motives analysis for joining gangs, we report the prevalences for the qualitative themes along with representative quotes of the associated themes that emerged for gang avoidance based on our thematic analysis.

## FINDINGS ON JOINING AND AVOIDING GANGS

### The Patterns of Gang Onset and Imprisonment

Figure 8.1 details whether the location of initial entry into gangs occurred on the street or in prison. Recall that 441 respondents self-identified as having been a gang member in their lifetime, and we were able to gather valid data on entry for all but one of these individuals. We find that gang membership is more likely to have its origins on the street than in prison, at least among a sample of prison inmates. A total of 18 percent of respondents indicated that they had been in a gang before becoming incarcerated. At the time of our pre-release (baseline) interview, 30 percent of our sample had a history of gang membership. In other words, a large number of inmates (12 percent) joined a gang for the first time in their lives while in prison. Gang membership, thus, is one of the collateral consequences of incarceration (Hagan and Dinovitzer 1999), one that could have lasting effects. While this finding is consistent with the popular view of prison, where inmates must join a gang to "survive" in prison, it is inconsistent with the broader literature on gang "career" patterns that anchor the onset of gang membership to adolescence. It is equally important to note that many inmates avoid gang membership altogether, whether on the street or in prison.

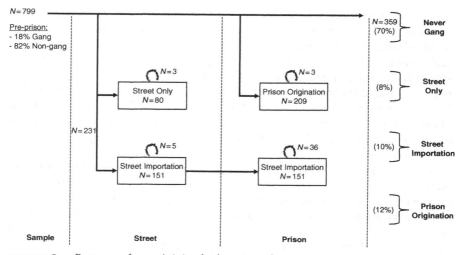

FIGURE 8.1 Patterns of gang joining by location of entry
Notes: Prevalences are weighted to correct for sampling; frequencies are unweighted. Circular arrows refer to the number of respondents in the associated box who joined a new gang.

Before we can reach any conclusion about the validity of importation and deprivation models, it is necessary to distinguish between individuals who did and did not continue their affiliations with gangs in prison. After all, one of the established findings in longitudinal street gang research is that gang membership is impermanent and typically lasts for only a few years. There are good reasons to argue for both importation and deprivation patterns of gang membership in prison.

About two-thirds of street onset gang members imported their affiliation or transitioned to a new affiliation in prison (although the weighted prevalences indicated greater parity). Here are two examples:

• A 51-year-old respondent in our sample joined a gang on the street at age 16, and despite having been in the custody of the Texas Department of Criminal Justice (TDCJ) for the last twenty-six years, is still an active Crips gang member.
• A 41-year-old former member of the Aryan Brotherhood, who has been in prison for the last sixteen years, indicated that he joined the gang on the street at age 18, only to leave in prison just three years ago.

Examples like this abound in our data. Part of the reason it makes sense to observe such high rates of importation has to do with prison adjustment. Around 65 percent of the 151 respondents who imported their gang affiliation into prison told us that being a gang member made the adjustment to prison easier. As the examples above illustrate, transitions across the life course – from adolescence to middle age – produce changes in the pattern of gang membership as well. Abandoning such affiliations could be physically and socially costly. Imagine rejecting the Crips or Aryan Brotherhood (both STGs) in prison?

Other respondents transitioned from a street to a prison gang upon becoming incarcerated. There were more gang-to-gang transitions among the street importation group than any other; over 75 percent of the transitions for the forty-seven multi-gang joiners occurred among this group in prison. For example, one of our respondents – a 44-year-old Latino male – has spent over half of his life in prison, entering into TDCJ custody at age 20. He was first a member of the Latin Kings, joining at age 14. He dropped out of the Latin Kings when he went to prison and transitioned into the Mexican Mafia, with whom he was affiliated for the next seventeen years. Examples like this, although not the norm, are common enough in our data to require attention.

Still, when we focus only on the inmates who were gang-active in prison, the street gang importation group was actually in the minority. Gang membership is more likely to originate in prison (12 percent) than on the street (10 percent), at least among those who were gang members in prison. Indeed, we find that prison origination accounts for about 55 percent of gang membership in prison. Examples of this pattern of gang onset cut across our data:

- a 42-year-old member of Barrio Azteca, who has been in prison for the last twenty-five years, joined the gang at age 20, only a few years after prison admission;
- a 55-year-old former gang member has spent the last twenty years in prison, and until he left the gang two years ago, eighteen of them have been with Tango Valluco;
- a 27-year-old former member of the Peckerwoods joined the gang at age 22 when he entered prison, only to leave last year in preparation for release.

As we will demonstrate shortly, we observe large demographic differences between street importation and prison origination gang members. But, before we can examine this issue, it is first necessary to learn about how and why people join gangs and whether there are differences in gang joining on the street, in prison, and across different types of gangs.

## Motivations for Joining Gangs

Why would people want to join a group that exploits their members, hurts people, and has lasting and cascading negative consequences over the life course? Figure 8.2 contains the motivations for joining a gang based on our consensus coding of open-ended responses for the 441 lifetime gang members in our sample, partitioned by the six comparative groups.

Normative influence was the leading motivation for joining a gang. We referred to this as a push factor because it represents environmental normative

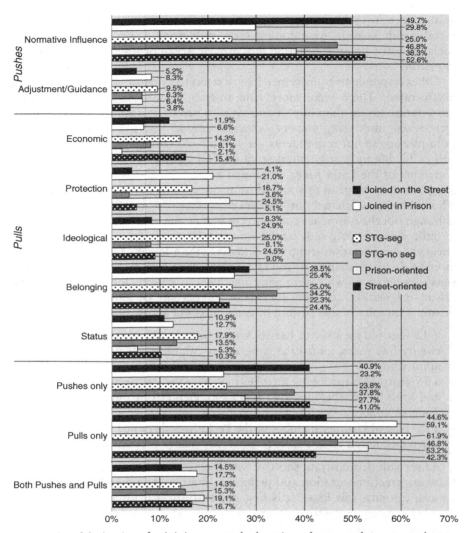

FIGURE 8.2 Motivations for joining a gang by location of entry and group typology

pressures – whether in the neighborhood, prison, or family – to become involved with a gang, which about 40 percent of our gang subsample identified as the main reason for their involvement. This is reflected in the quote from a respondent who transitioned to the Tangos from the Surenos in prison:

All of the street gangs in Dallas normally fight in Dallas, but they come together, West, North, South, and East Dallas, in prison you all unite. I joined them because all of my friends joined them and because you cannot run with a street gang in prison.

Notice the normative subtleties in this line of reasoning, which include peer, city, and prison affiliations. The ability to set aside street beefs in order to gain power in numbers is the sign of groups who have control over their members, although the Tangos are perhaps the most decentralized and horizontally structured gang in the Texas prison system.

The role of peer associations was especially strong among prison gang members, and there is a reason that social learning theory occupies a central place in research on gangs (Winfree and Freng 2015). This former member of the Mexican Mafia, who is now old enough to qualify for social security benefits, joined when the "war years" broke out in Texas prisons:

Because they were my friends at that time. It was predominantly from San Antonio, I connected with them, so I knew them. There was a war against TS [Texas Syndicate] and I joined to help my friends.

Yet, normative influences seemed to matter more among street-oriented gang members and for joining gangs on the street than in prison. Indeed, half of the respondents who joined gangs on the street identified normative influences compared to only 30 percent of respondents who joined gangs in prison. Take for instance the following quotes from respective members of the Bloods and Crips:

Because it was really all I seen growing up, family members, friends, uncles. It is what I thought you were supposed to do.

The environment. Just being around it all the time. My oldest sister was a Crip and being around other Crips you just kind of naturally join.

Both of these respondents joined gangs before age 15, a period where such influences are especially strong and serve as models for behavior, identity, and status. The role of normative influence for members of non-segregated STGs, such as Bloods and Crips, was much greater than for members of segregated STGs, who were the least likely to offer up such explanations.

The next most common motivation for gang joining, found among 27 percent of the subsample, was seeking the sense of belonging that is found in gangs. This response was endorsed at the same rate statistically across all six of the comparative groups, although the "type" of belonging varied across groups. Belonging often cut across other categories, although this former member of the Aryan Brotherhood was uniquely classified in this category:

I was raised a military brat and I missed the chance to join the Marines because I caught a case [was arrested for a crime and charged]. So when I came to TDCJ, the AB [Aryan Brotherhood] offered me the brotherhood and camaraderie that I was missing [by not being in the military].

Such a case is notable, given that incarceration may have been the difference between serving in the military and serving in one of the most notorious prison gangs in the country.

Belonging is such a strong pull for many prospective members because of the companionship that gangs offer. Even in a sample of prisoners, the backgrounds of gang members are marked by greater socioeconomic disadvantage and marginalization than non-gang members, which heightens the value of and need for comradery. This is evident in quotes from the respective members of the 52 Hoover Crips and Gangster Disciples, both of whom joined their gangs in their early teen years:

That's where I got the love from. I was always around it. It felt like, you know, you grow up with people, all of my homeboys, as we got older we all got down with the same thing. It was my time, everyone looked at me, saying it was my time to join.

Just what was in the neighborhood. It was the sense of belonging, what I didn't get at home. Like if you grow up with a bunch of brothers or sisters you're close to versus you grow up without it. You envy others who have it and you go over to the gang to find that.

It is clear that both of these men, around age 40 when we interviewed them, found that the gang was an avenue to satisfy social needs. In addition, there was considerable overlap between belonging and normative influence, particularly for the role of neighborhood and friends.

The distinction between joining a gang in prison and on the street was sharpest for the next two most common motivations: ideological (16 percent) and protection (12 percent). Those who joined on the street rarely mentioned (less than 10 percent) ideology or protection as a reason to join, but nearly one-quarter of respondents who joined in prison identified these as motivations to join a gang while incarcerated. To be sure, ideology is a new addition to the research on motivations for gang joining; research with street gang members rarely identifies the beliefs and norms of gangs as reasons for joining a gang, much less race, religion, or shared conflict or rivals. Note both the ethnic and religious tones in this quote from this former member:

I joined because they were talking about our Hispanic culture, Mexico, our Sun God, Virgin Mary. I wanted to learn more about my culture. But I was tricked. Once I was in they made it about being a mafia.

Of course, the name of the gang he joined was the Mexican *Mafia*, but aside from that, it is notable how this respondent (and many others) viewed the gang as exploiting culture to entice his involvement. Many respondents identified race or ethnicity as a motivating factor. Although perhaps an extreme example, this active member of the Mexican Mafia, who joined the gang in prison, stated:

My heart and my mind desired it, desired to go with my race. I cannot explain it, it felt like it was my destiny. The way I grew up was my destiny and my heart was in it.

And notice this quote from an active member of the White Knights of America, who joined while he was incarcerated:

It's not a violent organization, it's more of a pro-white group that fights for our culture.

The former reads like a line out of *American Me* or *Blood In, Blood Out*, with the emphasis on race and destiny, and the latter reads like a quote from a KKK leaflet or a talking point for Richard Spencer.

But where ideology stood out most strongly was in terms of the Tangos. The word Tango stands for "Together Against Negative Gang Organizations," a phrase we heard numerous times over the course of our interviews as well as in the qualitative data. If gangs in prison have to compete for members, it is apparent that the Tangos are now winning the competition against the "families," or the traditional Latino gang structures, as our respondents call them (e.g., see Chapter 3). Some of this ideology takes on softer tones, for instance, in this quote from an active member of the Tango Orejones, who joined a gang at age 19 when he was incarcerated:

When you get locked up you see a bunch of different things and how people carry themselves and how they act. I wasn't down with the families and I wanted to do my time and kick it with the people who live in my city, so I joined them.

The responses from others took on a harder tone.

What they stood for. That's it. In the 1980s there was a big war. Being Hispanic coming to prison, they wanted you to join one. You had to pick one gang. [The families or] I picked together against negative gang organizations.

Many of the Tangos view themselves in the role of protectors in the prison. Comments to this effect from members of the Tangos include: "To stop a lot of the bullying that was going around," "To keep control in the prison system to counteract the dominant organizations," and "To stop certain individuals from overpowering who weren't affiliated." And the respondent who issued the last quote added, "Tango Blast is not really even considered a prison gang." Of course, he is wrong about that. The vast majority of the members of the Tangos consider themselves a gang, as does the prison system. But he is right in noting the protective and reactive function of the Tangos – they were born out of the need to prevent the predatory actions of the families against young Latino males.

Which brings us to protection. It is commonly believed that protection is the predominant motivation for joining a gang in prison, but our data do not support that belief. What is notable is that there were marked differences in reporting protection by race. With only two exceptions, Latinos and whites were the ones who identified protection as a motivation to join. For Latinos, the reasons underlying the endorsement of protection had to do with the tension between the Tangos and the families, as we described above. While intra-ethnic tensions appeared to drive such responses for Latinos, it was interracial tensions for whites. This former member of the Aryan Brotherhood stated:

Here's the situation. When I first went to state jail, it was a really bad time for white people. Everyone in the unit was [black], 85 percent black. It was right after when that guy drove that black dude to death in Jasper. Us white people got really close.

He is referring the tragic death of James Byrd in 1998, who was chained by his ankles, tied to a pickup, and dragged to death on an asphalt road in east Texas by known white supremacists who offered him a ride home. The quote above alludes to the ramifications of what happens on the street for inmates in prison. Indeed, this respondent joined a gang when he was nineteen years old, right around the time of the trial that resulted in death sentences for two of the perpetrators.

An active member of the Peckerwoods, also a white gang, alludes to similar points about the context of the unit where inmates are housed:

It was when I got to a maximum security unit. The main reason was because I wanted to just in case shit pops off. If there is a race riot, motherfuckers are going to have my back. Blacks can't stomp me because the Woods got my back. It's hard in here for a white guy.

We could not identify a single instance of Latino–white conflict as a motivation for joining, although that does not mean it did not exist. Indeed, in Chapter 7 the rivalry network of gangs included several edges between Latino and white gangs (refer to Figure 7.1). The long-standing conflict between blacks and whites in Texas prisons was clearly a motivation for whites, but not blacks, to get involved in prison gangs. And of the two instances of blacks identifying protection as a motivation for joining, only one had to do with racial tension: a former member of the Mandingo Warriors who joined in the late 1980s, not long after the conclusion of the war years.

Overall, while there appears to be overlap in the motivations for joining a gang in prison or on the street, there are also sharp distinctions between the two. Whereas belonging, status, and economic motivations were largely consistent in both settings, normative influences were stronger on the street while ideology (especially racial identification) and protection were stronger in prison. And, whereas there were few differences in motivations between joining non-segregated STGs and street-oriented gangs, the motivations for joining segregated STGs and prison-oriented gangs differed slightly from each other and even more sharply from the other gangs. If there are differences in *why* people join gangs by the location of entry and the type of gangs joined, it raises the question: Are there also differences in *how* people join gangs?

## Methods for Joining Gangs

The methods for joining can be thought of in terms of duration and intensity. Some methods are high in duration and low in intensity, while others are low in duration but high in intensity. In contrast to the motivations for joining gangs, the methods for joining – specifically how someone becomes a member – exhibited far more consistency across the comparative categories. That is to say, with only a few important exceptions, the methods for joining a gang on the street were comparable to those for joining a gang in prison and there were few differences across the categories of the gang typology. The few differences that we observed, however, were rather large and, quite frankly, compelling in what they said about the types of gangs with which they were associated. The quantitative results can be found in Figure 8.3.

The most common method of entry was getting jumped in (53 percent), a low duration–high intensity method. This practice entails a prospective gang member subjecting himself to a many-on-one fight with members of the gang. To many Latino gangs, this is called a *corrache*, or a "heartcheck." Why do they do this? After all, many-on-one is a losing proposition for the solo fighter. Two different members of the West Texas Tangos, both in their early thirties, who joined the gang in prison, told us:

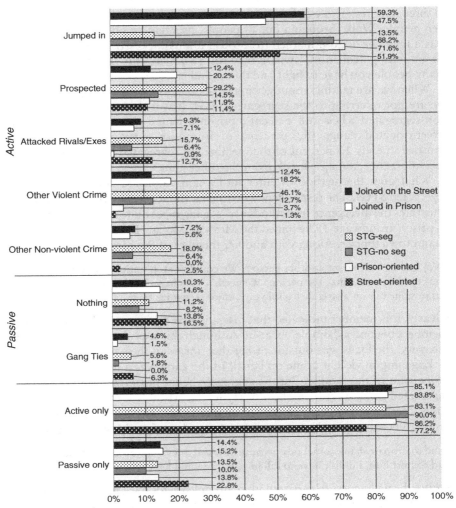

FIGURE 8.3 Methods for joining a gang by location of entry and group typology

I had to do a heartcheck. Two on one. Get cliqued in. If you fold or don't fight back, then they see that as being weak or whatever and that will be a reason for you not to be recruited.

They line up three guys and you fight each of the three guys for forty-five seconds and it's called a corrache, a heartcheck. It's just to see if you can stand up and last if you have to go to battle. Just fists. It's mainly from the neck down.

The *corrache* took on many different forms. Although we consider this a low duration–high intensity method, both the duration and intensity differed across gangs and gang members. We counted over a dozen variants of each. Fifty-nine seconds. Thirty seconds. Forty-five seconds. Fifty seconds. Two minutes. Two to three minutes. Three to five minutes. Two people. Three people. Five people. Ten people. Walk through a line of people, fists flailing about. And then there was a member of an unnamed (to protect anonymity) street gang who told us about getting "rolled in," where they roll two dice, and "the first dice is how many people you have to fight and the second is for how long you had to fight."

When we are talking about getting jumped in as a method of joining a gang, we are not referring to the segregated STGs. It was the norm for members of non-segregated STGs (68 percent), prison-oriented gangs (72 percent), and street-oriented gangs (52 percent) to formalize entry into the gangs. In contrast, merely 13 percent of the members of segregated STG gangs reported such a practice, a major break from the other gangs.

What does the method of entry into a gang look like for the members of segregated STGs? The respondent who told us about getting "rolled in" with dice illustrates the divergence in methods across gang types quite nicely. When he went to prison around age 19 he joined the Mexican Mafia. His role transitioned from victim to victimizer. Along with another member of the Mexica Mafia:

[We] had to beat down another person. We couldn't stop until blood was coming and you could not recognize the person. We needed to fight so hard that they were air lifted out or gone out on a stretcher until you cannot recognize them.

Clearly, this member indicated that his gang was asking something else of their members beyond a "simple" beat-in. Although this was also low duration–high intensity, the locus was outside rather than inside of the gang.

Engaging in violent crime on behalf of the gang was a method identified by 15 percent of the sample. But the aggregate belies just how different the STG-segregated gangs were from the other types. Nearly half of the members of these gangs carried out violence as part of their entry ceremony, the modal response among STG-segregated gang members. A member of the Mexican Mafia stated:

I had to drop or shank somebody because he owed money. I was lucky at the time. I only had to hurt him, I didn't have to kill him, but I would have.

Notice the willingness to carry out ultimate violence for the gang. Some people told us "I had to kill someone" or "I had to hurt people." Some people were purposefully vague on details, which we did not mind given that this project resulted in many communications with our university Institutional Review Boards. Others would specify the number of bones broken, stab wounds, and "body count" over a gang career. In some ways, it was a badge of honor for gang members to share the information, not unlike how sports legends rattle off their career accomplishments.

Many identified that a specific target needed to be hurt in order to enter, however. For example, a member of an unnamed (to protect anonymity) cartel indicated that he had to kill a "fellow member that the cartel wanted me to take care of, he turned snitch or something like that." Snitches and ex-gang members were typically named as the targets of this form of violence. Other gangs tasked prospective members with more indiscriminate tasks, like targeting someone of a different race or gang for violence. Nearly all of the most explicitly race-based descriptions came from current or former members of the Aryan Brotherhood; these are a sampling:

Inflict harm on black people.

Stab a black guy.

Fought others, especially along racial lines.

Beat a black guy pretty bad.

Fight one other person from a different race.

Blood ties to the gang, and I had to do a hit, cannot be on the same race.

You don't have to necessarily kill someone but you have to commit a racially charged fight on a non-white person. Need to beat them up really bad or kill them.

It is striking that there were few other race-based violent methods for entry among white gangs, let alone gangs of other races or ethnicities. In contrast, there were a number of instances of general violence against rival gangs, where it really did not matter who they targeted, provided it was a member of the rival gang.

The final method that distinguished the segregated STGs from other gangs involved prospecting. While over 16 percent of the entire subsample reported this method, nearly 30 percent of the members of STG-segregated gangs reported this. A member of the Aryan Brotherhood described it as follows:

I had to prospect for two years. Prospecting for two years means that you are not an official member and you have a sponsor that is an active gang member and you kind of do dirty work for them such as fight, collect money, etc.

The duration, although important, matters less than the intensity of the task. Some report prospecting for as few as ninety days, whereas others, like the member of the Aryan Brotherhood, reported one year or more.

But across the board, prospecting is a purposive action. It involves education, "mentoring" and training, and there are rituals, not unlike completing graduate school or training to become a police officer. Another member of the Aryan Brotherhood shared the finer details of this commitment:

You have to sign a blind faith commitment to one person that is going to teach you. You have to put all of your trust and faith in that person blindly. He taught me the history of it, set of by-laws which were the same things you already know to be a man or adult. The gang is based on race. You have to be taken under a vote. If they feel you are ready and learned what you need to learn, then you are in. You have to be tied in through blood, meaning, you have to show your loyalty by spilling blood of someone outside of the gang.

This quote illustrates that prospecting is distinguished from other methods of entry by its duration *and* intensity. The time and commitment invested in this group bear similarity to intensive trade schools. And it makes getting beaten down for a minute look like a much more attractive method of entry.

Prospecting is a process in which recruits must engage in a wide variety of violent and non-violent criminal behaviors, along with becoming educated to the history, beliefs, and norms of the gang. This point is underscored by this former member of the Aryan Circle's comment:

You do what you are told for one year. You are on the bottom of the totem pole. You have to take care of things that need to be done. You have to do the dirty work. If one of our guys was disrespected, then you have to go beat the disrespecter up and teach them a lesson. You fight so they can see where your heart is. You can't be scared to fight. You have to learn a lot of information about the family and where they come from. You have to memorize it. There is a constitution, twenty-something pages, you have to learn it all.

Prospecting also took on other variants. Some described a business component to prospecting, where the gang would test prospective members in a different way. A former member of the Texas Syndicate perhaps illustrated this best:

You have to be asked to join. To do that, you had to have heart for the beliefs and the needs of the gang. That you would do what was necessary to make the gang grow, progress, make money for the family. Services. We have restaurants, tattoo shops. If anyone wasn't connected to the gang they wanted to have, sell food, have tattoo shops, sell art work, they had to pay us a percentage, 20 percent, or their business was going down. They wanted to see if I had the potential to take care of people that were problems for the gang. You do what they ask you to do. They send you to the sergeant of arms, guys who supply the arms. Then you went to carry your business. When they see you have heart, then you are automatically a member.

It is rare to describe entry into gangs in these terms. Some members of street-oriented and prison-oriented gangs described the methods of entry like this, but rarely was it described as thoroughly or consistently across members of the gang.

There were also low duration–low intensity methods of entry, although such passive methods were the exception in this sample, even for the street-oriented gangs. Although the differences were not statistically significant, the street-oriented gang members appeared to be the most likely to rely upon passive rather than active methods of entry. Most respondents just said "nothing," although a few provided more detail, like this former Nazi Low Rider:

You don't have to do nothing to join the gang but you just have to be an active participant in the things that the gang does.

That seems simple enough. A member of the Bloods who joined on the street as a teenager said that he "just told them he wanted to be in it and he was in." Compared to prospecting, much less getting jumped in, these methods lack the ceremony or formality. Others noted that they could enter the gang by using passive methods because they had a connection, typically a family member or friend, like this former member of the Mexican Mafia:

It was supposed to be a hit, a stabbing or something that draws blood, but I never actually did it. Because I know someone higher who had rank, so I got in without having to do the hit.

Overall, these results indicate that active methods are the most common form of entry into a gang, particularly methods that are of low duration and high intensity. Masked in an analysis of the full subsample of gang members is the uniqueness of methods for entry into STG-segregated gangs. Put simply, the methods for getting into these gangs differs markedly from the others. Violence is outward rather than inward and membership is proven over time rather than minted over the span of a TV commercial. Thus, talking of "prison gangs" as a homogenous group is a misnomer, particularly when it comes to the methods of joining such gangs.

There are differences both small and large in the methods and motives for joining gangs on the street and in prison, as well as across different gang types. As such, it may also be the case that the people who join these gangs in these places may also differ, and this could be based on demographic, environmental, health, social, attitudinal, criminal justice, or gang factors. It is important to find out if such differences do exist. Indeed, understanding these differences is the crucial first step when considering how to best prevent and intervene in gang membership in prison, much less advance theory and research on the topic.

### Correlates of Different Pathways into Gangs

Table 8.1 contains descriptive statistics for three categories of inmates: (1) street-only gang members, (2) street-to-prison importation gang members, and (3) prison origination gang members. We are interested in the extent to which these three groups evince similar characteristics across the domains, but also where they diverge from one another.

In terms of demographic characteristics, there were sharp and rather fascinating differences across the three groups. The most striking difference to us was in terms of race and ethnicity. Put simply, blacks do not join gangs in prison. Only 4 percent of the prison origination group was black, which means the gang membership originated on the street for 93 percent of black inmates

TABLE 8.1 *Correlates of street-only, street-to-prison importation, and prison origination gang membership*

| | Street only | | Street-to-prison import | | Prison origination | |
|---|---|---|---|---|---|---|
| | N = 80 | | N = 151 | | N = 209 | |
| | Mean/% | (SD) | Mean/% | (SD) | Mean/% | (SD) |
| **Demographic** | | | | | | |
| Age in years | 35.60 | $(7.85)^c$ | 34.34 | $(8.06)^c$ | 38.57 | $(10.25)^{ab}$ |
| Latino | 36.3% | $^c$ | 27.8% | $^c$ | 59.3% | $^{ab}$ |
| Black | 45.0% | $^c$ | 44.4% | $^c$ | 3.8% | $^{ab}$ |
| White | 10.0% | $^c$ | 8.6% | $^c$ | 28.2% | $^{ab}$ |
| Married | 12.5% | | 14.0% | | 16.7% | |
| In a relationship | 18.8% | | 20.7% | | 15.3% | |
| Father | 68.8% | | 73.5% | | 72.2% | |
| Military veteran | 2.5% | | 6.0% | | 2.9% | |
| Education | 11.10 | (1.54) | 11.11 | $(1.68)^c$ | 10.74 | $(1.70)^b$ |
| IQ | 89.88 | $(11.30)^c$ | 89.74 | $(12.19)^c$ | 93.53 | $(11.65)^{ab}$ |
| Low self-control | 1.33 | $(0.78)^b$ | 1.68 | $(0.76)^{ac}$ | 1.41 | $(0.77)^b$ |
| **Environment** | | | | | | |
| Informal social control | 2.68 | (1.02) | 2.53 | (1.02) | 2.68 | (0.99) |
| Prison social control | 1.75 | (0.83) | 1.67 | $(0.92)^c$ | 1.88 | $(0.87)^b$ |
| Good place to live | 56.3% | $^c$ | 54.3% | $^c$ | 70.8% | $^{ab}$ |
| Gangs in neighborhood | 69.6% | | 78.1% | $^c$ | 61.1% | $^b$ |
| Disorder in the prison | 7.89 | $(1.94)^b$ | 8.66 | $(1.96)^a$ | 8.33 | (1.81) |
| Unstructured routines | 2.38 | (3.84) | 2.68 | (3.33) | 2.09 | (3.25) |
| **Health** | | | | | | |
| Stress | 0.87 | (0.63) | 1.01 | $(0.59)^c$ | 0.88 | $(0.59)^b$ |
| Self-rated health | 2.11 | $(0.84)^b$ | 2.33 | $(0.75)^{ac}$ | 2.14 | $(0.83)^b$ |
| BMI | 28.89 | (6.29) | 27.63 | (5.51) | 27.89 | (4.84) |
| Exposure to violence | 1.83 | $(1.08)^b$ | 2.50 | $(0.85)^{ac}$ | 2.03 | $(1.02)^b$ |
| Self-esteem | 2.20 | (0.55) | 2.16 | (0.55) | 2.07 | (0.56) |
| Projected age of death | 87.41 | (20.74) | 87.19 | (21.38) | 86.32 | (21.12) |
| **Social connections** | | | | | | |
| Embeddedness in gangs | −0.31 | $(0.78)^{bc}$ | 0.85 | $(1.02)^{ac}$ | 0.25 | $(1.12)^{ab}$ |
| Social distance | 0.94 | (0.49) | 1.04 | (0.51) | 1.04 | (0.49) |
| Family social support | 2.56 | (0.61) | 2.51 | (0.65) | 2.39 | (0.76) |
| Friend social support | 1.70 | (0.98) | 1.89 | (0.94) | 1.72 | (0.98) |
| Criminal peers | 0.80 | $(0.73)^b$ | 1.09 | $(0.80)^{ac}$ | 0.89 | $(0.80)^b$ |

*(continued)*

TABLE 8.1 *(continued)*

| | Street only | | Street-to-prison import | | Prison origination | |
|---|---|---|---|---|---|---|
| | N = 80 | | N = 151 | | N = 209 | |
| | Mean/% | (SD) | Mean/% | (SD) | Mean/% | (SD) |
| **Attitudes and beliefs** | | | | | | |
| Code of the street | 2.10 | $(0.91)^b$ | 2.44 | $(0.73)^{ac}$ | 2.23 | $(0.90)^b$ |
| Convict code | 2.71 | (0.57) | 2.81 | $(0.57)^c$ | 2.68 | $(0.58)^b$ |
| Legitimacy | 1.22 | (0.60) | 1.11 | $(0.57)^c$ | 1.24 | $(0.60)^b$ |
| Procedural justice | 0.99 | (0.60) | 0.93 | $(0.55)^c$ | 1.07 | $(0.61)^b$ |
| Ethnic ID – cultural | 3.20 | (0.50) | 3.14 | (0.64) | 3.17 | (0.54) |
| Ethnic ID – social | 3.24 | $(0.66)^c$ | 3.18 | (0.75) | 3.06 | $(0.69)^a$ |
| Spirituality/religiosity | 2.87 | (1.00) | 2.85 | (1.06) | 2.74 | (1.11) |
| **CJ system** | | | | | | |
| Age at first arrest | 17.84 | (4.33) | 17.37 | (5.44) | 17.64 | (3.89) |
| Number of arrests | 9.03 | $(5.61)^c$ | 8.48 | $(5.34)^c$ | 10.76 | $(6.51)^{ab}$ |
| Prison stints | 2.09 | $(1.35)^b$ | 1.78 | $(0.95)^{ac}$ | 2.31 | $(1.26)^b$ |
| Years incarcerated | 4.28 | $(4.43)^b$ | 5.84 | $(5.46)^a$ | 5.34 | (5.96) |
| Violent offender | 35.0% | $^b$ | 49.7% | $^{ac}$ | 34.9% | $^b$ |
| **Gangs** | | | | | | |
| Age at first joining | 14.51 | $(2.66)^c$ | 14.28 | $(3.93)^c$ | 22.38 | $(5.02)^{ab}$ |
| Current gang members | 7.5% | $^{bc}$ | 46.4% | $^{ac}$ | 30.6% | $^{ab}$ |
| Years since leaving | 11.30 | $(7.85)^{bc}$ | 4.47 | $(4.23)^{ac}$ | 7.30 | $(6.59)^{ab}$ |
| Years in gang | 10.75 | $(7.75)^b$ | 17.30 | $(7.37)^{ac}$ | 11.12 | $(6.98)^b$ |
| STG-seg | 6.3% | $^{bc}$ | 16.6% | $^{ac}$ | 40.2% | $^{ab}$ |
| STG-no seg | 50.0% | $^c$ | 53.0% | $^c$ | 7.2% | $^{ab}$ |
| Prison-oriented | 2.5% | $^{bc}$ | 17.9% | $^{ac}$ | 46.9% | $^{ab}$ |
| Street-oriented | 37.5% | $^{bc}$ | 11.9% | $^{ac}$ | 3.8% | $^{ab}$ |

*Note:* Superscripts indicate a statistically significant difference between the focal group (column) and street only ($^a$), street-to-prison import ($^b$), and prison origination ($^c$) derived from equality of proportions and means z- and t-tests.

who had been in a gang over their lifetime. The gang-involved black inmates in prison imported their affiliation from the street. This stands in contrast to white inmates whose gang joining was nearly the inverse of that for black inmates, in that most gang-involved white inmates initiated gang membership in prison (71 percent), and only a minority of them (19 percent) imported gang affiliation from the street to prison. There was a more even mix of joining patterns among Latinos. But when we speak about gang membership that originates in prison, we are talking about Latino and white inmates, not blacks. There were other individual differences across the groups, although much less compelling than race and ethnicity, where self-control was the lowest among the street importation gang members and IQ was highest among the prison origination gang members.

When turning to environmental factors such as social control, disorder, and the "neighborhood," there were fewer consistent differences across the groups. In general, prison origination gang members reported that they lived in "better" neighborhoods, where gangs were less common. The street importation gang members perceived more disorder in prison than the street-only gang members and perceived lower informal social control in prison than the prison origination gang members. This could be a reflection of their intensity of involvement in gangs and misconduct.

The health findings are notable because of how street importation members stand apart from the other groups. All three groups maintain statistically similar values for BMI, self-esteem, and projected age of death. However, those who imported their gang membership into the prison from the street view themselves as healthier than the other two groups. This is despite the fact that they report higher levels of stress and exposure to violence than the other groups. Again, this further fuels our suspicion that the street importation gang members are more deeply involved in gangs and misconduct activities while in prison. This supposition underscores that importation, exportation, and prison origination can be working side-by-side in the same prison.

The findings from the social connections domain confirm this suspicion regarding the street importation group with evidence of gang embeddedness. The street importation gang members are rather deeply embedded in the gang, well over a full standard deviation more embedded than street-only gang members and over one-half a standard deviation more embedded than prison origination gang members. Put simply, the street importation gang members are still in the thick of gang life, which could explain some of the environmental, health, and social differences across the groups. Whereas prison origination and street-only gang members reported comparable scores on criminal peers, these scores were lower than what the street importation gang members reported. It is clear that the social networks are different across these groups, which in turn has implications for the remaining domains.

The attitudes and beliefs of gang members did not diverge as sharply as the above findings would have suggested. The major difference across the groups is in terms of adherence to the code of the street, where (as expected) street importation gang members exhibited higher scores than both street-only and prison origination gang members. The remaining differences were between the two groups who were active in prison, oddly enough. Street importation gang members more strongly endorsed the convict code than prison origination gang members (but statistically equivalent to street-only gang members), while also reporting lower procedural justice in their experiences with correctional officers and lower legitimacy in the authority of correctional officers. The sole difference between street-only and prison origination gang members was in terms of social ethnic identification – the former were more open to interracial/ethnic social interactions.

Our final comparisons focus on the criminal justice system and gang involvement, and this is where we observe some of the most striking differences across the three groups. First, the street importation gang members were most likely to be serving a sentence after being convicted of a violent crime. Second, whereas the street-based gang members joined, on average, in their early teenage years (consistent with survey-based research) the prison origination gang members joined a gang in their early twenties. In other words, incarceration was concomitant to gang membership for the former group, but the antecedent to gang membership for the latter group.

Third, and related to gang embeddedness, about half of the street importation gang members report a current affiliation with the gang, compared to only 8 percent and 31 percent of the street-only and prison origination groups. Fourth, the gang careers of the street-only and prison origination groups are similar to one another – around eleven years in the gang – and are comparatively shorter than the seventeen years the street importation group have spent in a gang.

Finally, as might be expected, the types of gangs these groups are part of differ considerably. Prison origination gang members tend to belong to STG-segregated and prison-oriented gangs. The street-only gang members tend to belong to STG-non-segregated and street-oriented gangs. The street importation gang members are most likely to be members of STG-non-segregated gangs. These findings continue to underscore just how different gang members who import their membership from the street are in the prison context.

The preceding sections have examined the methods and motives for joining gangs, the patterns of entry into gangs in relation to imprisonment, and the correlates of these patterns. With this groundwork established, it is time to shift our focus from the "gang members" to the "non-gang members" to learn about gang avoidance practices. After all, the people who join gangs in prison are the minority of inmates, constituting slightly over 10 percent of our sample of Texas prisoners. And less than one-third of our sample had ever been involved with a gang over their lifetime. How and why did 70 percent of inmates avoid the attractive features and pernicious influences of gangs on the street and in prison?

## Avoiding Gangs on the Street and in Prison

Figure 8.4 reports the *potential* for joining a gang on the street and in prison for the respondents who were not involved in a gang in the respective setting. For most of these respondents, gang membership was not even a consideration – only

15 percent in either setting told us that they even considered joining a gang. Yet, there was at least some pressure to join, as evidenced by 40 and 51 percent of these subgroups revealing that they were recruited by a street or prison gang, respectively. And a whopping 81 percent of non-gang inmates told us they were "checked" by gang members in prison, that is, asked about their gang affiliation upon admission to a reception facility or new unit. It is clear that prison gangs are keeping tabs on the affiliations of "new fish." If gang members are central to the social order of prisons, this is exactly what we would expect to observe. As gang members "churn" out of prison, their ranks must be replenished if the gang is to maintain its control over their own members and other inmates. Given the incongruence between interest and pressure to join a gang, we are interested in uncovering why and how our respondents avoided gangs in the respective street and prison locations.

In terms of motivations to resist gang membership reported in Figure 8.5, the similarity in avoiding gangs across the settings (street and prison) was strong. In fact, less than a five-percentage point difference exists in the motivations for avoiding gangs on the street and in prison across the six most commonly reported themes. The most common reason for avoiding gangs is actually a common reason why gang members leave gangs (that we explore in the next

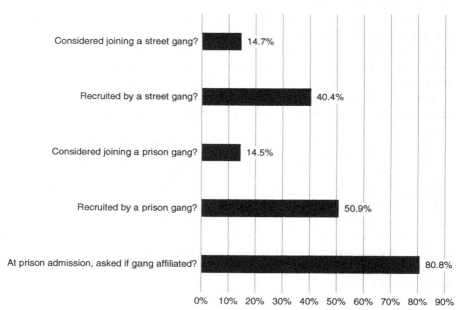

FIGURE 8.4 Potential for gang involvement on the street and in prison, non-gang respondents
Note: The denominators for the prevalences reported only include valid responses for respondents who self-reported non-gang membership on the street ($N = 477$) or in prison ($N = 448$).

chapter): gangs sell their members a bill of goods. As noted by this 29-year-old Latino inmate:

They paint a pretty picture for you, but that is not what it is. If anything, you really just get yourself in more trouble.

This 59-year-old white inmate stated:

I don't have a need for it. I didn't need companionship, protection, or feeling of family, or [the gang] to make decisions for me. I make my own decisions.

This 58-year-old black inmate makes a similar point, but from a different perspective:

Because when I work hard, I'm not sharing it with you. When I come home, I don't want you in my house. What you do out there, I don't want to have to pay your debt. I'm not gonna bleed to be your friend. I don't need nobody's protection to protect me.

These men simply are not buying what gangs have to offer. Of course, many recognize that the need for gangs ebbs and flows in prison, which is reflected in this quote from a 47-year-old white inmate:

You don't get anything out of it. Many of them are washed up and it's not like how it used to be in the 1980s. I've been doing time since 1987 when it was very rough and strict. Gangs were more disciplined. They still have control in prison and check paperwork. I heard that gang members are going to be coming out of seg [solitary confinement], so once they get out to general population, the risk will change in GP.

It appears that the worry projected by inmates, correctional officers, and prison administrators alike is that the Texas prison system will return to a deadlier era if the members of STG-segregated gangs are released from solitary confinement.

Themes of independence from and disinterest in gangs were also quite common among non-gang members. This 41-year-old black inmate stated this rather sharply:

I don't need a bunch of people. I roll by myself. Gangs in prison are a bunch of homeboy stuff. It is really messed up. The whole gang situation is nothing to me. Once you get in trouble, they ain't going to help you. They won't see you or nothing. It's weak to me.

The independence from gangs resonated strongly across the sample of those who avoided gang membership. Respondents referred to the members of gangs as "crash test dummies" who are used and abused. They viewed gangs as nothing more than a group that will exploit you and get you in trouble. Some simply expressed dismay about the possibility of gang membership. These Latino inmates, one age 25 and the other 53, said as much:

I think it is stupid. Being a follower is stupid. A gang is always having trouble. Stabbing. Fighting. Stuff like that. I didn't want to be part of that.

Because I think it is wrong. They break laws. Beat people up. I have seen twenty guys on one guy, and it was for a [postage] stamp! That is just wrong.

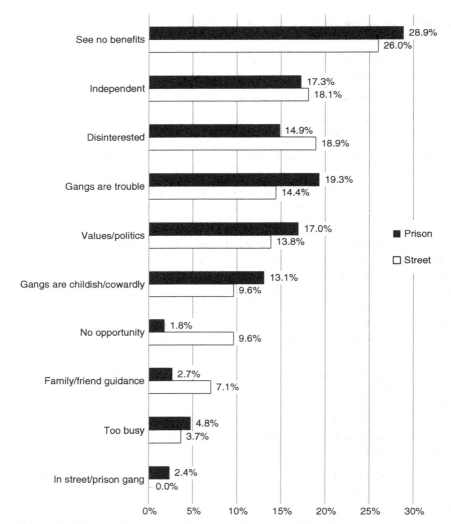

FIGURE 8.5 Motives for gang avoidance on the street and in prison
Note: The denominators for the prevalence reported only include valid responses for
respondents who self-reported non-gang membership on the street (*N* = 354) or in prison
(*N* = 336).

And other gang members noted the ideological component of it. This white
inmate, age 24, stated:

It's political. Me being white. It would make me an anti-black gang member, and I'm not
anti-black.

The greatest divergence between why our respondents avoided gangs on the street and in prison was opportunity. Simply put, the opportunity structure in prison is more constrained and controlled than that on the street. This is as much of a question of "how" as it is a question of "why," that is, opportunities in prison are more controlled than those on the street. This is the reason we now turn to the methods for gang avoidance in prison.

Figure 8.6 shows that, unlike the motives, there were sharper differences in gang avoidance on the street and in prison, and those differences reflected the

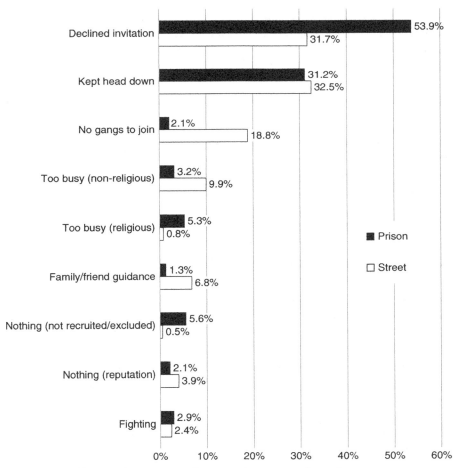

FIGURE 8.6 Methods for gang avoidance on the street and in prison
Note: The denominators for the prevalence reported only include valid responses for respondents who self-reported non-gang membership on the street (*N* = 382) or in prison (*N* = 375).

most common theme in our data: respondents who flat-out declined the invitation to join. On the street, this was reported in the qualitative data among 32 percent of our sample. In prison, over half of our sample told us this is how they avoided gang membership.

Declining invitations to join the gang took on different features in both settings. On the street, it was almost as simple as Nancy Reagan's "Just say no" campaign against drugs. In analyzing the qualitative data, there were numerous mentions of "I just told them no." In fact, it was hard to identify individuals who elaborated on this point, perhaps an indication of declining as a straightforward method of avoidance, although this 38-year-old black respondent stated:

I never even entertained them. When I ran into gang members, I told them I wasn't interested in it. I heard people say they were forced in a gang in Houston, but I was never forced or anything like that. They [those people] were forced by telling them that they have no choice. If they don't want to get beat up every day, if you need our help, you have to be in the gang. A lot of them are weak minded, they think it is cool.

This is not to say that some people did not have to fight on the street or were not pressured or bullied. However, in prison, our impression is that a simple "just say no" does not fly like it does on the street. In fact, we identified variants of declining an invitation to join, such as claiming independence, identifying themselves as having poor qualities for gangs, referencing future orientations, and street gang ties. This 31-year-old white inmate appealed to higher loyalties in declining the invitation:

I just told them no, and told them that I was a religious man trying to stay in the word [of God] and remain solo. I said that God's more important than some prison gangs. Just got to hold your ground, they're going to keep on asking you.

A 21-year-old Latino inmate echoed similar points, but recognized that your "jacket" follows you from the street to prison:

It's a choice. Yes or no. And that's it. They respect it. To be in a gang in prison, you get evaluated before you get to prison, when you are in county jail, to see if you are worthy of being a member. They watch your action and evaluate your character. Some people use the Bible to avoid getting involved.

Some people also had characteristics that precluded gang membership, such as age, sexual orientation, or charge. For example, this 29-year-old white inmate noted:

I just told them my charge. They wouldn't ask me about joining since they knew about it. You can tell when they are hinting at affiliation, but tell them I'm a sex offender shuts it off entirely.

This may mark one of the few benefits associated with a sex offender status. Others also noted that the dynamics in prison have changed, although not enough to allow sex offenders in. This 37-year-old white inmate stated:

I told them no. They respected it. They have no choice. They don't force people. Gangs today are not the gangs of when I first came down, are not the gangs of twenty-five years ago. Twenty-five years ago you joined to survive. When I first came down, if you can stand on your own, then you stand on your own. Guys that can't stand on their own will join gangs today. Gang members join because they need protection, they can't fight their way out of a paper bag. I wouldn't have any problems in the prison population as a non-gang or non-family member.

Even if the gangs have changed, it appears that even younger inmates can resist the will of the group. This 22-year-old black male reported a strategy that involved appealing to independence and family:

I just stayed to myself and told them I'm a loner that is trying to go home, and that I have people that care about me on the outside. I love my family too much to worry about a prison gang.

But sometimes it requires more than a "no" with a valid explanation. Although this was rare, a handful of respondents said that they needed to fight to ward off a gang. The more common active method of avoidance was "kept my head down," which was endorsed by about one-third of the sample, equally split across street and prison settings. This 41-year-old black inmate said:

I just stayed to myself. After I told them I was not affiliated, they respected that. They only asked me one time. If you lie about gang affiliation, the gang will send word to the street to check that, if you are not but said you were, then you will get smashed. If you are a gang member but lie, then you will also get smashed.

As this quote illustrates, there is still interaction between gang and non-gang inmates. This also drives home the point about vetting the gang credentials of inmates, both face-to-face and "back home," seeking discriminating and honest signals to lessen the asymmetric information between gangs and new inmates. Still, respondents would report taking steps to actively avoid even the appearance of involvement with gangs. This 57-year-old black inmate told us:

I wasn't associating with them or any of their affiliates. On my unit, they have GRAD [the Gang Renouncement and Disassociation program]. If they came from the GRAD chapter, then they were not affiliated anymore. If I saw affiliates, I didn't get involved with them. I avoided conversation and contact with them.

And others noted that such a strategy was effective, partly because the gangs appeared to respect this decision. This Native American inmate in his early sixties said:

I didn't partake in any activities. I didn't get involved in gangs. Gangs don't really bother people who are doing their own thing.

The only other feature of gang avoidance methods that bears mention is the opportunity structure. As our colleague James Densley has stated, if there is no gang, then there is no gang member. And that was the case here. Many of the respondents in our sample were located in neighborhoods or communities with no gangs. This rarely occurred in prison. As one might suspect, the prevalence of gang members and the confined spaces of institutions make it practically impossible to avoid interactions with gangs. The handful of respondents who reported no gangs in prison were either non-violent/minimum security inmates or housed in isolation.

The street was a different story, as evidenced by nearly 19 percent of our sample stating that they avoided gangs simply because there were no gangs to join. The responses are what most would expect:

I wasn't running around street gangs growing up. I lived in a white middle class neighborhood.

No gangs out in the country.

Right where I come from in California, there really isn't a white group street gang. They are mainly race gangs, black and Hispanic.

My town is really small, so there was no gang influence.

Clearly there were racial connotations associated with this response, and this does not mean that only whites grew up in gang-free neighborhoods. Yet, 16 percent of blacks and 11 percent of Latinos said that there were no gangs in their neighborhood, compared to 29 percent of white inmates. It is hard enough for most to envision going to prison, but imagine transitioning from an area where gangs are nonexistent to the Texas prison system. We believe that those who avoided gangs in prison, an environment where gangs are ever-present, have something to teach us about gang prevention and intervention in prison, and perhaps on the street as well.

CONCLUSION

This chapter examined the important topics of gang joining and avoidance in prison. It is necessary to place this chapter in context: roughly 20 percent of Texas inmates have a history of gang involvement in prison (and 30 percent when street gang involvement is included). This makes claims that gang members are ubiquitous in prison, that they control the prisons, and that individuals must affiliate with a prison gang to maintain their safety or access to contraband difficult to sustain. The picture of gangs we draw in earlier chapters – that they exert less control over prison life than has been suggested, that their organizational structure has been flattened, and that while gang members still commit more violence and prison infractions, they by no means control prison violence and contraband as they once did – is reflected in the joining and avoiding of prison gangs. In addition, and we believe importantly, there is substantial diversity in the motives and methods of gang joining as well as the correlates of individuals who join gangs while in prison. Much of this variability was explained by the location of entry (street or prison) or gang structure (four-part typology).

Like many things in prison, race and ethnicity play key roles in the processes of joining and avoiding gangs. Although we did not formally test for race and ethnicity, these differences could be inferred from our qualitative data and the racially and ethnically homogenous gangs that were joined. The patterns of gang joining among black, Latino, and white inmates differ in stark terms. Black inmates tend not to join gangs in prison; many of them come to prison with a prior gang affiliation that is maintained in a comparable prison gang. However, both Latino and white inmates do join gangs while in prison and in substantial numbers. That said, the motives and methods for gang joining showed considerable variation across race. For blacks who imported their membership from the street, there was a certain level of proving their toughness that was expected. Latinos were less likely to engage in gang joining that involved violence and whites were least likely to do so. The motives for gang joining also varied as Latinos demonstrated more cultural (ethnic pride) motives than did blacks whose motives for joining were more strongly oriented toward violence and contraband. Whites who joined a gang in prison identified protection and safety as primary reasons for joining. Few white prison gang members belonged to a gang before they came to prison.

Many of the motives for joining a gang on the street were not as strongly endorsed by prison gang members as we had expected. We used the common distinction between pushes and pulls in assessing motives for joining a gang. We found that pushes were particularly strong motivations for individuals who were members of street gangs. We also found evidence of normative influences for gang joining to be stronger among street gang members than prison gangs, whether they be STG or just prison-oriented. However, we found pulls to be stronger motives among individuals who had joined a gang in prison. Protection was the strongest pull for prison gang members, and differentiated them from both STG-non-segregated gangs as well as street gangs. A similar observation existed for ideology, which was endorsed more strongly in prison than the street, as well as among STG-segregated and prison-oriented gang members.

Interestingly, we found that methods of joining gangs differed little across those who joined their gang on the street or in prison, regardless of whether that prison gang was an STG or a clique. These groups were more likely to describe their method of joining as "active" rather than "passive" by nearly a six-to-one ratio. That said, the kinds of things regarded as active steps to join a gang generally fell short of the use of extreme forms of violence.

We regard gang avoidance as a major new contribution to the literature on understanding gang joining, particularly among prison gang members. While there is scant mention of this in the street gang literature, we are unaware of any prior research on this topic in the prison gang literature, although findings from Narag and Lee (2018) in the Philippines come the closest. We found avoidance among each of the major divisions of race/ethnicity in our sample, but it was greatest among older and white members of the sample. Many who avoided joining a gang indicated that they desired to serve their time and expedite their return to family and their life as it was before imprisonment. It is instructive to examine the primary methods for avoiding gang joining among those who were street gang members and those who joined in prison. There were few differences between the groups, and the modal categories were "declining the invitation to join" and "keeping their head down." Over half (54 percent) of prison inmates who avoided the gang said that "declining the invitation to join" was the method they used to avoid gangs, while nearly one-third (31 percent) "kept their head down." Neither of these two "methods" seem particularly sophisticated nor do they seem like strategies that would be effective against groups that were well organized and effectively violent. The large number of gang avoiders and the techniques they used to avoid joining gangs suggest that the "iron fist" of prison gangs did not have a strong grip on prison life. After all, how strong could a group be if "just saying no" was an effective way of avoiding their influence?

Our findings on gang joining suggest that media and even the public pronouncements of correctional officials regarding the influence of prison gangs may be misunderstood. To be sure, prison gangs are not benevolent organizations looking out for the well-being of inmates. Many of their members have brutal histories on the street and in prison. That said, the institutional locus of control appears to have weakened, perhaps in the face of widespread application of restrictive housing (née solitary confinement) and the splintering of gang control brought about by mass incarceration. Regardless of its origins, gang joining is by no means a certainty in contemporary settings. The finding of gang avoidance suggests that individuals who are resolute and feel that they can count on some level of protection inside the prison can say "no" to a gang, particularly if they do not bring a history of gang membership with them to prison.

# 9

## Continuity and Change in Prison Gang Membership

The phrase attributed to the Greek philosopher Heraclitus, "There is nothing permanent except change," is aptly applied to gangs and gang members. As this book has shown, transitions characterize the lives of prison gang members even in highly structured institutional settings. Gangs exert considerable influence on their members whether on the street or in prison. This influence can be measured in the involvement in crime and misconduct in prison, as well as in the disruption of many positive socializing forces such as employment, marriage, religion, and school. In the previous chapter, we examined the transition into gangs on the street and in prison. This chapter examines instances where gangs' control over individuals weakens and their members sever their ties to the group and transition out of gangs on the street and in prison. If people are able to leave gangs, it is important to understand the reasons they do and how they go about disengaging, as well as the potential consequences of leaving. Unfortunately, there is little research on this topic. With roughly one million gang members in the United States, many of whom are in prison or have been in prison, these questions require good data, careful analysis, and policy applications.

In the classic movie, *American Me* (1992), Edward James Olmos traces the lives of young Angelinos from the street to prison. The protagonist expresses a desire to leave the gang but faces the reality, one that he created, that the only way out of the gang is death. Such imagery is powerful, but is it reality? Both street and prison gangs engage in a considerable amount of "mythologizing." Malcolm Klein (1995) argues that such mythologizing is functional for the gang in that it creates expectations for behavior and reinforces group cohesion. Decker and Van Winkle (1996) reported that part of gang mythology in St. Louis was that you could only leave your gang by killing your mother. Nearly every subject knew someone who had left their gang, but no one reported knowing anyone who had killed their mother. Such mythology reinforces the bonds of membership and creates "respect" for the gang as being "hard" or "tough." Such beliefs need not be true if they fulfill a function such as keeping individuals in their gang. While the research in intervening years has taught us that most street gang members do leave their gang, we have very little knowledge about whether this is true for prison gang members. The mythology of "blood in, blood out"[1] (the need to spill blood to enter and exit gangs) and the physical and social isolation of prison reinforce images about the permanency of prison gang membership. Similar to corporations, athletic teams, and religious congregations, gangs have an interest in minimizing turnover in membership in a competitive marketplace. Successfully navigating intergang competition requires strength in numbers, part of which is achieved through preventing gang exit.

This chapter examines disengaging from gangs in prison. We focus on a series of questions about leaving a gang: (1) Do gang members leave gangs while in prison? (2) Why do they leave the gang? (3) How do they leave the gang? (4) Who or what helps facilitate the transition? (5) What types of consequences are associated with leaving a gang? (6) Who continues their involvement in gangs, and why? As with the prior chapters in this book, our aim is to elucidate how gang behaviors and processes differ in prison from the street, which is why we contrast these questions across respondents who left gangs in either location. Leaving a gang in prison may be very different – in frequency, motivation, method, and consequence – from leaving a gang on the street, although there is little hard data to bear on this question. We are further interested in whether the grip of the group is stronger among some gangs than others, which is why we also contrast these questions across our four-part typology of Security Threat Group (STG)-segregated, STG-non-segregated, prison-oriented, and street-oriented gangs. It may also be the case that leaving certain gangs may occur less frequently, require different motives and greater effort, and involve graver consequences than others. Either way, our goal is to learn about gang disengagement among our respondents in the LoneStar Project.

## UNDERSTANDING DISENGAGEMENT FROM GANGS

Approaches to understanding disengagement from street gangs have generally relied on life-course criminology, with its emphasis on transitions and turning points within a structure of criminal careers (Roman, Decker, and Pyrooz 2017). Rather than adopting a static view of subjects' lives, it treats change as a central element in understanding how individuals enter into crime and persist or desist in offending careers. The role of transitions and turning points (Laub and Sampson 2003; Piquero, Farrington, and Blumstein 2003) is central to this perspective. Turning points may be the product of many

---

[1] *Blood In, Blood Out* (1993) was the title of a Hollywood film about gangs in East Los Angeles and San Quentin prison (where it was partially filmed) featuring Benjamin Bratt, before the movie was retitled *Bound by Honor* upon release, owing to worries about gang violence in the aftermath of the 1992 Los Angeles riots.

sources, including *relationships* such as friendship, marriage, and parenting, as well as *opportunities* such as employment, education, and military service. But relationships and opportunities are not restricted to legitimate sources; instead, there is a broad marketplace of possible relationships, especially in prison. Such a marketplace includes relationships with offenders as well as criminal opportunities. Exposure to such opportunities is enhanced in prison where inmate organization and activity may involve violations of prison rules as well as the criminal law, and one's choice of associates is restricted (on the inmate side) to convicted felons. However, incarcerated individuals are also exposed to programming and often face life-course changes involving shifting relationships with family members, aging out, and other challenges (violence) that may work individually or in concert with transition away from their gang, involvement in wrongdoing, or both.

Gang disengagement has been conceptualized as the process of disembedding oneself from the gang and the event of de-identifying as a gang member (Sweeten, Pyrooz, and Piquero 2013). The former refers to the declining level of embeddedness over time while the latter refers to crossing a threshold, or a tipping point, where "gang" no longer occupies one's primary identity. Decker, Pyrooz, and Moule (2014) described the stages of gang disengagement in terms of role transitions, drawing on Helen Ebaugh's (1988) work on role exits. The role transition literature focuses more on changes in identity – self-concept – than it does on external and institutional factors that may produce change. Consistent with Maruna's (2001) work on the role of scripts in change among ex-inmates, this approach finds that self-concept and self-definition both reflect changes in behavior and help to change behavior. From Ebaugh's formulation, role exits contain four interrelated stages.

The first stage of role transitions begins with "first doubts" about the current identity. Such doubts often emerge from challenges to identity or exposure to new identities; there is no commitment to leave the gang, but questions arise about the gang's utility. This stage is followed by a consideration of alternative roles; for example, a smoker may consider what not smoking would mean for their associations and activities or a drug user may weigh the benefits of not using any longer. People may begin to "try on" new roles privately, known as "anticipatory socialization," such as the classic scene in *American History X* where a reformed Edward Norton, Jr., standing shirtless in front of a bathroom mirror, covers the swastika tattoo on his chest with his hand. The third stage – turning points – is the critical stage where an individual sheds old self-conceptions and adopts a new role identity. Whereas the prior stages are largely cognitive and internal, during this stage there is an alignment between self-concept and behavior, brought about by experiences (e.g., disillusionment, victimization) or imperatives (e.g., family, religion). The final stage is confirmation of the new role by third parties. In the case of former offenders, this stage would be represented by friends or authorities who no longer reacted to the individual as an offender but as a "former" or "non" offender. In the case of gang members, this is the stage where the "ties that bound" are truly unwound. We see this as a general process, one that applies to leaving behind gangs, hate groups (Simi et al. 2017), and terrorist groups (Bjorgo and Horgan 2008), among others.

## KEY FEATURES OF LEAVING GANGS

It is ironic that until recently there has been little attention to exiting gangs, or for that matter exiting groups involved in crime such as terrorists, extremists, drug smugglers, and human traffickers. If we better understand why and how individuals leave such groups we may be able to apply those lessons to policy and programs, and avoid actions that strengthen gang membership (Roman et al. 2017). Not only is this area of theory, research, and behavior poorly developed, it is generally plagued by myths, particularly about the possibility of being able to leave such groups. Street gang research has a growing body of theory and evidence (Carson and Vecchio 2015; Densley and Pyrooz 2017) that documents the motives, methods, and correlates of gang leaving on the street, which is informative for considering disengagement from gangs in prison. What does this research tell us about leaving gangs?

Studies of the motives for leaving gangs have focused on the role of "pushes" and "pulls" in disengagement, similar to joining gangs. Pushes include intrinsic factors to the gang such as experiences with violence, growing disillusionment with gang life, or changing identities, and typically reflect something negative. For example, Bubolz and Simi (2015) theorize that gang members become disillusioned with the gang upon realizing that promises of kinship, safety, and wealth are rarely realized; gang members have been sold a "bill of goods." Decker and Lauritsen (2002) documented how violence eventually takes an emotional and physical toll on gang members and as such threatens gang cohesion and may hasten exits from the gang. Alternatively, pulls represent a positive force such as the birth of a child, having a partner or spouse, or securing employment. For example, Pyrooz, McGloin, and Decker (2017) recently found that becoming a parent for the first time universally leads females to leave the gang, but its disengagement potential for males is contingent upon residing with the child. Research that documents the motivations for leaving gangs has determined that those who successfully disengage from a street gang typically have multiple motives for leaving. Three studies conducted in the last decade confirm this point, where both pushes and pulls combined to motivate exit from gangs. This was found among 78 percent of the 260 former gang members in a five-city high-risk justice-involved sample (Decker and Pyrooz 2011), 85 percent of the 51 former gang members in a network-based justice-involved sample in Philadelphia and Washington, DC (Eidson, Roman, and Cahill 2016), and 44 percent of the 473 instances of gang leaving in a seven-city school-based sample of youth (Carson, Peterson, and Esbensen 2013).

The methods for exiting a gang challenge conventional portrayals of this process. Movies such as *American Me* and *Blood In, Blood Out* highlight the role of sometimes lethal violence that members incur when attempting to leave the gang, particularly a gang with roots in prison. But the preponderance of street gang research has not found exits involving violence to be commonplace. Indeed, leaving through some "passive" means (e.g., walking away) is the modal method of disengaging from a gang. Pyrooz and Decker (2011) found that members who left the gang for what could be viewed as "legitimate" pull reasons – family, children, and jobs – did not undergo hostile exits, such as getting jumped out ("blood out"). However, gang members who left for "push" reasons, such as violence, disillusionment, or criminal justice system involvement, were more likely to face violence in the course of the exit process.

A review of the street gang literature also suggests that while most gang members expect to face residual consequences of gang membership, there were very few observations of its occurrence. Indeed, few of the individuals who left their gang faced consequences for doing so, either from their own gang or a rival gang. It is possible that processes and groups that facilitate exit can be found within prison, such as programs or religion, along with more traditional life-course processes and relationships such as family or experiencing violence. What happens to those who do leave their prison gang? After all, some street gang members who disengage from their group report threats or real forms of retaliation. There is good reason to suspect that this may occur in a closed environment like prison. We turn to the small body of research to gain a preliminary glimpse into disengagement from gangs in prison.

## PRIOR RESEARCH ON LEAVING GANGS IN PRISON

Much of what is known about leaving gangs in prison is from anecdotes related to prison policies or tangential commentary on the mythology of prison gangs. With regard to the former, this typically occurs in the context of policies that result in the placement of gang members in solitary confinement, where scholars note that the only way out of prison gangs and solitary confinement in places like California was to "snitch, parole, or die" (e.g., Reiter 2012; Tachiki 1995; Toch 2007). With regard to the latter, it is common for works to portray prison gang membership as a lifelong commitment. Crouch and Marquart (1989, 208) cited transcripts of two affiliates of the Aryan Brotherhood, who stated: "Once in, always in. This holds true even if the member leaves the prison and goes home." Skarbek (2014, 115), citing a criminal indictment (*US* v. *Rubalcaba et al.* Indictment Federal District Court, Northern District of California, April) of Nuestra Familia, a Latino prison gang in California, details: "membership, once achieved, was for life, as symbolized by the organization's membership phrase, blood in, blood out." Other evidence based on systematic longitudinal tracking of serious offenders in Philadelphia and Phoenix reveals that people do indeed leave gangs while incarcerated (Pyrooz, Gartner, and Smith 2017), but understanding disengagement processes was not the primary focus, nor was it clear whether leaving occurred in prison or county jail and juvenile halls.

Two very different studies lend insights into prison gang leaving. The first (Fong and Vogel 1995) is over twenty-five years old, and based on a small number ($n$ = 48) of gang members in Texas. An anonymous questionnaire was administered to former gang members housed in protective custody via prison mail by a "gang specialist" (Buentello) who was a prison employee. What was notable to us from the outset was the authors' use of the term *defector* to describe former gang members, language we would anticipate being applied to soldiers, spies, and citizens engrossed in international conflict. The gangs from which inmates "defected" included the Mexican Mafia (twenty-four members), Aryan Brotherhood (eleven members), Texas Syndicate (seven members), and Texas Mafia (six members), all of which were well established and by reputation powerful and violent gangs (and all represented in the LoneStar Project as STG-segregated gangs). None of the forty-eight people in the study had been in a gang on the street; as Chapter 8 revealed, prison onset was the norm, not the exception. Eight reasons for leaving gangs were identified and included only push factors (it was unclear in their report if these were canned or open-ended responses). The leading explanations accounted for forty-two of the forty-eight individuals in their sample, and included "loss of interest" (21%), "refusal to carry out hit on a non-gang member" (19%), "disagreed with gang direction" (15%), "refusal to carry out hit on a fellow gang member" (13%), "violated a gang rule" (10%), and "grew out of it" (10%). "Loss of interest" hardly seems a likely reason to give for leaving the most notorious and violent prison gangs in Texas. While the authors acknowledge the small size of this non-probability sample, their findings suggest that gang leaving in prison occurs, although leaving was contingent upon the use of protective custody housing, and the reasons for leaving may not involve profound rejections of gang life or a focus on new opportunities.

Recent work by Johnson and Densley (2018) conducted inside two Brazilian prisons suggests a mechanism that facilitates gang leaving in prison. Using signaling theory, which is aligned with the stage-based model of role exits (Densley and Pyrooz 2017), they argued that religious commitment – particularly among Pentecostals – provides an outlet by which gang members may signal their preparedness to disengage from prison gangs to fellow gang members as well as authorities. Engaging in religious rituals in prison communicates the desire for a new status and credo, a desire that elevates religious beliefs and practices above gang membership. This is consistent with others who have argued that religion constitutes a viable disengagement pathway, particularly for Latinos (Brenneman 2011; Deuchar 2018; Flores 2013; Ward 2012). While not a direct test of gang leaving, this study documents – in a different yet also harsh prison environment – that disengagement occurs and does not involve "blood out." Religion constitutes a credible commitment that is respected by a rather tense relationship between the gangs and religious groups in Brazilian prisons.

## METHODS TO LEARN ABOUT DISENGAGEMENT FROM GANGS

The increasingly sophisticated research on disengagement from street gangs, along with the early (Fong and Vogel 1995) and recent (Johnson and Densley 2018) work on leaving gangs in prison, is no doubt informative. But what is missing from this work is a systematic examination of gang disengagement, one that includes a large, diverse, and representative sample of former gang members who have exited a variety of gangs. To guide our approach to the study of gang disengagement in the LoneStar Project, we drew on our earlier work with the Google Ideas study, where we aimed to uncover the key features of leaving street gangs.

In this chapter, we examine gang disengagement in prison beginning with a fundamental question: Do people leave gangs in prison? Among the respondents who have left gangs, we compare the frequency of dropping out of a gang in prison to that of dropping out of a gang on the street. This is followed by an examination of the motivations for leaving gangs. While we recognize that leaving the gang is often the product of multiple influences, we examine pushes and pulls individually as well as through a typology (pushes and pulls) of multiple motives. We next move to an examination of the methods for leaving the gang, where we compare active and passive methods of gang departure, as well as develop a typology that includes multiple methods of leaving the prison gang. In examining the motives and methods for leaving the gang, we use both quantitative and qualitative data, the latter of which are based on open-ended questions asked of each respondent about gang leaving. In this way, we hope to convey a fuller sense of the disengagement process, about which we know so little. From here, we examine the most important source of help in facilitating gang exit. We consider the possibility that multiple sources contributed to the decision to leave. In addition, we consider the role of programmatic and other institutional resources in gang exits. Many street gang members find themselves with few programmatic or alternative resources to facilitate leaving their gang; however, such programs do exist in prisons such as in Texas. We then examine the residual consequences of leaving the gang, including those that are real and those that are perceived.

Finally, like in Chapter 8, we flip our original questions on their head and instead of learning about why people leave the gang, we assess what encourages people to stay. We do this with both qualitative and quantitative data. We then extend this line of questioning a step further: What distinguishes people who stay in gangs from those who leave, on the street and in prison? We compare these three groups quantitatively across a wide range of domains (demographic, environment, health, social connections, attitudes and beliefs, the criminal justice system, and gangs). This, combined with why people stay, should inform efforts to intervene in the lives of gang members. Indeed, we are keenly interested in highlighting the variables that may be manipulated to enhance disengagement through policy or programming.

We expect that the grip of the gang is not ironclad, that it waxes and wanes in prison not unlike on the street. Thus far, our work has characterized the structure of prison gangs as a web of complex relationships with other prisoners, both gang and non-gang alike, as well as with street gangs and gang members. Gangs exert a strong influence on individuals, circumscribing their behaviors and relations in prison. Some of this has to do with the forces imposed by gangs (e.g., group process); some of this has to do with formal social controls enacted in response to gangs (e.g., solitary confinement). In this context, the roles of importation and exportation assume importance in understanding the interactions between the prison and the street. Life-course processes, so important to understanding continuity and change among individuals on the street, may also be at work for individuals in prison. Maturational reform, familial obligations, and gang disillusionment play important roles in leaving street gangs. But do they also play a similar role in prison? And how do they play out across different types of gangs? We know very little about these questions. While the preceding chapters present evidence that the street and prison settings share much in common, leaving the gang is a strong test of the complementarity of life-course processes across street and prison gang members.

## Measuring Key Features of Gang Disengagement

We gathered detailed information about the key features of gang disengagement in our interview-based surveys. To begin, and as we have described previously (Chapter 7), we were interested in the occurrence of gang leaving. Any of our respondents who indicated that they had been a member of a gang were asked: "Have you left this gang?" A "yes" response would then trigger a battery of questions related to disengaging from gangs. What is perhaps most important to this chapter is the question that immediately followed: "Were you incarcerated at the time you left?" Those who responded "no" were recorded as *Exited Gang on the Street*, while those who responded "yes" were recorded as *Exited Gang in Prison*. We then queried respondents about when they left their gang, including their age and/or year of leaving.[2]

---

[2]   Attempting to identify precisely when someone left a gang is not always a cut-and-dried matter. As we have described above (and in earlier work; Decker, Pyrooz, and Moule 2014), leaving a gang is messy, replete with fits and starts. Based on the wording of our location of leaving question, there is the possibility that some people left a gang – or potentially experienced the first doubts or triggering events of disengagement – while in a county jail rather than prison unit. However, a review of the most recent and prior prison admission and release dates and gang leaving dates/ages indicated extensive overlap between the two.

To understand the motivations for leaving, we asked former gang members to provide us with the reasons why they left the gang with which they were most recently involved with. While we now know a fair amount about the motivations for exiting gangs on the street, we know very little about leaving gangs in prisons, which is why we allowed former gang members to provide us with open-ended rather than canned responses to this question. As with gang joining in prison, this proved to be a good decision. As we describe below, new themes for exiting gangs emerged early and often, all of which fell within the push/pull motivational framework that we use to organize our findings. Pushes refer to forces or factors internal to the gang that motivate leaving, while pulls refer to forces or factors found outside of the gang. Consensus coding of qualitative themes produced the following motives:

- Disillusionment (push): maturational reform, seeking independence from gang lifestyle, tired of engaging in violence, shifts in gang politics, and bill of goods;
- Triggering events (push): discontent with the gang crystallized via personal victimization, vicarious victimization, and exasperating non-violent actions;
- Criminal justice involvement (push): leaving prison, punishment due to gang affiliation, and punishment due to gang obligations;
- Gang structure (push): forced out by the gang, dissolution of the gang, and transitioned to another gang;
- Family (pull): sense of responsibility to family, spending time with family, sadness about missing important events, and household obligations;
- Work (pull): job responsibilities, job training, and seeking employment;
- Positive influences (pull): pressure, monitoring, or disappointment of a romantic partner, parent, child, or role model;
- Religion (pull): finding God, attending religious services, reading scripture.

Whereas the motivations for leaving a gang address questions of "why," the methods for leaving tackle questions of "how." We asked former gang members: "What did you have to do to leave your gang?" Since our only prior knowledge of this comes almost exclusively from the street gang literature, much like motivations, we allowed former gang members to provide us with open-ended responses. Again, this was a good decision. While many of the themes we coded overlapped strongly with the street gang literature, additional themes emerged that certainly bring new meaning to the exit process in prison. Following similar consensus coding procedures, we organize the methods for leaving a gang into active/passive processes. Active exits entail a communicative exchange between the gang member and the gang, which can range from verbal to physical. Passive exits lack such communication and occur without ceremony or hostility. The categories include:

- Intervention (active): typically the Gang Renouncement and Disassociation program, but also includes formal non-government organization intervention;
- Jumped out (active): undergoing a physical beating by members of the gang as ceremony to mark the departure of a member;
- Permission/meeting (active): the departing member seeks permission from leadership to exit, and a meeting is held to accept the request and determine exit procedures;
- Giving notice (active): the departing member notifies the gang of leaving, and may or may not give an explanation;
- Moving (passive): leaving occurs by chance or purpose by moving to a new city, neighborhood, prison unit, or cell;
- Stopped associating (passive): walked away from the gang without notice, typically on good terms due to rank or status;
- Nothing/no explanation (passive): did nothing to leave, just left the gang.

Both the motivations and methods for leaving a gang are centered primarily on the former gang member. But leaving a gang involves more than that, as there are important stakeholders who can facilitate or complicate the process (Densley and Pyrooz 2017). We shift our attention to another key feature of gang disengagement, where we aim to uncover whom or what facilitated leaving the gang. What got the former gang member from Stage 1 (first doubts) to Stage 4 (post-exit validation)? Unlike the methods and motives, however, we provided respondents with ten possible responses, which included: (1) no one or nothing; (2) leaving prison; (3) a romantic partner; (4) a parent or family member; (5) a mentor or non-familial role model; (6) education, taking classes, or getting training (e.g., vocational); (7) church or attending religious services; (8) a job or going to work; (9) a program or agency that helps people get out of gangs; or (10) moving to a different neighborhood, cell, or unit. We also included an "other" category as a catch-all, although all of the responses provided fell within the aforementioned categories and were generally more precise explanations of what facilitated exit.

Mythologizing about gangs on the street has produced a warped reality about the ability to leave a gang alive and unscathed. Does this also apply in prison? We asked all of our gang-involved respondents, including current and former gang members: "Are there consequences if someone drops out of his gang in prison?" And since we were interested in the physical and social costs of gang leaving, anyone who responded "yes" to the prior question was asked to share with us what they viewed these consequences to be. We divided their responses up into "violent" and "non-violent" consequences.

We then asked former gang members about their post-exit experiences, both real and perceived, consistent with our prior work on the topic (Decker, Pyrooz, and Moule, 2014). In terms of the actual residual consequences, we queried former gang members about the following experiences since leaving the gang:

(1) being attacked by their former gang, (2) being attacked by rival gangs, (3) the former gang attacking their family, and (4) being treated as a gang member by police or correctional officers. We then asked these same former gang members how worried they were about each of these actions occurring *today*. All of the residual consequences include two response categories: whether an action occurred/worries exist or not.

### Measuring the Correlates of Active and Former Gang Membership

The final portion of our analysis includes both active and former gang members. Rather than focus on what promotes disengagement from gangs, we ask an equally important question about persistence: What encourages active gang members to stay? And, perhaps more tellingly, when do they plan on leaving? Active gang members were posed these questions, including the projected time to departure (upon leaving prison, within six months post-release, six to twelve months post-release, one to five years post-release, more than five years post-release, and never). Based on this, we then asked respondents an open-ended question on why they plan to leave the gang or not.

We also aimed to distinguish former from active gang members across a number of characteristics. Recall that a core argument in this book is that gang members are distinguishable from non-gang members owing to what drives people to gangs (i.e., selection) and how the gang influences people (i.e., coercion and persuasion). This same argument applies to former gang members, who have selected out of the gang and are no longer/less vulnerable to gang-related group processes. We differentiate active and former gang members – including those who left the gang on the street and those who left in prison – along a number of characteristics, which we organize into domains of demographics, environment, health, social connections, attitudes and beliefs, criminal justice system involvement, and gang-related, similar to Chapters 4 and 8.

### Analytic Plan

Our plan of analysis for this chapter begins by evaluating whether leaving gangs in prison is even possible. We report gang members' views on the possibility of leaving gangs in prison without consequence, along with the types of consequences that our respondents believe exist. Representative quotes are reported to give readers a sense of how gang-involved respondents viewed the violent and non-violent consequences for leaving gangs in prisons. This provides a good starting point for then assessing the normativity of leaving gangs on the street and in prison.

Next, we turn our attention to the motives and methods for leaving gangs. We report why people leave gangs, how they leave gangs, and who/what facilitated leaving. Based on our consensus coding of qualitative data, prevalence scores are reported for each of these outcomes. We also distinguish these outcomes across multiple strata: (1) location of where someone left a gang, whether it was on the street or in prison; and (2) the four-part gang typology, which includes STG-segregation, STG-no-segregation, prison-oriented, and street-oriented gangs. Representative quotes are provided for the motives and methods for leaving gangs to illustrate common responses along with differences across our comparison groups.

Since it is unclear whether the mythologizing about the barriers impeding leaving a gang also exist in prison, the next portion of our analysis focuses on the residual consequences of gang membership. Using the same comparative groups described above, we report the real and perceived negative consequences of post-gang life.

The final portion of our analysis focuses on what distinguishes active gang members from former gang members. We first report when active gang members intend to leave their gang, along with explanations for their responses, including representative quotes. We then quantitatively compare active gang members and former gang members who left their gang in street and prison settings across demographic, environment, health, social connections, attitudes and beliefs, criminal justice system, and gang-related domains.

## FINDINGS ON DISENGAGING FROM GANGS

Of the 802 prison inmates we interviewed in the LoneStar Project, over half (441) revealed to us that they had been a member of a gang in their lifetime. As we noted in Chapter 8, 47 of these individuals had been a part of a second gang, which brings us to 488 person-gang observations in total. Only around 30 percent of the gang-involved respondents in the study were still active in these gangs when we interviewed them. While that figure is not insubstantial, and certainly has consequences for misconduct and victimization, as we demonstrated in Chapter 7, it is also notable that over two-thirds of our gang-involved subsample have left the gang behind. Did this occur years or even decades ago on the street, when most people get involved in gangs as adolescents? Or was leaving a gang only possible for the people who got involved with groups with low levels of organization and structure? The mythology surrounding disengagement from gangs is quite strong on the street, and perhaps even stronger in prison. In what follows, we aim to pull back the curtain to learn about leaving gangs in prison.

### The Myth and the Reality of Leaving Gangs in Prison

Eight out of every ten gang-involved respondents in the LoneStar Project reported to us that there are consequences associated with leaving a gang in prison. It was surprising just how little variability there was across our comparative groups. Indeed, there was little difference between street (79%

said "yes") and prison (86%) gang joiners or street (75%) and prison (81%) gang leavers. The only notable distinction was between the members of STG-segregated gangs, where 94% endorsed these consequences, compared to a low of 74% of the STG-non-segregated gangs (both prison-oriented and street-oriented gangs were in the lower 80s).

What was universal across all the comparisons was the belief that the consequences of dropping out of a gang included violence. Roughly 91 percent of the respondents who told us that there were consequences for leaving a gang in prison indicated that violence was one of them. The most common response was getting "jumped out" of the gang. As an active member of the Tangos told us:

You have to get "smashed" out. You got "blasted" in and now smashed out. Go a couple of rounds if you are leaving with respect. If not, you get stomped. Some people died but definitely not normal procedure for people sliding back.

This quote reflects the subtleties of leaving gangs. It is viewed as typical to get jumped out for members in good standing, particularly those who are stepping away for legitimate reasons. Others note that it is possible to walk away without any violent consequences, but "it depends on how long he's been a member and his rank and rep," according to a member of La Raza Unida. Gangs appear to weigh the résumés of members when making these decisions. A former member of the Bloods noted:

It varies. Because it is political. Favoritism. He may want to drop out, but if he is the main contributor, then there would be no consequences. But for someone who is less of a contributor, I've seen severe and not severe consequences.

Yet, for members with shorter or blemished résumés, that is, those who have not "put in work" or are not in good standing, it is more complicated and the consequences may extend beyond getting jumped out. Indeed, nearly one-third of our gang-involved respondents told us that death may be a consequence of leaving a gang. Why? A veteran of the Texas Syndicate indicated:

They don't like exes. They know too much. They are afraid if he gets busted then he will snitch. Sometimes they are taken out completely, especially if they know too much. If he is a potentially weak-minded person they will take him out before he has the opportunity.

Of course, we do not have a way to validate such a claim since all of the members we interviewed were alive and could not have experienced the ultimate punishment. Overall, while nearly every gang-involved respondent indicated to us that consequences are possible, whether or not they are carried out appears to be conditional on rank, reputation, and reasoning.

Do gang members leave gangs in prison? Absolutely. Figure 9.1 extends the information reported in the previous chapter on gang joining to gang leaving. The three categories of gang onset – street only, street importation, and prison

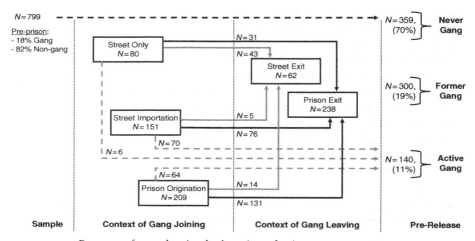

FIGURE 9.1 Patterns of gang leaving by location of exit
Notes: Black dotted line refers to never gang members; gray dotted line refers to active gang members; gray solid line refers to leaving a gang on the street; black solid line refers to leaving a gang in prison. Counts (N) are unweighted and % are weighted to correct for oversampling.

origination – are linked to the location of gang leaving. At the time of the pre-release or baseline interview, 300 people in the LoneStar Project were former gang members while 140 people were active gang members, constituting 19 and 11 percent of our representative sample based on weighting, respectively. For the sake of parsimony, we only report exits based on the gang our respondents were most recently a part of (there were actually 342 observations of gang leaving in our data, owing to transitions to different gangs).

There are two findings that strike us as particularly noteworthy. First, it is more common to leave a gang in prison than on the street. Second, it is more common to leave a gang than join one in prison. These findings seem to fly in the face of popular perceptions of gang membership in prison. While most (54 percent) of the street-only gang members left the gang before they went to prison, 39 percent dropped out upon arriving to prison. The remaining six respondents claimed to retain an affiliation that was street-based only. In other words, they were not gangbanging in prison. For this group, "street only" meant that gang affiliation did not extend into prison.

Nearly half of the respondents who imported their gang affiliation into prison also ceased that affiliation in prison. In other words, prison may contribute to continuity in gang membership, exacerbating ties to the gang, but it also may produce change in prison gang affiliation. By the time we interviewed these men, over half of the street importation group had dropped their affiliation with the gang. Of course, we lack a counterfactual to compare what would have occurred if they had not been incarcerated. But this suggests to us that leaving a gang is possible in prison, even if one's affiliation stretches far back in the life course (as we demonstrate shortly).

Most of the prison origination group – those who joined a gang for the first time in their life upon imprisonment – had dropped their affiliation by the time we interviewed them. In fact, only 31 percent of this group were active gang members at pre-release and many indicated to us that they would leave once they experienced freedom in the upcoming days of release. Still, the prison origination respondents overwhelmingly left their gang in prison (90 percent), with the remaining respondents leaving behind their affiliation on the street after a prior spell in prison.

These findings are notable because they reveal that leaving a gang in prison is possible. Just as we thought about prison as a turning point for gang onset for a sizable proportion of inmates (around 12 percent of Texas inmates), prison may also be a turning point for gang exit for an even larger proportion of inmates. Findings such as these lay the groundwork for considering prison as an opportunity for both prevention and intervention. Left unexplored in these findings, though, is whether the process of disengagement diverges across important points of stratification: street vs. prison, STGs vs. cliques, prison gangs vs. street gangs. Understanding these differences is important to theory and policy alike.

## Motivations for Leaving Gangs

Why would gang members want to leave a group that purportedly offers them identity, kinship, pride, safety, and wealth? In an increasingly stratified society that marginalizes the very youth who select into gangs, these benefits are hard to come by on the street, just as they are in the prisons that strip away identity, impose strict routines, and provide insufficient protection. Understanding the motivations for leaving gangs is not only important for the scientific enterprise to illuminate the contours of gang membership, but also to inform the policy, programming, and practices that aim to respond to gangs and gang members. Figure 9.2 contains the motivations for leaving a gang based on our consensus coding of open-ended responses, partitioned by our six comparative groups.

The leading motivation for leaving a gang is disillusionment, which was defined by Bubolz and Simi (2015, 336) as "unmet expectations produc[ing] a psychosocial state of discontent." We adopt a broad definition of disillusionment to capture discordance between personal identity, beliefs and values, and personal goals versus those of the gang. Over three-fourths of former gang members identified disillusionment as a motivation for leaving. Although the former members of street-oriented gangs were the least likely to endorse it, disillusionment was still their most common motivation for leaving. A former member of Barrio Azteca [STG-segregated] conveys this line of thinking quite nicely:

I got tired. Also a spiritual awakening. One day I looked at my older brother who is active still, turned around, told him I was tired and didn't want to live this life anymore. Believe it or not, the year prior I lost thirteen close members who were friends and family, all because of that lifestyle. My mom passed away too; her prayers finally caught up to me. I was all in the money and the dope, all in the lifestyle, then I had a *moment of clarity* and I wondered what the hell am I doing with my life? (emphasis added).

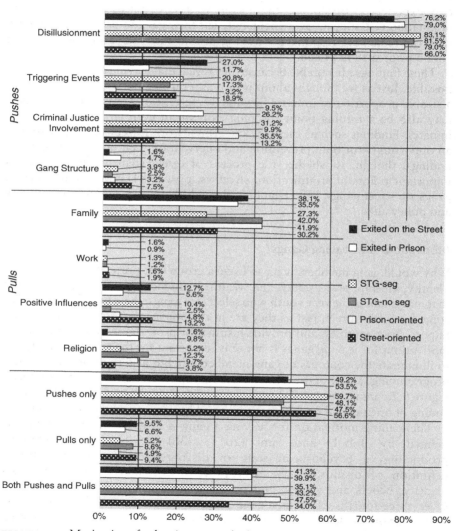

FIGURE 9.2 Motivations for leaving a gang by location of exit and group typology
Notes: Mean number of responses provided by group: Full Sample (N = 277) Mean = 2.20; Exited on the Street (N = 63) Mean = 2.05; Exited in Prison (N = 213) Mean = 2.24; STG-seg (N = 77) Mean = 2.45; STG-no seg (N = 81) Mean = 2.09; Prison-oriented (N = 61) Mean = 2.26; Street-oriented (N = 53) Mean = 1.94.

This respondent clearly checks off a number of boxes, but what stands out to us is the crystallization of discontent, which is a rather representative comment among former gang members. Indeed, many former gang members could point to the exact moment when they realized "this is not who I am, I'm done," which signaled an identity reformation, or the tipping point noted above. Usually such thinking was accompanied by feelings of being "too old" or "too tired" to continue the gang lifestyle. When these respondents wake up and look at themselves in the mirror, "gang member" is no longer what they see.

Although many of these moments of clarity occurred without apparent rhyme or reason, about 15 percent of former gang members reported triggering events, that is, an experience that prompted a recalculation of devotion to the gang. One theme that resonated quite strongly was a feeling of betrayal. A former member of 18th Street [street-oriented] gang said:

Because I saw that none of my homeboys wrote me once I got locked up. There was no loyalty within the gang.

Those feelings seemed to extend to a lack of visits in prison or at the hospital, or the gang not having their back during a personal crisis. For example, a former Blood [STG-non-segregated] told us about a robbery at his apartment, where his father was tied up and had a gun to his head:

[The robber] was a crackhead and tried to steal the drugs from the apartment. He didn't steal the jewelry or the drugs. Mom came in and told him she was calling the cops. They ran out the back of the apartment and I run after them with a gun on the golf course. I told [my parents] not to call the cops. I went looking for people and went to my homeboy's house, a Blood, and asked him to help kill this guy but no one from the gang would help me. So I left the gang.

Others realized it when they were committing crimes, according to a former member of the Mexican Mafia [STG-segregated]:

Sometimes when we went to collect the 10 percent for selling drugs, we went to condemned houses and people with run-down cars. When we were slapping around this guy, he was crying and trying to put food on the table. I was the sergeant, that hurt me in a way. At that point I thought, "what am I doing," especially for those who were trying to help their family.

Of course, triggering events also occurred with personal victimization and threats to personal and family safety, as others have noted (e.g., Decker and Lauritsen 2002), but it is clear that the tolerance for actions and experiences in the gang clearly has an upper limit.

Family, the second most prevalent motivation among our respondents, was often paired with disillusionment. It appeared as if the reference group for gauging self-worth and life satisfaction changed, as seen in this quote from a former Blood [STG-non-segregated] gang member:

I grew up and I found out what I was doing and what I was affiliated for was wrong. I no longer had the same desires. I thought about my son, family, and future. I see things from a different viewpoint. I learned more about myself. I was more confident in myself and just being me.

Family took on a number of flavors in motivating leaving gangs. A former member of the Aryan Brotherhood [STG-segregated] put it rather succinctly: "My family needed me more than the gang did." It seemed as if many of the former gang members in our sample maintained what could be thought of as a gang ledger, where they weighed the costs and benefits of continuity against that of change. Such conflict between competing demands and interests is apparent in the reflections of a former member of the Tangos [prison-oriented]:

Came in [to prison] with a different attitude, got a family, got kids, can't worship two gods. Can't do two things. Can't do good and evil. Can't do both. Made my decision to stay away from all the negative stuff.

While gangs maintain an attraction that may allow members to neglect relationships over a period of time, eventually those compelling forces begin to wear on people. This was apparent across all of the comparative groups, and especially among the former members of STG-non-segregated and prison-oriented gangs.

In due course, gang members no longer view the gang through rose-colored glasses. A former member of the Texas Syndicate told us: "they became more of a liability than an asset." All the appeal and glamour of life in the gang eventually wanes, especially once members scratch beneath the surface of the group, as exemplified by a former member of the Texas Mafia [STG-non-segregated], who touches on a number of core factors:

It is a bunch of bull crap – when you first get into it the picture that is painted that it is loyalty between everyone and it is not that. The only thing it does is keepin' you in prison. It doesn't help you or your family. Everything is a power struggle where everyone wants to be in charge and take over. Don't believe in the same things anymore . . . dealing drugs and stealing is now wrong . . . loyalty is only for gangs rather it is for family, real family. While in prison none of my gang people wrote or sent me money but my real family did.

At first glance, he is describing being sold "a bill of goods," a source of disillusionment that Bubolz and Simi (2015) put at the core of their cognitive-emotional theory of gang disengagement. The former members of prison-oriented gangs were the least likely to endorse being sold a bill of goods, but our sense is that the mythologizing around groups like the Tangos and Peckerwoods is less sensational than the STG-segregated gangs. After all, they view themselves as protective groups, not criminal organizations. The above response also taps emerging themes that, to our knowledge, are new to research on disengagement from gangs: shifting gang politics and imprisonment as a motivation for change.

Gang politics was a somewhat common refrain among former members, noted by about one-quarter of our sample, and especially among the STG gangs. Some referred to the "young guys" taking over and wanting power. Others were frustrated by allowing certain people in the gang. For example, a former member of the Aryan Circle noted that a leader of the "AC was a sex offender and [they] are not allowed in." But we also identified a stronger ideological dissonance. Motivations expressed along ideological lines typically focused on the purpose of the gang – generating income, protection of racial group, or friendship. A former member of the Mexican Mafia [STG-segregated] told us that gang politics was a motivation for leaving because:

For one, the way they were doing things. They were going to start taxing people, take commissary from people, abuse and use people for prostitution. There was a lot of hate and violence. I didn't like that. If anything, I try to help people. It was pretty bad.

Likewise, a former member of the Aryan Brotherhood [STG-segregated], who had been incarcerated a number of times, noted that:

When I got locked up again this time, it seemed like no one had their head on straight, no one knew what we were supposed to be about. It was pointless.

If gang members look to gangs for purpose, it appears that the lack thereof drove people away.

Research with street gang members commonly finds trouble with the law as a motivation for leaving, but our sample further highlights the perils of gang membership for punishment in the system. This was a notable distinction between the people who left gangs on the street and people who left gangs in prison. Many former gang members viewed continued involvement as preventing them from returning home: "It was more important to go home than belong to a gang," according to a former member of the Tangos. But the specter of punishment ran much stronger than that, and tapped the collateral consequences of gang membership (Pyrooz and Mitchell 2019). Another former member of the Tangos [prison-oriented] told us:

I am trying to make it home. Too much politics, favoritism, wrong decisions made, nonsense, BS. It's just not worth it. It wasn't what I'd thought it would be at the beginning. It stayed on my record, parole denies you for being confirmed [as a gang member], you don't qualify for certain TDCJ [Texas Department of Criminal Justice] activities when you are confirmed. There was too much tension, stress, headaches for me.

The latter half of this statement recognizes that continued gang membership is not just about imprisonment, but also parole challenges, access to programming in prison, and even mental health, a point we return to below. And then there is the issue of segregation. A former member of the Aryan Brotherhood [STG-segregated] said, "I wanted to make parole and get out of seg," which would have been almost impossible without leaving the gang, owing to housing policies. Indeed, segregation was a particularly acute point among the STG-segregated members. As a former member of the Aryan Circle [STG-segregated] put it, he wanted to get out of "state-sponsored torture."

All of our comparative groups typically identified two reasons for leaving the gang. But Figure 9.2 makes it apparent – for all six of our comparative groups – that leaving the gang is rarely motivated by pulls alone. Less than 10 percent of our sample only identified pulls as the motivation for leaving, whereas pushes alone was the modal category for all groups, and especially for the former members of STG-segregated gangs. In other words, gang members are motivated to leave the gang primarily due to dynamics internal to the gangs. When those dynamics are paired with pulls external to the gang, it appears to be a recipe for behavioral and cognitive change. But when this realization takes place, how do they begin to unwind the ties that bind together members of a gang? After all, motivation may undergird action, but it does not guarantee it (Densley and Pyrooz 2017), which is why we need to examine the methods of exit.

### Methods for Leaving Gangs

If the perception is that there are serious, often violent consequences for leaving a gang in prison, what is the reality? Figure 9.3 reports these results.

What is perhaps the most notable finding is that only 15 percent of our sample reported being jumped out or, as the Tangos termed it, "smashed out" of the gang. And it was indeed the prison-oriented gangs that were driving this value, particularly the Tangos. Here is what a former member of the Tangos had to say:

I got jumped out by twenty or thirty people beating me up for a long time. That is when my ribs were broken. I was supposed to be dead, but by the grace of God I was able to live.

Although this former member did not allude to the background behind his departure, at least based on perceptions of leaving, he likely left the gang without the status, rank, or experience to avoid undergoing such a brutal exit. The former members of other gangs reported getting jumped out, too. For example, a number of former members of the 52 Hoover Crips told us that they had to fight several guys for "52 seconds." Some former members of STGs-segregated indicated that they were jumped out, although this was rare, and seemed to take a sinister turn. A former member of the Mexican Mafia stated:

I had a choice between death (which would have been quick) or get beaten (which would have been a slower process). I was lowered in rank to get the choice. Was originally a sergeant. Got lowered to a normal member.

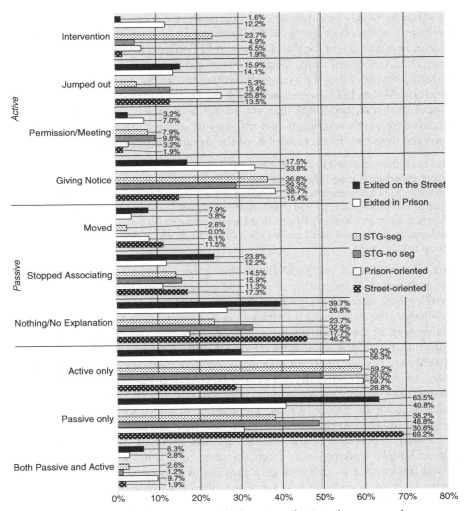

FIGURE 9.3 Methods for leaving a gang by location of exit and group typology
Notes: Mean number of responses provided by group: Full Sample (N = 276) Mean =
1.13; Exited on the Street (N = 63) Mean = 1.13; Exited in Prison (N = 213) Mean = 1.13;
STG-seg (N = 76) Mean = 1.16; STG-no seg (N = 82) Mean = 1.07; Prison-oriented (N =
62) Mean = 1.18; Street-oriented (N = 52) Mean = 1.10.

Overall, there appears to be far more mythologizing about violent exits than
actual violent exits. After all, the majority of the sample was able to leave a gang
without violence.

The methods for leaving are highly contingent upon comparative groups,
much like what we observed for getting jumped out, especially for other active
methods for leaving. In particular, intervention as a method for leaving was

identified by nearly one-quarter of STG-segregated former gang members, but rarely among the other gangs. In the Texas prison system, the primary way out of solitary confinement for the members of STG-segregated gangs is through the Gang Renouncement and Disassociation program (Burman 2012). Being deemed a threat is based on gang affiliation, and as one former member of the Mexican Mafia [STG-segregated] put it, this "clear[ed him] from being a security threat, prov[ing] that you're not a member." When members are prepared to leave the gang, they notify an investigator in the prison system, as conveyed here by a former member of the Aryan Brotherhood:

> I had to contact someone in the gang and tell them that I was going to attend GRAD [the Gang Renouncement and Disassociation program]. Had to write an I-60 to gang intelligence [the STG management office] and tell them I wanted to renounce being a member of the Aryan Brotherhood. I had to tell someone at rank [a major] of Aryan Brotherhood. I shot him a kite [a letter] explaining that I was wanting to get out. Doesn't mean I got his good graces, just means that I can do what I have to do and it doesn't mean that I won't be retaliated against.

Part of the reason we highlighted this quote is that it reflects the joint communication a member has with the gang and the prison system before invoking on a nine-month journey through GRAD.

Whereas the street gang literature does not place much emphasis on the role of the gang in the disengagement process (Densley and Pyrooz 2017), such a position is at odds with our data on leaving gangs in prison. First, there is a twenty-six percentage point difference in active methods for leaving gangs in prison than gangs on the street. Put simply, street exits are far more likely to be passive than prison exits. Second, and what is a new contribution to our understanding of leaving gangs, highlighted in the quote from the former member of the Aryan Brotherhood, is that leaving gangs in prison, particularly STGs and prison-oriented groups, involves what we term *giving notice*. Simply walking away from the gang in prison or gangs with strong prison links is not as common of a practice as it is on the street. This is not particularly surprising, as it is far more difficult to hide in prisons – even in protective custody or administrative segregation, inmates have the ability to gather information about the individuals in their cellblocks or pods.

Many former gang members tell us that they had to seek permission from the gang, as reflected in this statement from a former Texas Syndicate member:

> Spoke with my fellow gang members and the leaders or the ones that were leading on the unit, the top rank. I told them what my plans were, what I wanted to do, that I wanted to get out, but still be in good standing. They asked me why. Said my age and I was just tired of this shit. They took a vote among the rank there, took it to the table which is the main man and let me know their decision. They got a positive response, favorable vote, and they put me in retirement . . . I don't have to look behind my back because I am in good standing.

Not all gangs react this way, of course. Since gangs are competing for control in prison, gangs are concerned about the message it conveys for members to be able to leave scot-free. As this former member of the Texas Chicano Brotherhood [STG-non-segregated] noted, in planning to sign denouncement papers:

I told TCB what I planned to do and if they had a problem with it, to take care of it. They didn't have a problem with it, but they wanted me to make sure to tell people that I was an ex-member because of my religion. So it would put out a better worldly image.

Other gangs were less compromising. Many former gang members told us that upon giving notice, the gang reacted by putting what is known as a "hit" on them – kill on sight. A former member of the Mexican Mafia [STG-segregated] recalled:

I wrote a letter and told them I didn't want anything to do with them anymore. They put a hit on me. Now there is two or three thousand ex-members. Now they don't mess with us. There's too many of us.

Still, most of the gangs – as we first discovered in street-based settings (Pyrooz and Decker 2011) – are largely understanding of the reasons for leaving. Of course, there may be differences, even among members of the same gang, as this former member of the Mexican Mafia told us:

I didn't have to do anything to leave. The rules are relaxed now. Membership heard about all of the BS that I went through and they understood. As long as you have a legitimate case it is okay – you cannot up and leave. They understood.

Giving notice specifically, and active methods for leaving generally, stand in contrast to what the former members of street gangs reported to us. In fact, over two-thirds of the former members of street-oriented gangs revealed that their exit from the gang was passive, and nearly half of them indicated that they did nothing to leave. Some indicated to us that they had to "slide back" and stop associating, but when we asked the question, most simply stated "nothing," as if it was a rather odd question that they would have had to do something to leave. While notifying a gang is one step in breaking the ties, it is very different to fully transition to a bona fide former gang member. Who or what helped facilitate this transition to post-exit validation?

## Facilitators of Leaving Gangs

Given the former gang members' responses to methods of leaving, perhaps it would be expected that a large proportion viewed their exit as entirely independent and on their own accord. We report this information in Figure 9.4. Around 41% of the former gang members told us that "no one" or "nothing" helped facilitate their exit from the gang. STG-segregated (33%) and prison-oriented (36%) former gang members were the least likely to

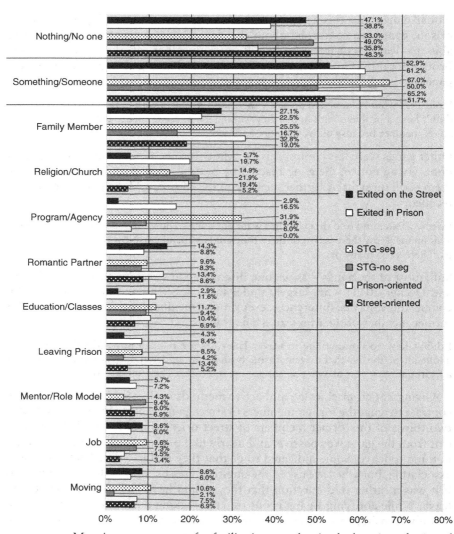

FIGURE 9.4 Most important source for facilitating gang leaving by location of exit and group typology

Notes: Mean number of responses provided by group: Full Sample (N = 323) Mean = 1.02; Exited on the Street (N = 64) Mean = 0.80; Exited in Prison (N = 235) Mean = 1.08; STG-seg (N = 93) Mean = 1.30; STG-no seg (N = 96) Mean = 0.90; Prison-oriented (N = 67) Mean = 1.13; Street-oriented (N = 58) Mean = 0.64.

endorse this viewpoint, where STG-non-segregated (49%) and street-oriented (48%) former gang members were the most likely. But when turning to the sources for facilitating exit from the gang, there were not a lot of statistically or substantively significant differences across the comparative categories.

Leaving gangs in prison, though, was more likely to be facilitated by a religious commitment or program/agency than leaving gangs on the street. As a former member of the Crips stated, "Because I found God. I needed God in my life, so I decided to serve God." Religion was viewed as a legitimate pathway out of the gang in prison, both to the departing gang member and to the gang being left behind. This further validates the findings of Johnson and Densley (2018) in Brazilian prisons, as well as Deuchar's (2018) comparative research in Glasgow and Los Angeles. Of course, we should not overstate the role of religion; while it is an established and respected pathway out of the gang, it applies only to a smaller subgroup of former gang members. There is nary a mention of religion among most (83 percent) of the former gang members in our sample.

In terms of interventions, about 17 percent of former gang members who exited in prison identified a program or agency to facilitate leaving, compared to only 3 percent of former gang members who left on the street. This difference was driven largely by STG-segregated former gang members, of whom nearly one-third stated that programs or agencies were what facilitated their exit from the gang, and overwhelmingly cited the GRAD program. A former member of the Aryan Brotherhood noted: "GRAD takes care of you. They take you to a unit that makes you safe although there are other gangs active on these units." Safety is a major concern for facilitating exit, especially when leaving gangs where there could be severe consequences. And if those continued consequences exist, how common are they?

## The Residual Consequences of Gang Membership

Figure 9.5 reports whether former gang members experienced actual consequences post-exit from the gang and their continued concerns about gang activity. In general, it was pretty rare for former gang members to be attacked by their gang or rival gangs. Not a single former gang member told us that their family was attacked, although around 10% reported that they had been attacked by their former gang (8%) or rival gangs (3.5%), and some were attacked by both. The former members of STG-segregated gangs were the most likely to report attacks by their former gang (14%), although there were no differences in being attacked by rival gangs. The only comparative group with members that seemed especially worried about the residual consequences of gang membership was the STG-segregated gangs, where nearly one-quarter worried about being attacked and 15% worried about their families.

Gangs are not the only concern of former gang members, as there are other important stakeholders in the disengagement process (Densley and Pyrooz 2017). The majority of former gang members agreed that police and correctional officers continued to treat them as active gang members, despite having left the gang. There seemed to be a feeling among members of our sample that GRAD would help reduce such consequences in prison. In response to this question, a former member of Hermanos de Pistoleros Latinos [STG-segregated] told us, "GRAD doesn't help you in the free world at all, only in prison." Indeed, a former member of the Mexican

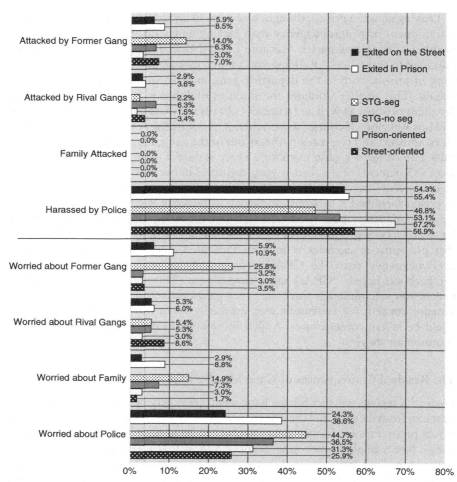

FIGURE 9.5 Residual consequences of gang leaving by location of exit and group typology

Mafia shared this sentiment, and he wanted to "send GRAD program [completion] paper to all criminal justice agencies to signify [that he is] not a gang member." Formally renouncing affiliation is a costly signal, one that burns bridges to the gang, which is why former gang members view it as valid and think that it can withstand the scrutiny from people in positions of power.

## Continuity in Gang Membership

If life in the gang is replete with violence, politics, and imprisonment, why do people continue their involvement? And, perhaps more importantly, why do members stay in a gang as long as they do? Our sample of gang-involved inmates reports an average of twelve years in the gang, much longer than school-based and representative non-institutional samples. We asked the 140 active gang members in the LoneStar Project when they planned on leaving their gang. Four of them either would not tell us or simply did not have an answer, but the remainder did, and their answers were telling.

About half of the active gang members said that they would never leave their gang (49 percent), or that they would leave in more than five years from now (6 percent). Those who said that they would never leave either maintained an intense loyalty to the gang or felt like they had no options other than the gang. A member of the Bloods [STG-non-segregated] described it as:

I guess I feel loyal for some reason, like I took an oath.

A member of the Crips [STG-non-segregated] blends together loyalty and obligation, noting:

I am dedicated to them. Once you join, then there is no getting out. When you get out, they actually try to hurt you. They feel like you are betraying them.

Mythologizing about gangs appears to play a role in his continued involvement.

Many of the respondents who remain active in the gang alluded to familial undertones to gang membership. A member of the Aryan Brotherhood [STG-segregated] told us: "Because they have been my family when I didn't have family. It's friendship and protection and leadership." This touches on themes related to motivations for joining and leaving gangs, where perhaps some active gang members simply do not feel like they have been sold a bill of goods. For example, this active member of the Tangos noted "It's not a violent gang. We made it to protect our homeboys and their families. TDCJ actually let us create our gang to stop the Mexican Mafia." Whether or not loyalty, obligation, or protection is factual hardly matters when one believes such virtues are true. After all, much of what drives gang dynamics is perceptual rather than objective (Klein 1995; Lauger 2012).

We can also learn much from those who tell us that they will be leaving. The responses we received from the sixty-one active members who intend to leave in the next five years bear a strong resemblance to the motivations for leaving a gang. A Tango gang member told us that

I am done with it. I don't want to do this no more. I don't want to do the penitentiary, this whole lifestyle. I don't want to come back.

Another member of the Tangos said that:

I don't want to carry that burden on my shoulders and my sons. I don't want my sons to tell me that they joined a gang because I did.

Yet another member of the Tangos offered a more practical take, recognizing that:

The gang stays in prison, so I will leave it [when I get out, but] if I come back to prison, I will join back up again.

Given the striking parallels between the active and former gang members revealed by qualitative data, it does lead us to wonder just how different these two groups are when compared along a range of attitudinal, criminal justice, demographic, gang, and social characteristics. Although we have shown that active gang members engage in more misconduct and violence, as well as experience more victimization behind bars than former gang members, it is unclear just how different or similar these two groups are in other domains.

### Distinguishing Active and Former Gang Members

Table 9.1 presents descriptive statistics on three categories of inmates: (1) current gang members, (2) former gang members who had left their gang on the street, and (3) former gang members who had left their gang in prison. We pay close attention to how the differences and similarities between these three groups shift as we move across domains.

In terms of demographic characteristics, the figure that jumps out immediately is age: current gang members are about five years younger than street-former gang members and six years younger than prison-former gang members. Of course, this is what we would expect, given that there appears to be an age-gang curve that is slightly positively distributed, but with central tendencies around the mid-twenties. When shifting to race/ethnicity, however, there are few differences across the three groups. Surprisingly to us, especially in light of Chapter 8 that revealed whites were most likely to join a gang in prison, the street-former gang members were statistically more likely to be white than the current or the prison-former gang members. Perhaps whites experience a different set of pressures for continuity and change in gang membership post-release than blacks and Latinos. Current gang members maintained lower self-control than former gang members, which is consistent with research showing that self-control predicts continuity in gang membership (Pyrooz, Sweeten, and Piquero 2013) and that self-control worsens during periods of gang membership (Matsuda et al. 2013).

The neighborhoods where current gang members lived before becoming imprisoned appeared to be worse off than those of former gang members. Both street-former and prison-former gang members reported that their neighborhoods had higher levels of informal social control and were less likely to have gangs than current gang members' neighborhoods, although all three groups were equivalent in their perceptions of their neighborhood as a good place to live. These groups also described the prison environment differently. Current gang members reported more disorder than former gang members, and, importantly, indicated that they maintained about 1.5 hours

TABLE 9.1 *Differences between respondents who remain in gangs and those who leave on the street and in prison*

| | Current gang[a] N = 140 | | Exited on the street[b] N = 62 | | Exited in prison[c] N = 237 | |
|---|---|---|---|---|---|---|
| | Mean/% | (SD) | Mean/% | (SD) | Mean/% | (SD) |
| **Demographic** | | | | | | |
| Age in years | 32.44 | $(7.83)^{bc}$ | 37.72 | $(7.75)^{a}$ | 38.70 | $(9.73)^{a}$ |
| Latino | | 44.3% | 41.9% | | 45.1% | |
| Black | 17.1% | | 11.3% | | 20.3% | |
| White | 24.3% | $b$ | 38.7% | $ac$ | 22.4% | $b$ |
| Married | 11.5% | | 21.0% | | 15.6% | |
| In a relationship | 22.3% | | 16.1% | | 15.2% | |
| Father | 68.6% | | 75.8% | | 73.4% | |
| Military veteran | 2.9% | | 3.2% | | 4.6% | |
| Education | 10.86 | (1.63) | 11.32 | (1.38) | 10.88 | (1.75) |
| IQ | 90.87 | (13.14) | 91.69 | (11.59) | 91.97 | (11.24) |
| Low self-control | 1.72 | $(0.71)^{bc}$ | 1.30 | $(0.77)^{a}$ | 1.40 | $(0.78)^{a}$ |
| **Environment** | | | | | | |
| Informal social control | 2.43 | $(0.99)^{bc}$ | 2.91 | $(1.04)^{a}$ | 2.68 | $(0.99)^{a}$ |
| Prison social control | 1.76 | (0.88) | 1.75 | (0.77) | 1.81 | (0.92) |
| Good place to live | 2.32 | (1.34) | 2.48 | (1.35) | 2.57 | (1.19) |
| Gangs in neighborhood | 83.2% | $bc$ | 59.7% | $a$ | 62.7% | $a$ |
| Disorder in the prison | 8.68 | $(1.81)^{bc}$ | 7.87 | $(2.50)^{a}$ | 8.30 | $(1.75)^{a}$ |
| Unstructured routines | 3.47 | $(4.62)^{bc}$ | 1.84 | $(2.74)^{a}$ | 1.81 | $(2.40)^{a}$ |
| **Health** | | | | | | |
| Stress | 1.03 | $(0.63)^{bc}$ | 0.77 | $(0.57)^{a}$ | 0.90 | $(0.58)^{a}$ |
| Self-rated health | 2.24 | (0.76) | 2.19 | (0.76) | 2.19 | (0.85) |
| BMI | 27.57 | (4.82) | 28.89 | (5.91) | 27.96 | (5.51) |
| Exposure to violence | 2.32 | $(0.98)^{b}$ | 1.68 | $(1.07)^{ac}$ | 2.17 | $(0.98)^{b}$ |
| Self-esteem | 2.11 | (0.55) | 2.26 | $(0.54)^{c}$ | 2.10 | $(0.56)^{b}$ |
| Projected age of death | 86.25 | (22.04) | 84.32 | (13.68) | 87.88 | (22.13) |
| **Social connections** | | | | | | |
| Embeddedness in gangs | 1.47 | $(0.59)^{bc}$ | -0.38 | $(0.75)^{ac}$ | -0.11 | $(0.92)^{ab}$ |
| Social distance | 1.06 | $(0.49)^{b}$ | 0.85 | $(0.43)^{ac}$ | 1.05 | $(0.51)^{b}$ |
| Family social support | 2.50 | (0.67) | 2.64 | $(0.65)^{c}$ | 2.39 | $(0.72)^{b}$ |
| Friend social support | 1.96 | $(0.88)^{c}$ | 1.84 | (1.00) | 1.65 | $(0.99)^{a}$ |
| Criminal peers | 1.18 | $(0.87)^{bc}$ | 0.74 | $(0.72)^{a}$ | 0.86 | $(0.74)^{a}$ |

*(continued)*

TABLE 9.1 *(continued)*

| | Current gang[a] N = 140 | | Exited on the street[b] N = 62 | | Exited in prison[c] N = 237 | |
|---|---|---|---|---|---|---|
| | Mean/% | (SD) | Mean/% | (SD) | Mean/% | (SD) |
| **Attitudes and beliefs** | | | | | | |
| Code of the street | 2.56 | $(0.75)^{bc}$ | 1.98 | $(0.73)^{a}$ | 2.19 | $(0.91)^{a}$ |
| Convict code | 2.89 | $(0.52)^{bc}$ | 2.54 | $(0.63)^{a}$ | 2.69 | $(0.58)^{a}$ |
| Legitimacy | 1.26 | $(0.49)^{c}$ | 1.41 | (0.57) | 1.42 | $(0.52)^{a}$ |
| Procedural justice | 0.87 | $(0.52)^{c}$ | 1.01 | (0.57) | 1.05 | $(0.54)^{a}$ |
| Ethnic ID – cultural | 3.16 | (0.60) | 3.27 | (0.44) | 3.14 | (0.59) |
| Ethnic ID – social | 3.04 | $(0.78)^{b}$ | 3.28 | $(0.61)^{a}$ | 3.15 | (0.68) |
| Spirituality/religiosity | 2.73 | $(1.04)^{bc}$ | 3.22 | $(0.61)^{a}$ | 3.08 | $(0.76)^{a}$ |
| **CJ System** | | | | | | |
| Age at first arrest | 17.42 | (5.46) | 18.91 | $(5.62)^{c}$ | 17.32 | $(3.49)^{b}$ |
| Number of arrests | 9.05 | (5.41) | 9.03 | (5.04) | 10.22 | (6.58) |
| Prison stints | 1.78 | $(0.94)^{bc}$ | 2.21 | $(1.36)^{a}$ | 2.24 | $(1.26)^{a}$ |
| Years incarcerated | 4.09 | $(4.02)^{c}$ | 4.04 | $(4.11)^{c}$ | 6.32 | $(6.33)^{ab}$ |
| Violent offender | 38.6% | | 35.5% | | 41.8% | |
| **Gangs** | | | | | | |
| Age at joining | 17.38 | $(5.98)^{c}$ | 15.98 | $(4.45)^{c}$ | 19.20 | $(5.95)^{ab}$ |
| Prison join | 61.4% | $^{b}$ | 24.2% | $^{ac}$ | 60.3% | $^{b}$ |
| Years in gang | 13.81 | $(8.17)^{b}$ | 9.31 | $(6.61)^{ac}$ | 12.68 | $(7.43)^{b}$ |
| Years since leaving | – | – | 12.38 | $(7.53)^{c}$ | 6.27 | $(6.07)^{b}$ |
| STG-seg | 15.0% | $^{c}$ | 17.7% | $^{c}$ | 34.6% | $^{ab}$ |
| STG-no seg | 30.7% | | 33.9% | | 30.0% | |
| Prison-oriented | 42.9% | $^{bc}$ | 6.5% | $^{ac}$ | 26.6% | $^{a}$ |
| Street-oriented | 10.0% | $^{b}$ | 37.1% | $^{ab}$ | 7.6% | $^{b}$ |

*Note:* Superscripts indicate a statistically significant difference between the focal group (column) and current gang member ($^{a}$), exited on the street ($^{b}$), and exited in prison ($^{c}$) derived from equality of proportions and means $z$- and $t$-tests.

more unstructured free time congregating with fellow inmates each day than former gang members.

When shifting to health, it is notable that while self-rated health is statistically equivalent across the gangs, the current gang members report higher levels of stress than street-former and prison-former gang members, and by a large margin (~0.5 standard deviations). Researchers are just beginning to uncover the physical and mental health consequences of gang membership (Coid et al. 2013; Watkins and Melde 2016). Whereas the prison-former and current gang members are likely to be susceptible to the violent environments constructed by gangs in prison, street-former gang members were the least likely to report exposure to violence in prison, which is what we would expect.

Social connections, particularly criminal capital, differed drastically across the three groups. As we anticipated, current gang members were the most embedded in gangs at the time of the interview, followed well behind by prison-former gang members and then by street-former gang members. Street-former gang members maintained the least social distance from correctional officers, while current and prison-former gang members remained equally socially distant. Family and friend social support did not vary considerably across the three groups, although prison-former gang members maintained the lowest family support while street-former gang members maintained the least friend social support. There was nearly a one-half standard deviation difference in criminal peers between current gang members and both groups of former gang members. After all, as people transition out of gangs, their peer groups change pretty remarkably (Sweeten et al. 2013; Weerman, Lovegrove, and Thornberry 2015).

Results for attitudes and beliefs are consistently in the same direction: current gang members hold more criminogenic views than street-former or prison-former gang members. In particular, current gang members adhere more strongly to the code of the street (over 0.5 standard deviations) and the convict code (around one-third standard deviation) than former gang members. Prison-former gang members maintain greater legitimacy in correctional authorities and report more procedurally fair experiences with correctional authorities, which is what we would expect with legal socialization theory and criminal punitiveness. Former gang members were also more religious than current gang members, perhaps a nod to the role of religion and spirituality in promoting disengagement from gangs.

The final results worth mentioning are in the gang-related domain. Prison-former gang members reported joining a gang at older ages (nineteen years) than current (seventeen years) and street-former (sixteen years) gang members. This reflects differences in the proportion of each group that joined their gang in prison; only one-quarter of the street-former gang members did, whereas three-fifths of current and prison-former gang members joined in prison. The street-former gang members had also been in gangs for a shorter portion of their lives – nine years, compared to fourteen and thirteen years among current and prison-former gang members, respectively. Lastly, it is notable that only a slim portion of current and prison-former gang members affiliated with street-oriented gangs, whereas that was the modal gang type for the street-former gang members. Perhaps more importantly, among those who leave their gang behind in prison, they are most likely to have been members of STG-segregated gangs, the groups that we demonstrated in Chapter 5 as having the highest level of organizational structure.

CONCLUSION

This chapter examined exiting the gang among our sample of 802 inmates. With estimates of over 200,000 prison gang members nationwide, this is an important topic. After all, gang membership on the street and in prison is linked to higher rates of offending, particularly violent offending. This puts the safety of correctional employees, other inmates, and gang members at risk and can be a major cause of disruption within prisons. A data-based understanding of leaving the gang in prison may pay dividends in pointing to successful or promising interventions and lead to penal institutions where programs can operate without as many challenges to their operation. There are also potential dividends to be reaped on the back end of incarceration, that is, once an individual has left prison and is at risk of recidivism.

To date the issue of gang leaving, especially prison gang leaving, has been characterized by more heat than light. That is, exceptional stories – blood in, blood out – have dominated thinking about the possibility of ever leaving a prison gang. Such mythologizing is functional for the gang and provides a key element of the prison gang code by depicting the prison gang as powerful, controlling, and ready to exact violent retribution at the first sign of members weakening their commitment to the gang. The few studies of leaving the prison gang that have been conducted are characterized by small and unsystematic samples but offer some insights to help shape our thinking about the possibility of leaving the prison gang. Perhaps the most important conclusion to draw from these samples is that they provide evidence that prison gang members do indeed leave their gang. This is a conclusion our work fully supports. Indeed, roughly two-thirds of our prison gang sample reported that they had left their gang. This stands in contrast to the belief held by most of our sample that they would face interpersonal violence if they were to leave the gang. It appears that the notion that one can never leave the prison gang represents an important gang value that has more symbolic importance than real-life consequences. We regard the prison setting as a strong test of the ability to leave a prison gang. After all, while a street gang member may move to a different neighborhood or city, prison gang members have no such mobility to escape retaliation for terminating their ties to the gang. In a total institution such as a prison, inmates must face fellow gang members or their associates on a daily basis, unless they are held in administrative segregation. Even then, the possibility of being the target of retaliation remains.

We were also struck by the reasons why they left, as well as the methods by which they left. We categorized the motivations for leaving as pushes (negative events or experiences that pushed them out of their gang) or pulls (positive relationships or events that attracted them to a non-gang lifestyle). Pushes far outnumbered pulls as motivations for leaving the gang. While some mentioned experiences with violence – both as a victim and an offender – far and above some form of disillusionment with the gang was the primary motivation for leaving the gang. We expected that single events would be more important than the accumulated disillusionment that led most of the gang-exiters to leave their gang. The method for leaving revealed a surprise for us. Rather than some formal process of being sworn or beaten out of the gang, many individuals simply "gave notice" that they were terminating their membership. This certainly flies in the face of the legend of "blood in, blood out" and more formal ceremonial processes for gang exit. Such passive exits were the norm and far outnumbered active forms of gang leaving, such as programming.

One thing shared in common in motivations and methods was that there were multiple motivations and methods at work in prompting gang leaving. We think this has implications for programming in prison, and possibly on the street. Individuals experiencing pushes (negative events) may be more vulnerable to the efforts of a program or a strengthened relationship with a family member. Looking to add pulls (positive events and relationships) to pushes experienced by inmates could pay dividends in reducing gang membership in prison. We do not want to lose sight of the importance of programming. While hardly the modal category for methods of leaving the gang, for many individuals, prison programming played an important role in their decision to leave and sticking with that decision, particularly among the most organized and structured gangs. The GRAD program in Texas prisons provides one avenue for individuals who want to leave their gang and escape most of the threats to their safety and serving their time (Burman 2012). A large number of individuals identified the gang as an impediment to doing their time and getting back to family.

While fear of retaliation from their own gang or a rival gang was certainly a concern voiced by many members of our sample, individuals who left their gang in prison faced little in the way of actual violence. This too stands in contrast to images of gang leaving in the media and in gang codes, suggesting that an information campaign may benefit individuals on the fence about leaving their gang.

In conclusion, it is important to note that for many individuals who left their gang in prison, life-course experiences were important. Age is inversely related to involvement in crime as well as recidivism. Obviously, age is not a variable that can be manipulated. However, other measures of the life course – marriage, parenthood – are also important factors in successful reintegration. Enhancing those whenever possible is likely to support exit. Values also seem to distinguish between those who have left their gang and those who remain members. This is seen in adherence to the code of the street and the convict code, whereby individuals with stronger embeddedness in groups that adhere to these codes are less likely to leave their gang.

We conclude with a final thought on gang leaving. Gangs provide many things for their members. One of the most important things they provide is a code of beliefs and guides for action. Thus, gang members know what to do in certain situations and have an underlying rationale for doing so. In many instances, leaving the gang means casting aside that guidance. Perhaps that is why so many of the former gang members score so high on the religiosity measures, significantly higher than current gang members. This is consistent with recent work by Deuchar (2018) and Johnson and Densley (2018) who found that spirituality was an important element in exiting from gangs. We suggest this be added to the (long) list of items on the gang research agenda. That said, violence, whether threatened or carried out, remains a strong undercurrent in prison gang leaving.

# 10

# Implications of Competing for Control

The LoneStar Project was initiated in the fall of 2014 with several ambitious goals. Key among those goals was the successful completion of interviews with gang and non-gang members. By the spring of 2018, the research team had completed two different types of interviews: the first included interviews with 802 inmates in two Texas prisons and the second included two post-release interviews conducted within the first year upon returning to the community. This book is the product of those interviews, official records for each individual, and the subsequent analysis and interpretation of those data. The primary focus of our work has been to produce a comparison of the culture, structures, processes, and behaviors of gang and non-gang members in prison and their roles in controlling prison life. Our approach was mainly quantitative and comparative, although qualitative accounts of these foci are important to this book. The results in this book are based on the in-prison interviews, which means that our representation of prison life in *Competing for Control* is based on what was communicated to us by inmates in custody. Such work is relatively rare in criminology, owing to difficulties of access to prisons and the numerous hurdles that must be overcome to complete such a research agenda, particularly for a sample such as ours.

This has led to what is largely a comparative work. We paid close attention both to the differences between and within gang and non-gang members in prison. A focus on both types of differences is important given the paucity of knowledge about incarcerated individuals in general. But a key to our work is the belief that prison gangs and gang members are not monoliths. That is, there is considerable variation between and within prison gangs and gang members. We made comparisons among gang members by focusing on gang status (current/former), the context of joining and leaving gangs (street/prison), and source of information about individuals (survey/prison). These are important comparisons to make and yielded substantial information about behavior, culture, and processes among gangs in prison. We also made comparisons among gangs in prison premised on the belief that they vary on several important demographic dimensions, such as race/ethnicity, as well as region of origin, history, and organizational structure of the gang. To facilitate such comparisons we examined a typology of gangs based on their locus of influence and organizational structure (Security Threat Groups [STGs] in segregation, STGs not in segregation, prison-oriented, and street-oriented). While such work is rare in prison research, we anticipate more work in this area in the future.

This analysis reflects our strong interest in the role of organizational structure on behavior. And, indeed, this was a consistent finding in our work: organizational structure varied across gang types and corresponded to different behaviors of the group and its individual members. We believe that this is an important feature of our research, with implications for research on gangs in both prison and street settings. The findings suggest that analyzing individual gang members is important, but it can only take us so far because there is additional knowledge that is only a product of group-level analysis. As Jim Short taught us in 1974, gangs matter because the sum of the parts is greater than just the individual members. This is an important focus as most crime is committed in groups and some of the most serious forms of crime (organized crime, drug and arms trafficking, terrorist acts) are committed in and facilitated by groups.

Our interest in process – specifically group process – is closely linked to our interest in groups and organization. This is largely new to the arena of prisons, especially with respect to gangs. Groups are more than a collection of individuals, they possess the ability to motivate and refocus individual attention to attempt and succeed at many tasks. The key elements of group process are both the impetus to try things that individuals may not, and the ability of the group to produce successful outcomes where a collection of individuals that lack cohesion may fail. These are characteristics of military units and "pelotons" in bicycle races, as well as gangs. Group process has been identified as a key element to gangs; its effects are evident in gang joining, "massing" for violent events, engaging in crime, and supporting the "brand" whether through expressive or instrumental acts. The significance of expressive acts to gangs is great and ignoring the group context and processes at work in gang membership is to miss a key ingredient of gang activity.

An emphasis on culture, largely through the inmate code, has been a staple of prison research for nearly eighty years (Clemmer 1940). Our research brings a focus on culture in prison and examines the convict code as well as other measures of attitudes, beliefs, scripts, values, and worldviews (e.g., code of the street, activism/extremism, gang embeddedness, legal cynicism, racial identification, and religiosity) that may be consequential for inmate behavior. This focus reflects our interest in the debate over the origins of prison social organization and activities that is largely captured in sociological theories of deprivation and importation. Codes reflect ties to external groups as well as previous associations, and we were specifically interested in the source and strength of values for group and individual conduct. Codes are also important in understanding relationships between the street and the prison, as they are more easily transferrable than goods (drugs, phones, weapons) and individuals. As such, they hold promise for explanations of the influence of one sphere (e.g., street) on another (e.g., prison).

We believe that gang behavior – either at the individual or group level – is a joint product of organizational structure, group process, and culture. Whether it is joining or leaving the gang, the actions taken to avoid gangs, transitioning from a street to a prison context or back to the street from prison, engaging in violence and other misconduct in prison, or preparing to return to society from prison, it is clear that this intersection is key to the understanding of such behaviors. We found that in prison the intersection of these three domains was important in accounting for affiliation, identity, misconduct, and relationships with the street (i.e., gangs on the outside). Affiliation and identity have a symbiotic relationship that strengthens ties to the gang.

## WHAT HAVE WE LEARNED ABOUT PRISONS AND GANGS?

Our goal in this section of the concluding chapter to the book is not to review the main findings. Rather, it is to identify four key areas where we have contributed to the literature on gangs and prisons, and their intersection.

### Identification and Identity

Identification and identity in prison reflect both the perspective of the institutional staff as well as the inmate. The way inmates are classified by staff has a good deal to do with their life in prison, as well as how they are perceived by staff and other inmates. Identification and identity relative to gang membership represent a key finding, not only because of the rare opportunity to examine official and self-reported results, but because of its importance to behavior, beliefs, and organization. The conventional wisdom about prison gangs is that their members will not talk to researchers as part of a strongly held code of silence. We found this not to be true, and what is more important, the responses of prison gang members, as measured against official records were as valid and reliable as those of non-gang members. We believe that this is one of the key findings from the study, not only because it flies in the face of much work on prison research but because it means that accessing either official records or inmate interviews could yield overlapping conclusions. In other words, prison staff and researchers are talking about the same group of people; the same cannot be said about law enforcement when studying gangs on the street. The finding regarding the overlap between self-reported and official classifications enhances the ability to conduct research in prison with a high degree of validity. We found that the overlap between prison records and self-reports as well as the willingness to participate in the research extended to individuals in administrative segregation. We found again and again that identity and identification were key elements of prison life. Identity was built not only on affiliations that were chosen (gangs, religious group, cell block) but also on ascribed characteristics such as race and ethnicity and city of residence. Such affiliations were important to inmate safety, social life, and inmate groupings.

## Life-Course Processes and Transitions

The second key area of findings concerns the processes and transitions experienced in prison. While an "inmate" or "prison gang member" may be described in static terms, the reality is far more complicated and features transitions through the life course that intersect with transitions in the prison experience. Prison itself can be a turning point in the life of an inmate, producing shifts toward conformity for many, while reinforcing criminal relationships and behavior patterns for others. The concept of prison as a turning point in the life course is, we believe, an important one. The first turning point may come when an individual enters prison, finding themselves shut off from familiar patterns of behavior, relationships, and opportunities they enjoyed on the outside. For some inmates, that means dropping their gang affiliation; for other inmates, that means initiating or strengthening an affiliation. For inmates serving longer sentences (say five years or longer) changes in the life course occur while they are in prison. The normal processes of aging do not vanish in prison, and prisoners encounter changes in their health, marital and family relationships, and employment prospects. As prisoners age, their physical, mental, and emotional needs change. The approach of a release date has an impact on this process as well. Just as with life on the outside, friendships, group affiliation, employment, and residential location are dynamic while in prison. These changes occur in a broader context that in some cases eases the transition and, in others, makes it more difficult. We found that a major transition – affiliating with a gang or exiting from a gang – occurred among a large number of the members of our sample. The involvement of inmates in misconduct also appears to follow key life-course patterns and processes, with older inmates participating less in such activities. The presence of gangs has a key impact on such processes and transitions, but once again, was not determinative in all cases. Instead, individuals were able to demonstrate agency and act in ways that challenged the authority of their gang. But release from prison is also a turning point, representing an opportunity to reenter both criminogenic and prosocial relationships and pursue opportunities.

## Inmate Behavior

We have focused a good deal of attention on "behavior" in prison. As criminologists, we are interested in crime and misconduct, as well as the violation of norms and rules, but our interest in behavior extends well beyond these categories. We also focus on victimization, an experience that on the street is inexorably linked to offending. The "victim–offender overlap" appears to be as important in prison as it is on the street. Beliefs, non-criminal activities, and background characteristics (health, family, employment, and residential location) also frame our assessment of "behavior" in prisons. The focus on crime and misconduct is built on two sources of data: survey responses from the inmates themselves and their official records. As we have demonstrated, we find more convergence than divergence between these two data sources and regard the convergence as an important finding from the study. Gang members were involved in more misconduct and experienced more victimization than non-gang members. But as our life-course orientation emphasizes, these patterns were not uniform across gang members and could be differentiated by whether or not a prisoner was a current or former gang member. This is consistent with our group process framework, where we held that inmates who are not actively involved in gangs will not be subject to the more intense influences of gang-related group processes. Further evidence of the importance of group processes was found in our efforts to disentangle gang-related misconduct and victimization; if not for these gang-related behaviors and experiences, the active gang members in our study, and to a lesser extent former gang members, would not be very different from the prisoners who were never involved in gangs. Other aspects of behavior we found important were transitions in and out of gangs. We found a good deal of gang joining and leaving among the members of our sample, and far more than popular accounts of inmate society would lead us to have expected. This suggests changes in other domains, such as identity, as well as having consequences for offending and victimization.

## Social Order and Control

Our focus on "social order" forms a key focus of the book. This focus is reflected in the title of the book, *Competing for Control*, a competition among prison gangs, other inmates, and staff with important consequences. The competition includes the role of the organizational structure of gangs, the extent and nature of their control of prison activities and group processes. Social order is often the product of a tenuous negotiation in prison, and we believe it is useful to think of the parties to the negotiation as the authorities (guards, rules, prison administration, criminal code), prison gangs, and the inmates writ large. From this perspective, social order is co-produced by inmates, guards, formal rules, and norms. Group structure (size, diversity, leadership, activities) is also a component of social order and as such receives attention in our analyses. While gangs have a role to play in the production of the social order of the prison, they do not hold primacy in that role. Their role may be disproportionately large relative to their size, but it is not the only voice in these efforts. It is clear that the balance of social order has changed in Texas prisons over the past generation, and that hybrid groups such as the Tangos now play a greater role than when the "families" dictated prison order largely through the exercise and threat of violence. Our observations portend a prison gang landscape that is more consistent with a street gang landscape. The dynamic nature of prison social order and inmate groups increases the need for more contemporary studies of life in the prison, particularly from the perspective of inmates. The role of group process, whether among gangs or other groupings of inmates, is important in understanding the formation and maintenance of social order in prison. Group process plays a key role in motivating behavior, whether that behavior is consistent with prison rules and regulations or not.

## WHAT ARE THE IMPLICATIONS OF OUR FINDINGS FOR POLICY AND PRACTICE?

This is not a book about policy and practice, but it is a book with implications for policy and practice. Our findings are primarily about the structures and processes in prison as experienced by gang and non-gang inmates. But our findings do suggest many insights into policy and practice that need to be highlighted. We organize these insights into the following themes, which are differentially relevant for policymakers and practitioners.

### Mass Incarceration and Gangs

Mass incarceration refers to the unprecedented growth of the US prison population over the last four decades. The rise in imprisonment is clearly and strongly linked to the growth of gangs in and out of prison. Some (e.g., Skarbek 2014) have gone so far as to contend that mass incarceration is a causal factor in the growth of gangs in prison. We find a lot of merit in this argument, although the mechanisms underlying this dual trajectory in growth still remain speculative. The findings from the LoneStar Project do not have a lot to say about this. However, it is apparent to us based on our data that, much like mass incarceration, the strategies to respond to gangs in prison are just as likely to be found *outside* of prisons as they are inside of them. There is little doubt in our mind that prison gangs and gang activity is co-produced by the street and the prison. Joan Moore (Moore et al. 1978, 93–128) was the first to observe – in the mid-1970s – such phenomena in the barrios of Los Angeles. Our evidence is less direct, but built from our observation that the origins of gang membership are roughly equally split between street and prison settings. There is also synergy between gangs on the street and gangs in prison, as evidenced by the coexistence of "prison gangs" in both prison and street settings. This extends beyond the cycling of members to and from prison, a key problem of recidivism for mass incarceration. Prison gangs would likely still exist in the absence of mass incarceration, but it is unlikely that they would be as entrenched as they are. Indeed, all of the gangs we studied emerged before the 1990s, right around the time of the buildup of prison population. Of course, Texas stands out from other prison systems, as the origins of gangs can be traced to litigated reform rather than other factors. That said, it is highly likely that gangs would have proliferated regardless in Texas, owing to racial dynamics, prison population growth, and a large and active street gang population in the state. Most police officers in gang units will share stories of tensions between and within street gangs when gang members return home from prison expecting to reexert their influence; correctional officers in STG units will share similar stories. The interplay between the two settings operates on three planes: first at the macro level with prison policy, second at the group level with gang dynamics, and third at the individual level with gang member roles and status. It appears more evident now than before that street and prison gangs cannot be treated as independent of one another. Efforts to curtail gangs on the street might pay dual dividends by blunting the influence of gangs in prison. In turn, efforts to curtail gangs in prisons may also yield dividends for gang activity on the street. Although if we were to make a prediction, reducing gang activity on the street would be more productive than in prison.

### Gang-Oriented Programming

It is difficult to imagine prisons being run without coherent policies for managing gangs. Most prison systems have policies for the classification and housing of gangs and gang members. On this score, prison systems clearly view this population differently, or at least as an important variable in the scheme of risk assessment. Our results should urge prison administrators to think more broadly than classification and housing policies and practices, and also concentrate on specialized programming for gang members. Our findings are in line with the argument of Krienert and Fleisher (2001) that gang members constitute a population in need of specialized programming owing to deficiencies in social skills and relationships. Compared to the non-institutional population, this is the case for prison inmates more generally. Yet these deficiencies are especially pronounced among gang members. But we see these as "risk factors" across many important domains, including behavior (e.g., misconduct, victimization), attitudes and beliefs (e.g., adherence to violent cultural scripts), social connections (e.g., gang embeddedness, social supports), criminal justice system involvement (e.g., immersion in the system), and socioeconomic (e.g., educational attainment, employability). Just as a one-size-fits-all model does not work on the street, it likely will not work in prison, either. The "plug-and-play" approach of programing to gang members may not produce the outcomes that prison officials are seeking. The risk factors for gang involvement in prison are distinctive enough to suggest that different approaches – whatever they may be – to dealing with gang members must be considered for development.

## Group Intervention in Prison

The description of prisons as total institutions implicitly points to the covert and overt monitoring that occurs in these facilities. Despite such high levels of monitoring, violence in prison remains an important concern for inmates and prison staff. Within the prison population, gang members are often the targets of heightened monitoring, subject to placement in solitary confinement, extensive classification and intelligence gathering, and prison responses to violence. Yet, gang members are still overrepresented as victims and offenders, as evidenced in our data. We also observed an overlap between involvement in misconduct and victimization; that overlap was even more pronounced for gang members. In prison, as on the street, victims and offenders are largely the same people. We think that the overrepresentation of gang members as offenders and victims points to the role of group process, especially considering that we accounted for many of the alternative explanations for such a relationship. Gangs and gang members in prison have rivals as our rivalry network illustrated, just as they do on the street. These rivalries are dynamic and evolve over time with changes in the prison population and routine conflicts among groups on the street and in prison (Gundur 2018; Ouellet, Bouchard, and Charette 2019; Papachristos 2009).

The implications for policy and practice are rather clear: group-based interventions represent one possible strategy for intervening in gang conflict. This may occur within or between gangs. There is evidence of success in group interventions with gangs in street settings, such as the Cure Violence (also known as Chicago Ceasefire) and Group Violence Intervention (also known as focused deterrence) approaches. These strategies, however, would require great care and effort to be applied to prison settings. After all, one of the major "sticks" in the focused deterrence approach, for example, involves clear messaging about the certainty and severity of punishment. If gang members are already in prison, and especially the gang members in solitary confinement, what possible additional punishment could prison officials mete out?

## The Grip of the Gang

The grip of the gang – as our colleagues Frank Van Gemert and Mark Fleisher (2005) termed it – refers to the differential ability of the group to exert influence over its members specifically and over the prison system generally. Deeply embedded gang members may be willing to "take the fall" for misconduct or engage in violence that is sure to attract the attention of prison authorities. This underscores how deeply embedded they are in their gangs. It is also possible to envision how non-gang inmates acquiesce to the demands of the gang for property or space in the presence of gang intimidation or threats. Some portrayals of prison gangs allude to an iron-fisted influence of gangs. We do not deny that this exists. Yet, we observed that this grip may not be as strong as the media and some prior scholarship have suggested. This was evidenced in our findings on gangs and the social order of prisons. Our findings suggest that there are possibilities for interventions with gangs and gang members in prison. We see intervention points as instances of potential vulnerabilities within gangs. This could occur for individual gang members, such as at the time of admission to prison, in preparation for release from prison, or at vulnerable moments in the life course such as the death of a family member or after personal victimization. This could also occur at the gang level, such as during times when the gang fractures or splinters or when there is a rift associated with gang politics. These are moments when gangs and gang members may be more receptive to messages about leaving their gang and the criminal capital and opportunities it poses. Of course, breaking the bonds of gang membership is a challenge, as perceptions of the grip of the gang are as important as reality.

### Prison as a Turning Point for Prevention and Intervention

We observed a considerable amount of joining and leaving gangs. Gang membership was found to originate in prison for over half of the people who were active in gangs in prison, with the origins found in the street for the other half. This suggests to us a major role for gang prevention in prison. Since about three-fourths of the sample were able to avoid gangs in prison, we think that there is much to be learned and translated in policy and programmatic efforts based on their motivations and methods for avoiding gangs. Few truly conceive of prison as a point of prevention, but our findings suggest that there is much to be gained from such a view. Indeed, to the extent that prison gang membership may result in higher rates of recidivism upon release, the role of gang prevention may take on added importance.

Contrary to popular view, prison also represents a context for gang leaving. Leaving a gang in prison was far more common than we anticipated. Over half of the gang members who imported their affiliation into prison also reported leaving in prison; nearly two-thirds of the inmates whose gang affiliation originated in prison reported leaving in prison. This suggests that prison can also function as a turning point for positive change. The Gang Renouncement and Disassociation (GRAD) program appears to be a big part of this. In the Appendix we report the results of a preliminary evaluation of GRAD, and the inmates who participated in the program fared much better in terms of gang membership status and gang embeddedness than a matched sample of inmates who did not (although rates of misconduct and victimization were no different).

Most importantly, if such a program is to have a role to play in reducing the negative influences of gang membership in prison, it must be subject to rigorous independent evaluation to assess its efficacy.

### Gang Variation May Require Different Policies and Practices

Just as gangs on the street show considerable variation, gangs in prison display differences. We introduced a four-part typology of gangs in prison. This typology described some of the more significant variation across gangs, but it also captured this variation quite nicely according to sensible descriptors (i.e., locus of influence, prison system perceptions of organization, and placement in solitary confinement). We found four key areas of differences across these groups: organizational structure, misconduct and victimization, perceptions of social order, and gang joining and leaving. These differences may be strong enough to support the use of an alternative approach to gang and non-gang members as well as between different types of gangs. Such an approach appears promising in the Texas prison system, although it was created in response to solitary confinement rather than gang-level variation. Indeed, the GRAD program was only available to inmates in administrative segregation. In other words, inmates who aimed to leave their gang and were not a confirmed member of an STG-segregated gang did not have the opportunity to enroll in GRAD. It is quite possible that the value we observe in GRAD is linked to the "carrot" or nudge of removal from solitary confinement. Nonetheless, it is important to conduct the type of auditing found in group violence intervention strategies on the street – documenting rivalries and alliances, recording criminal behaviors, detailing organizational structure, and identifying key players and members – before seeking to implement an intervention with gangs in prison. As we documented, the gang landscape is evolving in Texas prisons, where groups like the Tangos, with their flat hierarchy and decentralized organization, are ascendant. Targeting the leadership of the Tangos would be a fool's errand, as such leadership is more consistent with functional roles attuned to specific situations rather than fixed and top-down across situations.

### Housing Gang Members

One of the long-standing questions surrounding the management of gang members is how to house them. There are only a fixed number of beds, pods, wings, and units in the prison system, yet the alliances and rivalries of gangs continue to evolve. What steps can prison officials take to preserve the peace and not inflame gang tensions? There are generally three solutions: dispersion, concentration, and isolation. Dispersion entails spreading members of a gang across multiple prison units so that they do not maintain "strength in numbers" in a single pod or unit. Sometimes there is a non-dominant mixture of rival or alliance gang members in the same pod or unit. Concentration, instead, aims to house the members of a gang together so that they are the only inmates on a pod or unit. The logic for concentration holds that this contains gang influence to a single location and does not "contaminate" non-gang members through association with gang members. There are obvious drawbacks for both strategies. Using our public health metaphor from Chapter 2, dispersion could result in the "infection" of gang culture among inmates and within pods that would likely be gang-free. Concentration, alternatively, could backfire by strengthening the cohesion of gangs and giving gangs more power than correctional officials would feel comfortable with. Our results do not have much to offer to such an important debate, unfortunately. A limitation of our work is that while we have great information on individuals and groups, we are largely missing the "community," that is, the ecology of the prison unit (Kreager et al. 2017; Steiner and Wooldredge 2018). Nonetheless, we submit that our findings on the frequency of joining and leaving gangs in prison should be taken into consideration when evaluating these policies. Status transitions into and out of gangs may be more fluid than once expected, which may be a function of housing.

Prison administrators look favorably upon isolation (Winterdyk and Ruddell 2010). Although it is expensive, typically two to three times the cost of general population housing, it is a direct method of formal social control of gang members. Yet, rarely do prison systems have enough beds to house all of their problematic gangs and gang members. In the case of Texas, it is not feasible to place all of the 10,000 or so members of the Tangos in solitary confinement. And solitary confinement remains under intense scrutiny from watchdog groups and the federal courts owing to practices that have been labeled as torture. As such, prison systems are generally moving away from solitary confinement as a way to manage gangs (Pyrooz and Mitchell 2019). Given that 5 percent of our sample was in solitary confinement, this constitutes one of the largest samples of in-depth interviews with inmates in solitary confinement. There was a sharp divide in the inmates' views of solitary confinement. On the one hand, it was a safe haven; thus it was harder for them to get "touched" by a rival gang. On the other hand, it was mentally, physically, and socially damaging; these interviews simply felt different. There is also little in the way of pre-release programming or readying inmates for reentry in solitary. But solitary confinement was the inspiration for many members to enroll in the GRAD program. As we noted above, in the absence of solitary confinement, it is possible the positive effects of GRAD could wash away. Still, it is possible that solitary confinement reinforces the structure and behavior of gangs by failing to offer alternatives. Responses to prison gangs must involve more than housing strategies, and especially a sole reliance on solitary confinement. Housing is an area of inquiry that should be of interest to researchers, policymakers, and practitioners alike.

## Multiple Methods for Understanding Prison Gangs

We observed strong congruence between survey and official data. The overlap was not perfect, but when prisoners told us that they were gang members,

Latino, married, Catholic, and a father, those same qualities were reflected in the records of prison administrative data. This is a good sign for current and future research with inmates, and important for a number of reasons; chief among them that researchers and practitioners are not talking past one another. It also suggests a common foundation on which to build researcher–practitioner partnerships. This finding should be the impetus for more cooperation between the two. Each group operates from different vantage points to understand a problem. Since we have established that this type of gang research is possible in prison, hopefully it can result in the opening of doors in other prison systems. Gangs are not just a Texas prisons problem; we demonstrated in Chapter 1 that they exist in nearly every prison system for which there are data. Understanding how to respond to gangs more effectively should rank high on the priority list of most prison administrators; researchers with the interests and priorities that mesh with those of correctional authorities could result in projects that produce lasting change in prison systems.

### Preparing Gang Members for Community Reentry

It is a truism that preparing inmates for release is a key to the effective management of prisons, as well as reducing recidivism. It is clear from our results that what inmates (especially gang members) do while they are inside prison affects their behavior once they leave prison. It is also clear from our results that gang members should receive more intensive reentry preparation as well as reentry support upon release. The findings in Chapter 4 underscore these conclusions. Indeed, gang members check off nearly all of the boxes for reentry failure outlined by Mears and Cochran (2015). We believe that gang affiliation constitutes an added burden for prison reentry, above and beyond the traditional indicators of recidivism specifically and reentry challenges generally. Gang members are subject to the group processes of the gang, obligations to assume long-standing and emerging rivalries, and the expectation of veteran or "OG" status upon returning to the community. As it stands, it is hard enough for former prisoners – whether they have been incarcerated for two years or two decades – to find employment, reunite with family, and reintegrate into the community. The burden is enhanced for gang members. The more that can be done to break the ties that bind while in prison, the more successful individuals can be when reentering society upon release.

### FINAL THOUGHTS

Gangs occupy a central place in the social order of prisons. They present serious challenges for individuals in prison as well as on the street. Such challenges are not limited just to other prison gang members, but extend to their families, non-gang inmates, prison employees, and the communities to which they return. The disruptive power of gangs on the street is well understood, but that of prison gangs is much less so. The struggle for control in prison does focus on contraband and other commodities exchanged in prison. But that struggle also goes on over the daily routines that structure life in prison. As such it affects the programming that both gang and non-gang inmates participate in. We know that the reentry process is fraught with challenges for individuals returning to their communities from prison. The disruptive presence of gangs in prison adds a further burden to that transition, and at a tenuous time for returning inmates it may be enough to swing the balance against a successful reintegration. We know from street gang research that gang membership has lasting consequences in the areas of education, employment, and family relationships. Our work in this book documents a range of similar consequences for prison gang membership.

While this book has strong links to the sociological tradition of prison research, it breaks new ground in several areas. Among the most important findings of the study is the feasibility of such research. While many have lamented the difficulties of prison research, pointing to issues of access and the reliability and validity of interview and official data, our results paint a far more optimistic picture. The dynamic nature of prison life, particularly the groups formed by inmates while incarcerated, creates a foundation for more research in these areas, as well as offers concrete information that could be used to guide responses to gangs in prison and on the street.

# APPENDIX

# Preliminary Evaluation of the Gang Renouncement and Disassociation Program

The question "what do we do about the gang members" is one that many ask but few have answers to. Any review of the evidence surrounding "what works" is even more sobering. For example, Paul Boxer and his colleagues (2011, 2015) found that gang members perform worse than non-gang members in Multisystemic Therapy (MST), a "best practice" program. Still, as Klein and Maxson (2006) observed, the conclusion reached about most gang responses is that they are promising only because they have not been evaluated. There has been some progress since Klein and Maxson made this observation about street gang interventions over a decade ago. Researchers can now point with confidence to strategies to prevent gang membership, such as the Gang Resistance and Education Training (Esbensen et al. 2013), to reduce reoffending among youth at high-risk for gang membership, such as Functional Family Therapy (Thornberry et al. 2018), and to intervene in gang violence, such as the Group Violence Intervention (Braga, Weisburd, and Turchan 2018). However, when it comes to responding to gangs and gang members in prison, we have no reliable programs to offer.

What can be done about gangs in prison? When Winterdyk and Ruddell (2010) surveyed correctional administrators about effective responses to gangs, the most highly endorsed strategy was segregated or isolated housing – 75 percent viewed the practice as "very effective" and 19 percent viewed it as "somewhat effective." A former classification supervisor in the Colorado Department of Corrections described segregation as a "silver bullet" (Vigil 2006, 34). There is, in fact, some evidence to suggest that segregation may reduce violence and rule infractions in Arizona (Fischer 2002) and Texas (Ralph and Marquart 1991) prisons. However, placing gang members in solitary confinement is a practice, not a program. As Krienert and Fleisher (2001) remind us, gang members maintain "social deficiencies" that are distinguishable from that of the non-gang inmate population. These deficiencies were great enough, Krienert and Fleisher argued, to warrant targeted programming for gang members.

What are prison systems doing to promote disengagement from prison gangs? Most do nothing. Pyrooz and Mitchell (2019) reported that only fourteen of the thirty-eight state prison systems included in their study included such strategies. Among the fourteen states that did include strategies directly addressing gang membership, the most typical response was "debriefing," which, like solitary confinement, is a practice, not a program. Debriefing involves informing correctional officials about the inner workings of the gang, such as naming members and identifying leadership and hierarchy (e.g., see Reiter 2016; Tachiki 1995; Toch 2007). While debriefing may result in a reclassification of gang status and a return to general population housing, the onus is not so much on debriefing policy to effect change as it is on the individual gang member to seek out the program. However, the Texas prison system is one of the few correctional agencies in the USA to introduce programming to facilitate disengagement from gangs, the Gang Renouncement and Disassociation program, better known as GRAD.

This analysis extends our interest in gang control of the behavior of their members. Such control can be expressed through norms and values or more coercive measures such as violence. It represents an exercise of "soft power" (Crewe 2012) over the lives of inmates, in contrast to the "hard power" exercised through the use of administrative segregation. GRAD is a challenge from administrative staff to the control of the lives of inmates by gangs. As such, it represents a test of the power of gang organization.

## WHAT IS GRAD?

As part of her doctoral dissertation in social work, Michelle Burman (2012) "wrote the book" on GRAD. Her aim was to understand how the program defined success, learn about the selection of gang members into GRAD, and examine staff views about the program. Her conclusions were based on sixteen interviews with security staff (Serious Threat Group [STG] management office staff and correctional officers in GRAD units), non-security staff (teachers and counselors in GRAD), and police officers with expertise in gang investigations. Notable by their absence were the participants in GRAD, not an uncommon observation in prison research where the inmates' views seem to be missing.

GRAD began in 2000 out of necessity more than noble intentions (Burman 2012, 216). There were simply not enough beds to house gang members in segregation, which was the standard practice for the confirmed members of gangs we outlined in earlier chapters. Burman described GRAD as a "happy accident" (p. 330), given that segregation was so expensive and there were large numbers of gang members. Although it was modified for Texas's considerable gang population, GRAD was modeled after a gang renunciation program developed in 1994 by the Connecticut Department of Corrections.

To be sure, GRAD is both a gang renunciation program and a solitary confinement step-down program. This is reflected in the GRAD mission statement, as follows:

To provide a safe and secure environment for those offenders who choose to voluntarily renounce their gang affiliation by affording a structured process that will furnish the proper tools to reintegrate offenders into the general population. (Burman 2012, 328)

The tension between these two goals – gang renunciation and step-down – is obvious in Burman's review. Some, particularly custodial staff, view GRAD's purpose primarily as breaking the grip of gang influence in prison: fewer gang allegiances, more social order. Others, particularly non-security staff, view GRAD's purpose primarily as reintegration. Many outside of GRAD are skeptical of the program.

We outline the GRAD process in Table A.1. GRAD is available to a select group of inmates who have avoided problematic behavior detected by the prison system for at least one year, which also includes STG activity. Inmates must also be confirmed gang members, housed in administrative segregation, and not assigned a custody level that would preclude GRAD participation. Most importantly, the entry process into GRAD is voluntary and inmates who meet those criteria must *request* to participate in GRAD. For evaluation purposes, this presents a selection problem, as the people who participate in GRAD are likely different from those who avoid GRAD despite sharing the eligibility characteristics.

After signing a GRAD "renouncement" form, inmates are assessed as part of a "Disassociation Investigation." The purpose, of course, is for GRAD to avoid adverse selection, filtering out individuals committed to the goals of the program from those seeking entry to the program for reasons other than change. If GRAD is to work, the leading research on gang disengagement tells us that it has to replace the attractions of the gang and revise the "scripts" of the gang member. This is a tall task to accomplish during a nine-month period of programming. Although the program has no explicit theory of change, it appears that GRAD has many of the necessary ingredients to support change, including intensive programming.

Step-down programs such as GRAD are consistent with what behavioral economists term "nudges," that is, small incentives to promote healthier behavior (e.g., Thaler and Sunstein 2008). Completing a twelve-month vetting period (it was two years before being reduced in 2012: Texas Department of Criminal Justice 2014) is a strong signal that gang members are ready for change. And change comes rather quickly. Indeed, gang members will go from spending years in solitary confinement without social interaction to spending recreation time with another inmate four weeks after entering GRAD. Four months later inmates are double-celled with someone of another race or a rival gang member. This does not happen without programmatic support, though.

TABLE A.1 *The features of the phases of the Gang Renouncement and Disassociation program*

|  | Stage | | | |
|---|---|---|---|---|
|  | Disassociation investigation | Phase I: Normalization | Phase II: Socialization | Phase III: Reintegration |
| Unit | Administrative segregation | Ramsey or Ellis "GRAD wing" <br> *Red wristbands* | Ramsey or Ellis "GRAD wing" <br> *Orange wristbands* | Ramsey or Ellis "gen pop" <br> *Blue wristbands* |
| Time | Twelve months | Two months | Four months | Three months |
| Contact | *None* | *Limited contact* <br> • single-celled <br> • first month, solo recreation time <br> • second month, "double rec" time | *Expanded contact* <br> • double-cell with inmate from historical rival (race, gang) <br> • group-based programming | *Standard contact* <br> • general population interaction |
| Privileges | *None* | *Limited privileges* <br> More in-and-out of cell privileges <br> One visit per weekend | *Phase I, plus:* <br> • different clothing (two-piece rather than white jumper) <br> • more programming and movement | *Phase II, plus:* <br> • regular visitation <br> • phone calls <br> • commissary <br> • half-day work assignments <br> • GRAD completion ceremony |
| Programming | *None* <br> STG management office investigates sincerity and commitment, conflicts, and eligibility <br> (Confidential informants and state's witnesses can bypass this phase) | *Stabilizing programming* <br> In-cell videotaped lessons: <br> • substance abuse <br> • domestic violence <br> • "thinking errors" <br> Counselor meetings | *Classroom programming* <br> • cognitive intervention (180 hours), including journaling <br> • 68 hours of substance abuse, anger management, and criminal addictive behaviors <br> • role playing, group activities | *Vocational opportunities* <br> • when educational classes are not in session, comparable to GP inmates |

As participants move through the phases of GRAD, they are increasingly exposed to programming designed to address the sources of problem behavior and equip them with the skills to manage life without the gang.

Based on her participant-observation and interviews of correctional staff, Burman (2012) reported that there were changes in the physical appearance of inmates. They cared more about hygiene, such as clean haircuts and pressed clothes. Participants began to shed the gang and prisoner identity. This was a gradual process but one that is reinforced by the GRAD staff. For example, staff establish that participants understand that they are students, not "ad seg" inmates, and that the classroom is the teacher's territory, not the territory of any gang. An important part of this process is that programming in Phase II – the critical phase of GRAD – occurs in groups. It brings about a sense of identity and cohesion to a given GRAD cohort. Teachers and counselors build up the "we," but also push to reestablish the "I" – after all, these are men who are about to return to general population, where they will have to fend for themselves.

The final phase involves reintegrating participants into the general population, where they are afforded the same privileges of the general population. The pushes and pulls that we outlined in Chapter 9 are also evident in the motivations (as told by correctional staff) for participating in GRAD: disillusionment with gang politics and ideology, wanting to see family for contact visits, wanting to make parole and return home, and some of the little things that general population affords, such as watching television. Commissary and work assignments are also available, quite the nudge to an inmate who has spent years in administrative segregation.

But does GRAD work? According to Burman (2012, 16), "little information, other than anecdotal evidence, is available to support or disprove its success." Nearly 5,000 inmates had participated in GRAD by the end of 2015 (Pyrooz 2016), yet the only measure of success offered is the prison system "reconfirming" a participant as a gang member. An article published in the *Houston Chronicle* (Pinkerton 2014) reported that only 19 of the nearly 4,000 prisoners who have gone through the GRAD program circa 2014 have been reconfirmed, a success rate (99.995 percent) that almost defies belief. There is a need to learn more about GRAD's effectiveness, a question we tackle in this appendix.

## IS GRAD EFFECTIVE? A PRELIMINARY EVALUATION

This is not a formal evaluation, and our findings should not be interpreted as such. There were fifty-three GRAD participants in the LoneStar Project. And since we knew the criteria for selection into GRAD, we could pair this "treatment" group to a "control" group to assess whether the promise found in the *Houston Chronicle* was one that could be kept. Our preliminary assessment of the effectiveness of GRAD includes the following outcome measures: contemporaneous measures of current and former gang membership (official and survey), gang embeddedness (aggregate construct, individual items), misconduct (official and survey), and victimization (survey) over the last six months. Focusing on contemporaneous measures helps us maintain the time order to help establish a causal relationship.

Our analysis compares fifty-three GRAD participants to sixty-four non-GRAD inmates. To be included in the treatment group, the Texas prison system must have noted the respondent participated in, but may not have completed (although 94 percent did) GRAD, which makes our findings "intent-to-treat" estimates. To be included in the control group, the respondent must be classified by the prison system as a member of an STG that also contains a member in the GRAD treatment group. Our final sample consisted of respondents in seven of the STG-segregated gangs and one of the STG-non-segregated gangs.[1] Although this helps eliminate sample bias, it is not a perfect fix.

We also took into consideration factors that are mostly rank-order time-stable and could bias the validity of our findings as control variables, such as demographics, relationship status, cognitive ability, criminal propensity, perceptions of honesty, and criminal history. These control variables only go so far, of course, as they limit bias related to the choice-marker but not the choice set. In other words, selecting into GRAD is an exercise in agency on the part of the participant; there are reasons why non-participants do not enroll, which in turn could relate to our outcomes of interest. Table A.2 provides readers with the descriptive statistics for the key outcome and confounding variables, along with a breakdown of the gangs, partitioned by the GRAD and non-GRAD participant groups. We then estimated a series of multivariate logistic regression models and report the adjusted predicted probabilities by GRAD status.

Figures A.1, A.2, and A.3 report the results of the differences between GRAD and non-GRAD participants for gang status, gang embeddedness, and misconduct and victimization outcomes, respectively. In terms of gang-related outcomes, it is evident in Figure A.1 that there are clear and sharp differences between the groups. The GRAD participants are less likely to be identified as a *current* gang member based on survey (eighteen percentage points) or official (forty-seven percentage points) measures and more likely to be identified as a *former* gang member based on survey (twenty-one percentage points) and official (forty-seven percentage points) measures. Given the link between GRAD participation and prison classifications of gang status, the results for official measures would be expected. Yet, and despite the divergent point estimates between data sources, our survey measures further back the point that GRAD participants differ in their gang status from non-GRAD participants.

---

[1] Texas Mafia was downgraded to STG-non-segregated, but GRAD participation occurred prior to the study.

TABLE A.2 *Descriptive statistics for the study variables in the analysis of GRAD*

| N | All 117 Mean/% | (SD) | Non-GRAD 64 Mean/% | (SD) | GRAD 53 Mean/% | (SD) | t or z |
|---|---|---|---|---|---|---|---|
| *Outcomes* | | | | | | | |
| Survey: current gang | 15.4% | | 26.6% | | 1.9% | | 3.68* |
| Survey: former gang | 81.2% | | 68.8% | | 96.2% | | 3.79* |
| Gang embeddedness | −0.22 | (0.95) | 0.14 | (1.08) | −0.66 | (0.51) | 4.93* |
| Official: current gang | 36.8% | | 62.5% | | 5.7% | | 6.35* |
| Official: former gang | 63.2% | | 37.5% | | 94.3% | | 6.35* |
| *Confounders* | | | | | | | |
| Age | 43.61 | (8.77) | 42.00 | (9.24) | 45.56 | (7.83) | 2.22* |
| Latino | 49.6% | | 48.4% | | 50.9% | | 0.27 |
| White | 40.2% | | 39.1% | | 41.5% | | 0.27 |
| Multi-racial | 10.3% | | 12.5% | | 7.5% | | 0.88 |
| Skin color | 1.83 | (1.00) | 1.97 | (0.99) | 1.66 | (0.99) | 1.70 |
| Married | 14.5% | | 14.1% | | 15.1% | | 0.16 |
| In a relationship | 10.3% | | 6.3% | | 15.1% | | 1.57 |
| Single | 75.2% | | 79.7% | | 69.8% | | 1.23 |
| Father | 69.2% | | 68.8% | | 69.8% | | 0.12 |
| IQ | 96.13 | (12.59) | 96.41 | (12.76) | 95.79 | (12.50) | 0.26 |
| Low self-control | 1.51 | (0.85) | 1.66 | (0.89) | 1.33 | (0.77) | 2.10* |
| Interviewer | 2.30 | (0.70) | 2.38 | (0.70) | 2.21 | (0.69) | 1.33 |
| TDCJ stints | 3.09 | (1.68) | 3.00 | (1.55) | 3.19 | (1.84) | 0.60 |
| Prior arrests | 11.50 | (6.56) | 11.11 | (6.93) | 11.96 | (6.12) | 0.70 |
| Violent offender | 37.6% | | 40.6% | | 34.0% | | 0.74 |
| *Gangs* | N | | N | | N | | |
| Aryan Brotherhood | 31 | | 18 | | 13 | | |
| Aryan Circle | 15 | | 5 | | 10 | | |
| Barrio Azteca | 8 | | 4 | | 4 | | |
| Hermanos de Pistoleros Latinos | 6 | | 3 | | 3 | | |
| Mexican Mafia | 23 | | 13 | | 10 | | |
| Raza Unida | 8 | | 3 | | 5 | | |
| Texas Mafia | 4 | | 3 | | 1 | | |
| Texas Syndicate | 22 | | 15 | | 7 | | |

*Note:* Statistical significance (* *p* <0.05) was determined using differences in means or proportions tests.

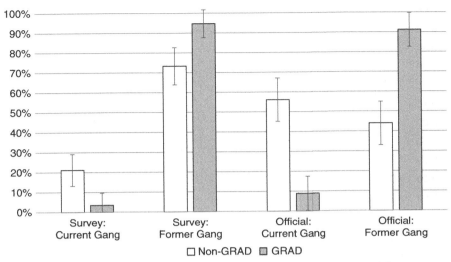

FIGURE A.1 Differences in survey and official measures of current and former gang membership by GRAD and non-GRAD respondents
Notes: Columns represent predicted values derived from logistic regression models holding constant age, race and ethnicity, skin color, relationship status, parenthood, IQ, low self-control, interviewer perceptions of honesty, number of prison spells, number of prior arrests, and violent offender conviction. Error bars are 95 percent confidence intervals derived from delta-method standard errors.

Figure A.2 displays the results for survey measures of gang embeddedness. The value of measuring gang embeddedness is that it avoids the black and white distinctions of gang status. The lines between "current" and "former" are often blurry and variable, and gang embeddedness allows us to shift our focus to immersion within gangs by concentrating on multiple relevant indicators. This is an important task when evaluating gang response programs. In terms of the overall construct, there is a substantively large difference between GRAD and non-GRAD participants – 0.62 standard deviations, which would be considered a large effect size. Position in a gang, importance assigned to the gang, and contact with the gang are the indicators that appear to be driving the overall differences in gang embeddedness. Of course, the sample size is small, which contributes to the wide confidence intervals and null differences for having friends in the gang and influence on gangs. Still, those features of embeddedness are often difficult to leave behind, as we have observed in our prior work on the aspects of life in the gang that far outlast affiliation.

Everything we have demonstrated thus far is promising: GRAD appears to be a sound pathway to break the grip of the gang on individuals. But does it correspond with changes in other areas that are important to the social order of prisons, namely, lowering misconduct and victimization? Figure A.3 lessens

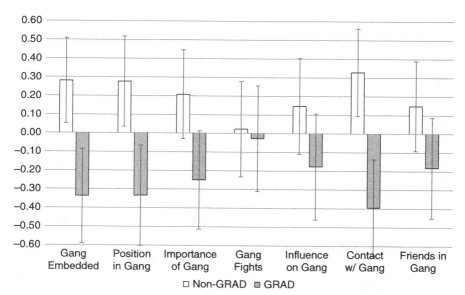

FIGURE A.2 Differences in aggregated and disaggregated survey measures of gang embeddedness by GRAD and non-GRAD respondents
Notes: Columns represent predicted values derived from OLS regression models holding constant age, race and ethnicity, skin color, relationship status, parenthood, IQ, low self-control, interviewer perceptions of honesty, number of prison spells, number of prior arrests, and violent offender conviction. Error bars are 95 percent confidence intervals derived from delta-method standard errors.

some of the enthusiasm surrounding GRAD. Indeed, regardless of the source of data or the type of misconduct or victimization, we observed no differences between the GRAD and non-GRAD participants. Thus it appears possible to reduce gang ties and embeddedness without producing important behavioral changes.

CONCLUSION

There are few evidence-based interventions in the lives of gang members. Texas stands apart from most prisons by having offered a viable program to facilitate disengagement from gangs. Michelle Burman's (2012) excellent case study of GRAD pulled back the curtain on the program, highlighting the implementation, processes, and potential benefits. But as a respondent in Burman's study noted, given the time, resources, and effort invested in GRAD: "we ought to be interested enough to see if it worked, to see if it truly worked, if it was a scam, or if they really have changed their ways and decided to do something else with their lives" (p. 356).

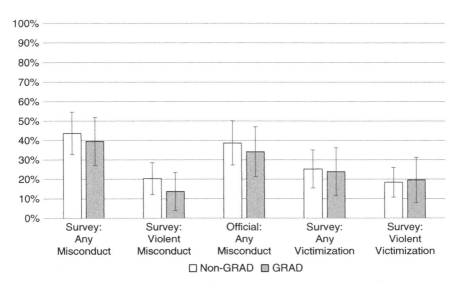

FIGURE A.3 Differences in survey and official measures of misconduct and victimization prevalence by GRAD and non-GRAD respondents, last six months
Notes: Columns represent predicted values derived from logistic regression models holding constant age, race and ethnicity, skin color, relationship status, parenthood, IQ, low self-control, interviewer perceptions of honesty, number of prison spells, number of prior arrests, and violent offender conviction. Error bars are 95 percent confidence intervals derived from delta-method standard errors.

We offer qualified support for GRAD. It appears to be a promising program that can facilitate disengagement from gangs in prison, as evidenced by our gang outcomes. Yet the data we have analyzed suggest that the ability of GRAD to effect change may not produce results in other areas that are important to the social order of prisons, namely misconduct and victimization. Of course, we recognize several limitations: that six months is a tight window for misconduct and victimization; that all of our respondents were preparing for release from prison; that our sample size is too small to reach definitive conclusions; and that we lacked information on program entry or completion. Our view is that any program that aims to promote disengagement from gangs also implies a focus on desistance from crime. After all, what is the value of a program that produces disengagement from gangs but not desistance from crime or misconduct? In our view, the value is negligible, lest we pathologize gang membership.

In the end, we view this preliminary investigation into GRAD as a call to implement and evaluate programs in prison that are designed to support disengagement from gangs and desistance from crime.

# References

Adamson, Christopher. 2000. "Defensive Localism in White and Black: A Comparative History of European-American and African-American Youth Gangs." *Ethnic and Racial Studies* 23 (2): 272–98. https://doi.org/10.1080/014198700329051.

Akers, Ronald L., Norman S. Hayner, and Werner Gruninger. 1977. "Prisonization in Five Countries: Type of Prison and Inmate Characteristics." *Criminology* 14 (4): 527–54. https://doi.org/10.1111/j.1745-9125.1977.tb00042.x.

Anderson, Elijah. 1999. *Code of the Street: Decency, Violence, and the Moral Life of the Inner City*. New York, NY: W.W. Norton & Company, Inc.

Association of State Correctional Administrators. 2013. "ASCA June 2013 Current Issues in Corrections Survey." Hagerstown, MD. www.asca.net/system/assets/attachments/6468/ASCA%20June%202103%20Current%20Issues%20in%20Corrections%20Surveyfin.pdf?1384359439.

Ayling, Julie. 2011. "Gang Change and Evolutionary Theory." *Crime, Law and Social Change* 56 (1): 1–26. https://doi.org/10.1007/s10611-011-9301-x.

Baćak, Valerio, and Christopher Wildeman. 2015. "An Empirical Assessment of the 'Healthy Prisoner Hypothesis'." *Social Science & Medicine* 138 (Supplement C): 187–91. https://doi.org/10.1016/j.socscimed.2015.05.039.

Beaird, Lester H. 1986. "Prison Gangs: Texas." *Corrections Today* 18 (July): 18–22.

Belknap, Joanne, and Molly Bowers. 2016. "Girls and Women in Gangs." In *The Wiley Handbook on the Psychology of Violence*, edited by Carlos Cuevas and Calliee Rennison, 211–25. New York, NY: Wiley-Blackwell.

Berg, Mark T. 2012. "The Overlap of Violent Offending and Violent Victimization: Assessing the Evidence and Explanations." In *Violent Offenders: Theory, Research, Policy, and Practice*, edited by Matt DeLisi and Peter J. Conis, 17–38. Burlington, MA: Jones & Bartlett Learning.

Bernard, H. Russell. 2012. "The Science in Social Science." *Proceedings of the National Academy of Sciences* 109 (51): 20796–9. https://doi.org/10.1073/pnas.1218054109.

Biderman, Albert D., and Albert J. Reiss Jr. 1967. "On Exploring the 'Dark Figure' of Crime." *The Annals of the American Academy of Political and Social Science* 374 (1): 1–15.

Biondi, Karina. 2016. *Sharing This Walk: An Ethnography of Prison Life and the PCC in Brazil*. Chapel Hill, NC: University of North Carolina Press.

Bjorgo, Tore, and John Horgan. 2008. *Leaving Terrorism behind: Individual and Collective Disengagement*. New York, NY: Routledge.

Boin, Arjen, and William A. R. Rattray. 2004. "Understanding Prison Riots: Towards a Threshold Theory." *Punishment & Society* 6 (1): 47–65.

Bolden, Christian. 2013. "Tales from the Hood: An Emic Perspective on Gang Joining and Gang Desistance." *Criminal Justice Review* 38 (4): 473–90.

Bouchard, Martin, and Andrea Spindler. 2010. "Groups, Gangs, and Delinquency: Does Organization Matter?" *Journal of Criminal Justice* 38 (5): 921–33. https://doi.org/10.1016/j.jcrimjus.2010.06.009.

Boxer, Paul. 2011. "Negative Peer Involvement in Multisystemic Therapy for the Treatment of Youth Problem Behavior: Exploring Outcome and Process Variables in 'Real-World' Practice." *Journal of Clinical Child and Adolescent Psychology* 40: 848–54.

Boxer, Paul, Kubik, Joanna, Ostermann, Michael, and Veysey, Bonita. 2015. "Gang Involvement Moderates the Effectiveness of Evidence-Based Intervention for Justice-Involved Youth." *Children and Youth Services Review* 52: 26–33.

Brenneman, Robert. 2011. *Homies and Hermanos: God and Gangs in Central America*. Oxford: Oxford University Press.

Bubolz, Bryan F., and Pete Simi. 2015. "Disillusionment and Change: A Cognitive-Emotional Theory of Gang Exit." *Deviant Behavior* 36 (4): 330–45. https://doi.org/10.1080/01639625.2014.935655.

Buentello, Salvador, Robert S. Fong, and Ronald E. Vogel. 1991. "Prison Gang Development: A Theoretical Model." *The Prison Journal* 71 (2): 3–14.

Burman, Michelle Lynn. 2012. *Resocializing and Repairing Homies within the Texas Prison System: A Case Study on Security Threat Group Management, Administrative Segregation, Prison Gang Renunciation and Safety for All*. Austin, TX: The University of Texas at Austin.

Butler, Michelle, Gavin Slade, and Camila Nunes Dias. 2018. "Self-Governing Prisons: Prison Gangs in an International Perspective." *Trends in Organized Crime*, March, 1–16. https://doi.org/10.1007/s12117-018-9338-7.

Camp, George M., and Camille Graham Camp. 1985. "Prison Gangs: Their Extent, Nature, and Impact on Prisons." Washington, DC: US Department of Justice, Government Printing Office.

Campbell, Donald T., and Donald W. Fiske. 1959. "Convergent and Discriminant Validation by the Multitrait-Multimethod Matrix." *Psychological Bulletin* 56 (2): 81–105.

Cantor, David, and James P. Lynch. 2000. "Self-Report Surveys as Measures of Crime and Criminal Victimization." *Criminal Justice* 4: 85–138.

Carlson, Peter M. 2001. "Prison Interventions: Evolving Strategies to Control Security Threat Groups." *Corrections Management Quarterly* 5 (1): 10–22.

Carson, Dena C., and Finn-Aage Esbensen. 2017. "Gangs in School: Exploring the Experiences of Gang-Involved Youth." *Youth Violence and Juvenile Justice* 17 (1): 3–23. https://doi.org/10.1177/1541204017739678.

Carson, Dena C., Dana Peterson, and Finn-Aage Esbensen. 2013. "Youth Gang Desistance: An Examination of the Effect of Different Operational Definitions of Desistance on the Motivations, Methods, and Consequences Associated with Leaving the Gang." *Criminal Justice Review* 38 (4): 510–34.

Carson, Dena C., and J. Michael Vecchio. 2015. "Leaving the Gang: A Review and Thoughts on Future Research." In *The Handbook of Gangs*, edited by Scott H. Decker and David C. Pyrooz, 257–75. Chichester, West Sussex: Wiley-Blackwell.

Carson, E. Ann. 2015. "Prisoners in 2014." NCJ 248955. Washington, DC: US Department of Justice, Bureau of Statistics.

"Prisoners in 2016." NCJ 251149. Washington, DC: US Department of Justice, Bureau of Statistics.

Carson, E. Ann, and Elizabeth Anderson. 2016. "Prisoners in 2015." NCJ 250229. Washington, DC: US Department of Justice, Bureau of Justice Statistics.

Clemmer, Donald. 1940. *The Prison Community*. New York, NY: Rhinehart.

Cloward, Richard A., and Lloyd E. Ohlin. 1960. *Delinquency and Opportunity: A Theory of Delinquent Gangs*. Glencoe, IL: Free Press.

Cohen, Sheldon, Tom Kamarck, and Robin Mermelstein. 1983. "A Global Measure of Perceived Stress." *Journal of Health and Social Behavior* 24 (4): 385–96.

Coid, Jeremy W., Simone Ullrich, Robert Keers, et al. 2013. "Gang Membership, Violence, and Psychiatric Morbidity." *American Journal of Psychiatry* 170 (9): 985–93.

Crewe, Ben. 2012. *The Prisoner Society: Power, Adaptation, and Social Life in an English Prison*. Oxford: Oxford University Press.

Crouch, Ben M., and James W. Marquart. 1989. *An Appeal to Justice: Litigated Reform of Texas Prisons*. Austin, TX: University of Texas Press.

Cullen, Francis T. 2011. "Beyond Adolescence-Limited Criminology: Choosing Our Future – The American Society of Criminology 2010 Sutherland Address." *Criminology* 49: 287–330. https://doi.org/10.1111/j.1745–9125.2011.00224.x.

Cullen, Francis T., Robert Agnew, and Pamela Wilcox. 2017. *Criminological Theory: Past to Present*. 6th ed. Essential Readings. New York, NY: Oxford University Press.

Cunha, Manuela. 2014. "The Ethnography of Prisons and Penal Confinement." *Annual Review of Anthropology* 43: 217–33.

Curry, G. David. 2000. "Self-Reported Gang Involvement and Officially Recorded Delinquency." *Criminology* 38 (4): 1253–74. https://doi.org/10.1111/j.1745–9125.2000.tb01422.x.

2015. "The Logic of Defining Gangs Revisited." In *The Handbook of Gangs*, edited by Scott H. Decker and David C. Pyrooz, 7–27. Chichester, West Sussex: John Wiley & Sons.

Curry, G. David, Scott H. Decker, and David C. Pyrooz. 2014. *Confronting Gangs: Crime and Community*. 3rd ed. New York, NY: Oxford University Press.

Decker, Scott H. 1996. "Collective and Normative Features of Gang Violence." *Justice Quarterly* 13 (2): 243–64. https://doi.org/10.1080/07418829600092931.

Decker, Scott H., Tim Bynum, and Deborah Weisel. 1998. "A Tale of Two Cities: Gangs as Organized Crime Groups." *Justice Quarterly* 15 (3): 395–425.

Decker, Scott H., and G. David Curry. 2002. "Gangs, Gang Homicides, and Gang Loyalty: Organized Crimes or Disorganized Criminals." *Journal of Criminal Justice* 30 (4): 343–52.

Decker, Scott H., Charles M. Katz, and Vincent J. Webb. 2008. "Understanding the Black Box of Gang Organization: Implications for Involvement in Violent Crime, Drug Sales, and Violent Victimization." *Crime & Delinquency* 54 (1): 153–72. https://doi.org/10.1177/0011128706296664.

Decker, Scott H., and Janet L. Lauritsen. 2002. "Leaving the Gang." In *Gangs in America III*, edited by C. Ronald Huff, 51–70. Newbury Park, CA: Sage.

Decker, Scott H., Chris Melde, and David C. Pyrooz. 2013. "What Do We Know about Gangs and Gang Members and Where Do We Go from Here?" *Justice Quarterly* 30 (3): 369–402. https://doi.org/10.1080/07418825.2012.732101.

Decker, Scott H., and David C. Pyrooz. 2010. "On the Validity and Reliability of Gang Homicide: A Comparison of Disparate Sources." *Homicide Studies* 14 (4): 359–76. https://doi.org/10.1177/1088767910385400.

Decker, Scott H., and David C. Pyrooz. 2011. "Leaving the Gang: Logging Off and Moving On." New York, NY: Council on Foreign Relations. www.cfr.org/sites/default/files/pdf/2011/11/SAVE_paper_Decker_Pyrooz.pdf.

Decker, Scott H., and David C. Pyrooz. 2015. "The Real Gangbanging Is in Prison." In *Oxford Handbook of Prisons and Imprisonment*, edited by John Woolredge and Paula Smith, 143–62. New York, NY: Oxford University Press.

Decker, Scott H., David C. Pyrooz, and Richard K. Moule Jr. 2014. "Disengagement from Gangs as Role Transitions." *Journal of Research on Adolescence* 24 (2): 268–83.

Decker, Scott H., David C. Pyrooz, Gary Sweeten, and Richard K. Moule Jr. 2014. "Validating Self-Nomination in Gang Research: Assessing Differences in Gang Embeddedness across Non-, Current, and Former Gang Members." *Journal of Quantitative Criminology* 30 (4): 577–98. https://doi.org/10.1007/s10940-014-9215-8.

Decker, Scott H., and Barrik Van Winkle. 1994. "'Slinging Dope': The Role of Gangs and Gang Members in Drug Sales." *Justice Quarterly* 11 (4): 583–604. https://doi.org/10.1080/07418829400092441.

Decker, Scott H., and Barrik Van Winkle. 1996. *Life in the Gang: Family, Friends, and Violence*. Cambridge, UK: Cambridge University Press.

DeLisi, Matt, Chad R. Trulson, James W. Marquart, Alan J. Drury, and Anna E. Kosloski. 2011. "Inside the Prison Black Box: Toward a Life Course Importation Model of Inmate Behavior." *International Journal of Offender Therapy and Comparative Criminology* 55 (8): 1186–1207. https://doi.org/10.1177/0306624X11383956.

Densley, James A. 2013. *How Gangs Work: An Ethnography of Youth Violence*. New York, NY: Palgrave Macmillan.

2014. "It's Gang Life, but Not as We Know It: The Evolution of Gang Business." *Crime & Delinquency* 60 (4): 517–46. https://doi.org/10.1177/0011128712437912.

2015. "Joining the Gang: A Process of Supply and Demand." In *The Handbook of Gangs*, edited by Scott H. Decker and David C. Pyrooz, 235–56. Chichester, West Sussex: Wiley-Blackwell.

2018. "Gang Joining." Oxford Research Encyclopedia of Criminology. https://doi.org/10.1093/acrefore/9780190264079.013.437.

Densley, James A., and David C. Pyrooz. 2017. "A Signaling Perspective on Disengagement from Gangs." *Justice Quarterly*: 1–28. https://doi.org/10.1080/07418825.2017.1357743.

Descormiers, Karine, and Raymond R. Corrado. 2016. "The Right to Belong: Individual Motives and Youth Gang Initiation Rites." *Deviant Behavior* 37 (11): 1341–59. https://doi.org/10.1080/01639625.2016.1177390.

Deuchar, Ross. 2018. *Gangs and Spirituality: Global Perspectives*. New York, NY: Springer.

DiIulio, John J. 1987. *Governing Prisons: A Comparative Study of Correctional Management.* New York, NY: The Free Press.

DiMaggio, Paul, Eszter Hargittai, W. Russell Neuman, and John P. Robinson. 2001. "Social Implications of the Internet." *Annual Review of Sociology* 27 (1): 307–36. https://doi.org/10.1146/annurev.soc.27.1.307.

Durkheim, Emile. 1951. *Suicide: A Study in Sociology.* Glencoe, IL: Free Press.

Ebaugh, Helen Rose Fuchs. 1988. *Becoming an Ex: The Process of Role Exit.* Chicago, IL: University of Chicago Press.

Eidson, Jillian L., Caterina G. Roman, and Meagan Cahill. 2016. "Successes and Challenges in Recruiting and Retaining Gang Members in Longitudinal Research: Lessons Learned from a Multisite Social Network Study." Youth Violence and Juvenile Justice, July. https://doi.org/10.1177/1541204016657395.

Esbensen, Finn-Aage, and Dena C. Carson. 2012. "Who Are the Gangsters? An Examination of the Age, Race/Ethnicity, Sex, and Immigration Status of Self-Reported Gang Members in a Seven-City Study of American Youth." *Journal of Contemporary Criminal Justice* 28 (4): 465–81. https://doi.org/10.1177/1043986212458192.

Esbensen, Finn-Aage, D. Wayne Osgood, Dana Peterson, Terrance J. Taylor, and Dena C. Carson. 2013. "Short- and Long-Term Outcome Results from a Multisite Evaluation of the G.R.E.A.T. Program." *Criminology & Public Policy* 12 (3): 375–411. https://doi.org/10.1111/1745-9133.12048.

Esbensen, Finn-Aage, Dana Peterson, Terrance J. Taylor, and Adrienne Freng. 2010. *Youth Violence: Sex and Race Differences in Offending, Victimization, and Gang Membership.* Philadelphia, PA: Temple University Press.

Esbensen, Finn-Aage, L. Thomas Winfree, Ni He, and Terrance J. Taylor. 2001. "Youth Gangs and Definitional Issues: When Is a Gang a Gang, and Why Does it Matter?" *Crime & Delinquency* 47 (1): 105–30. https://doi.org/10.1177/0011128701047001005.

Fagan, Jeffrey. 1989. "The Social Organization of Drug Use and Drug Dealing among Urban Gangs." *Criminology* 27 (4): 633–70.

1990. "Social Processes of Delinquency and Drug Use among Urban Gangs." In *Gangs in America,* edited by C. Ronald Huff, 183–219. Newbury Park, CA: Sage.

Fahmy, Chantal. 2018. *Physical Health, Social Support, and Reentry: A Longitudinal Examination of Formerly Incarcerated Individuals.* Doctoral Dissertation. Phoenix, AZ: Arizona State University. https://repository.asu.edu/attachments/207476/content/Fahmy_asu_0010E_18214.pdf.

Farrington, David P., and Brandon C. Welsh. 2008. *Saving Children from a Life of Crime: Early Risk Factors and Effective Interventions.* New York: Oxford University Press.

Federal Bureau of Prisons. 2017. "Our Locations." www.bop.gov/locations/list.jsp.

Felson, Marcus. 2006. "The Street Gang Strategy." In *Crime and Nature.* Thousand Oaks, CA: Sage.

Fischer, Daryl R. 2002. "Arizona Department of Corrections: Security Threat Group (STG) Program Evaluation." Final Report. Washington, DC: National Institute of Justice, US Department of Justice.

Fishman, Joseph Fulling. 1934. *Sex in Prison: Revealing Sex Conditions in American Prisons.* New York, NY: National Library Press.

Fleisher, Mark S. 1989. *Warehousing Violence.* Newbury Park, CA: Sage.

Fleisher, Mark S., and Scott H. Decker. 2001a. "Going Home, Staying Home: Integrating Prison Gang Members into the Community." *Corrections Management Quarterly* 5: 65–77.

Fleisher, Mark S., and Scott H. Decker. 2001b. "An Overview of the Challenge of Prison Gangs." *Corrections Management Quarterly* 5 (1): 1–11.

Flores, Edward. 2013. *God's Gangs: Barrio Ministry, Masculinity, and Gang Recovery*. New York, NY: New York University Press.

Fong, Robert S. 1990. "The Organizational Structure of Prison Gangs: A Texas Case Study." *Federal Probation* 54: 36–43.

Fong, Robert S., and Salvador Buentello. 1991. "The Detection of Prison Gang Development: An Empirical Assessment." *Fed. Probation* 55: 66.

Fong, Robert S., and Ronald E. Vogel. 1995. "Blood-in, Blood-out: The Rationale behind Defecting from Prison Gangs." *Journal of Gang Research* 2 (4): 45–51.

Fox, Kathleen A. 2013. "New Developments and Implications for Understanding the Victimization of Gang Members." *Violence and Victims* 28 (6): 1015–40.

Fox, Kathleen A., Jodi Lane, and Ronald L. Akers. 2010. "Do Perceptions of Neighborhood Disorganization Predict Crime or Victimization? An Examination of Gang Member versus Non-Gang Member Jail Inmates." *Journal of Criminal Justice* 38 (4): 720–9. https://doi.org/10.1016/j.jcrimjus.2010.04.046.

Fox, Kathleen A., Jodi Lane, and Susan F. Turner. 2018. *Encountering Correctional Populations: A Practical Guide for Researchers*. Oakland, CA: University of California Press.

Gaes, Gerald G., Susan Wallace, Evan Gilman, Jody Klein-Saffran, and Sharon Suppa. 2002. "The Influence of Prison Gang Affiliation on Violence and Other Prison Misconduct." *The Prison Journal* 82: 359–85. https://doi.org/10.1177/003288550208200304.

Gaston, Shytierra, and Beth M. Huebner. 2015. "Gangs in Correctional Institutions." In *The Handbook of Gangs*, edited by Scott H. Decker and David C. Pyrooz, 328–44. Chichester, West Sussex: John Wiley & Sons.

Gibson, Chris L., Marc L. Swatt, J. Mitchell Miller, Wesley G. Jennings, and Angela R. Gover. 2012. "The Causal Relationship between Gang Joining and Violent Victimization: A Critical Review and Directions for Future Research." *Journal of Criminal Justice* 40 (6): 490–501.

Goffman, Erving. 1968. *Asylums: Essays on the Social Situation of Mental Patients and Other Inmates*. New Brunswick, NJ: AldineTransaction.

Goodman, Philip. 2008. "It's Just Black, White or Hispanic: An Observational Study of Racializing Moves in California's Segregated Prison Reception Centers." *Law & Society Review* 42 (4): 735–70.

Gottfredson, Michael R., and Travis Hirschi. 1990. *A General Theory of Crime*. Stanford, CA: Stanford University Press.

Gravel, Jason, Blake Allison, Jenny West-Fagan, Michael McBride, and George E. Tita. 2018. "Birds of a Feather Fight Together: Status-Enhancing Violence, Social Distance and the Emergence of Homogenous Gangs." *Journal of Quantitative Criminology* 34 (1): 189–219.

Griffin, Marie L., and John R. Hepburn. 2006. "The Effect of Gang Affiliation on Violent Misconduct among Inmates during the Early Years of Confinement." *Criminal Justice and Behavior* 33 (4): 419–66.

Gundur, R. V. 2018. "The Changing Social Organization of Prison Protection Markets: When Prisoners Choose to Organize Horizontally Rather than

Vertically." Trends in Organized Crime, February, 1–19. https://doi.org/10 .1007/s12117-018–9332–0.

Hagan, John, and Ronit Dinovitzer. 1999. "Collateral Consequences of Imprisonment for Children, Communities, and Prisoners." *Crime and Justice* 26: 121–62.

Hagedorn, John M. 1994. "Homeboys, Dope Fiends, Legits, and New Jacks." *Criminology* 32 (2): 197–219.

Hart, Timothy C., and Callie Marie Rennison. 2003. Reporting Crime to the Police, 1992–2000. Washington, DC: US Department of Justice, Office of Justice Programs.

Hensley, Christopher. 2000. "Attitudes Toward Homosexuality in a Male and Female Prison: An Exploratory Study." *The Prison Journal* 80: 434–41.

Hepburn, John R. 2013. "Keynote Address: Get Dirty. WSC Conference, 2013, Berkeley, California." *Western Criminology Review* 14 (1): 1–5.

Hill, Cece. 2009. "Gangs/Security Threat Groups." *Corrections Compendium* 34 (1): 23–37.

Hill, Karl G., James C. Howell, J. David Hawkins, and Sara R. Battin-Pearson. 1999. "Childhood Risk Factors for Adolescent Gang Membership: Results from the Seattle Social Development Project." *Journal of Research in Crime and Delinquency* 36 (3): 300–22. https://doi.org/10.1177/0022427899036003003.

Howell, James C. 2015. *The History of Street Gangs in the United States: Their Origins and Transformations*. Lanham, MD: Lexington Books.

Howell, James C., and Elizabeth Griffiths. 2015. *Gangs in America's Communities*. 2nd ed. Thousand Oaks, CA: Sage.

Huebner, Beth M. 2003. "Administrative Determinants of Inmate Violence: A Multilevel Analysis." *Journal of Criminal Justice* 31 (2): 107–17. https://doi.org /10.1016/S0047–2352(02)00218–0.

Huebner, Beth M., Kimberly Martin, Richard K. Moule Jr., David Pyrooz, and Scott H. Decker. 2016. "Dangerous Places: Gang Members and Neighborhood Levels of Gun Assault." *Justice Quarterly* 33 (5): 836–62. https://doi.org/10.1080/07418825 .2014.984751.

Huebner, Beth M., Sean P. Varano, and Timothy S. Bynum. 2007. "Gangs, Guns, and Drugs: Recidivism among Serious, Young Offenders." *Criminology & Public Policy* 6 (2): 187–221.

Huey, Meredith P., and Thomas L. Mcnulty. 2005. "Institutional Conditions and Prison Suicide: Conditional Effects of Deprivation and Overcrowding." *The Prison Journal* 85 (4): 490–514. https://doi.org/10.1177/0032885505282258.

Huff, C. Ronald, and Matthew Meyer. 1997. "Managing Prison Gangs and Other Security Threat Groups." *Corrections Management Quarterly* 1 (4): 10–18.

Hughes, Lorine A. 2013. "Group Cohesiveness, Gang Member Prestige, and Delinquency and Violence in Chicago, 1959–1962." *Criminology* 51 (4): 795–832. https://doi.org/10.1111/1745-9125.12020.

Hummer, Don, and Eileen M. Ahlin. 2018. "Exportation Hypothesis: Bringing Prison Violence Home to the Community." In *Division on Corrections & Sentencing Handbook*, edited by Natasha A. Frost and Beth M. Huebner. Vol. 3. Columbus: OH: American Society of Criminology.

Hunt, Geoffrey, Stephanie Riegel, Tomas Morales, and Dan Waldorf. 1993. "Changes in Prison Culture: Prison Gangs and the Case of the 'Pepsi Generation'." *Social Problems* 40 (3): 398–409.

Irwin, John. 1970. *The Felon.* Cliffs, NJ: Prentice Hall.

———. 1980. *Prisons in Turmoil.* Boston, MA: Little, Brown and Company.

Irwin, John, and Donald R. Cressey. 1962. "Thieves, Convicts and the Inmate Culture." *Social Problems* 10: 142–55.

Jacobs, James B. 1974. "Street Gangs behind Bars." *Social Problems* 21 (3): 395–409.

———. 1977. *Stateville: The Penitentiary in Mass Society.* Chicago, IL: University of Chicago Press.

———. 2001. "Focusing on Prison Gangs." *Corrections Management Quarterly* 5 (1): vi–vii.

Jennings, Wesley G., Alex R. Piquero, and Jennifer M. Reingle. 2012. "On the Overlap between Victimization and Offending: A Review of the Literature." *Aggression and Violent Behavior* 17 (1): 16–26. https://doi.org/10.1016/j.avb.2011.09.003.

Johnson, Andrew, and James Densley. 2018. "Rio's New Social Order: How Religion Signals Disengagement from Prison Gangs." *Qualitative Sociology* 41 (2): 243–62, https://doi.org/10.1007/s11133-018-9379-x.

Johnson, Brian D. 2010. "Multilevel Analysis in the Study of Crime and Justice." In *Handbook of Quantitative Criminology*, edited by Alex R. Piquero and David Weisburd, 615–48. New York, NY: Springer. https://doi.org/10.1007/978-0-387-77650-7_30.

Katz, Charles, Andrew Fox, Chester Britt, and Phillip Stevenson. 2012. "Understanding Police Gang Data at the Aggregate Level: An Examination of the Reliability of National Youth Gang Survey Data." *Justice Research and Policy* 14 (2): 103–28. https://doi.org/10.3818/JRP.14.2.2012.103.

Katz, Jack, and Curtis Jackson-Jacobs. 2004. "The Criminologists' Gang." In *The Blackwell Companion to Criminology*, edited by Colin Sumner, 91–124. Malden, MA: Blackwell Publishing.

Kirk, David S., and Andrew V. Papachristos. 2011. "Cultural Mechanisms and the Persistence of Neighborhood Violence." *American Journal of Sociology* 116 (4): 1190–1233. https://doi.org/10.1086/655754.

Kissner, Jason, and David C. Pyrooz. 2009. "Self-Control, Differential Association, and Gang Membership: A Theoretical and Empirical Extension of the Literature." *Journal of Criminal Justice* 37 (5): 478–87.

Klein, Malcolm W. 1971. *Street Gangs and Street Workers.* Englewood Cliffs, NJ: Prentice-Hall.

———. 1995. *The American Street Gang: Its Nature, Prevalence and Control.* New York, NY: Oxford University Press.

———. 2005. "The Value of Comparisons in Street Gang Research." *Journal of Contemporary Criminal Justice* 21 (2): 135–52. https://doi.org/10.1177/1043986204272911.

Klein, Malcolm W., and Lois Y. Crawford. 1967. "Groups, Gangs, and Cohesiveness." *Journal of Research in Crime and Delinquency* 4 (1): 63–75. https://doi.org/10.1177/002242786700400105.

Klein, Malcolm W., and Cheryl L. Maxson. 2006. *Street Gang Patterns and Policies.* New York, NY: Oxford University Press.

Kreager, Derek A., and Candace Kruttschnitt. 2017. "Inmate Society in the Era of Mass Incarceration." Annual Review of Criminology, October. https://doi.org/10.1146/annurev-criminol-032317-092513.

Kreager, Derek A., David R. Schaefer, Martin Bouchard, Dana L. Haynie, Sara Wakefield, Jacob Young, and Gary Zajac. 2016. "Toward a Criminology of

Inmate Networks." *Justice Quarterly* 33 (6): 1000–28. https://doi.org/10.1080/07418825.2015.1016090.

Kreager, Derek A., Jacob T. N. Young, Dana L. Haynie, Martin Bouchard, David R. Schaefer, and Gary Zajac. 2017. "Where 'Old Heads' Prevail: Inmate Hierarchy in a Men's Prison Unit." *American Sociological Review* 82 (4): 685–718. https://doi.org/10.1177/0003122417710462.

Krienert, Jessie L., and Mark S. Fleisher. 2001. "Gang Membership as a Proxy for Social Deficiencies: A Study of Nebraska Inmates." *Corrections Management Quarterly 5* (1): 47–58.

Krohn, Marvin D., and Terence P. Thornberry. 2008. "Longitudinal Perspectives on Adolescent Street Gangs." In *The Long View of Crime: A Synthesis of Longitudinal Research*, edited by Akiva M. Liberman, 128–60. New York, NY: Springer.

Krohn, Marvin D., Terence P. Thornberry, Chris L. Gibson, and Julie M. Baldwin. 2010. "The Development and Impact of Self-Report Measures of Crime and Delinquency." *Journal of Quantitative Criminology* 26 (4): 509–25.

Lane, Jeffrey. 2018. *The Digital Street*. New York, NY: Oxford University Press.

Laub, John H., and Robert J. Sampson. 2003. *Shared Beginnings, Divergent Lives: Delinquent Boys to Age 70*. Cambridge, MA: Harvard University Press. http://psycnet.apa.org/psycinfo/2003-88395-000.

Lauderdale, Michael, and Michelle Burman. 2009. "Contemporary Patterns of Female Gangs in Correctional Settings." *Journal of Human Behavior in the Social Environment* 19 (3): 258–80. https://doi.org/10.1080/10911350802694766.

Lauger, Timothy. 2012. *Real Gangstas: Legitimacy, Reputation, and Violence in the Intergang Environment*. New Brunswick, NJ: Rutgers University Press.

Lessing, Benjamin. 2010. "The Danger of Dungeons: Prison Gangs and Incarcerated Militant Groups." *Small Arms Survey* 6: 157–83.

———. 2016. "Inside Out: The Challenge of Prison-Based Criminal Organizations." Washington, DC: The Brookings Institution.

———. 2017. "Counterproductive Punishment: How Prison Gangs Undermine State Authority." *Rationality and Society* 29 (3): 257–97. https://doi.org/10.1177/1043463117701132.

Lopez-Aguado, Patrick. 2016. "'I Would Be a Bulldog': Tracing the Spillover of Carceral Identity." *Social Problems*, March, spw001. https://doi.org/10.1093/socpro/spw001.

———. 2018. *Stick Together and Come Back Home: Racial Sorting and the Spillover of Carceral Identity*. Oakland, CA: University of California Press.

Lyman, Michael D. 1989. *Gangland*. Springfield, IL: Charles C. Thomas.

Maitra, Dev, Robert McLean, and Chris Holligan. 2017. "Voices of Quiet Desistance in UK Prisons: Exploring Emergence of New Identities under Desistance Constraint." *The Howard Journal of Crime and Justice* 56 (4): 437–53. https://doi.org/10.1111/hojo.12213.

Maruna, Shadd. 2001. *Making Good: How Ex-Convicts Reform and Rebuild Their Lives*. Washington, DC: American Psychological Association.

Matsuda, Kristy N., Chris Melde, Terrance J. Taylor, Adrienne Freng, and Finn-Aage Esbensen. 2013. "Gang Membership and Adherence to the 'Code of the Street'." *Justice Quarterly* 30 (3): 440–68.

Maxson, Cheryl L. 1998. "Gang Members on the Move." Washington, DC: US Department of Justice, Office of Juvenile Justice and Delinquency Prevention.

2012. "Betwixt and between Street and Prison Gangs: Defining Gangs and Structures in Youth Correctional Facilities." In *Youth Gangs in International Perspective*, edited by Finn-Aage Esbensen and Cheryl L. Maxson, 107–24. New York, NY: Springer.

Maxson, Cheryl L., Charlotte E. Bradstreet, Danny Gascón, et al. 2012. *Gangs and Violence in California's Youth Correctional Facilities: A Research Foundation for Developing Effective Gang Policies*. Irvine, CA: Department of Criminology, Law and Society, University of California, Irvine.

Maxson, Cheryl L., and Malcolm W. Klein. 1995. "Investigating Gang Structures." *Journal of Gang Research* 3 (1): 33–40.

Maxson, Cheryl L., Monica L. Whitlock, and Malcolm W. Klein. 1998. "Vulnerability to Street Gang Membership: Implications for Practice." *Social Service Review* 72 (1): 70–91. https://doi.org/10.1086/515746.

McGloin, Jean M., and Megan E. Collins. 2015. "Micro-Level Processes of the Gang." In *The Handbook of Gangs*, edited by Scott H. Decker and David C. Pyrooz, 276–93. Chichester, West Sussex: Wiley-Blackwell.

Mears, Daniel P., and Joshua C. Cochran. 2015. *Prisoner Reentry in the Era of Mass Incarceration*. Thousand Oaks, CA: Sage Publications.

Mears, Daniel P., Eric A. Stewart, Sonja E. Siennick, and Ronald L. Simons. 2013. "The Code of the Street and Inmate Violence: Investigating the Salience of Imported Belief Systems." *Criminology* 51 (3): 695–728. https://doi.org/10.1111/1745-9125.12017.

Melde, Chris, and Finn-Aage Esbensen. 2011. "Gang Membership as a Turning Point in the Life Course." *Criminology* 49 (2): 513–52.

2014. "The Relative Impact of Gang Status Transitions: Identifying the Mechanisms of Change in Delinquency." *Journal of Research in Crime and Delinquency* 51 (3): 349–76. https://doi.org/10.1177%2F0022427813507059.

Melde, Chris, Terrance J. Taylor, and Finn-Aage Esbensen. 2009. "'I Got Your Back': An Examination of the Protective Function of Gang Membership in Adolescence." *Criminology* 47 (2): 565–94. https://doi.org/10.1111/j.1745-9125.2009.00148.x.

Miller, Walter B. 1975. *Violence by Youth Gangs and Youth Groups as a Crime Problem in Major American Cities*. Washington, DC: Department of Justice, Law Enforcement Assistance Administration, Office of Juvenile Justice and Delinquency Prevention, National Institute for Juvenile Justice and Delinquency Prevention.

Mitchell, Meghan M., Chantal Fahmy, David C. Pyrooz, and Scott H. Decker. 2017. "Criminal Crews, Codes, and Contexts: Differences and Similarities across the Code of the Street, Convict Code, Street Gangs, and Prison Gangs." *Deviant Behavior* 38 (10): 1–26. https://doi.org/10.1080/01639625.2016.1246028.

Mitchell, Meghan M., Kallee McCullough, Jun Wu, David C. Pyrooz, and Scott H. Decker. 2018. "Survey Research with Gang and Non-Gang Members in Prison: Operational Lessons from the LoneStar Project." Trends in Organized Crime, March, 1–29. https://doi.org/10.1007/s12117-018-9331-1.

Mizzi, Shannon. 2015. "The Behavioral Economist's Case for Prison Gangs." *Wilson Quarterly*. March 2. https://wilsonquarterly.com/stories/behavioral-economists-case-for-prison-gangs/.

Moore, Joan W., Robert Garcia, Joan W. Moore, and Carlos Garcia. 1978. *Homeboys: Gangs, Drugs, and Prison in the Barrios of Los Angeles*. Philadelphia, PA: Temple University Press.

Morenoff, Jeffrey D., and David J. Harding. 2014. "Incarceration, Prisoner Reentry, and Communities." *Annual Review of Sociology* 40 (July): 411–29. https://doi.org/10.1146/annurev-soc–071811–145511.

Moule, Richard K. Jr., David C. Pyrooz, and Scott H. Decker. 2014. "Internet Adoption and Online Behaviour among American Street Gangs: Integrating Gangs and Organizational Theory." *British Journal of Criminology* 54 (6): 1186–1206. https://doi.org/10.1093/bjc/azu050.

Mumola, Christopher J. 2005. "Suicide and Homicide in State Prisons and Local Jails." Washington, DC: US Department of Justice, Bureau of Statistics. www.prisonpolicy.org/scans/bjs/shsplj.pdf.

Narag, Raymund E., and Sou Lee. 2018. "Putting out Fires: Understanding the Developmental Nature and Roles of Inmate Gangs in the Philippine Overcrowded Jails." *International Journal of Offender Therapy and Comparative Criminology* 62 (11): 3509–35. https://doi.org/10.1177/0306624X17744726.

National Gang Intelligence Center. 2011. "2011 National Gang Threat Assessment – Emerging Trends." Washington, DC: Federal Bureau of Investigation, National Gang Intelligence Center. www.fbi.gov/stats-services/publications/2011-national-gang-threat-assessment/2011-national-gang-threat-assessment-emerging-trends.

National Research Council. 2014. *The Growth of Incarceration in the United States: Exploring Causes and Consequences*, edited by Jeremy Travis, Bruce Western, and Steve Redburn. Washington, DC: National Academies Press.

New York Times. 1931. "Penologists Back Wickersham Data." *New York Times*, October 23.

Noonan, Margaret, Scott Rohloff, and Scott Ginder. 2016. "Mortality in State Prisons, 2001–2014 – Statistical Tables." Washington, DC: US Department of Justice, Bureau of Statistics.

Nye, Joseph S. 2004. *Soft Power: The Means to Success in World Politics*. New York, NY: Public Affairs.

—— 2009. "Get Smart: Combining Hard and Soft Power." *Foreign Affairs*: 160–3.

Orlando-Morningstar, Dennise. 1997. "Prison Gangs." *Special Needs Offender Bulletin* 2 (August): 1–13.

Ouellet, Marie, Martin Bouchard, and Yanick Charette. 2019. "One Gang Dies, Another Gains? The Network Dynamics of Criminal Group Persistence." *Criminology* 57 (1): 5–33. https://doi.org/10.1111/1745-9125.12194.

Owen, Barbara, James Wells, and Joycelyn Pollock. 2017. *In Search of Safety: Confronting Inequality in Women's Imprisonment*. Oakland, CA: University of California Press.

Paoli, Letizia. 2014. *The Oxford Handbook of Organized Crime*. Oxford Handbooks. Oxford: Oxford University Press.

Papachristos, Andrew V. 2009. "Murder by Structure: Dominance Relations and the Social Structure of Gang Homicide." *American Journal of Sociology* 115 (1): 74–128.

—— 2011. "The Coming of a Networked Criminology?" In *Advances in Criminological Theory*, edited by John MacDonald, 17: 101–40. New Brunswick, NJ: Transaction Publishers.

Papachristos, Andrew V., David M. Hureau, and Anthony A. Braga. 2013. "The Corner and the Crew: The Influence of Geography and Social Networks on Gang

Violence." *American Sociological Review* 78 (3): 417–47. https://doi.org/10.1177/0003122413486800.

Papachristos, Andrew V., Tracey L. Meares, and Jeffrey Fagan. 2012. "Why Do Criminals Obey the Law: The Influence of Legitimacy and Social Networks on Active Gun Offenders." *Journal of Criminal Law and Criminology* 102: 397–440.

Pelz, Mary E., James W. Marquart, and C. Terry Pelz. 1991. "Right-Wing Extremism in the Texas Prisons: The Rise and Fall of the Aryan Brotherhood in Texas." *The Prison Journal* 71 (1): 23–37. https://doi.org/10.1177/003288559107100204.

Perkinson, Robert. 2010. *Texas Tough: The Rise of America's Prison Empire.* New York, NY: Metropolitan Books.

Petersilia, Joan, Sara Abarbanel, John S. Butler, Mark Feldman, Mariam Hinds, Kevin E. Jason, Corinne Keel, Matthew J. Owens, and Camden Vilkin. 2014. "Voices from the Field: How California Stakeholders View Public Safety Realignment." SSRN Scholarly Paper ID 2395498. Rochester, NY: Social Science Research Network. https://papers.ssrn.com/abstract=2395498.

Peterson, Dana, Dena C. Carson, and Eric Fowler. 2018. "What's Sex (Composition) Got to Do with It? The Importance of Sex Composition of Gangs for Female and Male Members' Offending and Victimization." Justice Quarterly, January. www.tandfonline.com/doi/ref/10.1080/07418825.2018.1424231?scroll=top.

Pfaff, John. 2017. *Locked in: The True Causes of Mass Incarceration – and How to Achieve Real Reform.* New York, NY: Basic Books.

Phillips, Coretta. 2012. "'It Ain't Nothing Like America with the Bloods and the Crips': Gang Narratives inside Two English Prisons." *Punishment & Society* 14 (1): 51–68. https://doi.org/10.1177/1462474511424683.

Phinney, Jean S. 1992. "The Multigroup Ethnic Identity Measure: A New Scale for Use with Diverse Groups." *Journal of Adolescent Research* 7 (2): 156–76.

Pinkerton, James. 2014. "Prisons Study Ways to Reduce Solitary Confinement." *Houston Chronicle*, March 15. www.houstonchronicle.com/news/houston-texas/houston/article/Prisons-study-ways-to-reduce-solitary-confinement-5321117.php.

Piquero, Alex R., David P. Farrington, and Alfred Blumstein. 2003. "The Criminal Career Paradigm." *Crime and Justice* 30 (January): 359–506. https://doi.org/10.1086/652234.

———. 2007. *Key Issues in Criminal Career Research: New Analyses of the Cambridge Study in Delinquent Development.* New York, NY: Cambridge University Press.

Pratt, Travis C. 2009. *Addicted to Incarceration.* Thousand Oaks, CA: Sage.

Prendergast, Alan. 2014. "After the Murder of Tom Clements, Can Colorado's Prison System Rehabilitate Itself?" *Westword*, August 21. www.westword.com/news/after-the-murder-of-tom-clements-can-colorados-prison-system-rehabilitate-itself-5125050.

Pyrooz, David C. 2014. "'From Your First Cigarette to Your Last Dyin' Day': The Patterning of Gang Membership in the Life-Course." *Journal of Quantitative Criminology* 30 (2): 349–72. https://doi.org/10.1007/s10940-013-9206-1.

———. 2016. "Gang Affiliation and Restrictive Housing in U.S. Prisons." In *Restrictive Housing in the U.S.: Issues, Challenges, and Future Directions*, edited by Marie Garcia, 117–64. Washington, DC: US Department of Justice, National Institute of Justice.

Pyrooz, David C., and Scott H. Decker. 2011. "Motives and Methods for Leaving the Gang: Understanding the Process of Gang Desistance." *Journal of Criminal Justice* 39 (5): 417–25. https://doi.org/10.1016/j.jcrimjus.2011.07.001.

Pyrooz, David C., Scott H. Decker, and Mark S. Fleisher. 2011. "From the Street to the Prison, from the Prison to the Street: Understanding and Responding to Prison Gangs." *Journal of Aggression, Conflict and Peace Research* 3 (1): 12–24. https://doi.org/10.5042/jacpr.2011.0018.

Pyrooz, David C., Scott H. Decker, and Emily Owens. 2018. "Does Administrative and Survey Data Tell the Same Story in Prisons? A Multi-Trait, Multi-Method Study with Application to Gangs." Working Paper. Boulder, CO: University of Colorado Boulder, Institute of Behavioral Science.

Pyrooz, David C., Andrew M. Fox, Charles M. Katz, and Scott H. Decker. 2012. "Gang Organization, Offending, and Victimization: A Cross-National Analysis." In *Youth Gangs in International Perspective*, edited by Finn-Aage Esbensen and Cheryl L. Maxson, 85–105. New York, NY: Springer.

Pyrooz, David C., Nancy Gartner, and Molly Smith. 2017. "Consequences of Incarceration for Gang Membership: A Longitudinal Study of Serious Offenders in Philadelphia and Phoenix." *Criminology* 55 (2): 273–306. https://doi.org/10.1111/1745-9125.12135.

Pyrooz, David C., Gary LaFree, Scott H. Decker, and Patrick A. James. 2018. "Cut from the Same Cloth? A Comparative Study of Domestic Extremists and Gang Members in the United States." *Justice Quarterly* 35 (1): 1–32. https://doi.org/10.1080/07418825.2017.1311357.

Pyrooz, David C., Jean Marie McGloin, and Scott H. Decker. 2017. "Parenthood as a Turning Point in the Life Course for Male and Female Gang Members: A Study of within-Individual Changes in Gang Membership and Criminal Behavior." *Criminology* 55 (4). https://doi.org/10.1111/1745-9125.12162.

Pyrooz, David C., and Meghan M. Mitchell. 2015. "Little Gang Research, Big Gang Research." In *The Handbook of Gangs*, edited by Scott H. Decker and David C. Pyrooz, 28–58. New York, NY: John Wiley & Sons Inc.

——— 2018. "The use of restrictive housing on gang and non-gang affiliated inmates in U.S. prisons: Findings from a national survey of correctional agencies." *Justice Quarterly*, 1–40.

——— 2019. "The Hardest Time: Gang Members in Total Institutions." In *Handbook on the Consequences of Sentencing and Punishment Decisions*, edited by Beth M. Huebner and Natasha A. Frost, 3: 361–78. ASC Division on Corrections & Sentences Handbook Series. New York, NY: Routledge.

Pyrooz, David C., Jr.Richard K. Moule, and Scott H. Decker. 2014. "The Contribution of Gang Membership to the Victim–Offender Overlap." *Journal of Research in Crime and Delinquency* 51 (3): 315–48.

Pyrooz, David C., and Gary Sweeten. 2015. "Gang Membership between Ages 5 and 17 Years in the United States." *Journal of Adolescent Health* 56 (4): 414–19. https://doi.org/10.1016/j.jadohealth.2014.11.018.

Pyrooz, David C., Gary Sweeten, and Alex R. Piquero. 2013. "Continuity and Change in Gang Membership and Gang Embeddedness." *Journal of Research in Crime and Delinquency* 50 (2): 239–71. https://doi.org/10.1177/0022427811434830.

Pyrooz, David C., Jillian J. Turanovic, Scott H. Decker, and Jun Wu. 2016. "Taking Stock of the Relationship between Gang Membership and Offending: A Meta-Analysis." *Criminal Justice & Behavior* 43 (3): 365–97.

Rabe-Hesketh, Sophia, and Anders Skrondal. 2008. *Multilevel and Longitudinal Modeling Using Stata.* College Station, TX: STATA Press.

Ralph, Paige H., Robert J. Hunter, James W. Marquart, Steven J. Cuvelier, and Dorothy Merianos. 1996. "Exploring the Differences between Gang and Non-Gang Prisoners." In *Gangs in America*, edited by C. Ronald Huff, 2nd ed., 123–36. Thousand Oaks, CA: Sage.

Ralph, Paige H., and James W. Marquart. 1991. "Gang Violence in Texas Prisons." *The Prison Journal* 71 (2): 38–49.

Raudenbush, Stephen W., and Anthony S. Bryk. 2002. *Hierarchical Linear Models: Applications and Data Analysis Methods.* Vol. 1. Thousand Oaks, CA: Sage.

Reid, Shannon E., and Shelley Johnson Listwan. 2018. "Managing the Threat of Violence: Coping Strategies among Juvenile Inmates." *Journal of Interpersonal Violence* 33 (8): 1306–26. https://doi.org/10.1177/0886260515615143.

Reisig, Michael D., and Gorazd Mesko. 2009. "Procedural Justice, Legitimacy, and Prisoner Misconduct." *Psychology, Crime & Law* 15 (1): 41–59. https://doi.org/10.1080/10683160802089768.

Reiter, Keramet. 2012. "Parole, Snitch, or Die: California's Supermax Prisons and Prisoners, 1997–2007." *Punishment & Society* 14 (5): 530–63. https://doi.org/10.1177/1462474512464007.

———. 2014. "The Pelican Bay Hunger Strike: Resistance within the Structural Constraints of a US Supermax Prison." *South Atlantic Quarterly* 113 (3): 579–611. https://doi.org/10.1215/00382876-2692191.

Reiter, Keramet A. 2016. *23/7: Pelican Bay Prison and the Rise of Long-Term Solitary.* New Haven, CT: Yale University Press.

Rogers, Everett M. 2010. Diffusion of Innovations. New York, NY: Simon and Schuster.

Roman, Caterina G., Scott H. Decker, and David C. Pyrooz. 2017. "Leveraging the Pushes and Pulls of Gang Disengagement to Improve Gang Intervention: Findings from Three Multi-Site Studies and a Review of Relevant Gang Programs." *Journal of Crime and Justice* 40 (3): 316–36.

Rosenberg, Morris. 1965. *Society and Adolescent Self-Image.* Princeton, NJ: Princeton University Press.

Roth, M. Garrett, and David Skarbek. 2014. "Prison Gangs and the Community Responsibility System." *Review of Behavioral Economics* 1 (3): 223–43.

Rothman, David J. 2002. *The Discovery of the Asylum: Social Order and Disorder in the New Republic.* New York, NY: Routledge.

Rozycki Lozano, Alicia T., Robert D. Morgan, Danielle D. Murray, and Femina Varghese. 2011. "Prison Tattoos as a Reflection of the Criminal Lifestyle." *International Journal of Offender Therapy and Comparative Criminology* 55 (4): 509–29.

Ruddell, Rick, Scott H. Decker, and Arlen Egley. 2006. "Gang Interventions in Jails: A National Analysis." *Criminal Justice Review* 31 (1): 33–46.

Ruddell, Rick, and Shannon Gottschall. 2011. "Are All Gangs Equal Security Risks? An Investigation of Gang Types and Prison Misconduct." *American Journal of Criminal Justice* 36 (3): 265–79. https://doi.org/10.1007/s12103-011-9108-4.

Rufino, Katrina A., Kathleen A. Fox, and Glen A. Kercher. 2012. "Gang Membership and Crime Victimization among Prison Inmates." *American Journal of Criminal Justice* 37: 321–37.

Sampson, Robert J., Stephen W. Raudenbush, and Felton Earls. 1997. "Neighborhoods and Violent Crime: A Multilevel Study of Collective Efficacy." *Science* 277 (5328): 918–24.

Schaefer, David R., Martin Bouchard, Jacob T. N. Young, and Derek A. Kreager. 2017. "Friends in Locked Places: An Investigation of Prison Inmate Network Structure." *Social Networks*: Crime and Networks special edition, 51 (October): 88–103. https://doi.org/10.1016/j.socnet.2016.12.006.

Schelling, Thomas C. 1967. "Economics and Criminal Enterprise." *The Public Interest* 7: 61.

Schiller, Dane. 2016. "Aryan Brotherhood in 'Chaos' after Federal Takedown." Houston Chronicle, August 7. www.houstonchronicle.com/news/houston-texas /houston/article/Aryan-Brotherhood-in-chaos-after-federal-9127170.php.

Schubert, Carol A., Edward P. Mulvey, Laurence Steinberg, Elizabeth Cauffman, Sandra H. Losoya, Thomas Hecker, Laurie Chassin, and George P. Knight. 2004. "Operational Lessons from the Pathways to Desistance Project." *Youth Violence and Juvenile Justice* 2 (3): 237–55. https://doi.org/10.1177/1541204004265875.

Scott, Daniel W., and Cheryl Lee Maxson. 2016. "Gang Organization and Violence in Youth Correctional Facilities." *Journal of Criminological Research, Policy and Practice* 2 (2). www.emeraldinsight.com/doi/abs/10.1108/JCRPP-03-2015-0004.

Scott, Greg. 2004. "'It's a Sucker's Outfit': How Urban Gangs Enable and Impede the Reintegration of Ex-Convicts." *Ethnography* 5 (1): 107–40.

Scott, Terri-Lynne, and Rick Ruddell. 2011. "Canadian Female Gang Inmates: Risk, Needs, and the Potential for Prison Rehabilitation." *Journal of Offender Rehabilitation* 50 (6): 305–26. https://doi.org/10.1080/10509674.2011.583717.

Sharkey, Patrick T., Nicole Tirado-Strayer, Andrew V. Papachristos, and C. Cybele Raver. 2012. "The Effect of Local Violence on Children's Attention and Impulse Control." *American Journal of Public Health* 102 (12): 2287–93.

Shelden, Randall G. 1991. "A Comparison of Gang Members and Non-Gang Members in a Prison Setting." *The Prison Journal* 71 (2): 50–60. https://doi.org/10.1177 /003288559107100206.

Short, James F. 1974. "Youth Gangs and Society: Micro- and Macrosociological Processes." *The Sociological Quarterly* 15 (1): 3–19.

1985. "The Level of Explanation Problem in Criminology." In *Theoretical Methods in Criminology*, edited by Robert F. Meier, 51–72. Beverly Hills, CA: Sage.

1996. *Gangs and Adolescent Violence.* Boulder, CO: Center for the Study and Prevention of Violence. www.colorado.edu/UCB/Research/cspv/publications/ papers/CSPV-004.pdf.

1998. "The Level of Explanation Problem Revisited – the American Society of Criminology 1997 Presidential Address." *Criminology* 36 (1): 3–36.

Short., James F., and Fred L. Strodtbeck. 1965. *Group Process and Gang Delinquency.* Chicago, IL: University of Chicago Press.

Simi, Pete, Kathleen Blee, Matthew DeMichele, and Steven Windisch. 2017. "Addicted to Hate: Identity Residual among Former White Supremacists." American Sociological Review, August. https://doi.org/10.1177/0003122417728719.

Simon, Thomas R., Nancy M. Ritter, and Reshma R. Mahendra. 2013. *Changing Course: Preventing Gang Membership*. Washington, DC: National Institute of Justice and Centers for Disease Control and Prevention.

Skarbek, David. 2011. "Governance and Prison Gangs." *American Political Science Review* 105 (4): 702–16.

2014. *The Social Order of the Underworld: How Prison Gangs Govern the American Penal System*. New York, NY: Oxford University Press.

Sparks, Richard, Anthony E. Bottoms, and Will Hay. 1996. *Prisons and the Problem of Order*. Oxford: Clarendon Press.

Spergel, Irving A. 1964. *Racketville, Slumtown, Haulbug*. Chicago, IL: University of Chicago Press.

Spergel, Irving A., and G. David Curry. 1993. "The National Youth Gang Survey: A Research and Development Process." In *The Gang Intervention Handbook*, edited by Arnold P. Goldstein and C. Ronald Huff, 359–400. Champaign, IL: Research Press.

Spindler, Andrea, and Martin Bouchard. 2011. "Structure or Behavior? Revisiting Gang Typologies." *International Criminal Justice Review* 21 (3): 263–82. https://doi.org /10.1177/1057567711419046.

Steiner, Benjamin, H. Daniel Butler, and Jared M. Ellison. 2014. "Causes and Correlates of Prison Inmate Misconduct: A Systematic Review of the Evidence." *Journal of Criminal Justice* 42 (6): 462–70. https://doi.org/10.1016/j.jcrimjus.2014.08.001.

Steiner, Benjamin, and John Wooldredge. 2014. "Comparing Self-Report to Official Measures of Inmate Misconduct." *Justice Quarterly* 31 (6): 1074–1101. https://doi .org/10.1080/07418825.2012.723031.

2018. "Prison Officer Legitimacy, Their Exercise of Power, and Inmate Rule Breaking." *Criminology* 56 (4).

Stewart, Eric A., Christopher J. Schreck, and Ronald L. Simons. 2006. "'I Ain't Gonna Let No One Disrespect Me': Does the Code of the Street Reduce or Increase Violent Victimization among African American Adolescents?" *Journal of Research in Crime and Delinquency* 43 (4): 427–58.

Stone, Sandra S. 1999. "Risk Factors Associated with Gang Joining among Youth." *Journal of Gang Research* 6 (2): 1–18.

Surowiecki, James. 2005. *The Wisdom of Crowds*. New York, NY: Anchor.

Sweeten, Gary. 2012. "Scaling Criminal Offending." *Journal of Quantitative Criminology* 28 (3): 533–57.

Sweeten, Gary, David C. Pyrooz, and Alex R. Piquero. 2013. "Disengaging from Gangs and Desistance from Crime." *Justice Quarterly* 30 (3): 469–500.

Sykes, Gresham M. 1958. *The Society of Captives*. Princeton, NJ: Princeton University Press.

Sykes, Gresham M., and Sheldon L. Messinger. 1960. "The Inmate Social System." In *Theoretical Studies in Social Organization of the Prison*, edited by Richard A. Cloward, Donald R. Cressey, George H. Grosser, Richard McCleery, Lloyd E. Ohlin, and Gresham M. Sykes, 5–19. New York, NY: Social Science Research Council.

Tachiki, Scott N. 1995. "Indeterminate Sentences in Supermax Prisons Based upon Alleged Gang Affiliations: A Reexamination of Procedural Protection and a Proposal for Greater Procedural Requirements." *California Law Review* 83 (4): 1115–49.

Tangney, June P., Roy F. Baumeister, and Angie Luzio Boone. 2004. "High Self-Control Predicts Good Adjustment, Less Pathology, Better Grades, and Interpersonal Success." *Journal of Personality* 72 (2): 271–324.

Tapia, Mike. 2013. "Texas Latino Gangs and Large Urban Jails: Intergenerational Conflicts and Issues in Management." *Journal of Crime and Justice* 37 (2): 256–74. https://doi.org/10.1080/0735648X.2013.768179.

Tapia, Mike, Corey S. Sparks, and J. Mitchell Miller. 2014. "Texas Latino Prison Gangs: An Exploration of Generational Shift and Rebellion." *The Prison Journal* 94 (2): 159–79. https://doi.org/10.1177/0032885514524694.

Taylor, Carl S. 1990. *Dangerous Society*. East Lansing, MI: Michigan State University Press.

Taylor, Terrance J., Adrienne Freng, Finn-Aage Esbensen, and Dana Peterson. 2008. "Youth Gang Membership and Serious Violent Victimization: The Importance of Lifestyles and Routine Activities." *Journal of Interpersonal Violence* 23 (10): 1441–64. https://doi.org/10.1177/0886260508314306.

Texas Department of Criminal Justice. 2007. "Security Threat Groups 'on the Inside'." August. www.tdcj.state.tx.us/documents/cid/CID_STGMO_FAQ.pdf.

———. 2014. "Administrative Segregation." Huntsville, TX: Texas Department of Criminal Justice. https://assets.documentcloud.org/documents/2089812/texas-adseg-programming.pdf.

———. 2017. "Unit Directory." www.tdcj.state.tx.us/unit_directory/index.html.

Texas Department of Public Safety. 2015. "Texas Gang Threat Assessment: A State Intelligence Estimate." Huntsville, TX: Texas Joint Crime Information Center, Intelligence & Counterterrorism Division.

Texas State Historical Association. 2017. "Texas Prison Rodeo." https://tshaonline.org/handbook/online/articles/xxt01.

Thaler, Richard H., and Cass R. Sunstein. 2008. *Nudge: Improving Decisions about Health, Wealth, and Happiness*. New Haven, CT: Yale University Press.

Thomas, Charles W., David M. Petersen, and Rhonda M. Zingraff. 1978. "Structural and Social Psychological Correlates of Prisonization." *Criminology* 16 (3): 383–94.

Thompson, Heather Ann. 2017. *Blood in the Water: The Attica Prison Uprising of 1971 and Its Legacy*. New York, NY: Vintage.

———. 2018. "How a South Carolina Prison Riot Really Went Down." *The New York Times*, May 1, sec. Opinion. www.nytimes.com/2018/04/28/opinion/how-a-south-carolina-prison-riot-really-went-down.html.

Thornberry, Terence P., Brook Kearley, Denise C. Gottfredson, Molly P. Slothower, Deanna N. Devlin, and Jamie J. Fader. 2018. "Reducing Crime among Youth at Risk for Gang Involvement." *Criminology & Public Policy* 17 (4): 953–89. https://doi.org/10.1111/1745-9133.12395.

Thornberry, Terence P., and Marvin D. Krohn. 2000. "The Self-Report Method for Measuring Delinquency and Crime." *Criminal Justice* 4 (1): 33–83.

Thornberry, Terence P., Marvin D. Krohn, Alan J. Lizotte, and Deborah Chard-Wierschem. 1993. "The Role of Juvenile Gangs in Facilitating Delinquent Behavior." *Journal of Research in Crime and Delinquency* 30 (1): 55–87. https://doi.org/10.1177/0022427893030001005.

Thornberry, Terence P., Marvin D. Krohn, Alan J. Lizotte, Carolyn A. Smith, and Kimberly Tobin. 2003. *Gangs and Delinquency in Developmental Perspective*. New York, NY: Cambridge University Press.

Thrasher, Frederic M. 1927. *The Gang: A Study of 1,313 Gangs in Chicago*. Chicago, IL: University of Chicago Press.

Toch, Hans. 2007. "Sequestering Gang Members, Burning Witches, and Subverting Due Process." *Criminal Justice and Behavior* 34: 274–88.

Toman, Elisa L. 2017. "The Victim–Offender Overlap behind Bars: Linking Prison Misconduct and Victimization." *Justice Quarterly*: 1–33. https://doi.org/10.1080/07418825.2017.1402072.

Trammell, Rebecca. 2012. *Enforcing the Convict Code: Violence and Prison Culture.* Boulder, CO: Lynne Rienner Publishers.

Trulson, Chad R., and James W. Marquart. 2010. *First Available Cell: Desegregation of the Texas Prison System.* Austin, TX: University of Texas Press.

Trulson, Chad R., James W. Marquart, and Soraya K. Kawucha. 2006. "Gang Suppression." *Corrections Today* 68 (May): 26–31.

Tyler, Tom R., and Jonathan Jackson. 2014. "Popular Legitimacy and the Exercise of Legal Authority: Motivating Compliance, Cooperation, and Engagement." *Psychology, Public Policy, and Law* 20 (1): 78–95.

Useem, Bert. 1985. "Disorganization and the New Mexico Prison Riot of 1980." *American Sociological Review* 50 (5): 677–88.

Useem, Bert, and Anne Morrison Piehl. 2008. *Prison State: The Challenge of Mass Incarceration.* New York, NY: Cambridge University Press.

Valdez, Avelardo. 2003. "Toward a Typology of Contemporary Mexican American Youth Gangs." In *Gangs and Society: Alternative Perspectives*, edited by Louis Kontos, David C. Brotherton, and Luis Barrios, 12–40. New York, NY: Columbia University Press.

Van Gemert, Frank, and Mark S. Fleisher. 2005. "In the Grip of the Group." In *European Street Gangs and Troublesome Youth Groups*, edited by Scott H. Decker and Frank M. Weerman, 11–30. Lanham, MD: AltaMira Press.

Varano, Sean P., Beth M. Huebner, and Timothy S. Bynum. 2011. "Correlates and Consequences of Pre-Incarceration Gang Involvement among Incarcerated Youthful Felons." *Journal of Criminal Justice* 39 (1): 30–8. https://doi.org/10.1016/j.jcrimjus.2010.10.001.

Vasquez, Eduardo A., Lisa Wenborne, Madeline Peers, Emma Alleyne, and Kirsty Ellis. 2015. "Any of Them Will Do: In-Group Identification, Out-Group Entitativity, and Gang Membership as Predictors of Group-Based Retribution." *Aggressive Behavior* 41 (3): 242–52. https://doi.org/10.1002/ab.21581.

Venkatesh, Sudhir Alladi, and Steven D. Levitt. 2000. "'Are We a Family or a Business?' History and Disjuncture in the Urban American Street Gang." *Theory and Society* 29 (4): 427–62.

Vigil, Daryl A. 2006. "Classification and Security Threat Group Management." *Corrections Today* 68 (2): 32–4.

Vigil, J. Diego. 1988. *Barrio Gangs: Street Life and Identity in Southern California.* Austin, TX: University of Texas Press.

von Lampe, Klaus. 2016. "The Ties That Bind: A Taxonomy of Associational Criminal Structures." In Illegal Entrepreneurship, Organized Crime and Social Control, edited by Georgios A. Antonopoulos, 19–35. Studies of Organized Crime 14. New York, NY: Springer. http://link.springer.com/chapter/10.1007/978–3–319–31608-6_2.

Wacquant, Loic. 2001. "Deadly Symbiosis: When Ghetto and Prison Meet and Mesh." *Punishment & Society* 3 (1): 95–133.

——— 2002. "The Curious Eclipse of Prison Ethnography in the Age of Mass Incarceration." *Ethnography* 3 (4): 371–97.

——— 2009. *Prisons of Poverty.* Minneapolis, MN: University of Minnesota Press.

Ward, T. W. 2012. *Gangsters without Borders: An Ethnography of a Salvadoran Street Gang*. New York, NY: Oxford University Press.

Watkins, Adam M., and Chris Melde. 2016. "Bad Medicine: The Relationship between Gang Membership, Depression, Self-Esteem, and Suicidal Behavior." *Criminal Justice and Behavior*, April. https://doi.org/10.1177/0093854816631797.

Webb, Vincent J., Charles M. Katz, and Scott H. Decker. 2006. "Assessing the Validity of Self-Reports by Gang Members: Results from the Arrestee Drug Abuse Monitoring Program." *Crime & Delinquency* 52 (2): 232–52.

Weerman, Frank M. 2003. "Co-offending as Social Exchange: Explaining Characteristics of Co-offending." *British Journal of Criminology* 43 (2): 398–416. https://doi.org/10.1093/bjc/43.2.398.

Weerman, Frank M., Peter J. Lovegrove, and Terence Thornberry. 2015. "Gang Membership Transitions and Its Consequences: Exploring Changes Related to Joining and Leaving Gangs in Two Countries." *European Journal of Criminology* 12 (1): 70–91. https://doi.org/10.1177/1477370814539070.

Wells, James B., Kevin I. Minor, Earl Angel, and Lisa Carter. 2002. *A Study of Gangs and Security Threat Groups in America's Adult Prisons and Jails*. Indianapolis, IN: National Major Gang Task Force.

Western, Bruce. 2018. *Homeward: Life in the Year after Prison*. New York, NY: Russell Sage Foundation.

Winfree, L. Thomas, and Adrienne Freng. 2015. "Gangs and Social Learning Theory: What We Know, What We Need to Know, and Why It Matters." In *The Handbook of Gangs*, edited by Scott H. Decker and David C. Pyrooz, 118–35. Chichester, West Sussex: John Wiley & Sons.

Winterdyk, John, and Rick Ruddell. 2010. "Managing Prison Gangs: Results from a Survey of U.S. Prison Systems." *Journal of Criminal Justice* 38 (4): 730–6. https://doi.org/10.1016/j.jcrimjus.2010.04.047.

Wood, Jane, and Joanna Adler. 2001. "Gang Activity in English Prisons: The Staff Perspective." *Psychology, Crime & Law* 7 (1–4): 167–92. https://doi.org/10.1080/10683160108401793.

Wood, Jane L., Emma Alleyne, Katarina Mozova, and Mark James. 2014. "Predicting Involvement in Prison Gang Activity: Street Gang Membership, Social and Psychological Factors." *Law and Human Behavior* 38 (3): 203–11.

Wooldredge, John D. 1998. "Inmate Lifestyles and Opportunities for Victimization." *Journal of Research in Crime and Delinquency* 35 (4): 480–502. https://doi.org/10.1177/0022427898035004006.

Wooldredge, John, and Benjamin Steiner. 2012. "Race Group Differences in Prison Victimization Experiences." *Journal of Criminal Justice*, The Prison Experience, 40 (5): 358–69. https://doi.org/10.1016/j.jcrimjus.2012.06.011.

——— 2014. "A Bi-level Framework for Understanding Prisoner Victimization." *Journal of Quantitative Criminology* 30 (1): 141–62. https://doi.org/10.1007/s10940-013-9197-y.

Worrall, John L., and Robert G. Morris. 2012. "Prison Gang Integration and Inmate Violence." *Journal of Criminal Justice* 40 (5): 425–32.

Wu, Jun, and David C. Pyrooz. 2015. "Uncovering the Pathways between Gang Membership and Violent Victimization." Journal of Quantitative Criminology, October, 1–29. https://doi.org/10.1007/s10940-015-9266-5.

# Index